The Household and the Making of History
A Subversive View of the Western Past

This book argues that a unique late-marriage pattern, discovered in the 1960s but originating in the Middle Ages, explains the continuing puzzle of why western Europe was the site of changes that, from about 1500, gave birth to the modern world. Contrary to views that credit political and economic upheavals from the late eighteenth century for ushering in the contemporary global era, it contends that the roots of these and other modern developments themselves are located in an event taking place more than a millennium earlier, when the peasants in northwestern Europe began to marry their daughters almost as late as their sons. The appearance of this late-marriage system, with its unstable nuclear household form, is also shown to have exposed for the first time the common ingredients whose presence has perpetuated apparently universal beliefs in the importance of gender difference and of a sexual hierarchy favoring men.

Mary S. Hartman holds the title of University Professor at Rutgers, the State University of New Jersey, where she directs the Institute for Women's Leadership. She specializes in European social and political history as well as in women's and gender studies. A former president of the Berkshire Conference of Women Historians, she is also a cofounder of the Berkshire Conference on the History of Women. Professor Hartman has written and edited a number of books, including *Clio's Consciousness Raised: New Perspectives on the History of Women, Victorian Murderesses,* and *Talking Leadership: Conversations with Powerful Women.* She has published reviews and articles in scholarly journals including *Feminist Studies,* the *Journal of Social History,* the *Journal of Modern European History, Raritan Review, Signs,* and *Victorian Studies.*

The Household and the Making of History

A *Subversive View of the Western Past*

MARY S. HARTMAN

Rutgers University

CAMBRIDGE
UNIVERSITY PRESS

PUBLISHED BY THE PRESS SYNDICATE OF THE UNIVERSITY OF CAMBRIDGE
The Pitt Building, Trumpington Street, Cambridge, United Kingdom

CAMBRIDGE UNIVERSITY PRESS
The Edinburgh Building, Cambridge CB2 2RU, UK
40 West 20th Street, New York, NY 10011-4211, USA
477 Williamstown Road, Port Melbourne, VIC 3207, Australia
Ruiz de Alarcón 13, 28014 Madrid, Spain
Dock House, The Waterfront, Cape Town 8001, South Africa

http://www.cambridge.org

First published 2004

Printed in the United States of America

Typeface Sabon 10/12 pt.   *System* LATEX 2$_\varepsilon$ [TB]

A catalog record for this book is available from the British Library.

Library of Congress Cataloging in Publication Data

Hartman, Mary S., 1941–
The household and the making of history : a subversive view of the Western past /
Mary S. Hartman.
p.   cm.
Includes bibliographical references and index.
ISBN 0-521-82972-0 – ISBN 0-521-53669-3 (pbk.)
1. Marriage – History.   2. Households – History.   3. Sex role – History.   4. Social history.
1. Title.
HQ515.H38   2004
306.81′09–dc22   2003061671

ISBN 0 521 82972 0 hardback
ISBN 0 521 53669 3 paperback

For Edwin M. Hartman and
Samuel M. Hartman

Contents

Preface and Acknowledgments

Many years ago when I first imagined this book, it presented itself as a perfectly straightforward undertaking. A modern European historian trained in political history but attracted to the new social history and the even newer women's history, I was intrigued by the then novel work of Peter Laslett and the Cambridge Group for the History of Population and Social Structure. I was fascinated as well by John Hajnal's remarkable discovery of a unique pattern of late marriage – for women, in particular – that is believed to have emerged as early as the medieval era in northwestern Europe. I devised a project in the late 1970s that would show how the subfields of women's history and family history, and the recent demographic findings about this strange marriage and household formation pattern, were bound to transform the ways we understand the Western past.

After taking what I believed was a temporary administrative post in the early 1980s, I continued to find as much time as I could to explore the effects, as well as the still-mysterious origins, of the distinctive late-marriage arrangements in northwestern Europe. At that point, I was convinced that the project was such an obvious one that it was likely to be pursued by many scholars. I was wrong about that, as things turned out. I was wrong, too, about the administrative post being temporary. Worse still, I was wrong about the project itself being straightforward. I explain why in the book.

What I was not wrong about was an initial intuition that the story waiting to be pulled together was bound to be a good one. It is true that the early enthusiasm among the new breed of social historians for the discoveries of the historical demographers faded. Despite John Hajnal's and Peter Laslett's imaginative insights suggesting that the discovery of a peculiar family and household system might dramatically alter widespread views about how Western history – and even global history – unfolded, historical studies took other directions. The past few decades have nonetheless been a heady time of expansion, with many new fields and subfields being born. And if practitioners of the new women's history that I was sure had so much to bring to the findings of the historical demographers chose to focus their attentions elsewhere, it was often to dazzling effect. A happy personal dividend, too, was that for long I enjoyed the luxury of countless unhurried conversations and written exchanges with many generous colleagues, friends, and, initially anyway, total strangers. Several of the ideas we discussed in those years have made their way into the book; others, thanks to their wise counsel, have been qualified, recast, or abandoned altogether.

My chief purpose here, however, is not to recount the long version of how this book came into being but to thank the many who offered their help along the way. In doing so, I wish to make it quite clear that not all these people endorse the book's arguments or are even aware of what finally emerged as those arguments. Yet, regardless of varying degrees of skepticism and enthusiasm, most were intrigued enough to engage in dialogues, some carried on for years, that have greatly informed and enriched the book. Early on, work-in-progress sessions gave me much appreciated feedback from Rutgers colleagues, including historians Sue Cobble, Dee Garrison, John Gillis, Martha Howell, Dorothy Ko, Suzanne Lebsock, Maurice Lee, Jr., Phyllis Mack, Jennifer Morgan, William O'Neill, David Oshinsky, Susan Shrepfer, Bonnie Smith, Peter Stearns, Judith Walkowitz, Marc Wasserman, Deborah Gray White, and Virginia Yans. Of these, Dee, John, Mo, and Bill not only commented on several early chapters but also provided much encouragement and support, and occasional good-natured goading. More recently, colleagues Rudy Bell, Philip Greven, Mary Hawkesworth, and Bonnie Smith read the entire manuscript and offered wise and beneficial guidance. In addition, Marlie Wasserman, director of the Rutgers University Press, gave invaluable advice at a time when it was badly needed. And near the end of production, sisters-in-law Charlie and Sue Hartman provided some impressive editorial wisdom.

In the interim, three Rutgers colleagues in anthropology – Robin Fox, Susan Gal, and Michael Moffatt – read several chapters and offered indispensable counsel. I also owe thanks for their comments to faculty and graduate student colleagues in the 1997–98 interdisciplinary seminar "Women in the Public Sphere," cosponsored by Rutgers's Institute for Research on Women and Institute for Women's Leadership. In addition, several women whom I encountered through the wonderful Berkshire Conference of Women Historians kindly offered their thoughts on the project. The late Margaret Judson, whom I met when she was a retired colleague from Douglass College at Rutgers, not only introduced me to the "Berks" but also shared with me her vast knowledge of English constitutional history. Well before her superb book on the French family household appeared, former student and now Berkshire stalwart Margaret Darrow offered cautionary advice that I hope she notices I took to heart. Natalie Davis graciously sent a copy of one of her articles on early modern French families, arguing a position on the importance of household decision making at all social levels that I linked to the peculiar northwestern European marriage pattern and present here as a central theme.

Other Berkshire members who have liberally given me help and caveats include Barbara Hanawalt, Lynn Hollen Lees, Mary Beth Norton, Joanne McNamara, and Judith Zinsser. Still others, both scholars and editors who either read chapters or offered important advice at various points, include Susan Bielstein, Nora Chiang, Jean Bethke Elshtain, Sarah Hrdy, Joyce Seltzer, Catharine R. Stimpson, the late Lawrence Stone, and Susan Cott Watkins. The full and astute comments of two anonymous reviewers of the manuscript went far beyond what authors typically receive; and despite the resulting extra labor entailed, I am enormously grateful.

My editor at Cambridge, Lew Bateman, was everything an author could wish – responding positively in less than a week to my initial inquiry about potential interest of the Press and thereafter being supportive, widely informed, wise, and, quite often, very funny. The other people with whom I had the pleasure to work at Cambridge were similarly knowledgeable, thoughtful, and professional, especially Sarah Gentile, Helen Greenberg, and Helen Wheeler. I was blessed, too, in having a fine graduate student, Sandrine Sanos, aid in the preparation of the manuscript for publication. I also enjoyed the helpful and efficient support of Pat Dooley, who contributed in multiple ways to the project. Finally there are Ed and Sam Hartman. They are my favorite companions – at home, at the seashore, and in the mountains. This book is dedicated to them.

How Northwestern Europe Was Strange

Marriage, Households, and History

In a sparkling little book with the engaging title *Big Structures, Large Processes, Huge Comparisons*, social historian Charles Tilly reminded colleagues in the mid-1980s of an awkward situation that is still with us.[1] He pointed out that despite many heroic efforts, scholars have still not sorted out what it was that made western Europe the site of changes that, from about 1500, ushered in the modern era – changes that are still making themselves felt around the globe. As one commentator lately inquired, "Why did a relatively small and backward periphery on the western fringes of the Eurasian continent burst out into the world in the sixteenth century and by the nineteenth century become a dominant force in almost all corners of the earth?"[2] While the role of western Europeans in giving birth to the first "models of modernity" has been variously portrayed, not to mention regularly decried, it is impossible to dismiss compelling evidence that it was events set in motion within that region that are continuing to transform the world – for good, arguably, as well as for ill. Yet there is still no consensus as to why that was so.

Fernand Braudel, distinguished interpreter of that change as well as an ardent proponent of the vanguard role of western Europe, puts the point boldly in his famous multivolume endeavor to explain just how the contemporary

---

[1] Charles Tilly, *Big Structures, Large Processes, Huge Comparisons* (New York, 1984).

[2] Gale Stokes, "The Fates of Human Societies: A Review of Recent Macrohistories." *The American Historical Review* 106, No. 2 (2001): 508–9. Books discussed in the review include Jared Diamond, *Guns, Germs and Steel: The Fates of Human Societies* (New York, 1997); David Landes, *Wealth and Poverty of Nations: Why Some Are So Rich and Some So Poor* (New York, 1998); Kenneth Pomeranz, *The Great Divergence: Europe, China and the Making of the Modern World Economy* (Princeton, N.J., 2000); Andre Gunder Frank, *ReOrient: Global Economy in the Asian Age* (Berkeley, 1998); R. Bin Wong, *China Transformed* (Ithaca, N.Y., 1997); and J. M. Blaut, *The Colonizer's Model of the World: Geographical Diffusionism and Eurocentric History* (New York, 1993).

capitalist world took shape in the years from 1500 to 1800.[3] Tilly cites
Braudel's pronouncement that as late as the sixteenth century,

the thickly settled regions of the world, subject to the pressures of large populations,
seem close to one another, more or less equal. No doubt a small difference can be
enough to produce first advantages, then superiority and thus, on the other side,
inferiority and then subordination. Is that what happened between Europe and the
rest of the world? ... One thing looks certain to me: The gap between the West and
other continents appeared *late*; to attribute it to the "rationalization" of the market
economy alone, as too many of our contemporaries still have a tendency to do, is
obviously simplistic.

In any case, explaining that gap, which grew more decisive with the years, is the
essential problem in the history of the modern world.[4]

Tilly argues persuasively, though, that even Braudel, despite his mag-
isterial grasp of the Mediterranean world in the early modern centuries,
never managed to explain that familiar gap. He even contends that Braudel
never made up his mind on the relationship or the contributions of the parties widely presumed most responsible for western Europe's peculiar role
in global transformation: the new capitalists on the one hand and the new
state-makers on the other.[5] In an effort to help interpreters think more clearly
about this puzzle of historical change and the nature of Europe's role, Tilly
uses his essay to reflect upon and catalog "the strengths and weaknesses
of the schemes we customarily use to analyze large social processes and to
speculate on their origins."[6]

In addition to his critique of Braudel, Tilly provides lively commentary on
the efforts of scholar upon scholar to explain finally what it was about western Europe after 1500 that set the world on a new course. He warns in the
first instance, however, that we need to discard much unreliable interpretive
baggage inherited from nineteenth-century European social commentators.
Those gifted but often bedazzled or outraged eyewitnesses experienced first-
hand the cumulative effects of centuries-long change in the turmoil of a novel
reorganization of production dubbed the "Industrial Revolution." They also
beheld the awesome and often violent consolidation of nation-states as the
most powerful European organizations of the era. While Tilly concedes that
their judgments can be compelling, he declares that these nineteenth-century
commentators could also be simplistic and tendentious; and he is troubled
that even now, their pronouncements continue to "encumber our thought."[7]
Among what he labels their "pernicious postulates" are the mistaken notions

---

[3] Fernand Braudel, *Civilisation Matérielle, économie, et capitalisme, XVe-XVIIIe siècle* (Paris,
   1979).
[4] Tilly, *Big Structures*, 72 from Braudel, Vol. II, 110–11.
[5] Tilly, *Big Structures*, 66–73.
[6] Ibid., ix.
[7] Ibid., 11.

that the world as a whole can be divided into distinct societies; that social change is a coherent general phenomenon; that large-scale change takes all societies through a more-or-less standard set of stages; and that times of rapid change necessarily entail a range of disorderly behaviors such as crime, suicide, and rebellion.[8]

Tilly recommends that if we are finally to succeed in the challenge of identifying and understanding the large-scale structures and processes of change that struck European commentators so forcefully by the nineteenth century, we must leave such notions behind and appeal instead to what he labels "huge (but not stupendous) comparisons."[9] Next, he provides a useful taxonomy of different sorts of comparisons, citing a variety of examples of historians and social scientists looking comparatively at wars and revolutions as well as political, economic, and cultural systems, juxtaposing developments in different nation-states, regions, continents, time periods, and more. Such approaches, he suggests, can enable interpreters to steer a sensible middle course between the futility of attempting "total history," in the style of Braudel, and the limitations of confinement to the necessary but insufficient terrain of traditional microhistory, with its tight focus on individualized and compartmentalized experience. Such a historically grounded, comparative approach, he argues, offers the best hope for finding better answers to large questions about the origins and course of major social change in the modern world.

In the end, however, like most of the theorists he cites and admires while, often enough, deftly bringing them down, Tilly himself appears to accept the same presumptions they do about where we must all return to renew our search if we are to shed more light on western Europe's role in initiating an ongoing, dynamic process of global transformation. As he declares in his conclusion:

For our own time, it is hard to imagine the construction of any valid analysis of long-term structural change that does not connect particular alterations, directly or indirectly, to the two interdependent master-processes of the era: the creation of a system of national states and the formation of a worldwide capitalist system.[10]

This book will hardly contest the importance of these two "interdependent master-processes," let alone the need for their consideration in any serious study of long-term structural change. What it will argue, however, is that each master-process was itself dependent upon a prior and distinctive development within western Europe – or, more precisely, within northwestern Europe. This extraordinary development has long been known but remains hidden in plain sight. I refer to the discovery in the mid-1960s of

---

[8] Ibid., 11.
[9] Ibid., 74.
[10] Ibid., 147.

an idiosyncratic and still unexplained household-formation system featuring late marriage that, by 1500, dominated in northwestern Europe and singled that region out among all the major agricultural regions of the world.[11]

That a solid connection has yet to be established between the detection of this huge anomaly in marriage and household arrangements and the distinctive ways Western history evolved after 1500 is in one sense not so surprising. Standard historical interpretation, after all, continues to take for granted that "the making of the modern world" was a performance generated almost exclusively from extra-domestic sites, and largely by elite men. It is true that from the 1960s a new social history, and an even newer women's history, have contested the latter assumption, arguing that the activities of more ordinary men as well as women must always figure into accounts of what makes history run. Yet even these interpreters have rarely contested the ingrained view that all the historical action that truly matters takes place in arenas beyond the household. Their disputes have centered instead, as Tilly's own sweeping account confirms, upon which one of those arenas deserves to be assigned priority – the most popular contenders being the political and the economic realms. Nor have these scholars tried to claim that women's agency in any arena, domestic or otherwise, counted much for developments long singled out as most significant for European and, ultimately, global history.

This study will argue, to the contrary, that these and more extra-domestic arenas, along with the course of modern history itself, owe their most noteworthy features to a prior and still largely overlooked marriage and household system. I will maintain, too, that within the anomalous households of northwestern Europe, women's behavior mattered at least as much as men's – not only for generating some novel gender and power arrangements within those households but also for shaping major developments beyond them. It is true that in all arenas, men were and remained the dominant actors, and that for long anyway, they were acknowledged as legitimately such. Yet what is remarkable is that a peculiar household system, which will be shown here to have been unstable compared to its counterparts elsewhere, not only required women and men alike to be more actively engaged as partners in creating and maintaining their households, but regularly prompted women to resist men's control.

Equally striking is evidence that the combined features of the strange household-formation pattern in northwestern Europe worked from the late medieval era to diminish the salience of biological sex as a marker of social identity. That finding will be argued to suggest a new hypothesis, grounded in historical experience, to account for pervasive cross-cultural beliefs in the high importance of gender differentiation, including in a sexual hierarchy favoring men, a condition that is too often explained through the universalist

---

[11] John Hajnal, "European Marriage Patterns in Perspective," in D. V. Glass and D. E. C. Eversley, eds., *Population in History: Essays in Historical Demography* (London, 1965), 101–43.

claims of psychology or sociobiology. The discussion will also provide a splendid opportunity to call upon one of Tilly's recommended huge – perhaps even stupendous – comparisons.

* * *

A claim to present a novel approach to understanding Western and ultimately global developments, including the sexual hierarchy that appears nearly everywhere to favor men, may seem foolhardy at best. Yet since I was hardly alone during the 1970s in imagining that historical demographers were the ones about to blaze just such a path, with newly minted family and women's historians following hard on their heels, I suspect others may also have pondered why we have achieved a new millennium without a fresh array of historical syntheses to draw upon. It is true that compensation has been amply provided in the form of an enormous growth in specialty fields including, especially in the United States, a marked new focus upon cultural history. The downside of this extraordinary proliferation of research fields, however, is that collective historical attention has been diverted before a number of critical issues in social history and connected fields – especially demographic, family, and women's history – were adequately addressed. What is more, risk-taking seems to have been invested more in claiming legitimacy for new specialties than in showing just how each expands historical understanding, resolves ongoing controversies, or upsets the existing consensus on various topics.

This book returns to some of the larger unresolved issues, and it sets out a new explanation of how and why modern Western societies developed in some peculiar and still puzzling ways. While the book is based upon existing research in different and often isolated fields, that research is reimagined here in an interpretive account that links disparate findings in a single line of argument. The object is not to offer a full-blown revisionist narrative of the Western past. It is instead to make a case, and propose some tools, for a radically altered approach to that past. Illustrations and comparative examples from the medieval to the contemporary era will serve to delineate the rough outlines of what such a history might look like, but my wider aim is to provoke reassessments of what we think we already know about the making of the modern world.

The focal point, as noted, will be the still unexplored ramifications for Western historical development of the eccentric northwestern European system of late marriage. The system was first described and analyzed in the 1960s by economic historian John Hajnal, who later noted that it "presumably arose only once in human history."[12] Although late marriage and several other features of household formation are now familiar to

---

[12] John Hajnal, "Two Kinds of Preindustrial Household Formation System." *Population and Development Review* 8 (1982): 476. Hajnal refers to this article as a "sequel" to the one of 1965.

demographic and family historians, they are less well known among historians of women and hardly familiar at all to mainstream practitioners.
As for the wider community of history enthusiasts, even the most avid sub-
scriber to the popular History Book Club is unlikely to be aware of the
strange marriage and household arrangements that came to be dubbed "the
Western family pattern."

To appreciate what set northwestern Europeans apart, it is useful first to be
reminded of how most marriages have been formed in the rest of the world's
agricultural societies, including many places to this day. While particular
household structures have varied widely, couples in southern and eastern
Europe, India, the Middle East, China, and parts of Africa typically married
early, with brides being seven to ten years younger than grooms. Families
ordinarily arranged their children's marriages, and few persons remained
single throughout their lifetimes. Newlyweds most often moved into the
existing residence of the groom's parents, carrying on multifamily or joint
households of two or more married couples.

Young persons in northwestern Europe, however, followed a different path, and for a long time. In England, the Low Countries, much of
Scandinavia, northern France, and the German-speaking lands, most women
as well as men from the medieval era on married comparatively late and were
much closer in age than their counterparts in early-marriage societies. A significant number, 10 to 20 percent – and more women than men – never
married at all. While it is true that the sons and daughters of titled and
well-to-do families long married younger, had family-arranged marriages,
and might even move in with the groom's parents, the vast majority of youth
behaved otherwise. From medieval times until the late eighteenth century
or so, young persons in their late teens and twenties played the major role
in selecting their own partners; and they usually did so as agricultural servants or apprentices residing in their employers' households. At marriage,
these couples typically pooled their resources and created simple or nuclear
households of their own, which meant that most residences in northwestern
Europe housed just one married couple.

John Hajnal's exploration of this late-marriage system, presented in a
collection of specialized scholarly papers on population history in 1965,
was overshadowed by the publication the same year of the distinguished
Cambridge scholar Peter Laslett's ground-breaking book *The World We Have
Lost: England Before the Industrial Age.*[13] This popular study of small-scale

---

[13] Peter Laslett, *The World We Have Lost: England Before the Industrial Age* (New York, 1965).
Laslett, who died in 2002, is in many ways the key figure inspiring this study, even though it
was John Hajnal who, as I will argue, identified in late marriage for women the single most
critical feature of northwestern European household-formation arrangements and who also
proposed that late marriage might be the key factor in western Europe's pioneering role
in industrial transformation. Peter Laslett's career was initially devoted to examining early
modern English political theory, especially that of Filmer and Locke, before he turned his

familial society drew upon some of the same demographic evidence that Hajnal's did, but focused far more on the nuclear composition of households, rather than late marriage, as the distinguishing feature of English family arrangements. Laslett did remark that English people were bound to be surprised to learn that their ancestors had not married young, a mistaken belief that he suggests is likely owing to their awareness of the teenage brides in Shakespeare. But he insists in this widely admired study that the more serious mistake English people have made in contemplating how their ancestors lived has been to imagine that their households were extremely large.[14]

In England and northwestern Europe generally, Laslett reported, average household size was actually quite constant for centuries at just four to six persons. It was these findings on household composition and their possible implications, then, that first captured the attention of the younger generation of scholars attracted to the new social history in the late 1960s and 1970s. For a time, it even seemed likely that a genuine historical revolution was underway, based upon these startling demographic discoveries. Yet the revolution was not to be; and within a generation, the high excitement created by accounts of those discoveries, and what they might mean, had dissipated.[15]

---

attention to the family and gathered around him other talented demographers and historical sociologists who became the Cambridge Group for the History of Population and Social Structure. In this sense, Laslett's own intellectual odyssey traversed and sought to link the still separated historical worlds of the household and wider politics. Much of his work and that of his followers explored the possibility for integrating those worlds that is being called for here.

[14] Ibid., 93.

[15] See Keith Wrightson, "The Family in Early Modern England," in Steven Taylor, Richard Connors, and Clyve Jones, eds., Hanoverian Britain and Empire. Essays in Memory of Philip Lawson (Woodbridge, Suffolk, UK, 1998): 1–22. In this useful paper delivered in 1996 to Laslett's Cambridge Group for the History of Population and Social Structure, Wrightson comments in a survey of the past thirty years of family history in early modern England that controversies of many sorts on this topic have died down of late without actually being resolved. He argues that there has long remained an impasse in assessments of the early modern English family between the assertions of vast change in that period, represented by adherents of Lawrence Stone's schematic presentation of overlapping phases of development in The Family, Sex and Marriage in England 1500–1800 (London, 1977), and the work of Laslett and others, especially Alan Macfarlane, which emphasizes continuity in family structure rather than change for the early modern period. While within such a characterization this study would emphasize the continuity side, it would argue that what Wrightson's analysis misses, along with most other assessments of Western family history at this time, is John Hajnal's early identification of the significance of late marriage, and especially late marriage for women. Wrightson does not even mention Hajnal's work in this paper, which heavily cites English as well as continental scholars, although he does note that in his view, while the history of the family in early modern England as of 1996 was still in an "interpretive quandary" between a model of immense cultural change (Stone's) and one of essential cultural homogeneity (Laslett's and Macfarlane's), the "single most important development of the last 15 years has been the emergence of an explicitly gendered account of family relationships,

News, then, that for hundreds of years the most typical marriage and household arrangements in northwestern Europe constituted a global anomaly produced no sustained response from the historical community at large. It is true that demographers themselves paid much attention from the 1960s to the 1980s to comparing households, and especially household size, in many locales around the world; yet their findings have not been assimilated into standard historical narratives. Nor, more importantly, has there been a sustained interest in determining whether a distinctive domestic regime might have influenced familiar northwestern European developments, either within households or beyond them. What attention there has been was confined to the prevalence of nuclear households in the region, rather than to the feature that John Hajnal, at least, held far more important – namely, late marriage, and especially late marriage for women.

*   *   *

As noted earlier, most chroniclers of the Western past, along with nearly everyone else, have never viewed ordinary households, even collectively, as genuine historical players. Reading back from a contemporary world in which families appear to be ever more fragile entities, ceaselessly reacting to change generated outside their porous boundaries, such interpreters might be excused for thinking that whatever the motors of Western history may be, they must surely be located outside family households. Proponents of social history and its several offspring – especially family and women's history – might nonetheless have been expected to embrace the discovery of the aberrant family-formation pattern. These practitioners, after all, have long maintained that ordinary men and women belong in the historical record. Yet even family and women's historians, after intense but short-lived interest in the findings of historical demographers, turned their attention elsewhere.

Although she does not discuss the odd northwestern European marriage pattern as such, historian Louise Tilly's comparison of family and women's history helps explain why neither of those then-emerging subfields made a priority of tracking down the implications of the discovery of that pattern for behavior within or beyond households.[16] First, historians of the family

rooted in a feminist critique of the earlier agenda of family history," Wrightson, "The Family in Early Modern England," 11.

In the remainder of this introductory chapter, I will second this view of the importance of the new women's history while at the same time attempting to explain why neither that field nor historical demography – nor social history more broadly – managed to make good on an early promise to use new information about how northwestern European families were formed, and what women did within those families, to set out new accounts of how the Western world evolved.

[16] For a full discussion, see Louise A. Tilly, "Women's History and Family History: Fruitful Collaboration or Missed Connection?" *Journal of Family History* 12, Nos. 1–3 (1987): 303–15.

did not really set out to challenge the prevailing low status of typical family households as historical players. Their intent was instead to make a case that families have had a history of their own, as well as to understand these entities through what she describes as "a taxonomy of 'approaches': demographic, household economics, and sentiments or attitudes."[17]

While some of their work stresses connections between the family and other social institutions, and while all of it deals at least implicitly with women as well as men, family historians have downplayed sex-specific or individual experience in favor of aggregates of persons, households, or other collectivities. Historians of the family have cited the wider societal influence of middling and upper-class families, in particular, not only in the political realm but also in promoting certain supposed "Western" attitudes, including individualism and even egalitarianism.[18] Yet they have rarely lodged similar claims, as will be done here, on behalf of the overwhelming majority of northwestern European households – that is, the households of peasants.

Women's history, by contrast with family history, was born in the context of a wider rights movement; and its early practitioners, at least, raised many questions about the complicity of historians in ignoring women's lives and contributions. Many early interpreters, too, explicitly named the family as "a central institution of women's oppression."[19] The new historians of women, Tilly explains, did not really adopt "family" as a category in which history is appropriately conceptualized. Family turns up as a feature that may condition women's entry into politics or shape their relationship to labor markets or to housework, but family is something that is, in her words, "distributed across other concerns rather than being an independent category."[20]

All this makes it easier to see why news from 1965 that northwestern European marriage arrangements had been deviant for centuries shook neither a historical establishment focused on traditional political and economic categories nor a gathering crowd of revisionist upstarts seeking to expand the universe of legitimate historical sites, topics, and actors. Family historians, for the most part, were not asking the sorts of questions about agency and causality that have long engaged the major fields of historical inquiry; and while new historians of women were in fact asking such questions, they

---

For a more recent discussion of these same issues in the English context, see Megan Doolitle, "Close Relations? Bringing Together Gender and Family in English History." *Gender & History* 11, No. 3 (November 1999): 542–54.

[17] Tilly, "Women's History and Family History," 305.

[18] See, for example, Lawrence Stone, *The Family, Sex and Marriage in England 1500–1800* (New York, 1977); and Randolph Trumbach, *The Rise of the Egalitarian Family: Aristocratic Kinship and Domestic Relations in Eighteenth-century England* (New York, 1979).

[19] Tilly, "Women's History and Family History," 304, from Ellen Dubois, "The Radicalism of the Woman Suffrage Movement: Notes Toward the Reconstruction of Nineteenth-Century Feminism." *Feminist Studies* 3, Nos. 1/2 (Fall 1975): 63–71.

[20] Tilly, "Women's History and Family History," 310.

shared the view of most other historians that the family is not where the action is.

It is true that family historians have since researched the economic and social institutions that illuminate demographic and household structures – conducting, for example, extensive surveys of different landholding and inheritance practices.[21] Yet a leading scholar in the field, Tamara Hareven, has commented in a comprehensive review of trends in the study of families that more extensive work is needed. Most relevant to the investigation here, she states that a future agenda must include determining more precisely how households have evolved. In particular, she says, scholars must identify which circumstances enabled the family to be more or less able "to control its destiny and to affect the larger social process," as well as which factors evidently caused the family as an institution to succumb to external forces.[22]

More clarity is required, Hareven adds, on the emergence of so-called modern family behavior, especially now that it is clear that industrialization did not produce the nuclear household, as was once generally thought. Suggestions that the commercial revolution of the sixteenth and seventeenth centuries was somehow responsible still do not explain the continuing mystery of "the existence of nuclear household patterns in the Middle Ages."[23] Nor, she might have added, do they explain the continuing mystery of why, from medieval times to the modern era, women in northwestern Europe

---

[21] As E. Anthony Wrigley commented, "Since the flow of income from the land formed such a large part of the total flow of income generated in pre-industrial economies, and since the size and structure of familial systems were much influenced by their economic circumstances, tenurial and familial systems were necessarily closely related. The inheritance rules by which land passed from one generation to the next were likewise of significance to family constitution and strategy. For example, where land can be bought and sold freely and in units of any size, it is feasible for a family to adjust its holding of land to its labor power as this varies over the life cycle of the family – acquiring additional land as sons grow to adolescence and shedding it again after they leave home. Where, on the other hand, land is inalienable, any symmetry between land and labor on a holding can only be secured by 'importing' labor from outside the current co-resident family group whenever the number of able-bodied workers falls short of the number required to work the holding to advantage. Conversely if the family has a surplus of labor, it can only be fully productive if the surplus is 'exported' to another holding. There is no necessary connection between inalienable land-holding and particular family characteristics, of course, nor is surplus labor always 'exported.' Many peasant societies in Asia today, for example, appear to prefer to retain surplus labor on the family holding even when marginal productivity drops below marginal consumption. But the system by which a pre-industrial society attempts to match productive land and productive workers is so important to its general functioning that it is natural to consider the matter when examining family life," in "Reflections on the History of the Family," in Alice S. Rossi, Jerome Kagan, and Tamara Hareven, eds., *The Family* (New York, 1978), 79.

[22] Tamara Hareven, "The History of the Family and the Complexity of Social Change." *American Historical Review* 96, No. 1 (February 1991): 111.

[23] Ibid., 119.

typically married ten years later than women in most other agricultural societies around the world.

As for the field of women's history, a future agenda also contains items that may be clarified, or even resolved beyond controversy, by exploring the possible effects of the odd northwestern European marriage and family pattern. For example, an interpretive tension remains to this day between the portrayal of women as independent social actors, on the one hand, and as eternal victims of forces beyond their control, on the other. What this has meant in practice is that family households have not only been regularly presented as permanent sites of women's oppression but have also been dismissed as places where women could be imagined as significant social actors.

Insofar as the new women's history presented its subjects as agents rather than as victims, it long overlooked domestic settings in favor of public ones, presenting women as making an entrance onto the "historical stage" only in the modern era, with their roles as factory workers or as participants in suffrage and other reform movements. Recent research nonetheless supplies much evidence for women's domestic agency, although the sources and meanings of initiatives women have taken within the household arena remain contested. Fundamental interpretive differences are thus still unresolved in narratives of women's movement from the medieval to the contemporary era.

If these observations help to explain why an indisputably major finding about most northwestern Europeans remains so little known, one more item should be added. Neither John Hajnal, nor Peter Laslett, nor the demographers from the Cambridge Group for the History of Population and Social Structure (who, under Laslett's leadership, took it upon themselves to promote this so-called Western family pattern), nor anyone else, for that matter, has since been able to determine when or why the pattern appeared or what its effects really were. Hajnal commented in 1982, seventeen years after publishing his findings on late marriage, that clues as to why this odd system of marriage and family formation emerged are likely to appear when populations adjacent to northwestern Europe are explored more fully, especially those in southern Europe, which often combined features of both systems.[24] Suggestive recent comparative studies will be reported here, although it can be said now that none confirms when or why the pattern turned up in the first place.

Prior to the remarkable discoveries of the mid-1960s, scholars had, of course, been aware that northwestern Europeans married late and lived in nuclear households; but most supposed that these features emerged only in the modern era with the reorganization of work that accompanied

[24] Hajnal, "Two Kinds of Preindustrial Household Formation System," 476.

industrialization.[25] They imagined, in other words, that northwestern European households had once been multifamily ones like those in many other parts of the world, but had become "streamlined" in the nineteenth century as a result of the new factory system, with its demand for a mobile workforce.[26] Some argued further that the system promoted a sharp new specialization of labor by sex, with male "producers" occupied outside the household and female "nurturers" inside it. (This portrayal was influenced by the Victorian ideology of separate sexual spheres, which continues to persuade far too many people that the so-called gender divide widened and hardened in the early industrial era, a view that will be contested here.)

Before the revelation that most households had been nuclear for centuries, it thus seemed perfectly reasonable to specialists that the requirements of a new industrial order had altered the entire structure of northwestern European households almost overnight. But when compelling evidence turned up in the 1960s that nuclear households had dominated the region for hundreds of years before industrialization, this assumption was quietly dropped. Few scholars since, however, have pursued an alternate hypothesis suggested by that discovery – namely, that change moved in the opposite direction, and that all those anomalous late-marriage households were themselves the catalyst for industrial transformation (and much else besides) rather than being its product.

*   *   *

Testing the hypothesis that industrialization owed something to the established simple structure and small size of northwestern European households was in fact one of the stated motives that propelled the Cambridge Group in the late 1960s to launch a famous comparative global project to examine the size and structure of residential groups.[27] Another motive for that project was the desire to see whether, in Laslett's words, "the liberal political theory

---

[25] See Edward Crenshaw, "The Demographic Regime of Western Europe in the Early Modern Period: A Review of Literature." *Journal of Family History* 14, No. 2 (1989): 177–89, for a discussion.

[26] See, in particular, William J. Goode, *World Revolution and Family Patterns* (New York and London, 1963).

[27] In his introduction to the now classic *Household and Family in Past Time: Comparative Studies in the Size and Structure of the Domestic Group Over the Last Three Centuries in England, France, Serbia, Japan and Colonial North America, with Further Materials from Western Europe* (Cambridge, 1972), editor and founder of the Cambridge Group Peter Laslett stated, "We wanted to judge whether what might be called English familial individualism had been an exceptional or quite an ordinary thing. This was particularly important in view of the peculiar position of English social and economic development in relation to the process of industrialization. England had been the first of the world's societies to undergo that remarkable and momentous change, and it seemed quite possible that her pioneering role might have had something to do with the simple structure and small size of English households before ever industrialization began," 49.

which emerged in seventeenth-century England was related both with the political theory which it replaced and with the actual structure of the society which gave it birth."[28] In each of these remarkable and pioneering inquiries, as I shall argue, the decision to make the nuclear household the central research target, rather than to follow John Hajnal's lead and pursue women's late marriage as the most critical feature of northwestern European family arrangements, carried a high price. Results of exhaustive comparative investigations were at best inconclusive in determining the influence of nuclear households on critical economic as well as political change.

Spurred by enthusiasm for the computer as a new research tool at that time, the Cambridge demographers by the early 1970s confirmed the dominance of the nuclear form in preindustrial Europe and the so-called joint or multifamily form in a sampling of other global sites.[29] The Group's conclusions also challenged prevailing sociological wisdom that multifamily households were much larger than nuclear ones. It turned out that in premodern contexts, both household types usually contained just four to six persons, but for very different reasons. Unrelated adolescent servants in residence raised the average numbers in nuclear households in northwestern Europe, while splitting of households at various stages of evolution reduced the numbers in multifamily settings elsewhere. The hypothesis that the Western family pattern contributed to industrialization, insofar as it rested upon smaller average household size, appeared to be disproved.

These findings were important. Yet the decision to focus first on the numerical composition of households – which reflected a keenness to ask questions that computers can answer best – had the added effect, intended or not, of enshrining the nuclear household itself as the presumptive centerpiece of the eccentric northwestern European marriage system.[30] More recent studies

---

[28] Ibid., 46.

[29] As it turned out, when Hajnal published his findings in 1965, the Cambridge scholars were already engaged in launching Laslett's related project comparing household size and structure in different regions of the world. While the resulting publication, *Household and Family in Past Time* (1972), did cite Hajnal's article in its bibliography, there is no discussion of it in the text. It seems likely, then, that Laslett and others began to absorb the possible wider implications of Hajnal's findings only after Hajnal visited Cambridge in the 1970s.

[30] Even before *Household and Family in Past Time* appeared, the Cambridge Group was attacked by critics who portrayed their computer-generated data as a series of isolated household "snapshots" that overlooked changes in household composition over the family life cycle that produce a kind of "accordion effect" in both types. Multifamily households, the critics said, often undergo a compressed "nuclear" phase when younger sons and their families leave, while nuclear ones regularly experience an extended phase in which, for example, members of three generations may live for a time under one roof. The Cambridge Group did not contest the former effect and was able to show that the latter was actually quite limited in northwestern Europe, but the effort consumed a great deal of energy.

A second set of comparative essays on family structure by the Cambridge Group in 1983, published just over a decade after the first, paid particular attention to these disputed issues of the family life cycle in different settings, making an effort to place households in broader

under the Cambridge Group's auspices in the late 1980s and 1990s feature painstaking family reconstitution for England and for certain areas of the European continent where similar data are available.[31] These provide for the first time comprehensive information on the range and variability of male and female marriage ages in the preindustrial era, as well as on changes then in fertility and mortality. While the family reconstitution evidence, drawn in the English case from rich parish registers for the entire period from 1580 to 1837, confirms earlier work pointing to marriage as the chief determinant of demographic change, it does so in more detail than ever before. The irony, however, is that by the time these data were published, historical demographers had long since lost the large and enthusiastic audience of social historians that they had enjoyed in the 1970s and early 1980s. What is more, they themselves were steering clear of the intriguing questions raised by their forebears a generation before.

In concluding what they presented in 1997 as the final volume of twenty-five years of demographic studies, the Cambridge authors in fact state candidly that "wider issues linking demographic with economic and social change have been almost entirely neglected, though they are ultimately of greater significance than the attempt to establish the facts of population history."[32] Their study remains a monumental achievement, but it is also true that among the many interpretive items the authors admit they abandoned – such as how the economic and social circumstances of individual families influenced their demographic behavior and vice versa – there is no mention of any need for scholars to distinguish men's behavior from women's. There is no discussion, for instance, of whether the data might help to answer questions about women's and men's relative positions in these aberrant nuclear households, as compared to multifamily ones, or about women's possibly distinctive input in decisions about marriage, fertility, work, or the daily exercise of domestic power.

Well before their labors of family reconstitution were complete, there was more than enough evidence to open up such inquiries; and enterprising scholars among them, Hajnal and Laslett included, had long since launched daring speculative forays of their own into these topics. Whether or not

---

economic and social contexts. Peter Laslett's own contribution refined his earlier argument that had stressed the dominant nuclear form in northwestern Europe. Richard Wall, Jean Robin, and Peter Laslett, eds., *Family Forms in Historic Europe* (Cambridge, 1983). See further discussion of Laslett's views here in Chapter 3.

[31] Two exemplary studies are John E. Knodel, *Demographic Behavior in the Past: A Study of Fourteen German Village Populations in the Eighteenth and Nineteenth Centuries* (Cambridge, 1988); and E. A. Wrigley, R. S. Davies, J. E. Oeppen, and R. S. Schofield, eds., *English Population History from Family Reconstitution, 1580–1837* (Cambridge, 1997).

[32] Wrigley, Davis, Oeppen, and Schofield, eds., *English Population History*, 551–52. The editors even state that the sheer richness of the data "led to this book focusing more on the trees than on the wood," 550.

the demographers in this case were actually averse to the messy business of exploring why their particular data turned up, they do appear to share a still widespread view that inquiries about sex-specific behavior, and women's behavior in particular, are largely irrelevant to their enterprise.

In an intriguing article entitled "If All We Knew About Women Was What We Read in *Demography*, What Would We Know?" Susan Cott Watkins, herself a demographer with that journal, states that in her survey from the journal's founding in 1964 until 1993, she was surprised to learn how much the articles drew on "taken-for-granted understandings of what women are like, and of the differences between men and women."[33] Her curiosity was initially piqued, she says, by the realization that although demographers did try to explain women's late marriage in northwestern Europe and its high proportion of single women, their "dominant explanatory framework emphasized the circumstances of men." In particular, that framework focused on "whether they [the men] could afford to set up a neolocal household, which was believed to be the prerequisite for marriage in Western Europe for many centuries."[34] Women's own circumstances, and any challenges they faced, were totally absent from these discussions.

A related factor in skewing interpretation here has been rooted assumptions about the sexes that are presumed by demographers (as well as others) to be shared by their subjects. Watkins says of her colleagues at *Demography* that in articles about fertility, marriage, and the family, "we clearly expect the men we study to behave like men, the women like women."[35] Such assumptions are founded in part on biology, she notes, and especially on the fact that women are the childbearers; but they also come from a presumption that the socially conditioned behavior of the sexes in these areas changed very little until the contemporary era. Demographers, she further suggests, brought to their analysis of all historical settings the static interpretive framework of the western European doctrine of "separate spheres" for the sexes, in which women's supposed natural habitat is held to be the household and men's the world – with men presumed to be rightfully in charge of both the public and domestic spheres.

While women had long been associated with domestic activity, the modern doctrine of separate sexual spheres was not formally articulated until the later eighteenth century. Any socially constructed gender behaviors specific to late medieval and early modern Europe, when the Western family pattern was in its heyday, were thus unlikely to be taken into account by demographers in assessing women's marriage and family behavior at that time. Watkins says that demographers need to be "more alert to ways in which the social

---

[33] Susan Cott Watkins, "If All We Knew About Women Was What We Read in *Demography*, What Would We Know?" *Demography* 30, No. 4 (November 1993): 566.

[34] Ibid., 551.

[35] Ibid., 566.

constructions of gender shape not only the behavior of the people we study, but also the theoretical frameworks that lead us to collect data about some behaviors or characteristics and not about others."[36] The admonition applies to many more would-be interpreters than the demographers.

Power is another issue central to women's interests but almost completely ignored in the pages of *Demography*. It is true that the term "women's status," which was used early on in the journal, was resurrected in the 1980s – presumably, as Watkins says, in response to rising feminist concerns. That term was still not understood, however, as referring to men's and women's relative power. In *Demography*, Watkins notes,

"women's status" is a new label for several of our conventional variables, particularly women's education and non-domestic labor force participation. The distribution of power thus remains a central question that we still must address explicitly. If women's interests in more or fewer children can be overruled by their husbands, by others in the family, or by their friends and neighbors, we need to know more about the characteristics of those others. To address this question requires expanding our collection of data beyond surveys of individuals: the distribution of power in the family and in the community is institutional and thus is not represented adequately by information on individuals.[37]

A lone member of the Cambridge Group who recognized early on the importance of considering women's family position and behavior apart from men's is Richard M. Smith, who has explored issues of women's power and decision making insofar as medieval and early modern data permit. While not touting the full case for the influence of women's late marriage to be set forth in these pages, he was already concerned by the late 1970s that even those familiar with the pattern believed somehow that it was men's late ages at marriage, not women's, that mattered most.[38] Aware that this message had not yet sunk in, Smith was still at it in the 1990s, reminding colleagues, as Hajnal had done a quarter century before, that "the uniqueness of the European pattern lies primarily in the high age at marriage of women."[39] By then, however, what had once been an eager crowd of nonspecialists, intrigued by the new social history and gripped by the discovery of an aberrant marriage and household pattern, had dwindled to an audience of highly

---

[36] Ibid., 568.

[37] Ibid., 566.

[38] See Richard M. Smith, "Some Reflections on the Evidence for the Origins of the 'European Marriage Pattern' in England," in C. Harris, ed., *The Sociology of the Family: New Directions for Britain, Sociological Review* No. 28 (Keele, 1979): 74–112. Smith cautioned in this article, "It is rightly noted that every scholar who has employed this explanatory variable [late age at marriage] has failed to realize that it is the rise in female age that is critical and not that of males," 86.

[39] Richard M. Smith, "Monogamy, Landed Property and Demographic Regimes in Pre-Industrial Europe," in John Landers and Vernon Reynolds, eds., *Fertility and Resources* (Cambridge, 1990), 167.

specialized historical demographers. The rest had long since moved on to other specialties; and by now, most of them may barely recall how these findings once raised burning new questions about marriage, families, and the course of Western history.

* * *

Those of us who encountered the strange northwestern European marriage and household pattern many years ago got the news about it, then, not from Hajnal's paper from 1965 on late marriage, but from members of the enterprising Cambridge Group. Lively commentators among them, especially Peter Laslett, selected accessible forums to present the then recent demographic discoveries.[40] What was not clear at the time was just how sharply their portrayals veered away from the ideas, emphases, and framework that John Hajnal had originally presented.

Many of us, for example, were initially intrigued by the idea that streamlined households as a long-standing feature of northwestern Europe might help to explain why economic change that led to industrialization first occurred in that region. By the end of the decade, however, this hypothesis was already under a cloud, in part, as noted earlier, because of the Cambridge Group's own finding that mean household size was comparable for most preindustrial nuclear and multifamily households alike. What we did not realize was that John Hajnal had based his own conjectures about links between family arrangements and economic change not on the size of northwestern European households but on the known behavior of their residents – especially that of the women – during the long period prior to marriage that was a distinctive feature of the system. Here again, a myopic focus on nuclear structure appears to have stalled interpretive movement.

Ironically, too, Alan Macfarlane, a historian and anthropologist who drew heavily on the notion explored by the Cambridge Group that nuclear households promoted industrial transformation, probably did more to discredit the hypothesis than to strengthen it. Starting with his *Origins of English Individualism* in 1978, he devoted the better part of three fascinating books to the proposition that a unique household structure explains why England ultimately created the first industrialized economy.[41] In Macfarlane's exuberant rendition, nuclear households liberated both sexes from the claustrophobic bonds of extended kinship. They released their "natural" acquisitive impulses, transformed familial into individual property, and promoted

---

[40] For a discussion of Laslett's perspectives here and his views on family history as a branch of historical sociology, see Peter Laslett, "The Character of Familial History, Its Limitations and the Conditions for Its Proper Pursuit." *Journal of Family History* 12, Nos. 1–2 (1987): 263–84.

[41] Alan Macfarlane, *The Origins of English Individualism* (New York, 1978); *Marriage and Love in England: Modes of Reproduction 1300–1800* (Oxford, 1986); and *The Culture of Capitalism* (Oxford, 1987).

market-based economic structures that swept away patriarchal loyalties and institutions.

Macfarlane's bold assertion that already by the thirteenth century England displayed a "capitalist-market economy without factories" scandalized his reviewers.[42] His work may even have helped postpone a more sober case (one version of which will be presented here) for causally linking northwestern European marriage and household arrangements not only with industrialization but also with many other developments peculiar to those societies. Despite the problems with his quirky if brilliant analyses, Macfarlane deserves mention here for tackling early on the implicit but still unanswered question that others sidestepped when they learned of the strange household pattern. Simply: "How should startling new information about the distinctive ways people routinely behaved for centuries in northwestern Europe as members of aberrant family households be related to what we already know, or think we know, of their distinctive behavior elsewhere?"

It is evident by now that neither Macfarlane nor any of the other interpreters of this strange northwestern European family-formation system has been able to make the discovery of this "missing piece" fit smoothly into any larger and more familiar jigsaw puzzle of the Western historical landscape. This is an embarrassment, since the piece of evidence in question is itself so very large. I will make a case here that the reason it does not fit anywhere is that it simply does not belong in any existing depiction. It is instead part of a canvas of the Western past that has not been painted before, one whose contours have barely begun to be imagined.

Before Macfarlane published his studies alleging links between nuclear households, the freeing of acquisitive instincts, and the first industrial revolution, Peter Laslett himself had made related and only apparently less sweeping claims in a paper circulated informally from 1973 and revised for publication in 1977. That paper outlines several features of northwestern European households in the early modern era and dubs them for probably the first time "the Western family pattern."[43] Laslett argued that these household features must surely have had a profound influence on collective personality formation throughout the region, an influence that was even

---

[42] Macfarlane, *Origins*, 196. Notable among these critical reviews are Stephen D. White and Richard T. Vann, "The Invention of English Individualism: Alan Macfarlane and the Modernization of Pre-modern England." *Social History* 8, No. 3 (1983): 345–63; and Lawrence Stone, "Illusions of a Changeless Family." *Times Literary Supplement* (May 16, 1986): 525–26.

[43] Peter Laslett, "Characteristics of the Western Family Considered Over Time." *Journal of Family History* 2 (1977): 89–115, later published in Peter Laslett, *Family Life and Illicit Love in Earlier Generations* (Cambridge, 1977). Laslett notes that the paper was first circulated in an unpublished version in 1973 and subsequently revised and expanded after Hajnal's visit to Cambridge in the mid-1970s. In usage here, I will employ the term "Western family pattern" owing to its widespread acceptance, but always with the understanding that the pattern was the dominant form just in northwestern Europe.

greater in preindustrial contexts where societies, as he puts it, were "arranged in families and households for almost all social and economic purposes, and the shape of the co-resident group was accordingly of far greater consequence than it has been since."[44]

More than any single publication at that exciting time, Laslett's paper made many of us think, falsely as it turned out, that a brand new interpretation of the Western past was being born among the Cambridge demographers. At the same time, Laslett's compelling account helps to explain, in retrospect, why we paid so little attention to the implications of the feature of women's comparatively late marriage. In Laslett's rendition, discussion of that feature was confined largely to women's reduced reproductive role in the nuclear household life cycle. This item was important, but overlooked and arguably far more important was women's distinctive nonreproductive behavior over hundreds of years.

In this famous paper, entitled "The Characteristics of the Western Family Considered Over Time," Laslett places the nuclear household at center stage, citing four of its features that he argues had a "simultaneous presence during the period of primary socialization" of all young persons.[45] First, the family group was confined to one set of parents and their offspring. Second, the age of the mother during childbearing was late, "both in the experience of the mother and also in the period of fecundity." Third, the years separating spouses were few, with many wives older than their husbands and marriages "tending towards the companionate." Fourth and last, many households contained unrelated servants, marking a "peculiarity in the individual life cycle of those who went out to service as well as a characteristic of the domestic group."[46]

What was so exhilarating about the paper at the time was its argument for an enduring common influence on personality formation of a singular set of family arrangements from medieval times forward. Laslett's claims, such as that children's exposure to the strangers who were resident servants gave them unique early contact with a wider world, opened immense possibilities. They conjured up a potential array of as yet unidentified but idiosyncratic experiences that were common to the bulk of northwestern Europeans but more or less alien to young persons raised in most other agricultural settings.

---

[44] Laslett, "Characteristics of the Western Family," 95. As E. Anthony Wrigley put it in "Reflections on the History of the Family," in Rossi, Kagan, and Hareven, eds., *The Family*, "The pre-industrial family was to a greater or lesser degree the chief unit of reproduction, production, consumption, socialization, education, and in some contexts, religious observance and political action. It was the institution to which the individual normally turned to cope with the problems of age, sickness and incapacity. Effective membership in society at large was attainable in many circumstances only by membership in a family through which a claim could be mediated," 72.

[45] Laslett, "Characteristics of the Western Family," 90.

[46] Ibid.

If these experiences could be pinpointed, it might mean that a whole set of familiar European developments already identified exclusively with extra-domestic institutions and actors depended as much or more, in the end, on attitudes and behaviors that were generated and nurtured at home, within those anomalous household settings.

Naming such items was (and remains) fraught with challenges, although several of Laslett's early conjectures have borne up well to later research. He pointed out, for example, that servants moving from house to house, often on annual contracts, could readily make the acquaintance of potential marriage partners – and that they could do so in the absence of parental supervision. This "life-cycle" domestic service was an experience without parallel in societies where early marriage is the rule. In such societies, girls typically move just once in their lives, from their father's house to their new father-in-law's, whereas boys, and especially eldest sons, reside in their natal households for life, marrying in their twenties pubescent brides who are imported into their fathers' households.

Less persuasive was Laslett's claim that household service was highly ex-ploitive, especially as he ignores some common experiences of young per-sons in more typical agricultural settings that are plausible candidates for at least as harsh an assessment. Nor does Laslett argue persuasively for his contention that the authority of the single adult man in these stripped-down northwestern European households was bound to have been vastly enhanced in the eyes of the children there. The large issue of domestic power and its distribution in early- and late-marriage settings will be considered in due course. Yet what is noteworthy here is that Laslett, whose prior work had explored the theories of conservative Robert Filmer and liberal John Locke on the subject of power in the family and in the state, was attuned early on to possible links between household and state power structures.[47] Even now, scholars of political theory overlook this crucial topic.

More problematic than any of Laslett's claims in this early paper, how-ever, was his failure to draw systematic distinctions between women's and men's experiences and, just as important, to pursue fuller comparisons with the shared experiences of young persons from more typical agricultural so-cieties. His account at once obscures and diminishes Hajnal's central point that women's lives in northwestern Europe differed far more from those of their counterparts in early-marriage settings than men's did from theirs. What is more, labeling the experiences that set northwestern Europeans apart as differences in "socialization" trivializes the extent to which late-marriage household arrangements literally molded the collective experiences and men-talities of women and men alike at every phase of the life cycle, and not just during childhood and youth.

---

[47] See especially John Locke, *Two Treatises of Government*, a critical edition with an introduction and *apparatus criticus* by Peter Laslett (Cambridge, 1960).

Turning at last to John Hajnal's often cited but still too little read article of 1965, what is at first striking is that he barely mentions the nuclear household structure that the Cambridge Group came to elevate as the centerpiece of the Western family pattern. Hajnal's aim, as he tells us in the opening paragraphs of this famous article, simply titled "European Marriage Patterns in Perspective," is to show that marriages in northwestern Europe right up to the modern era were unique for displaying two features: "(1) a high age at marriage and (2) a high proportion of people who never marry at all."[48]

To drive these points home, Hajnal presents census data showing the persistence of these features into twentieth-century northwestern Europe, despite marriage ages there having declined steadily for both sexes from the late eighteenth century. In 1900, for example, around three-quarters of women aged twenty to twenty-four in most northwestern European countries were still unmarried, as were about 90 percent of the men. By contrast, over three-quarters of women in that age group in eastern Europe were already married, with even higher percentages elsewhere, including over 90 percent in India, Morocco, and Korea.

As for the numbers remaining single for life, Hajnal shows that even by 1900, many men and women in northwestern Europe never married – about 10 to 12 percent of men and slightly higher percentages of women. We now know that in the classic era of the Western family pattern, from the sixteenth through the late eighteenth centuries, the numbers were even higher. Up to a fifth of all persons are estimated to have remained single, thereby failing to achieve what was held at the time to be full adult status. In the early-marriage societies of eastern Europe, however, fewer than 5 percent of women remained single, with even smaller percentages elsewhere. For example, only 2 percent never married in Japan in 1920 and just 1 percent in India in 1931. In the early-marriage regions, the number of men who were single for life exceeded that of women, although the figures Hajnal cites never reach double digits.[49] While in early-marriage societies the married state was almost universal, then, especially for women, in the late-marriage region of Europe, marriage amounted to an achieved status that large numbers of women and men would never attain.

Another topic barely touched upon in the early studies of the Cambridge Group is the contrast in the age-sex composition of early- and late-marriage populations at marriageable ages. Hajnal notes that late-marriage societies

---

[48] Hajnal, "European Marriage Patterns in Perspective," 101.
[49] Ibid., 101–4. About three-quarters of women were unmarried in 1900 in Great Britain, Belgium, Denmark, Holland, Norway, Switzerland, and Sweden – as were 71% in Germany, 60% in Italy and 58% in France. Figures for men remaining single for life ranged from 9% in Denmark and Germany to 11% in France, 12% in Great Britain, and 20% in Ireland. Women's percentages were typically higher.

typically displayed either equal sex ratios or ratios slightly favoring females, whereas early-marriage societies frequently had sex ratios favoring males. He states that despite the natural or biological excess of 105 boys to 100 girls at birth, higher male mortality is the rule thereafter, due mainly to greater male susceptibility to disease in the early years. In northwestern Europe, the higher male mortality during youth meant that the ratios of men to women in modern census data were often roughly comparable by the time young persons reached marriageable ages, when there might even have been a female surplus.

Noting by contrast the relatively high sex ratios favoring males that often turn up, for example, in parts of India and China, Hajnal contests the then common explanation that there was systematic undercounting of females, arguing instead that much of the reported excess of males was genuine, owing to practices of female neglect and sex-selective infanticide.[50] Recent discussions of this topic will shortly be reviewed here, but it is remarkable that it was not until the 1990s that Western scholars paid much attention to these practices. Even now, there is little appreciation outside demographic circles of Hajnal's early observation that different marriage and family structures can have a powerful influence on the survival chances of females.

Reminding readers that his primary theme of postponed marriage is not a new one, Hajnal remarks that Thomas Malthus in the late eighteenth century had already called attention to the importance of "delay of the marriage union" as a check to population outpacing the food supply.[51] Hajnal's contribution is nonetheless highly original, not only for its emphasis on the historical longevity of late marriage and the large numbers of single adults but also for his insistence that "the uniqueness of the European pattern lies primarily in the high age at marriage of women (often with relatively small difference between the age of husband and wife), rather than in a high age at marriage for men."[52] The differences between men's age at marriage – from the early to mid-twenties in early-marriage societies and the mid- to late twenties in late-marriage ones – was, after all, but a few years.

Hajnal made another original contribution by hypothesizing that it was women who played the critical role in the changes that ultimately led to industrial transformation. As an economist, Hajnal was understandably intrigued by possible connections between the marriage pattern and what he cites as the relatively high living standards in northwestern Europe, and especially in England, in the eighteenth century.[53] Many people, not just the rich, he says, appear to have enjoyed quite decent housing, clothing, and food – well before the industrial era. (This conclusion has been borne out since in

50 Ibid., 125–30.
51 Ibid., 130.
52 Ibid., 134.
53 Ibid., 131.

numerous studies).[54] Hajnal speculates that the late-marriage system, and women's work in particular, help to explain this evidence:

The economic system influences the marriage pattern through the arrangements by which the economic basis for the support of a couple and their children is established. It is equally true that the marriage pattern influences the economic system. The traditional argument, that late marriage retarded population growth, has already been mentioned but other possible effects need to be explored. In the European pattern, a person would usually have some years of adult life before marriage; for women especially this period would be much larger than outside Europe. It is a period of maximum productive capacity without responsibility for children; a period during which saving would be easy. These savings (e.g. by means of the accumulation of household goods in preparation of marriage) might add substantially to the demand for goods other than the food etc. required for immediate survival. In this respect delayed marriage may be similar to income inequality in stimulating the diversion of resources to ends other than those of minimum subsistence; but when later marriage is the norm the total volume of demand generated might be much larger than that which can be caused by a small class of wealthy families in a population at subsistence level. Could this effect, which was uniquely European, help to explain how the ground-work was laid for the uniquely European "take-off" into modern economic growth? [55]

This hypothesis has yet to be seriously pursued, even though there is more evidence now than in 1965 that the contribution of women to household economies in northwestern Europe was both larger and older than even Hajnal first thought. He sees, too, that women's late marriage raises other sweeping issues – issues that by now ought to have summoned the talents of many more specialists than his demographer colleagues:

An inquiry into the origins of the European marriage pattern will inevitably take one into fundamental issues of economic and social history. This is so not only because of the connexions just discussed between marriage and births and deaths. There are other links. A marriage almost by definition requires the establishment of an economic basis for the life of the couple and their children. The arrangements current in a society for achieving this must fit in with the marriage pattern: they will shape it and will be in turn influenced by it. Unmarried men and women must be attached to households in some way, or form independent households. The structure and size of households and the rate of formation of new households and disappearance of old ones, therefore, depend on the marriage pattern. In societies where the household is the principal unit of economic production as well as consumption, all this means that

---

[54] For a recent statement of the view, see Roger Schofield, "Family Structure and Demographic Behavior," in John Walter and Roger Schofield, eds., *Famine, Disease and the Social Order in Early Modern Society* (Cambridge, 1989), 279–304.

[55] Hajnal adds this striking footnote: "The mere presence in the labour force of a large number of adult women not involved in child-bearing or -rearing must have been a consider-able advantage to the eighteenth-century European economies," Hajnal, "European Marriage Patterns in Perspective," 132. See the further discussion of industrial transformation in Chapter 7.

the marriage pattern is tied in very intimately with the performance of the economy as a whole. The emotional content of marriage, the relation between the couple and other relatives, the methods of choosing or allocating marriage partners – all this and many other things cannot be the same in a society where a bride is usually a girl of 16 and one in which she is typically a woman of 24. These things are perhaps obvious, but they have not been much explored, at least not in histories which trace the emergence of modern Europe. A full explanation of the background of European marriage patterns would probably lead into such topics as the rise of capitalism and the protestant ethic.[56]

Save for a few efforts with little effect to date on reigning interpretations of the Western past, these arresting final comments remain as valid now as when Hajnal first made them. Yet even he turned away from the speculative audacity of this early paper. Not until seventeen years later, in 1982, did he publish a less bold but important piece, "Two Kinds of Preindustrial Household Formation System," that he billed as a sequel to the first.[57] Featuring the comparative composition of households that was the Cambridge Group's trademark, the article looks at nuclear and joint or multifamily regimes by juxtaposing data from early modern Denmark and mid-twentieth-century India. It uses the census of 1951, when 80 percent of the population was still classified as rural and most Indians spent at least a portion of their lives in multifamily households.

Both Danish and Indian households had an average of five persons and the same number of resident children, although in India the number of sons far exceeded that of daughters, mainly, he says, because so many daughters had already left their natal households to marry, leaving their brothers behind. (There is no reference to the lesser reason of sex-selective neglect and infanticide that he had noted earlier.) In the Indian census, the "missing" daughters are located in the "other relatives" category in their new households, a large grouping that also incorporated additional kin. In Denmark, while numbers in the "other relatives" category were negligible, servants and "other unrelated persons" were numerous. The Indian households, by contrast, consisted almost entirely of kin.

Another notable feature was the status of married persons. In Denmark and throughout northwestern Europe, most married couples were in charge of their own individual households, whereas in rural India only 64 percent of married men were also heads of households. Scattered data from more than a century earlier give much the same picture, showing that there had long been many households in India with two or more married couples living together – most being married sons in households headed by their fathers.

---

[56] Ibid.
[57] The article pays homage to the Cambridge Group, with which Hajnal was closely allied by then. Hajnal, "Two Kinds of Preindustrial Household Formation System," 449–94.

Early household splitting was common, though, explaining why household size in both societies was about the same.

Hajnal is careful to note that although these were the two chief systems of household formation in agricultural societies, there were endless variations within each. He cites, for example, a census of an estate of Russian serfs in the late eighteenth and nineteenth centuries whose average household size, at nine, ensured that most men died without ever heading a household. He also notes instances in southern Europe of "hybrid" societies with features of both household-formation types. Acknowledging such broad variations did not, however, stem attacks from critics who from the beginning accused demographers who cited the distinctive northwestern European household features of a bias that privileged "the West" and lumped together all "the rest."[58]

Unfortunately, the fact that the Cambridge Group early on emphasized nuclear household composition as the all-important variable in the northwestern European family regime made it easier for such critics to dispute suggestions that particular developments there were owed to distinctive household arrangements. They could simply point to the immense variety of household composition both within that region and elsewhere. Hajnal, however, stressed that the item that mattered most was late marriage for women – a more straightforward indicator, in any case, than the disputed item of household composition. Late marriage will be presented here not only as the most hardy ingredient of an aberrant marriage regime but also as the variable that mattered most for the distinctive ways that northwestern European families and societies behaved, including the distinctive ways they entered the modern era.

In his article from 1982, Hajnal did embed several items that advanced his earlier ideas about women's status in the late-marriage regime. Noting the uniqueness of a system of life-cycle service that was roughly as common among women as among men, he made the case that women in late-marriage societies were obliged by household structures themselves to exercise more autonomy and responsibility than women in early-marriage societies:

This [household service] was an aspect of the apparently greater independence of women in preindustrial Northwest Europe compared with women in joint [or multifamily] household populations. While in service, women were not under the control of any male relative. They made independent decisions about where to live and work and for which employer. There was also financial independence even though women servants' wages were lower than men's. Savings accumulated during service were probably often a substantial contribution to the economic basis of a woman

---

[58] Anthropologist Jack Goody, for example, has made an avocation of disparaging scholars who make such claims, accusing them of harboring a "West is best" interpretive prejudice. See especially *The Development of the Family and Marriage in Europe* (Cambridge, 1983). The theme is also developed in his more recent *The East in the West* (Cambridge, 1996).

servant's subsequent marriage. This was probably the reason why women marrying laborers (for whom such a contribution was important) were on average older at first marriage than women marrying farmers. The future wives of laborers would have needed a substantial period of service to accumulate the necessary savings.

The fact that marriage in Northwest Europe joined together two mature adults must have affected considerably the nature of the relationship between the spouses. Indeed this relationship was generally initiated by way of a period of courtship, whereas in the joint household populations the practice of marriage arranged by the parents seems to have been nearly universal, often arranged marriage in the full sense that the couple had little or no acquaintance with each other before the wedding. The joint household system must also affect the relationship between husband and wife after marriage because, in contrast with the Northwest European situation, the young couple is often not the only couple in the house. The young husband's parents will often be in charge of the household. The young wife is under the dominance of her mother-in-law at an age at which, in Northwest Europe, she would often have been in service under an unrelated mistress. Her husband may continue to have a closer relationship with his mother, who is present in the household, than with his wife.[59]

For whatever reasons, Hajnal excised these insightful comments on women and domestic power relationships when he revised this previously published piece for inclusion in the Cambridge Group's popular collection *Family Forms in Historic Europe* (1983).[60] While somewhat at odds with Laslett's condemnation of service as exploitive, they might have intrigued the new social historians then still avidly devouring the Group's work. It is, of course, a large claim that late-marriage arrangements compelled women to become more independent social agents than their counterparts in early-marriage settings. Yet that claim will be warmly defended in the next chapters, along with another of my own, which is that men's attitudes and behavior were also profoundly influenced by those distinctive domestic arrangements.

In his "sequel" article of 1982, Hajnal revisits the question of when the northwestern European marriage system might first have appeared. While he had previously argued that the system had emerged only in the sixteenth century, he now stated that new research suggested a much earlier date. He remarked, too, that even in the absence of complete demographic information, evidence for residential life-cycle servants, for example, points to the likely prevalence of the late-marriage pattern in a region. Data on retirement contracts are another such indicator, for in societies where most children of both sexes leave the parental household, there are no built-in "social security" arrangements for the older generation, as in the early-marriage system. Hajnal reports that contractual arrangements appeared early, allowing a

---

[59] Hajnal, "Two Kinds of Preindustrial Household Formation System," 474–75.
[60] See Hajnal, "Two Kinds of Preindustrial Household Formation System," in Wall, Robin, and Laslett, eds., *Family Forms in Historic Europe*, 65–104.

couple to retire in return for a formal guarantee of upkeep, often by nonkin. Evidence of public provision for the poor, usually by the local community, is yet another indicator of extra-domestic practices and institutions devised to meet needs that smaller and less enduring households could not readily handle on their own. Hajnal states that "for England, at least, it seems likely that these features – life-cycle service, retirement contracts, and public provision for the poor – can be traced back for perhaps four centuries prior to 1600."[61] Whatever its origins, then, the northwestern European regime appears to have had deep roots in the past.

* * *

A run-of-the-mill dispute from a sixteenth-century English church court in the diocese of Ely provides as good a window as any on the peculiar way most northwestern Europeans by that time were creating their marriages and their households. The principals were two young persons of modest country background: a woman named Joan Wigg and her suitor, John Newman, of the village of Royston in Hertfordshire. In the mid-1530s, Newman brought Wigg to court, claiming she had reneged on her promise to marry him. He was seeking a ruling that would allow him to enforce that promise, but Joan Wigg did not wish to marry, at least not yet. She admitted that she had once told Newman she would marry him, but denied that she had contracted before witnesses in any way that amounted to a formal betrothal. When Newman presented friends to testify to the contrary, Wigg subjected her suitor to a spirited cross-examination:

John Newman, I marvel what you mean.... You follow some evil Counsel. I cannot deny but I have made a promise to you to my husband; but shall we need to marry so soon? It were better for us to forebear and [have] some household stuff to begin withal.[62]

Joan Wigg's protest has a strikingly contemporary ring. Not only does this woman not want to be rushed, she dares to speak out sharply on her own behalf. She does not try to argue, as might be expected, that her family forbids the match. Instead, she contends that the obstacle to marriage is the couple's lack of "household stuff." The union should be put off until both have managed to work and accumulate resources sufficient to set up housekeeping on their own. This, at any rate, is the argument Joan Wigg chooses to present. Presumably it is also the one she deems likely to work best for her with the court.

Yet consider for a moment the circumstances underlying this dispute. The union at issue would evidently have taken place without contest if the two

[61] Hajnal, "Two Kinds of Preindustrial Household Formation System," 477.
[62] Laslett, *The World We Have Lost*, 151. See also the full discussion in John Gillis, *For Better, For Worse: British Marriages, 1600 to the Present* (New York, 1985), 22.

parties themselves had simply agreed to it. Unlike the pubescent brides of twelve to sixteen in more typical agricultural settings, Joan Wigg was likely to have been in her early to mid-twenties, with considerable independent wage-earning experience as well as substantial leverage in the choice of a spouse. The ecclesiastical court's role was not to sanction a union arranged by parents or other third parties, but rather to determine whether whatever had transpired between Wigg and Newman amounted to a formal betrothal.[63] It is true that couples like this pair typically sought and obtained parental approval of their choices, especially if they anticipated contributions in goods, money, and/or land. Yet it is also true that relatively late marriage ages meant that most young persons were likely in any case to have lost at least one parent by the time they married.[64]

Besides illustrating spousal selection as the prerogative of couples themselves, admittedly with kin and community exercising a strong influence, the case of Joan Wigg and John Newman displays something else that was basic to northwestern European marital arrangements, at least by the early modern period from about 1500 to 1750.[65] That is a requirement that both parties to a marriage not only contribute to the startup costs of their new households but also have a reasonable expectation of future economic independence. There is no such requirement for young persons in early-marriage societies, which helps to explain the more universal incidence of marriage in those societies. Wigg and Newman evidently disagreed not only about whether they were officially betrothed but also about the amount of "household stuff" they needed. Yet the marriage postponement proposed by Wigg was in itself hardly unusual.

When population rose throughout the region in the sixteenth century, in fact, land and other resources required for a livelihood became increasingly squeezed, and already high marriage ages rose still higher. It is true that landed elites and the urban patriciate with significant property at stake continued to marry their daughters relatively young. For the majority in northwestern Europe, however, the age at marriage climbed from the early to the mid- and even late twenties from the sixteenth to the eighteenth century. From 1610 to the 1730s in England, for example, grooms averaged between twenty-seven and twenty-eight and brides between twenty-five and

---

[63] Scholars have known that the Church's canon law admitted mutual consent by the couple as a valid basis for matrimony; but only recently through pioneering studies on early modern marriage, such as that by John Gillis cited previously, have they realized that throughout northwestern Europe, ordinary people like Joan Wigg and John Newman had long been accustomed to playing a major role in selecting their spouses.

[64] Peter Laslett makes this point in "Characteristics of the Western Family," 107.

[65] For a careful recent discussion of this transitional era, see the fine and nuanced study by Diana O'Hara, *Courtship and Constraint: Rethinking the Making of Marriage in Tudor England* (Manchester, 2000).

twenty-six.[66] Similarly, in Crulai, France, from 1674 to 1742, women were just over twenty-five at marriage and men almost twenty-seven.[67] Despite these late ages at marriage, demographers estimate that illegitimacy throughout northwestern Europe was extremely low. In England, where parish registers permit the determination of ratios of illegitimate baptisms to all baptisms, these range, in the decades from 1538 to 1754, from 1.2 to 4 percent, with illegitimacy ratios in most decades between 2 and 3 percent.[68] These were considerably less that the typical illegitimacy figures for early-marriage societies.[69]

There is, of course, nothing remarkable, these days anyway, about young persons being close in age at marriage, or taking charge of selecting their spouses, or saving to support themselves in households of their own. Postponed marriage and lifelong singleness, moreover, not only affect many people in contemporary societies but have emerged as voluntary conditions more than ever before. What is surprising and puzzling, however, is the sheer longevity of these features in northwestern Europe. From the Middle Ages, that region almost alone featured late marriage and nuclear households at a time when early-marriage and multifamily households – arrangements that are actually far better suited to the needs of agricultural societies – dominated in the rest of the world.[70] While textbooks by now may make

---

[66] Wrigley, Davies, Oeppen, and Schofield, eds., *English Population History*, 135. The editors remark that from the 1730s to the 1830s, men's age at marriage fell from about twenty-seven to twenty-five, whereas women's average marriage age dropped even more, from twenty-six to twenty-three and a half.

[67] John Hajnal cites these data from a study of the French village of Crulai published in 1958 by Etienne Gautier and Louis Henri, showing the mean age at first marriage at 26.6 for men and 25.1 for women. Hajnal, "European Marriage Patterns in Perspective," 111.

[68] Cited in Richard Adair, *Courtship, Illegitimacy and Marriage in Early Modern England* (Manchester, 1996), 50.

[69] See the comparative discussion by Richard M. Smith, "Marriage Processes in the English Past," in Lloyd Bonfield, Richard M. Smith and Keith Wrightson, eds., *The World We Have Gained: Histories of Population and Social Structure* (Oxford, 1986), 43–99. See also the discussion in Crenshaw, "The Demographic Regime of Western Europe in the Early Modern Period," 177–89.

[70] Alan Macfarlane has recently compared the two island nations of England and Japan for the different ways each managed to escape the "Malthusian trap," in which mortality crises typically arrest economic growth. He notes that, unlike northwestern Europe, which relied upon late marriage as the primary means to control fertility, Japan had more than one mechanism for that purpose. From the seventeenth to the nineteenth centuries, the low birth rate in Japan was influenced by significant marital abstinence, with large numbers of prostitutes readily available for married men. Female infanticide was also practiced. In addition, and significantly for the discussion here, the age at marriage for Japanese women, at eighteen to twenty-two from the seventeenth to the nineteenth centuries, was somewhere in between that for most agricultural societies – namely, the early to mid-teens – and that for England, which ranged from twenty-five to twenty-seven in the seventeenth century. On the other hand, marriage was nearly universal in Japan, whereas only in northwestern Europe did significant numbers of women never marry. Remarriage was also far less frequent in Japan

passing reference to the practice of late marriage in northwestern Europe, their failure to describe the far more common early-marriage system means that Westerners persist in the mistaken impression that their own marriage arrangements are somehow natural or optimal, rather than the global oddity that they remained for such a very long time.

The saga of Joan Wigg and John Newman offers a glimpse of real people confronting issues of establishing a marriage (or, in their case, postponing doing so). To their counterparts in early-marriage societies, however, the tale of this pair's altercation over their betrothal would have been incomprehensible. Despite countless variations in their own families' practices, such young persons, whether from China, India, or the Middle East, would have understood accounts of youthful brides and arranged marriages in one another's societies. Such features, after all, had typified agricultural households like theirs for millennia. Ironically, though, since the late-marriage pattern is increasingly becoming the norm in many societies around the globe, it is the early-marriage system that is more and more being perceived as aberrant. Arranged marriages that were once the way of the world are now declared barbaric, and parents who marry their adolescent daughters to strangers ten or more years their senior are attacked as ignorant and cruel.

Such critics fail to appreciate that compelling reasons have prompted societies to adopt and perpetuate these practices, reasons that make good sense in the context of the shared concerns of agricultural peoples. This helps to explain evidence that the early-marriage system, which is agreed to be by far the older of these two family-formation systems, emerged independently in several regions of the world and lasted such a very long time – in China even surviving massive twentieth-century revolutionary upheaval.[71] What still needs explaining, however, is what lies behind the spectacle of Joan Wigg and John Newman quarreling before the ecclesiastical court in Ely – which is to say, what lies behind the strange features of the marital regime that turned up in medieval northwestern Europe. An attempt will be made here to explain when, why, and how that system emerged, but what matters finally are less the system's origins than its likely effects.

Contrary to the near-universal orthodoxy that would discount the household as a place where history is made, this book will contend that the course of northwestern European history, including the regions settled by

---

than in northwestern Europe, so the overall demographic characteristics in Japan were still closer to those of early-marriage societies; *The Savage Wars of Peace: England, Japan and the Malthusian Trap* (Oxford, 1997).

[71] Margery Wolf reports that despite the increase since the revolution in nuclear or elementary households, "most young people still spend some part of their married lives under the domination of an older married couple. The youngest son and his wife, or the only son and his wife, will live jointly with the parents until their deaths. No farm woman would consider living with her daughter and her daughter's husband if she has a son," *Revolution Postponed: Women in Contemporary China* (Stanford, Calif., 1985), 190.

northwestern Europeans and ultimately beyond, was critically affected by a peculiar marriage and household regime. Contemporary experience admittedly discourages the idea that domestic arrangements might loom large in any new portrayal of the Western past. Accustomed to seeing their own households as embattled and weakened, many would dismiss the suggestion that there was ever a time when typical household settings exercised immense influence, not only in structuring women's and men's daily lives but also in generating lasting change beyond households and in setting crucial conditions on the nature of that change. In the contemporary world, after all, we are used to the idea that the arrow of change always moves from institutions back to households, that households are always reactors to outside developments and never places from which far-reaching transformation might emanate.

Compelling evidence that the marriage and household system in northwestern Europe was unique and established well before the modern era nonetheless makes it possible to reimagine the ways change might have taken place in the Western past. It permits observers to recognize how a peculiar set of choices and constraints within idiosyncratic household settings could have established critical preconditions for the entire range of familiar developments associated with modern Western societies – not just economic transformation but everything from Protestant upheaval to scientific revolution, mass democratic movements, and major alterations in the relations between the sexes. Much of the change that will be argued to have flowed from these deviant arrangements was less calculated and more haphazard than the standard accounts of these developments would have it, but that hardly diminishes the main point. Women and men in ordinary household settings will be presented here as having played indispensable roles in placing Western societies, from the medieval era, on a distinctive historical path.

One of the most striking features of the case to be made here is that the household regime appeared not within the elites of Western societies, but instead among the masses of women and men who worked the land. The system also showed up in the medieval era among humbler residents of the growing towns, including servants, day laborers, shopkeepers, and apprentices. Many of these, including disproportionate numbers of single women, were migrants from the countryside. Their social betters meanwhile, namely, the newly wealthy commercial groups and the older landed elites, continued to practice early marriage for their daughters, even though, by the industrial era, they too came to adopt many of the marriage and household practices pioneered by their social inferiors. All this raises the possibility that vitally important changes in men's and women's attitudes and behavior did not trickle down from the more privileged upper reaches of northwestern European societies, as is usually thought, nor were they otherwise imposed from above. Such changes appear instead to have been owing to the prior agency of a relatively poor and illiterate majority.

In other important ways, within that very large group it was the women, even more than the men, whose collective activity set these households apart. In a real sense, it is the spunky Joan Wigg, insisting before the court upon her own account of a promise to marry John Newman, and her own reasons to postpone their marriage, who needs to be foregrounded in new renditions of the Western historical drama. Her experiences contrasted more sharply with those of her counterparts in early-marriage settings than did those of the men with theirs. They also made a greater difference for directions that Western history has taken in the modern era, both in the household and in the wider world.

Discussions here will explore shifts noted earlier in domestic power relations, arguing that the marriage regime itself had the effect of augmenting women's capacity to take action, including challenging men's control, on both the domestic and extra-domestic fronts. The late-marriage system also appears to have sharply reduced the domestic authority of men as heads of household that is structurally reinforced in the early-marriage regime. Since new brides and grooms were typically the only resident adults in brand new households, shared decision making in running those households was more likely to occur from the outset, especially as women often brought resources they themselves had earned to the creation of those households. By contrast, in the early-marriage system, multifamily households were likely to be ongoing, patriarchally run entities, controlled by a network of two or more generations of resident male kin.

The comparatively greater mutuality in decision making in late-marriage settings appears, however, to have been less than entirely welcome. There is abundant evidence, in fact, that the increased overlapping of women's and men's experiences that I will contend was a major effect of the late-marriage regime was an ongoing source of friction and conflict within marriage, especially during the early modern period. To this day, a recognition that both partners share decision-making authority leads to regular marital clashes, although men continue to display more concern about this situation than women for reasons to be explored.

Attentiveness to how late-marriage societies worked will be argued to provide new clues to some old mysteries, including the very large one about the source of a widespread insistence upon gender differentiation, as well as upon a hierarchy favoring men. What I shall present as a fairly swift undercutting of material and ideological buttresses for such beliefs and related practices, owing to late-marriage arrangements, raises serious questions about theories that continue to invoke universal and inexorable mechanisms, whether biological or psychological, to account for what is labeled "male dominance." Observable elements of family structure will be argued instead to go a very long way toward explaining the pervasiveness and longevity of patterns of gender differentiation and hierarchy.

These elements, as noted at the outset, will also make it easier to explain otherwise baffling evidence that in a rather brief period of time, the ways people spent their daily lives in northwestern European-based societies came to have less to do than ever before with whether they were biologically male or female. An advantage of taking comparative household and family-formation systems into account in addressing the conundrum of a still pervasive insistence upon differences between the sexes is that unlike most other explanations, this one will be shown to be amenable to empirical scrutiny and applicable, with predictive as well as analytical force, to gender arrangements anywhere.

This book, then, will contend that the innovation of a comparatively flexible if unstable marriage and family-formation system that appeared first in medieval Europe had huge if still mostly unrecognized consequences. That system will be proposed to hold immense potential to explain better what we already know of women's and men's behavior on the domestic front, as well as of their activities beyond the household. It will be argued to provide more coherent accounts for developments long held up as peculiar Western achievements, such as industrial transformation and the emergence of mass democratic political movements. It also will be shown to go some way toward explaining a number of issues that have long puzzled historians, such as the appearance of intense hostility toward homosexuality in Western societies from the later Middle Ages, as well as the rise in those societies of massive witch hunts.

The late-marriage system of family formation will be presented as the vehicle most responsible for generating novel political structures, transformed means of livelihood, and fresh social, cultural, and intellectual systems in the period known as the "early modern era," from the sixteenth to the late eighteenth centuries. Along the way, I will also show how the system's very instability exposed for the first time the common ingredients whose presence has ensured, in nearly all societies, the familiar impulse to differentiate roles, qualities, and status by sex. A concluding chapter will trace a number of the ways that late-marriage features have continued to influence developments in the modern era, both within European-based societies and beyond.

The exercise as a whole represents a means to use what we already know in new ways to get closer to a credible account of western Europe's role in the making of the modern world. It selects several "big structures, large processes, and huge comparisons" of its own to sketch out an altered version of the past, one that I like to think helps to support early insights of social and women's historians that ordinary persons, women as well as men, truly did make history and did shape the world. These, in any case, are the outlines of arguments to be set out in these pages.

2

Marrying Early and Marrying Late
Divergent and Parallel Lives

In concluding *Utopia* (1516), his fantasy blueprint for a model society, Thomas More makes a sly disclaimer. He says that he hardly shares the enthusiasm for the island commonwealth of his imaginary narrator and interlocutor, Raphael Hythloday, who has just regaled him with the tale of an extended visit there. More further declares that many of the laws and customs of Utopia are ridiculous. "But I freely admit," he adds in the very last words of his classic account, "that there are many features of the Utopian Republic which I should like – though I hardly expect – to see adopted in Europe."[1]

The precaution of putting his description of Utopia into the mouth of a fictitious visitor has long been understood. This was a time when expressing a subversive opinion could land a person in the Tower of London; and Thomas More, after all, was considering appointment to high office in Henry VIII's government at the time he was writing the book. Yet in all the controversy about what More actually thought about the features he invented for his island republic, modern commentators seldom tarry on the institution that he presents as the cornerstone of Utopian society: namely, a multifamily, multigenerational patriarchal household. Here is Hythloday's description:

Now I'd better explain their social arrangements – how society is organized, how they behave towards one another, how goods are distributed, and so on. Well, the smallest social unit is the household, which is virtually synonymous with the family. When a girl grows up and gets married, she joins her husband's household, but the boys of each generation stay at home, under the control of their oldest male relative – unless he becomes senile, in which case the next oldest takes over.

Each town consists of six thousand households, not counting the country ones [there are fifty-four towns, which are the main population centers, although women and men alike are required to spend time living in the countryside, performing agricultural work in addition to their regular urban craft employments]; and to keep the

[1] Thomas More, *Utopia*, tr. and intro. Paul Turner (New York, 1987), 132.

population fairly steady, there's a law that no household shall contain less than ten or more than sixteen adults – as they can't very well fix a figure for the children. This law is observed by simply moving supernumerary adults to smaller households....

But let's get back to their social organization. Each household, as I said, comes under the authority of the oldest male. Wives are subordinate to their husbands, children to their parents, and younger people generally to their elders.[2]

Elsewhere in the tale we learn that premarital sex is strictly forbidden in Utopia. Anyone caught engaging in such behavior is severely punished and disqualified from marrying unless pardoned by the town mayor. Utopians, we are told,

are very strict about that kind of thing, because they think very few people would want to get married – which means spending one's whole life with the same person, and putting up with all the inconveniences that this involves – if they weren't carefully prevented from having any sexual intercourse otherwise.[3]

In view of all this, it is startling to learn that when young Utopians are seeking a spouse – women must be at least eighteen to marry and men twenty-two – they are permitted (if accompanied by a chaperone) to inspect a prospective bride or groom stark naked. This practice, our traveler remarks, merely acknowledges the need for making an informed choice in view of the lifetime of sexual fidelity expected of all married persons. Theoretically, divorce by mutual consent is obtainable on grounds of incompatibility, but the required permission is rarely granted. Adulterers, moreover, are sentenced to penal servitude for a first offense, while a second conviction brings an automatic death penalty. Most married Utopians, unsurprisingly, are faithfully monogamous. To encourage domestic harmony, wives are required before the sacred festivals at the end of each lunar month to kneel down before their husbands (and children before their parents)

to confess all their sins of omission and commission, and ask to be forgiven. This gets rid of any little grudges that may have clouded the domestic atmosphere, so that everyone can attend divine service with an absolutely clear mind.[4]

While occasionally noting these family and household arrangements, scholars have focused attention on Utopian institutions outside of the household.[5] What has captivated them is the extraordinary portrayal, in the early sixteenth century, of a full-blown urban-based welfare state. Religiously

---

[2] Ibid., 69–70.

[3] Ibid., 103.

[4] Ibid., 126.

[5] A recent critical edition that contains extensive background material and commentary, for example, presents no discussion of the household form that More incorporates, even though a large selection of classical and biblical sources is presented as well as essays by eight distinguished historians and literary critics. See Robert M. Adams, tr. and ed., *Utopia, a Revised Translation: Backgrounds, Criticism* (New York, 1992).

tolerant and representatively governed, the Utopian republic ensures food, clothing, employment, housing, education, health care, and short working hours (six per day) for all citizens. In contrast to More's opening description, via Hythloday again, of a Europe of rapacious and warring rulers and an England of selfish landowners, disinherited farmers, and unemployed vagabonds, More's invented society has no social divisions based upon individual wealth and no poverty.

Local government is based on election by households, which are divided into groups of thirty for the annual naming of District Controllers. Each town has 200 such officials, all evidently male; but the priests, who are also elected, may be female so long as they are elderly widows. (Few women are chosen, we are told.) The District Controllers are responsible for selecting a mayor for life from among nominees named by the whole electorate, and the system includes representative councils to protect the people's interest in case any mayor should develop dictatorial impulses. At the national level, there is a parliament to which each of the fifty-four towns sends three representatives.

These elected officials, along with priests and diplomats, belong to a small intellectual elite that is not closed to studious young people who seek promotion into it. For the rest of the men and for all women (save for those few female priests), training and practice in a trade are required, in addition to the farm labor already mentioned, "though the weaker sex are given the lighter job[s], like spinning and weaving, while the men do the heavier ones."[6] There is no problem with productivity despite the short working day. This is partly because consumer goods are limited to the modest basics – there are no tailors or dressmakers, for instance – but mostly because nearly all the women, both married and single, are in the labor force. In most other countries, More declares, "practically all the women – that gives you nearly 50 percent for a start" – are "totally unemployed."[7]

Utopians live simply but well in a republic whose codes leave no room for greed, laziness, or pride. All must wear nearly identical plain garments and eat in communal dining halls, each serving thirty households and supplied with nurseries for the infants. The precious metals and jewels accumulated through trade are occasionally used to hire foreign mercenaries; but since this peace-loving people opts for diplomacy over armed conflict whenever possible, the jewels are mostly used as baubles to amuse small children, while the gold and silver are melted down for humble domestic items such as chamber pots. Citizens are content when not working to pursue self-improvement through education or to perform volunteer service for the common Utopian good.

Utopia has long been recognized as an indictment of what the Christian humanist Sir Thomas More held to be the meanest features of English and

[6] More, *Utopia*, 77.
[7] Ibid.

European society of his time. Historians are aware that many aspects of Utopian life, while influenced by classical and biblical sources, are responses to real situations in sixteenth-century England. For example, the absence of distinctions based upon personal wealth presents a stark contrast with a country showing such a gap between rich and poor that a single individual, as one critic notes, "could enjoy an income of fifty thousand pounds a year, while thousands of people starved, or were hanged for stealing food."[8]

Yet while practices outside households in Utopia have been recognized as responses to actual sixteenth-century social ills, commentators have not attempted to analyze in the same way the households More fashioned. His multifamily residences, with each Utopian bride moving into an existing household headed by the eldest man in the groom's family, were hardly common in England save in the upper classes. Most English households, as More well knew, had but one married couple in residence. True, Utopian couples were closer in age than those in most early-marriage societies, and in this regard they resembled English ones. But the obsequious handmaidens of Utopia would never be confused with the spirited and aggressive mistresses of real English households.

Just as his portrait of Utopian life beyond households is recognized as More's critique of English society, Utopian domestic arrangements need to be seen as a critique of actual English households. That More showed such exquisite care in devising a stable, almost static, household system as the foundation for all other institutions in Utopia was no accident. He obviously recognized that the single-family households that dominated in England were rather precarious. In Utopia, More could expressly invent laws and customs to shore up households. Better still, he could supply the base of enduring multifamily residences that functioned like those in more typical early-marriage societies, where adult sons stayed put from one generation to the next. He could also control disruptive demographic growth by holding population constant in each town.

Yet as More knew best, early-sixteenth-century England was hardly Utopia. Population expansion from the end of the fifteenth century, as well as ongoing enclosure of agricultural land by rich property owners to provide sheep pastures for the wool trade, resulted in floods of unmarried and unemployed rural migrants into the towns. This meant a dramatic increase in crime, agricultural riots, poverty, and vagrancy – all of which are discussed at length in the first part of *Utopia*. More knew that in a society in which public law enforcement structures are weak, and in which household heads are relied upon to help ensure order within communities, changes that destabilize households will likely diminish the capacity of government to maintain authority.

[8] Ibid., 15.

The related aim of ensuring women's obedience to their husbands was also easier to achieve in Utopia than in the real-life contexts More knew best. There, women were acquiring a reputation for assertive and unruly behavior as wives, and men from all ranks were responding to a perceived usurpation of their rightful authority by engaging in a kind of collective taming of the shrews. Thomas More himself joined in the popular misogyny, as this example of his antifemale aphorisms attests: "If you let your wife stand on your toe tonight, she'll stand on your face first thing tomorrow morning."[9]

Scholars long took this pervasive misogyny for granted. Only with the rise of women's history have they noted that women at this time were widely perceived to be gaining the upper hand within households.[10] While the late-marriage pattern has yet to be named as a prime causal factor, interpreters have begun to connect these perceptions with the more deadly sentiments fueling the great European witch hunts that were launched not long before More wrote *Utopia* and that continued for 300 years. Researchers have finally begun to ask why women were the chief targets of these witch hunts as well as why married women and widows, especially in northwestern Europe, were held up at just this moment in the Western past as the most dangerous creatures in society.[11]

The period from 1500 to 1750 has long been seen as a time of social instability, and more recently as a period of rising tensions in relations between the sexes. Yet, unlike Thomas More, modern commentators have not imagined that household arrangements might be implicated in these developments. Prevalent complaints about a breakdown of the present-day "family" are occurring in a kind of interpretive vacuum, unconnected to any acknowledged historical trajectory for the shape and functions of households relative to other institutions. Rather than being seen as a new phase in a long-standing concern about families and gender roles in Western societies, today's alleged breakdown of families and obsession with gender and sexuality are seen as recent developments, often enough as the fault of persons who are still with us.[12]

---

[9] Ibid., 14.

[10] There is a growing literature in the field, much of it discussed in Judith M. Bennett, "Misogyny, Popular Culture and Women's Work." *History Workshop* 31 (Spring 1992): 166–88. See, in addition, Katharine Rogers, *The Troublesome Helpmate: A History of Misogyny in Literature* (Seattle, 1966); and Linda Woodbridge, *Women and the English Renaissance* (Urbana, Ill., 1984).

[11] For full recent discussions, see Robin Briggs, *Witches and Neighbors: The Social and Cultural Context of European Witchcraft* (New York, 1998), especially Ch. 7: "Men against Women: The Gendering of Witchcraft," 257–86; and James Sharpe, *Instruments of Darkness* (Philadelphia, 1996), especially Ch. 7: "Women and Witchcraft," 169–89.

[12] For an excellent discussion that touches on these themes in the more limited context of American family history, see Daniel Scott Smith, "Recent Change and the Periodization of American Family History." *Journal of Family History* 20, No. 4 (1995): 329–46.

Most historians, too, would agree that the roots of these developments lie entirely in the modern era. While they might differ on specifics, they would concur that the causes of the present instability in family households, as well as of our endless preoccupation with male and female roles, authority, and identity, can be traced back only as far as the late eighteenth century. Their account, reasonably enough, would run as follows: democratic and industrial upheavals of that era altered the ways people conceived of legitimate authority as well as how labor was organized, thereby transforming the position of families and the roles of the sexes. Everyone had to adjust to change that diminished the household as the basic social unit and called into question established views about who women and men are. These upheavals, which are still playing themselves out on their home territory, are now being diffused around the globe, everywhere helping to replace authoritarian regimes with democratic ones and, through new modes of production, bringing shifts in women's and men's roles, status, and options.

While there is no question that the democratic and industrial upheavals had major effects on households and gender roles, there is a problem with this familiar analysis. It assumes that major concerns about family instability and about appropriate male and female behavior began only with changes launched in the late eighteenth century from sites beyond households. But as already seen, there is abundant if undigested evidence that such anxiety long antedated the modern era in northwestern Europe. Sir Thomas More was hardly alone in his unease over unstable households and uppity women. Arguably, too, these things owed at least as much to prior and distinctive marriage arrangements as to any changes imposed on households from the outside.

The features identified with the aberrant northwestern European family pattern – that is, comparatively late marriage, especially for women; significant numbers who never marry; life-cycle domestic service; a preponderance of nuclear households; and relatively equal sex ratios at marriageable ages (an item included by Hajnal) – were all on display in most households from about 1500 to 1750. Several of these, as noted, had likely been in place for centuries.[13] That a lone adult couple resided in most households goes far

[13] Richard M. Smith points out that while Englishmen's age at marriage over the two centuries from 1550 to 1750 in a group of English villages varied between 27.2 and 28.2 years, women's ages were more volatile, moving between 24.8 and 27.0 years and rising in some communities between three and four years: "Some Reflections on the Evidence for the Origins of the 'European Marriage Pattern' in England," in C. Harris, ed., *The Sociology of the Family: New Directions for Britain, Sociological Review* No. 28 (Keele, 1979), 96. Without more data from earlier centuries, it is hard to make definitive statements, but it is worth noting that at 24.8 years in 1550, women's age at marriage was already higher by about a decade than that in most other agricultural societies. Just how long women had been over twenty at marriage in most regions of northwestern Europe is unknown, although there is further discussion of this issue in Chapter 3. Smith does point to hard evidence from the thirteenth and fourteenth

to explain the shakiness that troubled More, especially since these households usually dissolved with the deaths of the partners. To appreciate more fully how early- and late-marriage systems influenced behavior and attitudes, however, it is necessary to compare women's and men's experiences in specific societies.

What emerges from the comparisons to be outlined here is dramatic. While specific experiences of the sexes in both systems may vary widely, a clear pattern runs across each type. In early-marriage societies, life cycles diverge quite sharply, with girls and boys, women and men, in many ways living separate lives in separate gendered universes. By contrast, in late-marriage societies, women's and men's life cycles tend to converge. Their daily lives are neither identical nor equal; but family structures themselves work to ensure that they are roughly parallel at every stage – with infancy, childhood, youth, and adulthood increasingly permeated by similar experiences.

This is not to say that such closeness between the sexes was celebrated. Quite the contrary. The unsettled and anxious behavior in early modern societies actually appears to have been a reaction all along the social spectrum to change that accompanied women's late marriage. An extended period of adjustment for both sexes ensued, and the repercussions are still with us. But that is jumping ahead. First, we must set out the case that at each stage of the life cycle in early modern northwestern Europe, women's and men's identities were vitally shaped by an idiosyncratic marriage and household system.

*   *   *

In most societies, ancient habits of sexual hierarchy are renewed with each new generation, signaled at the outset of the life cycle when a baby boy is welcomed more warmly than a girl. Expressions of this nearly universal preference for sons nonetheless vary widely.[14] Agricultural societies display a sharp preference for sons that has often been linked to an allegedly higher value on men as workers and as heirs. Among these societies, though, little attention has been paid to the contrasting receptions for the newest members of early- versus late-marriage households. Hajnal noticed that in the former, the preference for sons often stretches to include systematic female neglect and infanticide. While he and others have also cited limited evidence for these practices in medieval Europe, it appears that for whatever reasons,

centuries for several other features of the Western family pattern, including at least some life-cycle service. He also notes limited but reliable data from fourteenth-century England of marriage ages for both women and men of around twenty-one years. In addition, he remarks that already by the thirteenth century, a study of the importance of kin in relation to neighbors reveals the greater importance of neighbors, "Some Reflections," 102.

[14] See, in particular, Martin King Whyte, *The Status of Women in Preindustrial Societies* (Princeton, N.J., 1978).

they were largely abandoned by the early modern era, when the full set of features of the Western family pattern came together.

While to this day boys are more eagerly received than girls in both early- and late-marriage settings, already by the sixteenth century in northwestern Europe the rationales for son-preference were far weaker than in most other agricultural societies. This was so even though 85 to 90 percent of people there were still modest rural householders who earned livings from the land and continued to do so right through the eighteenth century.[15] According to an account from still largely rural India in the 1960s, the reasons for the strong son-preference in that early-marriage society were

(1) the transmission of family property and name, (2) economic support for the parents when they grow old or in case of earlier disability, (3) performance of the ancestral (*sraddra*) rites for the father after his death to ensure the peace of his soul, and (4) financial interests since a family must provide a dowry for the marriage of a daughter while no payment is necessary for a son's marriage and since there is the added advantage of bringing in a bride with her dowry.[16]

Most northwestern European heads of household did try whenever possible to favor sons in transmission of property, especially landed property. Yet already by the late medieval era, parents were not counting on offspring of either sex for maintenance of their households or for care in old age, even though both practices were common enough in some regions. In cases where there were daughters only but no sons to inherit their property, parents readily accepted in-marrying sons-in-law. They also were prepared to sell property to nonkin when their own offspring migrated to other communities. Where dowries persisted, young women in late-marriage societies usually made contributions to them from their own earnings, which meant that daughters were hardly the burden on parental generations that they remained in early-marriage settings.

A son's duty in India to perform rites after a father's death, a role with parallels in many cultures, did not apply in Catholic Europe by the early modern era, as the Church had long since assumed a function that continued to be performed in the household in most early-marriage societies.[17] Children of either sex by the medieval era might conduct prayers and found masses for either parent. Mourning was also restricted in length and intensity there, whereas in early-marriage settings, a man might spend a portion of every day of his life performing rituals for a deceased father. With the emergence

[15] Olwen Hufton, *The Prospect Before Her: A History of Women in Western Europe, 1500–1800* (New York, 1996), 69.

[16] Barbara D. Miller, *The Endangered Sex: Neglect of Female Children in Rural North India* (Ithaca, N.Y., 1981), 160.

[17] See Francis L. K. Hsu, *Under the Ancestors' Shadow* (Stanford, Calif., 1971).

of Protestantism even purgatory disappeared. As Natalie Davis puts it, for Protestants "all the forms of exchange and communication between souls in the other world and the living were to be swept away."[18] Since the souls of the saved were present with Christ and the damned were already in hell, there was no longer any special intercessory role for surviving kin of either sex.

While female neglect and infanticide have ceased to be ascribed by Western interpreters to benighted heathen attitudes, the role of entrenched marriage patterns in perpetuating these practices is still not widely understood. Although early-marriage households literally depend upon the supply of sons, it is less necessary for couples in late-marriage societies to have sons or, for that matter, to have children. A childless nuclear household, or one with daughters alone, is not necessarily ruined since livelihood does not depend so completely on family labor and households are not ongoing entities. Parents also depend little upon resident sons and daughters-in-law for care in old age.

In early-marriage societies, to be childless, or to have only daughters and confront the choice of an in-marrying son-in-law or the end of an established household, is not just a disappointment: it is a calamity. In a hamlet in present-day Morocco, where peasants with holdings that supply only a quarter of their needs still give priority to agricultural work, women are liable to be divorced not only if they bear no children but also if they bear only girls.[19] A son alone can confer status on a woman, including the right to stay on in her husband's family as a widow. All this goes far to explain why men and women alike in early-marriage societies display such intense preference for boys, whereas in late-marriage societies, couples who may prefer a boy are usually quite ready to raise a girl.

A recent study of Chinese demography cites evidence for female infanticide as far back as the first millennium B.C.[20] Contrary to widespread belief, however, infanticide was just one strategy among many in a larger system of controls on marital fertility. A variety of measures, including sexual abstinence, were monitored collectively within multifamily households and worked to contain fertility centuries before the official policies mandated by the state in the 1970s. Marital fertility was actually far lower in China than in early modern northwestern Europe, where late marriage and high

---

[18] See Natalie Zemon Davis, "Ghosts, Kin, and Progeny: Some Features of Family Life in Early Modern France." *Daedalus* 106 (April 1977): 94–95.

[19] Vanessa Maher, "Possession and Dispossession: Maternity and Mortality in Morocco," in Hans Medick and David Warren Sabean, eds., *Interest and Emotion: Essays on the Study of Family and Kinship* (Paris and Cambridge, 1984), 103–8.

[20] James Z. Lee and Wang Feng, *One Quarter of Humanity: Malthusian Mythology and Chinese Realities, 1700–2000* (Cambridge, 1999), 105.

celibacy were long the primary checks on fertility.[21] We now know, too, that the Chinese system did ensure adequate living standards.[22]

Early-marriage structures still played a large role in conditioning households in their familiar dread of daughters and celebration of sons. In describing nineteenth- and early-twentieth-century China, for example, ethnographers are emphatic:

> Daughters were goods on which one lost money. They could contribute little or nothing to their natal families in the way of enhancing their status, increasing their wealth, or providing for their care in their old age. They could not, except in very special circumstances, provide descendants who could worship the family's ancestors. And when the time came for a girl to be sent off to another family in marriage, most of the bride price [a traditional amount paid to the bride's parents by the groom's parents for the loss of the daughter's services] had to be spent on a dowry if the family was not to lose its standing within the community. Unfortunately, the cultural stereotypes about the nature of women did nothing to make up for their structural handicaps. Women were narrow-hearted.... They were ignorant and stupid and irresponsible. Worse yet, women were dangerous. Their menstrual secretions, if handled improperly, could cause men to sicken, gods to turn away in disgust, and families to decline into poverty. Their sexuality could drain men of their strength or drive them insane with lust.[23]

While it used to be thought that in the West, prejudicial treatment of daughters at no time included female infanticide, a survey of *Inquisitiones Post Mortem* in England revealed a shift from an equal ratio of male to female children in the mid-thirteenth century, when the records begin, to a 4 to 3 ratio in favor of males prior to the mid-fourteenth-century Black Death, when population pressure rose.[24] Similarly, a recent study of London children who were wards of the court in the fourteenth and fifteenth centuries

---

[21] Ibid., 107. This control of marital fertility actually had a greater effect in limiting population growth in China than female infanticide, although from the eighteenth to the twentieth centuries, as undeveloped rural areas in the frontier provinces were opened up, fertility controls within marriage were relaxed and population almost tripled. As a hedge against all these plans failing, moreover, Chinese couples often turned to adoption as insurance against mistaken calculations, taking in girls to ensure daughters-in-law and, more infrequently, boys to guarantee an heir.

For a discussion arguing that celibacy rates rather than age at marriage accounted for most of fertility variation in England before 1750, a view now generally accepted, see also David R. Weir, "Rather Never Than Late: Celibacy and Age at Marriage in English Cohort Fertility." *Journal of Family History* 9 (Winter 1984): 340–54.

[22] Lee and Wang, *One Quarter of Humanity*, 136.

[23] Kay Ann Johnson, *Women, the Family and Peasant Revolution in China* (Chicago, 1983), 1–2.

[24] J. C. Russell, *British Medieval Population* (Albuquerque, N. M., 1948), 147–49 and 166–68. See also Barbara Kellum, "Infanticide in England in the Later Middle Ages." *History of Childhood Quarterly* 1, No. 3 (1974): 367–88.

shows that overall, there were 10 percent fewer girls than boys, with figures rising to 14 percent with overpopulation in the early fourteenth century.[25]

Unsurprisingly, a preference for boys remained strong among the upper classes. French childrearing practices among the seventeenth-century elite displayed favored treatment for male infants that could have boosted their survival rates. There was less wet-nursing (notorious for high mortality), longer breastfeeding, better overall nutrition, and more parental solicitude.[26] Parents of the English nobility and gentry also expressed a special desire for sons and greater solicitousness for sons' well-being. One new mother, Anne D'Ewes, wrote to her husband in 1641:

It hath pleased God now again the ninth time to restore me from the peril of childbirth; and though we have failed in part of our hope by the birth of a daughter yet we are likewise freed from much care and fear a son would have brought.[27]

In the poorer classes, a survey from eighteenth-century Paris also found a slightly higher incidence of female than male infant abandonment. By that time, unwanted babies were often brought to the foundling hospital by midwives, nursemaids, parents, or provincial agents. Periods of rising abandonment coincided with times of rising grain prices, and it is noteworthy that a fifth to a third of abandoned infants were legitimate. It can be inferred from the very small sex differentials, however, that by the eighteenth century, save in extreme conditions, parents were prepared to raise a child of either sex.[28]

---

[25] Barbara Hanawalt, *Growing Up in Medieval London* (New York, 1993), 53.

[26] Elizabeth Marvick, "Nature versus Nurture: Patterns and Trends in Seventeenth-Century Child-Rearing," in Lloyd de Mause, ed., *The History of Childhood* (New York, 1974), 259–93.

[27] Cited in Sara Mendelson and Patricia Crawford, *Women in Early Modern England, 1550–1720.* (Oxford, 1998), 81. Mendelson and Crawford's study points out, too, that Amy Erickson's *Women and Property in Early Modern England* (London and New York, 1993) found little evidence of preference for sons below the gentry level; see *Women in Early Modern England,* 82.

[28] Claude Delasselle, "Abandoned Children in Eighteenth-Century Paris," reprinted in Robert Forster and Orest Ranum, eds., *Deviants and the Abandoned in French Society: Selections from the Annales, Economies, Sociétés, et Civilisations,* 4 (Baltimore, 1978), 47–82. Historical as well as contemporary data on female neglect and infanticide are hardly lacking, but what continues to be missing is an appreciation of the ongoing role of marriage and household structures in promoting and reinforcing these practices.

In twelve Chinese provinces from 1776 to 1850, for example, men always outnumbered women, from a fifth to as much as a third. A provincial governor-general showed his understanding of his native Shansi province in these comments: "The first female birth may sometimes be salvaged with effort, but the subsequent births are usually drowned. There are even those who drown every female baby without keeping any.... This is because the poor worry about daily sustenance...and the rich are concerned over future dowries," William Langer, "Infanticide: A Historical Survey." *History of Childhood Quarterly* 1, No. 3 (1974), 60.

Another account from a local history of 1864 underscores the suffering its author says was typical of parents who made the hard choice to kill a baby daughter: "The rustic people

The threat a daughter might represent in early-marriage households is reflected in many things, including naming practices. Nineteenth-century Chinese peasants might call a baby girl "Little Unpleasantness" or "Little Mistake," or they might select generic names for daughters to avoid choosing an individual name for a creature seen as a temporary and expensive guest.[29] In the late-marriage regions of the medieval West, peasant daughters received individualized names, although clear distinctions marked a gender hierarchy favoring boys. In a fourteenth-century English manor, for instance, men's names came from a limited range. John, William, Richard, and Robert were often repeated in each generation, underscoring a boy's more important association with his family's past and future as well as "the greater value that inheritance customs gave to male children."[30] Women's names, by contrast, were more varied. They included the standard Matilda, Agnes, and Alice, but also idiosyncratic or one-time entries such as Mariaunt, Strangia, and Sibilla. "Medieval parents might have loved their daughters as much as their sons," says one authority, "but they also expected daughters to contribute less than sons to the family's continuation in the next generation."[31]

Intriguingly, these distinctions softened by the early modern era. At that time, daughters, like sons, increasingly bore the name of a same-sex parent or godparent. In colonial New England, sons as well as daughters were often named after relatives on their mother's side, illustrating once more the evolution being argued here for more parallel experience of the sexes.[32] The new recognition for women nonetheless brought some problematic issues in a mini-trend of naming girls after traits they were intended to display or cultivate, such as Patience, Obedience, Charity, Reliance, and even Submit and Silence.[33] These were times of a new anxiety about womanhood – and about manhood.

To the extent that Western scholars are likely to be aware of life-threatening practices at the far end of a continuum of son-preference, it

---

of Hupei and parts of Hunan customarily rear two sons and one daughter at most. Any further birth is often disposed of. It [the custom] is particularly against female infants. This is why in this area women are proportionately scarce and single unmarried men abound. When a baby girl is born, she is usually killed by drowning. Her parents, of course, cannot bear this, but none the less they close their eyes and turn their backs while continuing to immerge [sic] her in the water tub until she ceases to utter her feeble cries and dies," Ping-ti Ho, *Studies on the Population of China, 1368–1953* (Cambridge, 1959), 558–59.

[29] Judith Stacey, *Patriarchy and Socialist Revolution in China* (Berkeley and Los Angeles, 1983), 43.

[30] Judith M. Bennett, *Women in the Medieval English Countryside: Gender and Household in Brigstock Before the Plague* (New York, 1987), 69.

[31] Ibid.

[32] Daniel Scott Smith, "Child-Naming Practices, Kinship Ties, and Change in Family Attitudes in Hingham, Massachusetts, 1641–1880." *Journal of Social History* 18, No. 4 (Summer 1985): 541–66.

[33] Ibid., 544.

is of current rather than historical examples, such as the rise of female infanticide in China after institution of the one-child-per-family policy of 1979.[34]
United Nations conferences, and attention from scholars such as economist
Amartya Sen, have penetrated resistance to this topic. Sen's powerful article
"More Than 100 Million Women Are Missing" states that the reported ratio of 94 women to 100 men in China and in South and West Asia actually
understates the deficit in the number of women:

> since, in countries where men and women receive similar care, the ratio is about 1.05
> [men to women], the real shortfall is about 11 percent. In China alone this amounts to
> 50 million "missing women" taking 1.05 as the benchmark ratio. When that number
> is added to those in South Asia, West Asia and North Africa, a great many more than
> 100 million women are "missing." These numbers tell us, quietly, a terrible story of
> inequality and neglect leading to the excess mortality of women.... If this situation
> is to be corrected by political action and public policy, the reasons why there are
> so many "missing" women must first be better understood. We confront here what
> is clearly one of the more momentous, and neglected, problems facing the world
> today.[35]

   While Sen does not invoke the influence of early- versus late-marriage
structures, he remarks that the simplistic "sexist East versus non-sexist West"
explanation that has been presented or, more often, implicitly assumed for
these practices will not bear scrutiny. There are too many divergent cases.
(Women outnumber men in many places including Thailand and Indonesia,
for example.) Nor does the contrast of developed versus underdeveloped
regions work as an explanation, especially since many places such as sub-
Saharan Africa have more women than men, as do several of the poorest
Indian states. The two most important variables in places where sex ratios
are more equal, Sen reports, are literacy and gainful employment, both of
which appear to enhance women's perceived value and give them greater
bargaining power within households and beyond.[36]

---

[34] See Susan Greenhalgh and Jiali Li, "Engendering Reproductive Policy and Practice in Peasant
   China: For a Feminist Demography of Reproduction." *Signs: Journal of Women in Culture and
   Society* 20, No. 3 (1995): 601–41.

[35] Amartya Sen, "More than 100 Million Women Are Missing," *New York Review of Books*
   (December 28, 1990): 61–66. The extent of the continuing practice of eliminating baby girls
   has not been fully documented or explained. In urban areas, where there is easier access
   to modern medical technologies, couples take action before birth. At one Bombay clinic,
   according to a 1991 Indian government report, of 8,000 abortions performed after amniocentesis, 7,999 were of female fetuses, in Sara S. Mittler, *Dharma's Daughters: Contemporary
   Indian Women and Hindu Culture* (New Brunswick, N.J., 1991), 115.

[36] Sen, "More Than 100 Million Women Are Missing," 64. When different regions of Asia and
   Africa are ranked from high to low for rates of employment outside the home and ratios of
   life expectancy for females, the two lists match almost exactly. The proportion of women
   relative to men in employment in descending order is: 1. sub-Saharan Africa, 2. southeastern
   and eastern Asia, 3. western Asia, 4. southern Asia, and 5. northern Africa. The rankings
   for life expectancy of men are the same except that the two last rankings are reversed.

In contemporary societies where women are perceived to contribute to their natal family's wealth through their labor, their value is automatically enhanced. Even in predominantly early-marriage settings such as India, women have been far less at risk for their lives in the south, owing to their work there in rice cultivation. In the north, where less productive work is available for women, sex ratios are more imbalanced in favor of men.[37] The role of early-marriage arrangements is beginning to be recognized, however, as a result of efforts to understand why there was a sharp increase in female neglect and infanticide after the Chinese government introduced the one-child-per-family policy. Research points to a complex interaction of traditional early-marriage practice, in which sons are still seen as required for their parents' support in old age, and more recent single-child policies of the party-state.[38]

The distance of late-marriage societies by now from a past that likely included female neglect and infanticide is great enough that any residues are hard to detect. Yet in places where such practices are at best a part of the recent past, the signs are everywhere. A report from a north Indian village in the 1960s spells out the effects on one woman of the birth of a boy and of a girl in a place where women remain an endangered species:

When Bipat's mother gave birth to a fourth son, a Thakur woman who was among the first to hear passed the word on to others. Her broad smile spoke for itself before she related the news and said, "Every time a boy is born in the village, I feel very happy. The whole day I can't think of anything else. I feel just as happy as I would feel if a boy were born in my own family." This same woman looked very downcast when a baby girl was born in her family not long afterward. Far more girls than boys had been born in her family in recent years, and the financial burden of their marriages was telling on the family reserve.... One day this Thakur woman held her baby granddaughter up in the air and said, "Now she should die. I tell her she should die. She is growing bigger and soon there will be the problem of finding a husband for her...." Often when she thought of the consequences of another female member of the family, she spoke in this way, but always in her personal relations with the baby,

In historical contexts as well as in the present day, these features correlate with life or death for many women. The Indian state of Kerala, for example, whose current ratio of women to men at 1.03 is closer to Europe's than to India's as a whole (0.94), does not stand out as a center for gainful employment but does have an exceptionally high female literacy rate. The tradition goes back nearly two centuries when this state, not part of British India, was ruled by a queen who established strong support for public education that has persisted. Punjab, however, has long been a region where women's lives were at risk. In 1852 there were nearly six boys for every five girls among children in the Hindu majority, and the three leading Rajput subcastes had three boys to one girl. The Punjab today, the richest yet most life-threatening Indian state for women, has the lowest ratio of employed women to men.

[37] See Miller, *The Endangered Sex*, especially Ch. 6: "Women's Work and Female Worth in Rural India," 107–32.

[38] For an excellent discussion of the effects of the one-child policy, see Greenhalgh and Li, "Engendering Reproductive Policy and Practice in Peasant China."

she was loving and affectionate. If the baby were to die, the grandmother would be greatly affected by the loss. No one could doubt this. But a baby girl is not just a person in her own right. She is also a member of her sex group and she places upon her parents many obligations and responsibilities.[39]

One effect of the late-marriage regime appears to have been the comparatively limited liability to a household of a decision to raise a girl. Yet since the greater burdens of raising a daughter in early-marriage settings remain little understood in the West, primary "credit" for sparing girls and for treating them more comparably with boys has often mistakenly been assigned to the Christian faith or even to a superior "Western civilization."[40] It is worth noting, though, that while the early abandonment of female neglect and infanticide was more likely a side effect of whatever led people in northwestern Europe to adopt late marriage for their daughters, the result was that the experiences of boys and girls were more similar, literally from the outset of the life cycle.

* * *

Turning next to the experience of childhood for the sexes, the first noteworthy distinction is in the cast of characters surrounding each child. In early-marriage households, the young grow up with grandparents, parents, siblings, and perhaps cousins, aunts, and uncles, whereas in late-marriage ones, there are just parents, siblings, and perhaps unrelated servants.[41] The difference is vitally important for socializing children to the notion that women and men have distinctive roles. With just one resident adult of each sex, late-marriage households simply cannot uphold the strict gender boundaries characteristic of early-marriage households. When a given task needs to be performed, an adult of the "right" sex is less likely to be at hand. Whatever notions children in these households absorb about an official division of roles by sex, they are destined to observe more day-to-day boundary crossing, even though, for reasons to be discussed, they will more often see mothers doing "male" tasks than fathers doing "female" ones.

---

[39] Miller, *The Endangered Sex*, 156–57, quoted by Mildred S. Luchansky, "The Life of Women in a Village of North India: A Study of Role and Status," unpublished doctoral dissertation, Cornell University, 1962.

[40] David Herlihy suggests that the Christian faith can be credited for more equitable treatment of women within marriage, in "The Family and Religious Ideologies in Medieval Europe." *Journal of Family History* 12, Nos. 1/3 (1987): 3–17. He also argues that the Catholic Church was primarily responsible, through its promulgation of a single sexual standard, for establishing a sexual morality that was the same for both sexes. The argument here is instead that while religious doctrine was not without influence in promoting monogamous marriage, the stronger causal factor in generating a single sexual standard was the distinctive late-marriage household pattern.

[41] The point was made by Peter Laslett, "Characteristics of the Western Family Considered Over Time." *Journal of Family History* 2, No. 2 (1977): 95.

This blurring of the lines between women's and men's roles could be offset by resident servants or, to an extent, by relatives living nearby. Yet recent work on England contends that, already by the thirteenth century, extended kinship bonds were declining.[42] A study of a West Midlands manor from the late thirteenth through the fifteenth centuries does argue that although over three-quarters of households there were nuclear, wider kinship ties remained strong, with 70 percent of tenants having kin on the manor by the late fourteenth century. By the fifteenth century, however, the tight family–land bond had eroded even there, as it appears to have done earlier in many other places in England.[43] It is true, as will be discussed in later chapters, that the family–land bond remained intact far longer in France and other places on the northwestern European continent, thereby working longer to buttress sharper gender role separation.

Researchers who have begun the daunting task of reconstructing the lives of late medieval peasants have not set out to demonstrate the roughly comparable experience of the sexes that is being argued here. Their evidence nonetheless supports that hypothesis while still exposing an unequal world for the sexes. For example, Barbara Hanawalt makes ingenious use of the English coroners' rolls, which identify the activity in which the deceased was

---

[42] See Barbara Hanawalt, *The Ties That Bound: Peasant Families in Medieval England* (Oxford and New York, 1986), 84 and the full discussion in Ch. 5, "Kinship Bonds," 79–89.

[43] Unlike most of the current generation of medievalists, Zvi Razi, author of *Life, Marriage and Death in a Medieval Parish: Economy, Society and Demography in Halesowen, 1270–1400* (Cambridge, 1980), maintains in both that study and in his more recent article "The Myth of the Immutable English Family." *Past and Present*, No. 140 (August 1993): 3–44 that a joint family system, featuring early marriage for women, must have been the norm in most parts of England in the thirteenth century, when he thinks nuclearization of the peasant family began. He argues, moreover, that despite the dominant nuclear form, families were "functionally extended" until at least the beginning of the sixteenth century, with individual households relying on extended kin networks, "The Myth of the Immutable English Family," 42.

H. E. Hallam presents considerable evidence for an established late-marriage pattern in England as early as the mid-thirteenth century. Although he acknowledges with Razi that it is possible that women married much earlier prior to that date, Hallam shows that late marriage was present in the five villages in the Lincolnshire fenland between 1252 and 1478, with the average marriage age for women being 22.4 and that for men 25.9 in his "Age of Marriage and Age at Death in the Lincolnshire Fenland, 1252–1478." *Population Studies* 39 (1985): 55–69. Lawrence R. Poos has made an even more impressive case for late marriage in fourteenth-century Essex in *A Rural Society After the Black Death: Essex: 1350–1525* (Cambridge, 1991), Ch. 7: "Marriage and Household Formation," 133–58. Other historians, such as Alan Macfarlane, see no reason in the absence of data to assume that an early-marriage pattern, with teenage brides, prevailed in the earlier medieval centuries, and are persuaded that there is more reason to believe that late marriage for women was established much sooner in the medieval past. Chapter 3 discusses this major issue in more detail.

engaged when a fatal accident occurred.[44] While she found that even young children spent more time in activities related to those of the same-sex parent, her basic finding was wide overlap in the experience of the sexes. Little girls were somewhat more likely to be killed in accidents in the home – falling into pots or spilling scalding liquid on themselves – while little boys more often fell into ditches or streams. Yet about half of toddler girls met their deaths outside the home compared to two-thirds of the boys.

Only at age seven or eight do the coroners' rolls start to reflect serious training for adult male and female activities, and even then the overlap is great. That boys had more fatal accidents around the home than adult men shows, in Hanawalt's plausible view, that girls and boys alike spent much of their youth relieving the workload of the housewife, freeing her for field work or for income-producing activities such as brewing. Girls sooner than boys settled into adult work patterns of women, while only in late adolescence, after achieving their full strength, did boys spend much time in the fields.

This sharing of tasks between the sexes continued into adulthood. While more women died in or near the home (29.5 percent as against 11.8 percent for men in Hanawalt's sample), women also had many fatal accidents away from home, especially at times when seasonal field work was intense. This wide overlapping of male and female tasks from childhood into adulthood already set England and northwestern Europe apart by the late medieval era. For reasons to be explored in the next chapter, field and household did not divide as neatly there as in most other agricultural regions into discrete male and female worlds.

By the sixteenth century, the experience of the sexes overlapped even more. A recent study of early modern England, for example, argues convincingly that outside the ranks of the elite, there was considerable congruity between the childhoods of girls and boys.[45] At least up to the age of ten, ordinary laborer and small farming households devoted the same resources to daughters as to sons.[46] Also, until they went into service in the early teens, children of both sexes were educated at home. Admittedly, girls alone were taught to preserve their chastity; and they also had even less formal education than boys, a situation reflected in their considerably higher estimated rates of illiteracy.[47]

It is true that upper-class girls in England and throughout northwestern Europe led quite different lives from their brothers. Boys typically left the

---

[44] Hanawalt, *The Ties That Bound*, 169–87. See also Barbara Hanawalt, "Childrearing Among the Lower Classes of Late Medieval England." *Journal of Interdisciplinary History* 7, No. 1 (Summer 1977): 1–22.

[45] For a fuller discussion of these sources see Mendelson and Crawford, *Women in Early Modern England*, Ch. 2: "Childhood and Adolescence," 75–123.

[46] Mendelson and Crawford, *Women in Early Modern England*, 85.

[47] Ibid., 90. See also David Cressy, *Literacy and the Social Order: Reading and Writing in Tudor and Stuart England* (Cambridge, 1980), esp. 118–21.

maternal orbit as early as age seven, often being clad in breeches at that point and sent away to school, whereas girls were likelier to remain at home to be educated by their mothers. More privileged and protected than their humbler sisters, these young women were also less independent; and their training emphasized modesty, obedience, and submission to future husbands. Well-to-do families, who were less dependent either upon daughters' work or wives' comanagement of households, married their daughters later and held out longer against the gender-leveling tendencies of the dominant marriage system. In this period, moreover, they declared and enforced new distinctions between women and men in matters ranging from dress to education, legal status and rights, religious observance, and social behavior.

On the popular level as well, there was a novel and urgent articulation of two notions previously taken for granted: that the sexes are profoundly different from one another and that women are inferior to men. Men stepped up as the authors of multiple discourses – medical, religious, legal, political, and social – aimed at naming and policing a whole new set of gender attributes and behaviors.[48] An oral and visual culture of ballads, broadsheets, and pamphlets stressed female inferiority and highlighted women's chief alleged defect: their insubordinate behavior toward men.[49]

Commentators have noted this heightened preoccupation with gender difference and female inferiority. They have not, however, presented the wider social context as one in which ordinary women's and men's lives were moving closer together, relative not just to their counterparts in other agricultural societies but also to their own forebears in medieval northwestern Europe. More commonly, interpreters have alleged the opposite: a new and deepened patriarchy, a widening gap between women's and men's lives, and a decline in women's status. Yet given evidence that late-marriage households were generating increasingly similar life cycles and shared power for the sexes, it makes more sense to see what happened as a male reaction to the growing proximity of their lives to women's.

Separate male and female roles and a hierarchy favoring males were less discussed in early-marriage societies largely, it appears, because such things were so obvious, being incorporated fully into the fabric of experience through marriage and household structures themselves. Contrasts between the childhood worlds of peasant girls and boys in these societies were much sharper, and China offers a striking example. From the decline of a feudal system after the ninth century A.D. until the fall of the Ch'in dynasty in 1911, China was dominated by small-scale peasant family farming. Yet while a minority of women worked in the southern rice-growing regions, as

---

[48] See Mendelson and Crawford, *Women in Early Modern England*, introduction and Ch. 1: "Contexts," 1–74, for a full discussion of the category "woman" as the "subject of endless discourse in early modern England," 15.

[49] Mendelson and Crawford, *Women in Early Modern England*, 58–65.

in India, women hardly worked at all in the vast dry-field regions of the north that could only absorb limited labor.[50] (A report from the 1930s shows that women averaged only 13 percent of agricultural labor for the whole country but performed almost no such work in the northern region.)[51] From earliest childhood, girls were more confined to the household.

For countless Chinese girls and women for over 1,000 years, restrictions on movement were also reinforced for life by the practice of foot-binding. Introduced by neo-Confucian court figures in the tenth century, foot-binding spread widely. It was slower to be adopted in the south, as it interfered with women's rice cultivation, although even there many rice workers had bound feet and toiled in the paddies on their knees.[52]

Foot-binding presents a striking if extreme example of the sharper divergence between female and male lives that is everywhere on display in early-marriage societies. At age five or six, girls alone underwent a procedure normally performed by mothers and often completed, at age twelve or thirteen, by their new female in-laws. A girl's toes were forced downward toward the soles of her feet and bandaged under pressure. The practice was deemed erotic as well as useful, according to Confucian patriarchs, in preventing "barbarous running around."[53] Attention has only lately begun to be paid to the practice, and it is now clear that the longevity of foot-binding depended upon the great strength of enduring family units. That strength helps to explain why the practice persisted for so long without direct force of law and even in express violation of imperial edicts.[54]

Historian Dorothy Ko cautions against viewing foot-binding simplistically as a male conspiracy to keep women subordinate. She argues in a study

---

[50] Stacey, *Patriarchy and Socialist Revolution in China*, 23.

[51] Ibid., 292. Stacey cites John L. Buck, *Land Utilization in China* (New York, 1956), a reprint of the land study from 1937.

[52] Ibid., 6.

[53] Ibid., 41, cited from Howard Levy, *Chinese Footbinding: The History of a Curious Erotic Custom* (New York, 1966).

[54] C. Fred Blake, "Foot-binding in Neo-Confucian China and the Appropriation of Female Labor." *Signs: Journal of Women in Culture and Society* 19, No. 3 (Spring 1994): 699. Blake describes the later phases of the foot-binding era as follows: "Although largely filtered through male voices during the period when foot-binding was under attack, testimonies of foot-bound women attempted to find words for the kind of pain experienced in binding – burning, throbbing feet swallowing the body in fire. . . . These accounts tell of girls losing appetites and sleep, running away, hiding, surreptitiously attempting to loosen their bandages, and enduring beatings while trying to comply with their mother's demands. But the girls were still at a tender enough age to retain the basic trust in the implicit goodness of their mother's intentions. The 'tradition' could not have passed from mothers to daughters if not for mothers' credibility as 'caring.' The conundrum of a mother's care consciously causing her daughter excruciating pain is contained in a single word, *teng*, which in the proverb cited above, [If you care for your son, care not if he suffers in his studies; if you care for your daughter, care not if she suffers in her feet], refers to 'hurting,' 'caring,' or a conflation of both in the same breath," ibid., 681–82.

of elite women in seventeenth-century China that the practice was part of female culture and "prepared a girl physically and psychologically for her future role as wife and a dependent family member."[55] It also reinforced the belief in separate male and female domains. "Through foot-binding, the doctrine of separate spheres was engraved onto the bodies of female children."[56] Experiences of girls and boys did not differ so dramatically in all early-marriage societies, but everywhere they diverged more than in late-marriage settings.

The next stage of the life cycle, adolescence, was the time when daughters in early-marriage households moved out, leaving their brothers behind. Specialists have identified the hardest period in a woman's life, in late imperial China anyway, as just after marriage, when as a very young bride she moved into her new husband's household. Studies of the nineteenth and early twentieth centuries also report this as a time in the life cycle when women's suicide rates, always higher at all ages than for men, soared.[57]

While stress periods for women and men in early modern northwestern Europe have been explored to a degree, they have not been causally linked to the marriage system there. Data that enable us to identify such periods confirm, however, what is predictable from a system in which most marriages are arranged not by parents but by young persons themselves. That is, by far the most troubled period in such settings was courtship, not the early months of marriage – and for both sexes, not just the women.

The records of a seventeenth-century English physician and astrologer of over 2,000 patients, mostly ordinary English villagers reporting a variety of illnesses and complaints, reveal that courtship stress was the largest single category of emotional disturbances. While women dominated the numbers, with problems including lovesickness, quarrels, jilting, seduction and betrayal, and broken marriage promises, men constituted a significant percentage of this group and registered every one of these complaints. Unsurprisingly, the largest occupational category for both women and men was that of servant. Few stated that their unhappiness was owing to parents' objections to a chosen partner – only 15 among the 118 women with courtship troubles and 2 among the 63 men.[58] This symmetry in women's and men's experience contrasts strikingly with the asymmetry of the Chinese case. Since most Chinese grooms remained in their fathers' households, they – unlike their brides – experienced no comparable stress of uprooting.

---

[55] Dorothy Ko, *Teachers of the Inner Chambers: Women and Culture in Seventeenth-Century China* (Stanford, Calif., 1994), 149. See also Ko's fuller treatment of foot-binding, *Every Step a Lotus: Shoes for Bound Feet* (Berkeley, 2001).

[56] Ibid.

[57] See Margery Wolf, "Women and Suicide in China," in Margery Wolf and Roxanne Witke, eds., *Women in Chinese Society* (Stanford, Calif., 1975), 111–41.

[58] Michael MacDonald, *Mystical Bedlam: Madness, Anxiety and Healing in Seventeenth-Century England* (Cambridge, 1985), 99.

In early-marriage societies, household structures literally reinforce control by the older generation over adolescents' rites of passage. A daughter knows that her marriage will be arranged at puberty and that her remaining rite of passage will be becoming a mother as soon as possible, ideally of a male heir. For sons, the marital rite of passage is one of a set of graduated rites that may or may not culminate with a household headship, an event usually coinciding with the death of the father. By contrast, the estimated 60 percent of youth in northwestern Europe from 1500 to 1750 who became servants, circulating among employers for five to ten years before marriage, accounts for the less automatic timing there of youthful rites of passage, as well as the comparatively smaller role of the older generation in those rites.[59] Also, since such rites were not so closely tied to biological events such as puberty, birth, or death, they all required more negotiation between the generations as well as more planning by the young people themselves.

Decisions about when to marry in the late-marriage region were based not upon biological events but upon young persons' employment opportunities, and were related to their own calculations about the optimal moment for establishing new households. The timing of weddings within the year has actually been shown to reflect the changing seasonal demand for agricultural work, with marriage peaks in autumn and in late spring that mirror the slack seasons after the fall harvesting of crops and the traditional spring lambing and calving of animal husbandry.[60]

Agricultural work was seasonal, governed by the annual rhythm of growth, and marriages moulded themselves to the seasonal matrix of work. Weddings, like other celebrations, were infrequent during the months of maximum work and risk; they then clustered in the weeks immediately following relief from work and risk. Why they clustered is probably overspecified: high harvest wages were paid to labourers; unmarried servants in husbandry were released from their annual contracts; one could posit a need to celebrate the end of a year's work; there certainly would have been a pent-up demand for weddings, strengthened by the revelation of prenuptial conceptions.[61]

Historian Ann Kussmaul has used the parish registers recording marriages for the early modern centuries to show further that for England, it is possible

---

[59] Peter Laslett estimated that only one in five of all young people escaped the experience of living with servants or of living as servants, "Characteristics of the Western Family Considered Over Time," 110. The most authoritative work on servants in England from this period is that of Ann Kussmaul, whose books treating the subject are *Servants in Husbandry in Early Modern England* (Cambridge, 1981) and *A General View of the Rural Economy of England, 1538–1840* (Cambridge, 1990).

[60] Noted in Ann Kussmaul, "Time and Space, Hoofs and Grain: The Seasonality of Marriage in England." *Journal of Interdisciplinary History* 15, No. 4 (Spring 1985): 755, from the study by Anthony Wrigley and Roger S. Schofield, *The Population History of England, 1541–1871: A Reconstruction* (Cambridge, 1981).

[61] Kussmaul, *A General View of the Rural Economy of England*, 3.

to identify by the later seventeenth century the evolution of more regional product specializations, with the eastern grain-growing areas ceasing to display the spring peaks of pastoralism and the western pastoral areas showing a decline in their autumn marriages. These shifts, she contends, show how improvements in transportation and the development of trade among different areas increasingly allowed regions to concentrate upon the products that were most suited to those places.

Kussmaul also uses the parish registers to trace a third pattern revealing quite volatile shifts in those regions where nonagricultural, rural industrial labor came to dominate in the early modern centuries. She is able to identify such regions by the fact that the marriage registration data are more evenly distributed throughout the months of the year and do not display a marked tendency toward peaks in either of the two agriculturally determined seasons. That, of course, ultimately became the pattern for the distribution of marriages in industrialized societies.[62]

An example of how the mature system of life-cycle domestic service worked in modestly prosperous families is recounted in the seventeenth-century diary of Puritan vicar Ralph Josselin, a small farmer living forty miles north of London, who rented much of his property to tenants.[63] Of his large family, two children had left home at age ten, two at thirteen, one at fourteen, and two at fifteen. Most went to London, where the girls became servants and the boys apprentices. A few had been to a nearby "petty" school, which set them apart since only a fifth of village boys, and fewer girls, received any formal education then. The Josselin children did not work for kin, and those in service had standard contracts with employers. They visited their parents on occasion; but when it was time to marry, they chose their own mates. All but one waited until the twenties to marry, saving earnings for the event. The vicar made comparable settlements on all his younger children at marriage, willing the bulk of his landed property to a son he had once threatened to disinherit for drunkenness, but who became the heir after the death in adolescence of a beloved first son.

The institution of service in northwestern Europe was especially important for women, who had fewer opportunities than their brothers for apprenticeship or formal education. Women also had comparatively less freedom of movement, so service played a more singular role in their exposure to life outside their natal households. A recent study of youth in early modern England underscores the importance of life-cycle service as a time when women learned to negotiate contracts, deal with strangers, and handle uncertainty. "Perhaps above all," the author concludes, "women brought with them into marriage the experience of long years during which they learnt to cope with

---

[62] Ibid., Ch. 6: 126–45.
[63] Alan Macfarlane, *The Family Life of Ralph Josselin: An Essay in Historical Anthropology* (Cambridge, 1970).

many tasks, and to switch between different skills, masters, and working environments."[64]

What is so striking from a comparative standpoint, however, and is not mentioned in such accounts, is just how aberrant these women's experiences were for their time. Employment featuring travel on her own and contact with many strangers would hardly have recommended any single woman in an early-marriage setting. To the contrary, such things would have made a young woman unmarriageable, regardless of whether she kept her virginity, as most did in northwestern Europe – at least until betrothal. Similarly, while early observations are quite correct that domestic service enabled young people to meet potential marriage partners on their own, what is extraordinary is that this institution evolved in late-marriage settings as a socially acceptable way for single young people to meet, evolve courting rituals of their own, and choose their life partners.

The contrast with the experience of young women in early-marriage societies is particularly arresting. The far more typical situation is outlined by Moroccan sociologist Fatima Mernissi, who notes that even today in her rapidly transforming country, over half of rural girls are married by their families before they ever reach puberty.[65] Especially in the countryside, traditional sexual segregation continues to divide all social space into male and female areas, and there is little interaction among marriageable young people. One effect is that young rural men visiting the modernized towns initially assume that any woman they see on the street must be sexually available.[66]

At an age when the adolescent Moroccan bride is already living with her husband's family under the daily supervision of her new mother-in-law, her early modern counterpart in northwestern Europe was a servant living with unrelated employers, likely to make a contract with another household for her services the next year, and unlikely to take a husband for years yet to come. In global terms, the anomaly was the servant. Yet since the few studies of life-cycle service stay within the northwestern European context, its genuine oddity goes unremarked.[67] When attention is paid to the peculiarity of men's and especially women's roles as servants in early modern Europe, it is easier to recognize a potential for opening a new window on the Western past.

It is true that Peter Laslett declared life-cycle service to be massive exploitation, charging that poor families offered up their children to rich ones "at the very time when those children were at the height of their productive

---

[64] Ilana Krausman Ben-Amos, *Adolescence and Youth in Early Modern England* (New Haven, Conn., 1994), 154.

[65] Fatima Mernissi, *Beyond the Veil: Male–Female Dynamics in Modern Muslim Society* (Bloomington, Ind., 1987), 101.

[66] Ibid., 143.

[67] See, for example, Kussmaul, *Servants in Husbandry in Early Modern England*.

powers."[68] By the eighteenth century, poor youth were in fact the ones most likely to be in service. Yet in most of the early modern era and before, service typically involved exchanges among families at comparable social levels as a way to handle changing labor needs in households where, owing to late marriage, the generations were further apart.[69] Northwestern Europeans, in any case, had no franchise on the exploitation of youth, which was hardly absent in early-marriage societies.

However the practice is judged, it remains true that for centuries, life-cycle service threw members of both sexes more on their own devices at tender ages. The youth of northwestern Europe automatically had to assume greater accountability for their lives than their counterparts in early-marriage households. For women in particular, there was also more exposure to unwanted sexual encounters with employers and strangers, as will be seen. Servanthood widened young people's experience of the world, then, while bringing the mixed blessing of greater personal responsibility for their fates.

The economic contributions of young women and men as single laborers over many centuries have finally begun to be reckoned in this long period of semifreedom, or semidependency, peculiar to the northwestern European life cycle.[70] Yet much remains to be sorted out in the chain of causes and consequences of late marriage. Not only do we not know why people married late in the first place, we understand too little about the effects on consciousness and behavior as an entire society early came to terms with a resulting loosening of the bonds of kinship that in so many other places continued to hold the generations of peasants together, often quite literally in the same place.

*   *   *

What happened to sexual behavior as couples postponed marriage until long after puberty, and as brides and grooms became age peers? Did women's and men's lives in this area, as in so many others, begin to display the convergence being argued here? Much evidence suggests that they did, although understanding of both the medieval and early modern eras suffers here, as well, from interpreters having overlooked how more typical agricultural societies actually work. Scholars are aware that single young people, especially those in service, had expanded opportunities for social and sexual interaction. They have also discovered that average illegitimacy rates in the early

---

[68] Laslett, "Characteristics of the Western Family Considered Over Time," 111.

[69] Hajnal, "Two Kinds of Preindustrial Household Formation System." *Population and Development Review* 8 (1982): 471.

[70] See especially among these studies John R. Gillis, *Youth and History: Tradition and Change in European Age Relations 1770–Present* (New York, 1974); and John Gillis, *For Better, For Worse: British Marriages, 1600 to the Present* (New York, 1985).

modern period from about 1500 to 1750 were far lower than in late medieval Europe and actually declined as the average marriage ages rose.[71]
The usual explanation for this oddity is that from the late fifteenth century, religious and secular authorities banded together in fierce and largely
effective campaigns to confine sexual activity to the marriage bed. The campaigns themselves have been well documented and extravagant claims made
that "sexual repression was stronger in the West than anywhere else in the
world."[72] Yet family historian Lawrence Stone once admitted to bafflement
as to why church and state might have campaigned so vigorously for "a
system that confined sexuality for men, now, as well as for women to heterosexual relations within marriage."[73]

As late as the mid-fifteenth century, popular European attitudes toward
sexuality were in fact similar to those in most other agricultural societies:
that is, accepting of men's pre- and extra-marital sexual activity but opposed
to any but married sex for women. Men had access to prostitutes, chiefly
in the towns, and, by the fourteenth and fifteenth centuries, to growing
numbers of municipally supported brothels. (In theory these were available
only to bachelors, but in practice they were open to all men.) This easy
attitude, however, came to a halt by the end of the fifteenth century, as
brothels were shut down and even the sexual activity of unmarried men

---

[71] Peter Laslett, *Family Life and Illicit Love in Earlier Generations* (Cambridge, 1977), 106. The
rates were estimated at less than 2% in England in 1700, for example, and just 1.2% in
France as late as the 1740s. See also Richard Adair, *Courtship, Illegitimacy and Marriage in
Early Modern England* (Manchester, 1996).

[72] Jean-Louis Flandrin, "Repression and Change in the Sexual Life of Young People in Medieval
and Early Modern Times," in Robert Wheaton and Tamara K Hareven, eds., *Family and
Sexuality in French History* (Philadelphia, 1980), 28.

[73] In 1985, Lawrence Stone declared that historians simply do not understand the widely recognized sexual repression of the sixteenth century. "The more we discover," he said, "about an
extraordinary system of control of sexual behavior in western society from the late Middle
Ages – a system that confined sexuality for men, now, as well as for women to heterosexual
relations within marriage – the less we understand about its causes, and the less we can explain the immense official efforts to police everyone's sexual behavior." He continued, "The
16th century was a period of destructive civil wars, declining real wages, rising population,
and increased unemployment and vagrancy. All states attempted to cope with these problems
by increasingly harsh measures to enforce law and order. But this hardly explains why the
drive to order should be so fiercely concentrated on deviant sexuality, not only on sodomy,
which almost everywhere was made a penal offense punishable by death, but also premarital
sex, fornication, concubinage and adultery. There was a powerful desire to repress, which
cannot merely be attributed to the growing power of the Renaissance state to control the
lives of its subjects. In any case, states, however powerful, usually have more important
things to do than to stamp out fornication and adultery.... The intermittent ebbs and flows
in the long history of the West of a passion for redefining the boundaries of the licit and the
illicit in sexual life are one of the most baffling phenomena facing the social historian, the
historian of ideas, and the historian of *mentalité*. Thanks to the meticulous research of many
scholars, we now know the broad outlines of the facts. But the causal mechanisms still elude
us," "Sex in the West," *The New Republic* (July 8, 1985), 37.

began to draw attack. A study of prostitution in southern France contends that what amounted to a European-wide shift in opinion emerged not from the church or the state but instead from lay society – preceding the more familiar repression from above.

This gradual change of lay sexual morality in the late Middle Ages laid the foundations for the dramatic transformation in morals which took place at the end of the fifteenth and throughout the sixteenth centuries and which were [sic] presented in a coherent manner in the theological works of the Reformation leaders and in the corpus of the canons of the Council of Trent. In general, their effect was to tighten sexual moral discipline by constructing a more coherent model of Christian marriage. Despite the important differences between the Catholic and Protestant models – Protestant marriage being neither a sacrament nor indissoluble – both resulted in the total condemnation of concubinage and the much stricter enforcement of laws against male adultery.[74]

The timing argued here – that is, a shift in lay morality followed by a formal tightening of discipline in Catholic and Protestant doctrine – makes more sense if one entertains the idea that it was the family household, not the church or the state, that played the catalytic role in generating a new sexual code with the same rules for both sexes. Claims for uniquely powerful external controls on sexuality in Western societies do not stand up in any case. Such controls on women, and to a lesser extent on men, are far stronger in early- than in late-marriage settings. Being built into family structures, however, they are less obvious.

In most agricultural societies, after all, early marriage is the key to the control of women's sexual behavior. Neither as daughters nor as wives are women themselves the guardians of their own sexuality. Concubinage and prostitution, meanwhile, offer approved outlets for men, especially single men among the peasant majority who are obliged to postpone marriage for so long. As a practical matter, however, most men are unable to take much advantage of this freedom, since available partners are limited to a scarce population of prostitutes and other women without male protectors. In practice if not theory, then, sexual denial is the usual lot of single men, although they are surrounded by nubile but untouchable sisters, sisters-in-law, and female cousins.

Ironically, in early-marriage societies, most women by age twenty have more sexual experience than men their age, many of whom are still unmarried and may remain so. The seclusion of women is one way these societies handle this awkward situation – whether formal, as in the Indian system of purdah, or informal, as in the Mediterranean practice of delineating separate

---

[74] Leah Lydia Otis, *Prostitution in Medieval Society: The History of an Urban Institution in Languedoc* (Chicago, 1985), 108.

male and female space within households and in wider communities.[75] That women are viewed by men in such settings as innately lascivious is thus hardly as bizarre as it may seem to persons raised in European-based societies. Appeals to a lustful, unruly female nature rationalize practical constraints that early-marriage populations place upon women while offering an excuse for men's lapses.

As later marriage was established in medieval northwestern Europe, distinctive ground rules for sexual behavior were bound to emerge as more women and men left home before marriage to work. A study of life on a manor in late-thirteenth- and fourteenth-century England argues that this freer association of young people helped fuel the late-thirteenth-century population increase, which included many illegitimate children.[76] Even with the established pattern of separate households for each married couple, children born out of wedlock at that time could be raised without much fuss, since they could still be brought up within a rooted network of neighboring kin.[77] By the fifteenth century, however, as the bond between kin and fixed property began to give way and as families became ever more mobile, it was no longer so easy to absorb illegitimate children into wider family groups. That

---

[75] See the classic article by Rayna Reiter, "Men and Women in the South of France: Public and Private Domains," in Rayna Reiter, ed., *Toward an Anthropology of Women* (New York, 1975), 252–82.

[76] Judith Bennett cites numerous fines for fornication among unmarried youth, as well as illegitimate births among them. It would appear that these young persons, nearly 700 years ago, were not only playing a substantial role in the selection of their marriage partners, but also experiencing far more sexual freedom than their counterparts in early-marriage societies. In Bennett's summary: "Adolescence, in short, ensured that young people were mature enough to choose their own spouses; instead of being barely more than children, they were young adults on the threshold of full majority. Moreover, the social effects of marriage simply were not extensive enough to warrant much familial coercion. Because marriage created a new household, it profoundly affected the principals, but redounded only indirectly and mildly upon their families.... Since marriage joined together two individuals, not their families, choice might well have rested primarily with the prospective bride and bridegroom," *Women in the Medieval English Countryside,* 96.
    That illegitimate births among daughters of the late medieval peasantry were relatively frequent as the age of marriage climbed is indirect support for the hypothesis to be argued here that daughters' marriages were initially postponed to take advantage of their productive activity on behalf of the household rather than to control fertility, as some have argued. Only with renewed population pressure by the sixteenth century, when age at marriage for both sexes moved up even further from the early to the mid- and even late twenties, does there appear to have been an appreciation of later marriage as a means to control fertility. By that time, too, elaborate courting arrangements enforced by young people themselves were more effectively limiting procreation during the long years before marriage, ibid., 100–3.

[77] See Hanawalt, *The Ties That Bound,* 73–74, for a discussion that underscores a lenient attitude toward bastardy in the thirteenth and fourteenth centuries. While complications were posed for inheritance, Hanawalt notes that bastards' rights might be recognized on many manors if they were the sole heirs, and that in any case they might receive lifetime use of landed property.

illegitimacy rates became so low by the early modern era, then, cannot continue to be credited to the repressive structures of church and state when a more plausible set of agents is nearer at hand. Although not without effect, these outside institutions appear to have been far less important than single young people's own reckoning of the negative consequences of an illegitimate child for their prospects of being able to work and save in order to marry and create new households of their own.

A recent study by Marjorie McIntosh of various forms of wrongdoing – including sexual misbehavior – in England from the late fourteenth through the sixteenth centuries bears out the view being argued here that the crackdown on sexual misconduct actually worked its way from the bottom up rather than the top down. This crackdown was exercised in the first instance by ordinary local parish notables who might be small landholders or perhaps craft or tradesmen who, for long anyway, were far more concerned about the increased social disruption posed by sexual misbehavior, including unwelcome illegitimate children who might become charges on the community, than they were about sexual morality per se.

Examining reports of misconduct from an array of 267 local courts in 255 communities, McIntosh finds that the offenses mostly fall into three categories: a disharmony cluster involving verbal misconduct known as "scolding" as well as eavesdropping; a disorder cluster including sexual misconduct, alehouse unruliness, and general bad behavior; and a poverty cluster involving vagrancy and vagabondage.[78] McIntosh explains that while only about an eighth of courts reported social offenses around 1400, there was generally a rise in reported instances of the disharmony and disorder offenses, with a peak in Elizabeth's reign at the end of the sixteenth century, whereas poverty offenses increased continuously from the mid-fifteenth century to the end of the period. There was, she says, less concern than many have supposed with female sexuality as such and more attention to regulating disorderly sexual behavior, wherever it took place, among both men and women. In addition, as she sums up:

This study demonstrates that new problems and solutions to them might well emerge first at the lowest level of government and courts, moving only gradually into the attention of higher authorities, an observation that reverses the directionality assumed by many analyses of national politics and law during the early modern period.[79]

---

[78] Marjorie Keniston McIntosh says, "Four types of courts handled misconduct between 1370 and 1600: at the local level, the public courts held in England's villages, market centers, and hundreds (the administrative units into which most countries were divided), plus the legal bodies of the cities and larger towns; and at the intermediate level, the church courts operating within dioceses or archdeaconries, plus country Sessions of the Peace," *Controlling Misbehavior in England, 1370–1600* (Cambridge, 1998), 7.

[79] Ibid., 15.

The real novelty of European sexual history from the late Middle Ages through the early modern era, in any case, appears not to have been repression from above of sexual behavior but rather a shift in the mechanisms for controlling youthful sexual activity. Whereas in most agricultural settings those mechanisms continued to be built into early-marriage structures and monitored by the older generation, later marriage for daughters entailed the slow but real surrender of control by the parental generation. The ferocity of an onslaught on pre- and extramarital sexuality by the outside authorities of church and state was real enough, but it was no match for the more powerful constraints on the young located within early-marriage households.

What set northwestern Europe apart was thus far more significant than sexual repression from the outside. It was instead the painful, protracted coming to terms with a new sexual order altogether, one in which real control over young women's and men's sexuality was ceasing to reside with the older generation, and especially with male elders acting in the larger service of family property and name. While church, state, and local community played a part in channeling youthful sexuality, and still do, what is striking about this region in the early modern era is its adjustment to the peculiar freedoms and constraints of distinctive family structures that obliged young women and men alike to assume responsibility for their own sexual behavior.

Despite the extended waiting period before marriage, now experienced by both sexes and providing yet another example of the growing alignment of their life cycles that is being argued here, couples hardly denied themselves all sexual activity. The important thing was to avoid having babies, and evidence on courting practices throughout northwestern Europe reveals that couples, especially those already betrothed, often engaged in socially sanctioned sessions of petting and fondling. They might be alone together in a bed, fully clothed, in ritualized all-night visits with parental consent. More commonly, they took advantage of seasonable nights in the fields, or stolen times indoors when the mistress was away, to indulge in what historian Jean-Louis Flandrin once described as "manual, oral, and bodily games."[80]

By the early modern era, when a single woman became pregnant, church or village authorities might become involved, for illegitimate children, by then, had emerged as undesirable community charges. The usual expedient was to pressure couples into marriage, tracking down any man who attempted to flee. Failing that, maintenance might be charged against the parents of the father, or another man might be found to marry the woman.[81] Court records feature accusations of fornication, seduction, and breach of promise; but for long, most such couples readily married, with no need for

[80] Flandrin, "Repression and Change in the Sexual Life of Young People in Medieval and Early Modern Times," 36.

[81] See G. R. Quaife, *Wanton Wenches and Wayward Wives: Peasants and Illicit Sex in Early Seventeenth-Century England* (New Brunswick, N.J., 1979).

outside intervention. The women were not exposed to the ostracism, or even death, that occurred in early-marriage societies, though they did endure social opprobrium. The commonest sexual encounters were between female servants and men, single or married, living under the same roof.

Beatrice Gottlieb's study of 800 late-fifteenth-century cases of marital and sexual disputes from two dioceses in northern France documents widespread sexual activity among unmarried servants.[82] Because the creation of a marriage then took so long, many disputes arose, especially as betrothal was popularly held to sanction sexual intercourse. A typical case featured Symon Ruillon and Isabelle Rosat from Nogent-sur-Seine, who lived and worked in the same house and began having sex one winter in a shed on the property. The following summer, Isabelle, evidently pregnant, contended in court that since Symon was betrothed to her, he should be made to marry her. He rejoined that Isabelle was free with her favors and that he knew at least six men who had slept with her. Isabelle prevailed in the end, and the pair married. They also paid the usual fine for consummating their marriage prior to its solemnization by the church.

While the church was always interested in upholding its long-fought rights as the arbiter of marriage, its interest in punishment for premarital sex has been overdrawn. Men and women alike sought out church courts of their own volition for resolution of disputes. Since these courts honored mutual consent as a basis for marriage, a pregnant young woman such as Isabelle Rosat might try her luck at salvaging her reputation and gaining child support, whether or not the story she told was true. In time, more women came to assert a right to refuse sexual relations until after marriage. For example, when her suitor tried to persuade Alice Wheeler in early-seventeenth-century Wiltshire to have sex with him on the grounds that they were already contracted to marry, Wheeler responded tartly, "I know . . . that I am your wife and you my husband, yet until such time as we are married [in church] you shall not have the use of my body."[83]

The late medieval rise in repression of sexual activity, especially in towns, was in part a response to the growing need to protect single working women. For example, when secular authorities prohibited traditional bachelor festivities that often included ritualized gang rapes, they were responding to the rising migration of young, single women in search of work.[84] Protective efforts after 1500 included new or reinforced measures against rape and sexual assault. Whereas in early-marriage societies protection for women destined

---

[82] Beatrice Gottlieb, "The Meaning of Clandestine Marriage," in Wheaton and Hareven, eds., *Family and Sexuality in French History*, 49–83.

[83] Mendelson and Crawford, *Women in Early Modern England*, 121.

[84] Jacques Rossiaud, "Prostitution, Sex, and Society in French Towns in the Fifteenth Century," in Philippe Ariès and André Béjin, eds., *Western Sexuality: Practice and Precept in Past and Present Times* (Oxford, 1985), 76–94.

to marry honorably was obtained by seclusion and youthful marriage, the protection of these growing numbers of single female workers was recognized to require new sorts of restraints by authorities located outside the family household.

Men surely experienced the new sexual restraints more keenly, partly because women's greater exposure now to pregnancies that could end their chances to marry encouraged them to see such restraints in a positive light. Safeguards against sexual attack helped enable single women to secure the paid employment in the world beyond the household that made them so unusual. The self-restraint required of both sexes during the long years until marriage contrasted sharply with the literal separation of the sexes for the same purpose – namely, preventing illegitimacy – in early-marriage societies. Young men and women together in northwestern Europe evolved a code of abstinence before marriage, and fidelity afterward, that in early-marriage settings applied only to women. Behavior could and did deviate from the code, but transgressors now included many more youth of both sexes and comparable social backgrounds.

* * *

Much has already been said about adulthood and old age, but what is noteworthy here is the continuing divergence of women's and men's lives in early-marriage contexts and their persisting convergence in late-marriage ones. Both parenthood and the world of work divided more sharply along gender lines in early-marriage households, with women assuming more responsibility for domestic work and childrearing and men engaged more exclusively in extra-domestic labor, including any dealings with the outside world. In late-marriage settings, parenthood and livelihood overlapped far more for the sexes, and the boundary between women's work and men's work was fuzzier.

Parenthood was also less prolonged and intensive in late-marriage households. That wives were older automatically ensured two to four fewer pregnancies.[85] Also, the institution of service meant that by the early modern era, most offspring would live under the parental roof for only ten to fifteen years before leaving home for good. True, daughters in early-marriage societies also leave home at or near that age, but in-marrying adolescent daughters-in-law usually replace them. First sons, moreover, remain in the parental household for life, while remaining sons and their families often live there at least until the death of the father. Fathers normally have far longer and closer relationships with their sons; but since fathers are considerably

---

[85] This assumes, of course, that marriage age and the rate of marriage were the prime determinants of the number of pregnancies, as they were in the areas of the Western family pattern. In China, as noted, despite women's far younger age at marriage, marital fertility was actually lower owing to the adoption of other previously noted preventive measures.

older than mothers, the most enduring parent–child connection is ordinarily that between mothers and sons.

Commentators exploring women's domestic lives in early-marriage societies describe how wives often create an "informal, mother-centered 'uterine family'" to gain influence in their husbands' households.[86] Based on a woman's ties with her children, uterine families embody patriarchal norms favoring sons, but for distinctive reasons:

> To a man, having a son fulfilled his sacred obligation as a man to ancestors and provided one further link in a patrilineal chain that existed before him and would exist after him. To a woman, a son provided a permanent mother–child relationship upon which she could center a family that would be tied to her for the rest of her life. Sons also provided a conduit through which a mother could hope to influence the world of male authority. The ideal son for a Chinese mother was one who, above all else, was personally loyal to her and who would serve as her "political front man" in domestic and even public affairs. A woman therefore invested a great deal in binding her son to her as she raised him.[87]

A mother who succeeded in such strategies could achieve a measure of household power, especially as a widow and matriarch, that was unavailable to her counterpart in northwestern Europe. Her success, though, depended as much on the accidents of being married to a man who became head of a household, and producing a surviving male heir, as on her own activity and skills. Her counterpart in northwestern Europe confronted different challenges in achieving a comfortable old age, which ordinarily depended more on her own initiatives and less on whether she had produced a son. She was likelier to spend far fewer years as a widow in any case, both because she was closer in age to her husband and was liable to remarry if he died. Yet even if she were well provided for, which depended in part on her husband, who usually controlled any property, she was unlikely to enjoy enhanced authority or respect in the eyes of the younger generation as she aged. By the end of the early modern era, in fact, a widow's children were apt to be scattered and the widow herself, in her last years, attended by paid caregivers.

As for the head of household, despite Peter Laslett's early pronouncement that the father's authority as the sole adult male was vastly magnified as a result of the Western family pattern, it seems obvious that stronger patriarchal authority over children is built into early-marriage households, resting on the head's dual position as chief of resident kin and as work boss.[88] In

---

[86] Johnson, *Women, the Family and Peasant Revolution in China*, 10.

[87] Ibid., 18.

[88] Peter Laslett says, "The perpetual presence of the father, the *paterfamilias*, the household head, must have had an enormous effect on the pre-industrial family and household. It follows that the influence of the shape of the family on the formation of the personality of the child must have been greater in the past than it is today. It follows further that this influence must have been strongest of all in the West, where the predominance of the nuclear family was most

northwestern Europe, the control of fathers was being displaced by the early modern era, as children of both sexes increasingly grew up knowing that they would soon leave home to work for others. First sons might still count on inheriting the family land, if there was any; but with rising population by the sixteenth century, sons and daughters alike knew that their chances to marry and manage their own households depended ever more on themselves.

In assessing the relative authority of husbands and wives, focus belongs on their positions within each household type and not on specific tasks or on whether work was paid or unpaid. In both systems, after all, wives mostly did domestic work, even though they were less likely to do field work in early-marriage households. What mattered, however, was that the wife in a late-marriage setting was literally more critical to her household's survival, for the simple reason that there was no other resident adult female who could assume her functions. One measure of the importance of the marriage partnership in northwestern Europe is that, for long, remarriage for either sex on the death of a spouse was swift. The rapidity of remarriage of widowers has been analyzed for several French regions in the seventeenth and eighteenth centuries. Most had a new wife within six months, and in some parishes more than three-quarters had remarried within that time. Here is an account from early-nineteenth-century France:

When a husband loses his wife or a wife her husband, the surviving spouse at once invites everyone to a meal: this sometimes takes place in the house where the corpse is still lying, and the guests laugh, drink, sing and make arrangements for remarrying their host or hostess. The widower or widow receives proposals, and gives reasons for acceptance or rejection; it is only rarely that the party comes to an end before the arrangement has been concluded.[89]

Fewer widows married again, then as now. Still, in sixteenth-century England, a quarter to a third of all widows remarried, and almost half of those did so within a year.[90]

By contrast, in early-marriage households, where a partnership of husbands and wives is less critical to a household's survival, remarriage of widows is uncommon and often proscribed by norms stressing the widow's duty of faithfulness to her dead husband's family. Remarriage occurs, particularly among the poor, although the option is commonly exercised not by the

pronounced, with children alone in the company of parents," Laslett "Characteristics of the Western Family Considered Over Time,"106. Laslett mentions that the greater maturity of western women may have increased women's authority over children, and he also says that a couple's closeness in age would produce more companionate marriages, 109; but he does not argue that either of these factors might have compromised the power of the *paterfamilias*.

[89] Jean-Louis Flandrin, *Families in Former Times: Kinship, Household and Sexuality* (Cambridge, 1976), 115.

[90] Mendelson and Crawford, *Women in Early Modern England*, 182–84. See also Amy Froide, "Marital Status as a Category of Difference: Singlewomen and Widows in Early Modern England," in Judith M. Bennett and Amy M. Froide, eds., *Singlewomen in the European Past, 1250–1800* (Philadelphia, 1999).

widow but by her in-laws. A woman who remarried in imperial China, for example, had no right to take property and no claims on her children, who belonged by custom and law to their father's family. Even now, despite revolutionary upheaval and a new marriage law to the contrary, the tradition that children belong to the dead man's family, not to his surviving widow, remains in force in many rural areas.[91]

Already by the medieval era in northwestern Europe, widows were comparatively independent legal actors since societies whose households contained but one married couple had to ensure support for a surviving spouse and children. Widows' options depended on economic conditions, age, skills, and property. In England, while legal charge of a girl belonged to her father, and that of a wife to her husband, widows could enter into contracts, run businesses, sue for debt, manage land, hire workers, and support their children's marriages. Settlements varied, but widows received a third of their husbands' property for lifetime use by common law. Assets from a deceased husband could even be brought into a new marriage, a practice that undermined patrilineal ties since those threatened most by the widow's freedom to take property into a new marriage were the heirs of her former husband.[92]

Widowhood was still a hard time, even for the well-to-do. Widows were vulnerable to threats against their property and their persons. Their frequent remarriage had little to do with the lust of which they were often accused and much to do with a concern to keep fragile households afloat. Widows with grown children might enjoy more independence than younger women, single or married; but as women who were liberated from men's authority, they were routinely subject to the suspicions of neighbors – or worse.

Responsibilities for managing households on their own did not often confront new widows in early-marriage societies. Yet as charges dependent upon their in-laws, widows were vulnerable in other ways, especially if they were young. A youthful widow was far likelier to be treated as a burden than in a late-marriage society, since her most valued reproductive contributions had probably been made, and any children could be raised by her deceased husband's resident female kin. A son might guarantee a widow's position if he was married and heading the household; but if still a boy, he could not be much of an advocate on his mother's behalf.

The "problem" of an abundance of widows was built in due to women's youthful marriage, and has sometimes been addressed by their actual elimination through such practices as *sati*, in which Hindu widows were burned alive on their husbands' funeral pyres. In orthodox Hindu belief, a widow was held responsible for a husband's predeceasing her, if not for sins in this

---

91 Margery Wolf, *Revolution Postponed: Women in Contemporary China* (Stanford, Calif., 1985), 202.
92 See Hanawalt, *The Ties That Bound*, Ch. 4, "Inheritance," 67–78 and Ch. 14, "Widowhood," 220–26.

life then for those in a previous one. She was also held incapable of being chaste without a husband to control her. A study of the persistence of
sati, despite prohibition under colonial rule, reports that widows were so devalued that the prohibition was perceived by many of them as a prized option
snatched away.[93]

While men in European-based societies are still likely to be the senior age
partner, married couples have been closer in age for centuries. In early modern times, it was even common for women to be the senior age partner. A
study of French villages then shows that 20 percent of brides were at least five
years older than their husbands.[94] In such cases, the wife, often a widow, typically brought landed property to the marriage. That she could do so shows
that inheritance structures had long since adapted to a family-formation
system that did not rest upon a unity of families and their property over time.

One could debate at length the drawbacks and advantages of each system,
but that has not been the object here. The aim instead has been to show how
household structures promoted the separation of women's and men's lives in
early-marriage settings and their overlapping in late-marriage ones. Evidence
of growing concern by the early modern era to delineate gender boundaries
and curb women's power has also signaled that shared decision making in
managing households was not necessarily welcome, especially to men. As
one more example of convergence owing to couples' closer marriage ages
and their pooling of resources to set up and run households, such sharing of
power appears to have been a major and ongoing source of conflict.

*   *   *

All this brings us back to Sir Thomas More, whose implied criticisms of
English households in *Utopia* speak to shortcomings of the dominant family regime from the viewpoint of a concerned head of state trying to ensure
stability in the polity, as well as of a troubled head of household trying to secure wifely obedience at home. The family arrangements More ordained for
Utopia can now be recognized as those of an early-marriage regime, but with
an important qualification. While mandating large multifamily households,
he retained what is being argued here as the chief feature of northwestern
European family arrangements, namely, later marriage for women.

In *Utopia*, it will be recalled, women under eighteen and men under
twenty-two were prohibited from marrying. While actual English marriage
ages for both sexes were higher at that time, More evidently approved of the
more mature and companionate, if not equal, marriages that long marked the
region. In addition, his insistence that even after marriage women, like men,
should pursue a trade took even further the shared employment of most
single women and men that was the hallmark of northwestern European

[93] Dorothy K. Stein, "Women to Burn: Suttee as a Normative Institution." *Signs: Journal of
Women in Culture and Society* 4, No. 2 (1978): 253–68.

[94] Edward Shorter, *The Making of the Modern Family* (New York, 1975), 337.

societies alone in this period. Eliminating money and enforcing a common standard of living removed the potential downside More identified from a resulting increase in productivity – namely, deepened social divisions – just as the enforcement of formal rituals of wifely deference headed off presumptions by women that their contributions merited a more exalted status.

It all worked in *Utopia*, but only because More said so. In real life, later marriage for women appears to have been exactly what made women so uppity in the first place – and, for that matter, families so unstable, youth so unchaste, and much else that troubled him. It appears that despite his weakness for somewhat later, companionate marriage, More recognized causal links between household structures and behavior within and beyond households. In any case, his perception in these matters was keener than that of most commentators, then or since.

In addition to compelling evidence that More was right to regard the households of his day as unstable, there is much evidence that he was correct in perceiving that women were gaining expanded influence within those households. While far from being generally accepted these days, this view will be defended in the chapters to follow, which will contend that late-marriage arrangements significantly enhanced most women's authority as wives and as widows, although not as mothers. Household fragility will be argued to have been the critical but as yet unacknowledged catalyst for generating early and dramatic change beyond households, beginning in northwestern Europe but reverberating, in due course, throughout the world.

First, however, it is necessary to pay some attention to why northwestern Europeans might have adopted such peculiar arrangements for establishing and running their family households. It is true that for the wider purpose of this inquiry – namely, setting out the case for the enormous but still unrecognized influence of this aberrant family-formation pattern – it hardly matters when or why the late-marriage pattern emerged, but only that it did so. Still, knowing more about likely reasons for the pattern's appearance should be helpful in making more informed assessments of later, more familiar developments. We already know that the cluster of Western family features did not turn up all at once, but we do not know which feature or features might have provided the original entry point, so to speak, or whether the system evolved by different routes in different regions.

The next chapter will present some of what we know and set out a hypothesis for why the late-marriage pattern was adopted that is at least consistent with scattered evidence that has come down to us. That analysis will make it easier to explain why the denizens of early modern European households were condemned to perpetual activity that, for better or worse, plunged them sooner into a wider world than their counterparts in societies where women married at much younger ages.

3

The Riddle of the Western Family Pattern

Medievalist Judith Bennett has an eye for the awkward but telling bit of evidence. She called attention a while ago to late-fourteenth- and fifteenth-century English manorial court records that cite single peasant women as purchasers of marriage licenses.[1] This seemingly inconsequential item had disruptive potential, as she well knew, since many scholars have long held that peasant households are governed by collective rather than individual economic activity. In such settings, the idea that a lone woman might earn and spend her own money, let alone select her own husband, is unthinkable.

The marriage licenses in question, called *merchets*, were fees paid by unfree peasants to the lord of a manor upon a woman's marriage. While historians had already remarked individual women among the purchasers, most persisted in treating *merchets* as taxes paid by households. Accustomed to portraying medieval households in northwestern Europe like those in most other agricultural societies – that is, as self-contained units of production, consumption, property-holding, and mutual support – they simply brushed anomalous evidence of this sort under their all-purpose interpretive rug.

In a clever analysis of over 400 *merchet* payments, Bennett, however, argues convincingly that the women recorded as purchasers in a third of the cases actually did buy the licenses with their own earnings. (Fathers of brides are recorded as buying a third, bridegrooms-to-be a quarter, and others, such as a bride's mother, 8 percent.) The money the women used likely came, she says, from their wage work in "road repair, manuring, thatching,

---

[1] Judith M. Bennett, "Medieval Peasant Marriage: An Examination of Marriage License Fines in *Liber Gersumarum*," in *Pathways to Medieval Peasants*, ed. J. A. Raftis, *Papers in Medieval Studies* 2 (Toronto Pontifical Institute of Medieval Studies, 1981): 193–246. See also the useful discussion by Barbara Hanawalt in *The Ties That Bound: Peasant Families in Medieval England* (Oxford and New York, 1986), 197–204. The characterization of the *merchet* here is Hanawalt's, ibid., 201. Hanawalt points out that the variations in the fee suggest that it was a tax based upon wealth, and that in all likelihood, the poorest women did not have to pay the *merchet*.

sheep-shearing, weeding, mowing, plowing and transporting corn."[2] That medieval women are now known to have performed such work supports the case that they were buying the licenses with their own funds, just as their low individual earnings may explain why women bought disproportionate numbers of the least expensive licenses. An estate treatise of the period urges the hiring of women, as they would work for "much less money than a man would take."[3]

It also appears that the female purchasers were older and more independent than the other brides-to-be. Compared to those whose fathers bought licenses, only half as many married unfree men from the same village; and a larger number bought the so-called general licenses, for which a groom was unspecified. Barbara Hanawalt suggests that the women who married freemen may have "sought independence not only from family but from the village. They probably met the freemen during employment away from the family."[4] For the other two-thirds of brides-to-be, it is possible, even likely, that families had a larger role in arranging their marriages.

What seems probable is that while young people in late medieval northwestern Europe may have put their earnings into a pooled family fund, many kept a portion for themselves. Recognizing a degree of autonomy for individuals hardly denies the continuing importance of family relationships and dependencies, but it does signal the presence by then of a household economy that is anomalous among peasant societies. Young women and men alike were evidently making decisions on their own about selling their labor in regional rural markets rather than always being directed by collective household interests.[5] The women, in particular, offer important clues to understanding change in the wider society and to imagining how the full set of features that became known as the Western family pattern might have emerged.

As evidence such as that about *merchets* continues to pile up, it begins to appear that most late medieval households in northwestern Europe, like the early modern ones already described, simply did not function like their counterparts in other agricultural settings. Yet medievalists have no larger framework into which to put their discoveries without disturbing rooted notions that they themselves share with other scholars about how history runs and how change takes place. Like most historians, they are not used to seeing behavior within households, especially women's behavior, as a catalyst for major developments anywhere. They are instead more likely to perceive their discoveries as aberrant items within a narrow historical subcategory labeled "how peasant households work." Even Judith Bennett, in

[2] Bennett, "Medieval Peasant Marriage," 207.
[3] Ibid., 208.
[4] Hanawalt, *The Ties That Bound*, 201.
[5] Ibid., 212.

calling attention to *merchets*, did not propose jettisoning the prevailing interpretive model of the "universal peasant household." She urged instead that
the "monolithc concept of the peasant family" be replaced with "a more
diversified and flexible view of the medieval peasant economy."[6] She was
perfectly aware of the possible wider consequences of her findings, however,
adding, "Because women frequently purchased their own marriage licenses,
we must re-consider many of our fundamental theories about the organization of medieval peasant families and the dynamics of medieval peasant
society."[7]

Scholars conducting these pathbreaking studies since the 1970s have not,
moreover, placed them in the context of the discovery of an atypical marriage
pattern. Demographer Richard M. Smith complained as recently as 1992 that
"to date only one, albeit brief, discussion of Hajnal's [late-marriage] model
has been made by a medievalist writing of medieval Europe."[8] While docu-
menting that most peasant households were nuclear and that most women
had paid work experience before marriage, these scholars have understandably had more interest in determining how much the recalcitrant records can
be made to yield about everyday peasant life. Yet as their accounts have appeared, describing for the first time what women and men did and even how
they felt about work, authority, sexuality, and more, it is clear that appeals
to expand the prevailing model of self-enclosed peasant households do not
go far enough. The typical late medieval household in northwestern Europe,
like the early modern one, was already a thing apart.

While they had no intention of doing so, these medievalists have bolstered
a previously unsubstantiated hypothesis that the cluster of features labeled
the Western family pattern emerged over a long period of several centuries or
more. By teasing astonishing amounts of data from intractable sources such
as manorial court records, poll tax records, wills, coroners' rolls, and guild
records, medievalists have done nothing less than supply critical empirical
grounding for a new approach to the European past.

Recent work confirms immense activity by individual household members, of which daughters making their own marriage arrangements is but a

[6] Bennett, "Medieval Peasant Marriage," 212–13. See also the discussion in Hanawalt, *The Ties
That Bound*, 107–23.

[7] Ibid., 215.

[8] Richard M. Smith, "Geographical Diversity in the Resort to Marriage in Late Medieval
Europe: Work, Reputation and Unmarried Females in the Household Formation Systems of
Northern and Southern Europe," in P. J. P. Goldberg, ed., *Woman Is a Worthy Wight: Women
in English Society c. 1200–1500* (Wolfeboro Falls, N.H., 1992), 27. Smith was referring to
David Herlihy's discussion in his *Medieval Households* (Cambridge, 1985), 155–56. Recent
studies are paying somewhat more attention to Hajnal. See especially Lawrence R. Poos, *A
Rural Society After the Black Death: Essex 1350–1525* (Cambridge, 1991), which takes full
account of the work of the Cambridge Group on the Western family pattern and, using more
intractable data from this earlier period, manages to demonstrate persuasively the presence
in late medieval Essex of several of the late-marriage features.

single example. Despite lords' efforts to restrict emigration, young women and men displayed astonishing mobility – leaving the manor of their birth temporarily for service on another, or permanently for marriage, or even abandoning manorial security altogether for the freedom of nearby towns. A remarkable study of late medieval Essex, for example, shatters any lingering images of a stable, immutable world. Lawrence R. Poos shows that even before 1350, only a quarter of people – mainly those with significant property – passed their entire lives in the parish of their birth. The rest, who were primarily wage earners, regularly moved about; and from the fourteenth century, these people with little or no land comprised the majority of the population.[9]

While service was a feature of earlier medieval centuries as well, scattered evidence from that era suggests that it was not yet fully developed on a life-cycle basis, and that rural servants might include, in the fourteenth century at least, married persons as well as unmarried day laborers hired for domestic and agrarian tasks.[10] In his study of late medieval Essex from 1350 to 1525, Poos nonetheless argues convincingly that there, at least, most youthful fourteenth- and fifteenth-century wage earners were unmarried persons in their mid- to late teens and twenties. These servants also resembled their early modern counterparts in typically residing with employers and moving annually, being under their masters' direct legal responsibility while working in their households. Wage-earning opportunities in fact shaped the peripatetic experience of most late medieval Essex residents. From at least the mid-fourteenth century, Poos says,

all these features of local demography and the culture of family formation that they imply were both part cause and part consequence of the economy with which they coexisted. Within the broader perspective of comparative preindustrial economies, wage-labour markets of sizeable proportions tend to be associated with mobile populations, most of whose children "are expected to leave home, accumulate their own wealth, choose their own marriage partners, and locate and occupy their own economic niche," and thus a distinctly non-familistic ideology of family formation. New households come into being in tune with the tempo of living standards and expectations of future opportunity.[11]

The peasantry also evolved complex social divisions, evidently reflecting the differential success of particular strategies their members chose to adopt. Already by at least the mid-thirteenth century in England, most manors

[9] Poos, *A Rural Society*, 290.
[10] See the discussion in Hanawalt, *The Ties That Bound*, Ch. 10: "Children and Servants at Home and in the Fields," 156–68.
[11] Poos, *A Rural Society*, 291. The internal quotation cited by Poos is from R. S. Schofield, "Family Structure, Demographic Behavior, and Economic Growth," in J. Walter and R. S. Schofield, eds., *Famine, Disease and the Social Order in Early Modern Society* (Cambridge, 1988), 285.

were roughly divided among three groups of about equal size: smallholding cottars with less than five acres, middling landholders with five to twenty, and large holders with twenty to forty acres.[12] We now know, too, that unfree tenant families by the late medieval era in northwestern Europe had long had effective control over the land they worked. While lords retained ultimate jurisdiction, families kept the land from one generation to the next, making their own arrangements for passing it on to heirs.[13] The custom, not only there but in most agricultural societies, was that wealth from a family's work on a property belonged to all the children, an ancient principle that originally applied to entire kindreds and that long survived in late- as well as early-marriage settings. Despite legal developments in western Europe denying inheritance rights to unfree peasants and setting out more individualized notions of property, manorial courts and the church long upheld older custom.[14]

Pressures of population growth on property, however, prompted serf families by the later Middle Ages to adopt a single-heir system throughout the manorialized region as a way of keeping their landed holdings viable as farming units. This practice typically meant that the eldest son inherited all or most of the land; but even then, other children long retained significant property claims. Daughters got dowries of movable goods, cash, and even small parcels of land, while younger sons received similar settlements and perhaps training for a trade. Buying, leasing, and selling of land for such purposes was common, and peasant parents at any time exercised a range of options.[15]

While life-cycle service may not have been experienced by most of the peasantry until the early modern era, there is abundant late medieval evidence that young single people not only put savings aside but also purchased or leased land with their earnings.[16] Such maneuvers enabled them to set up

---

[12] Cited in Judith M. Bennett, *Women in the Medieval English Countryside: Gender and Household in Brigstock Before the Plague* (New York, 1987), 50, from E. A. Kosminsky, *Studies in the Agrarian History of England in the Thirteenth Century*, ed. R. H. Hilton (Oxford, 1956). See also the fuller discussion of late medieval landholding patterns in England in Poos, *A Rural Society*, especially Ch. 1: "People, Land and Occupations," 11–31. Poos finds from a survey of tenancy sizes on seven manorial rentals in Essex in the period from 1288 to 1340 that as many as three-fifths of all tenants would be classified as smallholders with tenancies of no more than five acres, *A Rural Society*, 16–17. He points out too that the significant numbers of totally landless are excluded from these data.

[13] See the discussion in Hanawalt, *The Ties That Bound*, Ch. 4: "Inheritance," 67–78.

[14] See Cicely Howell, "Peasant Inheritance Customs in the Midlands, 1280–1700," in Jack Goody, Joan Thirsk, and E. P. Thompson, eds., *Family and Inheritance: Rural Society in Western Europe, 1200–1800* (Cambridge, 1976), 112–55.

[15] See the discussion in Hanawalt, *The Ties That Bound*, Ch. 4: "Inheritance," 67–78.

[16] Richard M. Smith, "Some Reflections on the Evidence for the Origins of the 'European Marriage Pattern' in England," in C. Harris, ed., *The Sociology of the Family: New Directions for Britain, Sociological Review* No. 28 (Keele, 1979), 100.

the separate households upon marriage that dominate northwestern Europe as far back as medieval records go, allowing young people to marry without waiting for parents to die. Until early modern times and despite moving about, many still lived near kin, often sharing work on family land despite residing in separate households.[17]

All this activity contrasts sharply with most other agricultural societies, where the integrity of family property is more sacrosanct and land markets tend to be inactive.[18] The restlessness of peasants in late medieval northwestern Europe has only begun to be linked to the likely influence of a long-established late-marriage pattern.[19] That all children save perhaps the heir to the main holding (if there was one) left the parental household meant that most people had to seek their way on their own.

Observers of early modern northwestern Europe have meanwhile found an important clue in the search for the elusive origins of the Western family pattern. They have discovered that the incidence of that pattern closely coincides with the classical feudal region of Europe.[20] This suggests that there was a hospitable climate for one or more of the pattern's features in the mixture of barbarian and Roman institutions and practices evolving from the fifth century with the disintegration of the Roman Empire.[21] Efforts to trace

---

[17] See the discussion by Zvi Razi, "The Myth of the Immutable English Family." *Past and Present*, No. 140 (August 1993): 3–44. See also Hanawalt, *The Ties That Bound*, Ch. 4, "Inheritance," 67–78, and Ch. 5: "Kinship Bonds," 79–89. In his earlier edited collection, *Land, Kinship and Life-Cycle* (Cambridge, 1984), editor and contributor Richard M. Smith provides an extended introduction to the then lively debate about the importance of systems of property transmission and whether these systems themselves determine preindustrial features of rural society such as household composition, marriage decision making, sex roles, and more. Essays ranging from the thirteenth to the nineteenth centuries show that much land in England, anyway, was transferred between living persons who were unrelated by blood or marriage. Smith reviews arguments for the notion that family forms have in effect been created by the ways property is transmitted and for the view that kinship arrangements are largely independent of such influences. The case to be made here follows Smith in viewing established marriage and household arrangements, if not kinship systems themselves, as more likely to determine systems of property transmission than the other way around in late medieval and early modern northwestern Europe.

[18] The contrast has been little discussed, though, since analyses have been conducted within a model that downplays individual economic behavior. Both Bennett, "Medieval Peasant Marriage," and Hanawalt, *The Ties That Bound*, 107–23, note that their own analyses involve stretching that model, attributed to the Russian economist A. V. Chayanov, *The Theory of Peasant Economy*, eds. D. Thorner, B. Kerblays and R. E. F. Smith (Homewood, Ill., 1966). It should be noted that Alan Macfarlane's previously cited studies, especially *The Origins of English Individualism* (New York, 1978), rely heavily on an analysis that traces the early evolution in English law of individual private property, but without tying that evolution directly to prior shifts within households, particularly in women's position.

[19] See Poos, *A Rural Society*, passim.

[20] Michael Mitterauer and Reinhard Sieder, *The European Family* (Oxford, 1982), 38.

[21] The most recent survey of the evolution of households in the European middle ages is David Herlihy, *Medieval Households* (Cambridge, 1985).

the origins of the so-called Western family pattern back to early medieval times still confront a daunting problem. It is not until the thirteenth century that sources begin to yield much more than isolated snapshots of how peasant households looked and worked. What is more, there are no continental sources comparable to the English manorial court records, although scattered data confirm much of what has been verified for England, suggesting that elements of the unique family pattern may have been in place there even longer. Yet we are no better able to document when or why specific features of the pattern appeared. Despite much new information about late medieval peasant life, a comment made in 1973 by Peter Laslett still holds:

> The further we go back, so it appears at the moment, the more elusive the origins of the interrelated characteristics of the Western family. As of the present state of our knowledge, we cannot say when "the West" diverged from the other parts of Europe.[22]

A decade later, in 1983, Laslett was no longer even prepared to characterize what happened in northwestern Europe as a "divergence" from a prior pattern. Responding to criticism that he had paid too little attention to change over the family life cycle and to regional differences within Europe, he located four European areas (west and northwest, central, Mediterranean, and east) on a descending scale of conformity to the Western family features he had outlined in 1973. Presenting a chart showing for each region whether new households were formed at marriage, marriage was early or late, the proportions marrying were high or low, and unrelated servants were employed in family work groups, he warned against hasty assumptions that there was an actual historical progression from one family type to another. Given our fragmentary information, he cautioned, there is no reason to regard any of the four variants as part of a developmental continuum, or even to claim that one set of arrangements necessarily came first.[23]

This pronouncement appears to have slowed inquiry into the origins of the Western family pattern by foregrounding yet again concurrent clusters of features, emphasizing households as work and kin groups rather than singling out women's late marriage and linked work roles as the critical items to track down. Research has also since shown that European households were even more complex than Laslett's revised picture, prompting allegations that such complexity compromises any claims for a distinctive Western family pattern.[24] Interpretation has been made more awkward, too, by a

[22] Peter Laslett, "Characteristics of the Western Family Considered Over Time." *Journal of Family History* 2, No. 2 (Summer 1977): 113. In a note to that paper, as indicated in Chapter 1, Laslett remarks that it was actually written in 1973.

[23] See Peter Laslett, "Family and Household as Work and Kin Groups," in Richard Wall, Jean Robin, and Peter Laslett, eds., *Family Forms in Historic Europe* (Cambridge, 1983), 513–63.

[24] See, for instance, the discussion by David I. Kertzer, "Household History and Sociological Theory." *Annual Review of Sociology* 17 (1991): 155–79.

contest between "continuity" theorists such as Laslett and Macfarlane, who tout evidence that the nuclear household reigned in northwestern Europe, at least, as far back as the records run, and "change theorists," who admit the early dominance of nuclear households but stress the importance of changing factors outside households.[25]

Unfortunately, this debate has shed little light on the origins of these family arrangements while making the task of uncovering them seem more hopeless than is warranted. Hajnal, it will be recalled, proposed a closer look at "hybrid" household systems in southern Europe that combined early- and late-marriage features. Richard M. Smith and his students have since done comparative studies with an eye to the effects of early and late marriage as well as of hybrid household formation patterns. Their work suggests that while southern European households might display features of both regimes, early marriage influenced behavior more decisively than nuclear structure. One study also shows that a big external event – the mid-fourteenth-century plague – played out differently in southern and northern Europe owing to differing marriage regimes.[26]

Comparing Italy and England, Smith's student P. J. P. Goldberg showed that in England, the labor shortage produced by the huge increase in mortality from the plague prompted an influx of unmarried women into the towns, a rise in marriage age, and an increase in the proportion of women never marrying. In Italy, however, the employment of single women did not increase much in the post-plague era, nor did women's marriage rate decline. Fewer than 3 percent of Italian women were unmarried by their mid-twenties in the early fifteenth century. New employment slots in Italian cities were filled by men from the countryside, producing high urban male sex ratios by contrast with low ratios in northwestern European cities, where women often outnumbered men.

While in Italy household service was deemed acceptable for older married or widowed women, the early-marriage tradition there ensured that eligible young women remained at home, despite the jump in potential employment opportunities. In England, however, young single women in the post-plague era, already accustomed to employment, chose to pursue new economic opportunities and further postpone marriage. Later, however, when demographic growth and urban slump combined to limit work opportunities at the end of the fifteenth century, women were displaced by men from productive

---

[25] These latter interpreters argue for an evolution in northwestern Europe from the collective behavior of traditional peasant households to more individualistic behavior, which they contend appeared only in the late medieval era and owed less to household structure than to changing conditions outside households. For a fuller discussion of this controversy, see Michel Verdon, *Rethinking Households: An Atomistic Perspective on European Living Arrangements* (London, 1998).

[26] P. J. P. Goldberg, *Women, Work and Life Cycle in a Medieval Economy: Women in York and Yorkshire c. 1300–1520* (Oxford, 1992).

work in the crafts. Confined to more traditional, less remunerative domestic employment, women at that time entered marriage at somewhat younger ages.

These findings are significant, for they show that preexisting marriage patterns themselves were an important determinant of people's aggregate behavior. In this case, when opportunities for work shifted owing to the same external event, women, especially, behaved quite differently, depending on whether they lived in early- or late-marriage regions.[27] The more parallel experience of the sexes being argued here for northwestern Europe was borne out again, too, as women and men alike made similar decisions in response to changing work options. It is noteworthy, though, that when employment opportunities became constricted by the turn of the sixteenth century, men adopted tactics such as restrictive guild membership to discourage competition from women.

Such examples show that change in the late medieval and early modern eras did not move almost exclusively from institutions or events beyond households back to households, as largely happens now. For long, in fact, the traffic in change seems to have been heavier from household sites to the wider world. Novel marriage and household arrangements, moreover, appear to have been responsible for much of the change that has been singled out as distinctive to northwestern Europe. A new look at the riddle of the origins of the Western family pattern will begin to explain why.

Taking into account findings summarized here, this chapter will introduce a new hypothesis for when, how, and why the peoples of northwestern Europe adopted a unique set of household arrangements. It will also speculate about which ingredients of that family pattern appeared first. Although there is no consensus on its origins, other theories will be reviewed along the way. A final section will return to familiar developments in the early modern era, using French examples this time, showing how a peculiar household system works better than the prevailing interpretations to explain many of these developments. Some change in this period has, of course, never been explained, and some has never been thought to require explanation. But the bulk has long since been assigned to factors and influences beyond households. It is likely, however, that to appreciate what made northwestern European societies so odd, it will be necessary to change the ways we have come to think about change itself.

*   *   *

That medieval records alone do not allow us to trace the origins of the early modern Western family pattern need not mean abandoning the search. Another way to approach this conundrum is to set aside the controversies around nuclear households and return to John Hajnal's idea of the pattern

[27] Ibid., 46.

as one of two basic models of household formation in societies of fixed agriculture.[28] While the precise origins of the dominant early-marriage model are likely lost forever in the mists of time, scholars suggest that the reason it turned up in many different places was that it responded so well to shared needs of agricultural peoples. That case, I will show, cannot be made as credibly for the late-marriage model.[29] Recognition that each met similar needs, though, makes it possible to focus more productively on the eccentric features of the late-marriage model, pinpointing conditions under which northwestern Europeans might have pursued some deviant paths.

Anthropologists agree, first, that agricultural societies themselves emerged quite late in the course of human affairs, and that hunting and gathering societies were the featured type throughout most of our species' history.[30] Since tools such as bows and arrows, spears, and digging sticks produced a limited food supply, those societies tended to be small, usually under fifty, with men hunting large animals and women and children gathering roots, plants, and berries. The first hoe societies are believed to have appeared in the Middle East about 10,000 years ago and the first plow societies about 5,000 years ago. Reasons for the shift to plant agriculture are unclear; but explanations stressing a gradual population rise that pushed foragers into

---

[28] In making this statement, I am following Hajnal's argument, recognizing as he does that there were a number of variations within the two primary family forms, in "Two Kinds of Preindustrial Household Formation System." *Population and Development Review* 8 (1982): 449–94. Anthropologists and other specialists who have chronicled specific household systems in different times and places correctly resist any rigid typology and point to the multiple variations, even within a given society at a given time. Still, it is possible, as Hajnal does, to acknowledge all the variations and yet to point out that early or late marriage for women remains an especially critical variable. Again, if Hajnal's formulation had prevailed, emphasizing late marriage as the critical variable in the Western system, the controversy over lumping together many variants within both systems would have been considerably diminished.

[29] Anthropologist Mildred Dickmann early proposed that the nuclear family form is best understood as a variant family form related to the multi- or joint family one, noting the importance of the fact that women in nuclear households were more likely to be early involved in productive wage labor. She also took data on female neglect and infanticide seriously long before this topic received wider serious treatment in the literature. Hers is ultimately a sociobiological interpretation that is not supported here, but her numerous articles on the subject have been most helpful. See in particular "Female Infanticide, Reproductive Strategies, and Social Stratification: A Preliminary Model" in Napoleon A. Chagnon and William Irons, eds., *Evolutionary Biology and Human Social Behavior* (Belmont, Calif., 1979), 321–67; and "The Ecology of Mating Systems in Hypergynous Dowry Societies." *Social Science Information* 18, No. 2 (1974): 163–95. I am grateful to my colleague Robin Fox for referring me to Dickmann's work and to his own fascinating *Tory Islanders: A People of the Celtic Fringe* (New York, 1978).

[30] This summary is based upon Joan Huber, "A Theory of Family, Economy and Gender." *Journal of Family Issues* 9, No. 1 (March 1988): 9–26; Martin King Whyte, *The Status of Women in Preindustrial Societies* (Princeton, N.J., 1978); and Jack Goody, *The Oriental, the Ancient and the Primitive: Systems of Marriage and the Family in the Pre-Industrial Societies of Eurasia* (New York, 1990).

increasing the food supply through cultivation have lately been challenged by a theory that the shift was owing to a decline in the number of large animals, perhaps as a result of advances in weaponry.[31]

In any case, in the Near East, Europe, and Asia, plows operated mostly by men came to replace the shifting, low-yield hoe agriculture dominated, and perhaps invented, by women.[32] Since the plow was more efficient than the hoe, it made possible significant food surpluses, enabling increased community size and social stratification as well as promoting the so-called Eurasian feudal system of a small political and economic elite, some low-ranking artisans, and masses of peasants, serfs, or slaves.[33] The iron that came to be used for plows was also used for weapons, and elites specialized in warfare while extracting food surpluses from those working the land. As sociologist Joan Huber puts it:

Land ownership became the basis for social stratification. The plow makes land the chief form of wealth because its use permits land to be used indefinitely, which increases its value. By contrast, hoe peoples had to move when soil fertility was exhausted.[34]

Intensive agriculture probably increased sexual as well as social stratification. Some argue that the way that happened was that the plow stimulated the domestication of large draft animals, thereby promoting male authority by placing a premium on men's greater average strength. That, in turn, enhanced the value to families of male infants. It now appears, though, that any effect of the plow on sexual stratification was less direct. A more compelling reason men came to monopolize the plow, and agricultural work generally, was its required use on large fields that had to be located some distance from population settlements. This made it harder than in hoe societies for women to combine agricultural work with sex-exclusive pregnancy and nursing as well as the linked tasks of child care.

Besides reducing women's participation in food cultivation, the introduction of the plow appears to have led to distinctive inheritance practices. Unlike hoe societies, in which marriageable women are commonly exchanged among families, with gifts of bridewealth going from a prospective husband's family to that of the bride, plow societies normally ensure that women receive their own share of their natal family's property through dowry and/or inheritance.[35] At the same time, measures are taken to guarantee that actual control of property – especially landed property – remains in men's

[31] Huber, "A Theory of Family, Economy and Gender," 16.
[32] See Ester Boserup, *Women's Role in Economic Development* (New York, 1970).
[33] Huber, "A Theory of Family, Economy and Gender," 19.
[34] Ibid., 19.
[35] The latter is anthropologist Jack Goody's term. See the discussion in Whyte, *The Status of Women in Preindustrial Societies*, 157.

hands. Women typically receive movable wealth in furniture, animals, or cash.[36]

Agricultural societies also early evolved constraints on sexuality, particularly women's sexuality, that have been remarkably persistent. Anthropologists concur that with fixed property as the chief form of livelihood, monogamy rather than polygyny came to predominate due to the need to limit heirs. Divorce was also discouraged for the same reason. The familiar concern for women's sexual purity in peasant societies owes a great deal to women's inescapable role in the transmission of fixed property, a role that goes far to explain the prevalence across so many societies of a double sexual standard.

With important economic and status differences based upon land, parents (especially well-off ones) are concerned about preserving the status of their offspring: their sons through inheritance of land, and their daughters through dowries. Dowries are inherently variable, and families will try to accumulate large dowries in order to attract a desirable mate for their daughter (i.e., one with substantial inherited land or prospects of such an inheritance). Given the importance of status considerations in marriage, females can wreck their parents' calculations by independently forming romantic ties and becoming pregnant. Therefore in such societies parents will try to strictly control marriage choices and will emphasize female purity and virginity at marriage. (Male romantic and sexual involvements are less of a threat as long as they can be kept casual, and thus a premarital double standard emerges.)[37]

---

[36] Ethnographer Martin King Whyte sums up rationales for these rules, based on comparative studies by anthropologist Jack Goody. Goody is most associated with developing the thesis that this practice of "diverging devolution" (his term), whereby women as well as men stood to receive family property in the major agricultural societies of the world – in the form of inheritance, dowry, or what he calls "indirect dowry" in the form of gifts from the groom's family to the bride's – counts seriously against what he maintains are prevalent notions that non-Western cultures are primitive and irredeemably sexist. In his book *The Oriental, the Ancient and the Primitive: Systems of Marriage and the Family in the Pre-Industrial Societies of Eurasia* (New York, 1990), Goody carries on an argument begun two decades ago on this theme. While many scholars would concur that early accounts in particular drew too sharp a distinction between supposedly enlightened Western patterns and those of the "primitive" East, others, whose view I share, point out that by carrying on in such polemical terms, Goody ignores Hajnal's and others' serious comparative treatments, with their genuine distinctions between early and late marriage and differing family regimes, while continuing to focus on straw men.

In a review of Goody's 1990 book in the *American Historical Review* 98, No. 4 (October 1993): 1208–9, Martin King Whyte states that while Goody is surely correct to emphasize the differences between "diverging devolution" of property in the plow agriculture societies, which acknowledge women's property rights, and the practices of sub-Saharan Africa, where such rights are not acknowledged, he has paid insufficient attention to major contrasts in family patterns that he lumps together, particularly contrasts between northwestern Europe and other parts of Eurasia. By now, in any case, the voices that Goody charges have been raised in celebration of Western superiority are less frequently heard in academic circles.

[37] Whyte, *The Status of Women in Preindustrial Societies*, 158.

It is already clear how familial and especially male labor sustained the households that emerged as the chief social and economic units. In most plow societies, as noted, women did little agricultural work; and their value was seen to reside in their reproductive roles. The common requirements associated with fixed agricultural property as the main source of wealth, then, help to explain the emergence of the familiar features of the early-marriage, multifamily household in scattered regions around the world.

The odd late-marriage model of family formation in northwestern Europe responded to the same concerns as the early-marriage one. Each enabled family households to ensure a labor supply for land they controlled, to help guarantee legitimate heirs, to manage intergenerational property transfers, to secure the care of elders, and to guard or enhance the social status of the new generation. Yet although each type addressed these basic requirements, the early-marriage one was not only dominant but by far the more successful – certainly if measured by longevity. The late-marriage system in northwestern Europe, at least in its declared "classic" form with resident domestic servants, existed in just one small region of the world, and then for only about 500 years. Early-marriage arrangements, by contrast, appear to have survived in many places such as China for thousands of years.[38]

Recognizing northwestern European arrangements as a variant household formation model for agricultural societies helps to explain the puzzle about the origins of that model. Just as the features of the early-marriage household have been shown to be interdependent, with women's youthful marriage tied to the need to replenish a household work force consisting exclusively of kin, the northwestern European features can be recognized as linked, with a lone pair of resident married workers, for example, obliged to call upon labor by unrelated servants. Such comparisons make it possible to identify the two models as cross-societal "cousins," with resemblances forged from similar needs.

More significant, since features of the dominant early-marriage system can readily be shown to address concerns anthropologists tell us are common to all agricultural peoples about work, inheritance, marriage, sexuality, and care in old age, instances in which corresponding features in the late-marriage system appear to compromise these concerns become vitally important to explain. For example, if people in all agricultural societies have compelling reasons to pursue early marriage for their daughters, it is necessary to explain what might have prompted northwestern Europeans to pursue the contrary and apparently risky course of postponing their daughters' marriages.

---

[38] One survey of more recent selected populations there shows that the mean female marriage age from the sixteenth century right up to the 1960s stayed within a narrow band of ages sixteen to nineteen, rising only by the mid-1990s to over twenty-two after government family planning policies promoted later marriage. James Z. Lee and Wang Feng, *One Quarter of Humanity: Malthusian Mythology and Chinese Realities, 1700–2000* (Cambridge, 1999), 67.

Under what conditions were the peasant majority willing to adopt a practice that automatically delayed and likely reduced their chances for heirs and workers, or did they have no choice? If concern to guard a daughter's virginity to ensure legitimate heirs was great enough in early-marriage societies that many daughters were literally sequestered, and most married at or before puberty, why were daughters in northwestern Europe allowed to leave home in adolescence and work for up to a decade in the households of total strangers before they married? Why would parents have exposed daughters to the risk of unwanted pregnancy and themselves to illegitimate heirs to their property? For that matter, since we know that most women in societies of fixed agriculture are little involved in agricultural work, how did it happen that women came to be so intensely involved in such work in northwestern Europe? Finally, why was it that women and men there were required to make their own arrangements for old age rather than living with, and being cared for by, their resident sons and daughters-in-law?[39]

Inheritance, as seen, was another area in which the late-marriage model was less reliable than the early-marriage one for keeping property intact over generations. First, late marriage by itself reduced a couple's total number of offspring, thereby lowering their chances for an heir surviving to adulthood. Second, since couples in late-marriage societies normally head their own new household rather than joining a preexisting one, they have no built-in safeguards for keeping property together. Even though both parties to a marriage are eligible to inherit in either model, enduring multifamily households provide surer means to keep landed property in the male line – a harder task for family households that are formed anew with most marriages. Why northwestern Europeans adopted a system that made it easy for prized landed property to be dispersed is unclear.

---

[39] Richard M. Smith gives evidence that from at least the thirteenth century, English people evolved the practice of formally contracted retirement arrangements as a "late-marriage" counterpart for the more typical practice in early-marriage, multifamily households of caring for the elderly in the context of the family itself. In this example, as in so many others in the late-marriage system, meeting a particular need, given nuclear arrangements, entailed an appeal to enforcement mechanisms through institutions outside the household, which were either created for the purpose or adapted to it. In this case, the manorial court became the mechanism through which individuals made their retirement arrangements, initially more often with kin but increasingly, by the fourteenth century, with nonkin. As Smith points out, "What is characteristic of these arrangements, whether they were made between close kin, neighbours, or those not linked by close residential propinquity, is that dereliction of duty to the elderly became a matter of *public* concern, or more specifically curial review, of possible censure and even intervention. What should be stressed is that although negotiations between parties, whether kin or unrelated persons, may have been a matter of individual bargaining, ultimately they would become a matter of concern for an institution outside the confines of the co-resident domestic group or the functionally extended family," in "The Manorial Court and the Elderly Tenant in Late Medieval England," 56, in Margaret Pelling and Richard M. Smith, eds., *Life, Death, and the Elderly: Historical Perspectives* (London, 1991), 39–61.

Since analysts have rarely compared the early- and late-marriage models for their capacity to meet the shared needs of agricultural peoples, and since they have even less frequently compared the experiences of the sexes in the two regimes, questions such as these have not been much addressed. It is true that scholars have finally stopped claiming that nuclear households emerged only lately to meet the needs of industrial societies; but most efforts to explain their appearance, or account for other features of the northwestern European model, are just as problematic. Some, for instance, contend that the requirement that newlyweds form economically self-sufficient households explains why couples married late in the first place.[40] It is true that by the early modern era such a requirement was in effect. But this "explanation" only moves the inquiry back to the issue of why such a peculiar requirement emerged at all, especially as couples in most other agricultural societies have never had to confront such a hurdle to marriage.

Commentators have also hypothesized that the limitation on fertility built into the Western family system through late marriage explains why that system was adopted.[41] Unfortunately for this theory, European-wide population

[40] See George Alter, "New Perspectives on European Marriage in the Nineteenth Century." *Journal of Family History* 16, No.1 (1989): 1–5. Alter makes the misleading statement about Hajnal's presentation of the family pattern that "The central feature of this behavior is the requirement that newly married couples must form economically self-sufficient households," 1.

[41] Commentators slip into the position that this system was governed by "economic rationality," contrasting it with one of youthful marriage in which custom rather than reason rules, and fertility is unchecked since a woman's marriage typically coincides with her arrival at puberty. It is true that by the later thirteenth and early fourteenth centuries, after several hundred years of sustained growth and population rise, pressure on resources presented European peoples with reason to contain their numbers. But it seems unlikely that this situation led to the rapid appearance and spread of the new pattern in just the northwestern region of Europe, especially since the population rise occurred in southern Europe as well, and also since several features of the pattern antedated the population pressure. Moreover, when the Black Death in 1348 suddenly reduced a European population of 80 million or so by about 25 million, there is no evidence for a sudden, widespread, and sustained adjustment downward of marriage ages. To the contrary, historian Wally Seccombe, who has devoted impressive attention to making the case, argues that this immediate post-plague era was the very time when the late-marriage regime became fully consolidated, at least in England. See Wally Seccombe, "The Western European Marriage Pattern in Historical Perspective: A Response to David Levine." *Journal of Historical Sociology* 3, No. 1 (March 1990): 50–74.

Recent demographic studies suggest, in any case, that the image of rational Europeans, on the one hand, controlling their fertility through postponed marriage, with most of the rest of the world, on the other, continuing to do what comes naturally is not just overdrawn but wrong. First, the notion that fertility is always high in premodern populations is simply false. In such populations, fertility is normally only 40 to 60 percent of what is possible in literal biological terms. What is more, such societies have now been shown to have developed their own self-regulating regimes to balance fertility, mortality, and migration as well as to restore equilibrium after any outside shocks to the system. For one example, the Chinese, see the study by Lee and Feng, *One Quarter of Humanity*.

Premodern peoples, then, including those of northwestern Europe, generally employed two sorts of strategies that maintained moderate rather than high levels of fertility. One was

pressure and hunger did not occur in the long medieval era until the turn of the fourteenth century, a time well past that during which late marriage now appears likely to have been adopted by the peasantry. From the sixteenth century, there is admittedly good evidence that people had come to appreciate later marriage as a means to limit their numbers.[42] But that is no proof that their ancestors postponed marriage in the first place as a means to control fertility.

A more audacious theory to explain the origins of the late-marriage model was proposed not long ago by anthropologist Jack Goody, who argued that while European marriage arrangements are indeed unique, they are owing to an event that occurred outside households in the fourth century A.D., namely, the formal adoption of Christianity by the Roman emperor Constantine. That event, he claims, prompted a remarkable set of calculations on the part of the Catholic Church fathers, all designed to undercut established strategies within kin groups to keep property within the family. The Church, Goody argues, fashioned counterstrategies to increase its landed patrimony that ultimately succeeded in making that institution the largest landowner in western Europe.[43]

Taking into account that women in Europe, as in agricultural societies generally, could inherit land, Goody contends that the Church's tactics, which included banning marriage within specified degrees of kinship and prohibiting adoption, polygyny, remarriage, divorce, and concubinage, all worked to make it harder for families to guard their property in the male line. This not only made it more likely that property would fall into women's hands and thus, he asserts, more readily into those of the priests, but also made it more probable that property would be separated from families through other means. As for late marriage, in Goody's view this was a rather insignificant by-product of the Church's property strategies, allegedly caused by delays as Christians became obliged to identify partners for their children outside their immediate kin groups.

Contesting this ingenious theory, Richard M. Smith says that, like several others, it fails to recognize that late marriage was primarily a feature of northwestern Europe, not of the whole continent. There was wide variation in the demography of popular marriage in the different, albeit Christianized,

---

customs surrounding marriage, including its postponement, to control the exposure of fertile women to pregnancy. The other was customs within marriage that limited fertility, including extended breastfeeding; taboos on the timing and purpose of sexual relations; neglect and nutritional deprivation of infants and children; and, finally, various forms of infanticide. All premodern societies were similar in employing strategies to limit fertility, then, although it is still fair to say that the late marriage and high celibacy arrangements in northwestern Europe set that region apart from other demographic regimes.

[42] See Richard M. Smith, "Fertility, Economy, and Household Formation in England Over Three Centuries." *Population and Development Review* 7, No. 4 (December 1981): 595–622.

[43] See Jack R. Goody, *The Development of the Family and Marriage in Europe* (Cambridge, 1983).

regions. If the theory were valid, late marriage should have dominated in the south as well as the north, but it did not. Smith was also able to show that in many places people long defied or ignored the Church's proscriptions. Betrothed couples regularly paid no attention to the prohibited degrees of kinship. Ecclesiastical hostility to remarriage ought everywhere to have increased the proportion of widows, yet they remained far more numerous in the south than the north. Campaigns against concubinage, moreover, did not for centuries produce popular acceptance of the doctrine that sexual relations should begin only after a marriage is blessed by a priest.

There is therefore little evidence to suggest uniformity in the demography of marriage in Christian Europe. Instead, there was a divide between the systems of north and south, with women's early marriage dominant in the south. Using scattered southern European data from the first century, Smith even argues that early marriage prevailed there not only long after the adoption of Christianity but well before. The Catholic Church, in short, does not appear to have been responsible for the late-marriage regime.[44]

*   *   *

Armed now with queries about why northwestern Europeans adopted a risky system of postponed marriage, evidence that different marriage patterns can cause whole regional populations to respond differently to the same event, and findings that the incidence of the Western family pattern in the early modern era coincided with the prior manorialized areas of Europe, it is time to outline a new hypothesis for the origins of that pattern. The first step is a look at the sparse records from early medieval manors, where features of that deviant family pattern now seem likeliest to have appeared.

In *Medieval Households*, David Herlihy describes the influence of late classical and barbarian households on early medieval ones and then summarizes what is known of domestic arrangements in the millennium from the decline of the Roman Empire through the mid-fifteenth century. He does not mention the Western family pattern as such, even expressing the view that by the later Middle Ages most northern and southern Europeans alike married early.[45] He holds, however, that from the dawn of the

---

[44] Smith, "Monogamy, Landed Property and Demographic Regimes in Pre-Industrial Europe," in John Landers and Vernon Reynolds, eds., *Fertility and Resources* (Cambridge, 1990), 174–75.

[45] See discussions in Herlihy, *Medieval Households*, Ch. 4: "Transformations of the Central and Late Middle Ages," 79–111, where Herlihy notes: "The data on marriage ages for women are very scattered and of varying reliability. Women of the nobility and of the towns dominate the listings. It is likely that peasant girls were older at first marriage than their urban or noble counterparts.... But if the evidence is scattered and uneven, it is nonetheless remarkably consistent. Girls in the central and late Middle Ages were usually very young when they first married. This seems not to have been exclusively a Mediterranean pattern, but marked the careers of medieval women wherever we can trace them," 107.

medieval era until the eleventh and twelfth centuries, marriage ages were late.[46]

Unintentionally but effectively, Herlihy's analysis makes it possible to imagine why the Western family regime emerged in the manorialized region of northwestern Europe and also to hypothesize that women's late marriage was the first feature to appear. With the decline of the Roman Empire from the fourth century, Herlihy reports, and especially with the drying up of sources of slave labor, new efforts were made by the great landowners to resettle abandoned fields on the basis of family farms.[47] As central authority in Rome waned, these landlords dealt with the shortage of field hands by offering lures to entice workers to resettle the land. Slaves were permitted to marry and set up their own households, with guarantees that their families would not be divided. Although they were obliged to pay rent to the lords, give them services, and acknowledge their ultimate dominion, these new householders gained in addition the all-important right to treat the land they worked as their own and to pass it on to heirs.

Coloni, or freemen with legal restrictions on their mobility and rights, received similar privileges, as did some contingents of barbarians – a practice that in itself testified to the Romans' desperation to promote cultivation. As Herlihy put it: "The slave economy of antiquity, an economy of coercion, was giving away to an agriculture based, at least in part, on incentives."[48] Barbarian kings and their warrior elites were also working to extend cultivated land, and thereby their own rents and services, through encouraging family farms. Both within and beyond the borders of the old Roman Empire, persons willing to improve the land received from barbarian and Roman alike "a right to hold it permanently, to claim the chief part of its fruits, and to pass it on to their heirs."[49]

Manorial records that begin to be fairly common from the mid-eighth century give detailed household surveys, often carried out by ecclesiastical lords eager to enforce claims for rents and services. These sources reveal that unlike the earlier Roman pattern of women marrying in their mid- to late teens and men in their late twenties, both sexes on the reorganized family farms married in their early to mid-twenties, with men only slightly older than women. Eighth-century Visigothic and Lombard codes even complain of the many marriages in which brides were older than grooms.[50]

Herlihy finds added support for later marriage in a ninth-century document from the monastery of Saint-Germain-des-Prés, which lists all persons among some 2,600 nuclei living on over 1,700 family farms. Household size

---

[46] Herlihy, *Medieval Households*, 157.
[47] Ibid., 59.
[48] Ibid., 60.
[49] Ibid., 60.
[50] Ibid., 75.

averaged just under six, with land controlled by each household increasing as the average number per household increased.[51] Nearly half of the households were nuclear, and just over half consisted of two or more same-generation couples and their children – mostly brothers and their families.[52] These laterally extended households, says Herlihy, support the likelihood of later marriage for both sexes, since that practice "would have lengthened the distance between the generations and diminished the chances that three or four generations would be found within the same house."[53] In the evidence of 86 widowers and just 133 widows overall, Herlihy also finds backing for women's later marriage. He says that if men had actually been much older than women at marriage, there should have been many more widows. In fifteenth-century Florence, where grooms were on average twelve years older than brides, he says, there were six times as many widows as widowers.[54]

While Herlihy builds an excellent case that women married late in the early medieval era – noting that evidence, while sparse and scattered, is at least consistent – he speculates little on the causes. Remarking that the Roman historian Tacitus in A.D. 98 said that women married late in the Germanic tribes, he states that in the early Middle Ages, the barbarian model was evidently adopted throughout the old Roman territories, replacing the early-marriage customs of classical Rome.[55] If we ponder the conditions Herlihy described, however, a more convincing reason can be found to explain why newly empowered slave households might have embraced later marriage for women.

---

[51] Ibid., 70. Herlihy notes that household size ranged from 4.41 to 8.21 persons, with land controlled by each household ranging from one to fourteen *bunaria*, with a *bunarium* being about 120 *ares* in size, *Medieval Households*, 69.

[52] Ibid., 71.

[53] Ibid., 72.

[54] Ibid., 76. In discussions of the central and late Middle Ages, Herlihy argues that girls were usually very young when they first married, although the evidence he cites is drawn chiefly from the urban and rural elites, not from the peasantry. The argument here is instead that relatively late marriage for women, by comparison with marriage in the mid-teens in multi-family households, was and remained the standard practice among rural populations from the early Middle Ages; that the depopulation of the mid-fourteenth-century plague did not much alter this established pattern; and that renewed population pressures in the early modern era pushed the age at marriage up to the high twenties and even beyond in many places for both sexes, ibid., 107.

See also the discussion of Herlihy by Richard M. Smith, "Geographical Diversity in the Resort to Marriage in Late Medieval Europe," especially 22–24. Smith notes Herlihy's assertion that despite the geographically widespread late marriage in the tenth and eleventh centuries, European households shifted to an early-marriage system in both the southern and northern regions in the later Middle Ages. Herlihy asserts moreover that this specific demographic outcome of earlier marriage was ultimately the result of measures undertaken by the Church to reform marriage rules. I argue here to the contrary that the primary decision making came from within households themselves.

[55] Herlihy, *Medieval Households*, 77.

It is important, first, to note that at this relatively late date in the evolution of agricultural societies, northwestern Europe was the only significant area on the Eurasian continent in which rich lands remained underpopulated and underexploited.[56] The offering of new incentives to attract peasants onto deserted but fertile land suggests a scenario in which recently settled families conceived interests of their own, as strong as if not stronger than those of their overlords, to call upon the labor of all possible workers in their households. Their overlords, after all, guaranteed their right to pass on any land they worked to their heirs. In these circumstances, householders may have taken the exceptional step of postponing their daughters' marriages for some years beyond puberty, taking advantage of their field work as a means to anchor and enhance family resources.

After all, the reason sons' marriages are postponed until well past puberty in early-marriage settings is to capitalize on their labor power, helping to build household reserves before new children come along. For the early medieval settlers, chances to expand land would clearly have increased by taking maximum advantage of all available family labor. A decision to call upon daughters' productive capacities offers a plausible entry point into what ultimately became the late-marriage system or, what Laslett came to call the Western family pattern. Daughters' position as workers contributing to their family households would thereby have become more comparable to that of sons, with both now required to postpone marriage in order to maintain and increase family holdings.

In his recent study of European conquest, colonization, and cultural change from 950 to 1350, Robert Bartlett highlights the activity of the peasantry in explaining why Europe was such an expansive society.[57] Noting that the culture began with the "core" of Frankish Europe and spread from a base of France, northern Italy, and western Germany, he argues that in addition to a warrior aristocracy, it was a peasantry eager to apply new techniques of landholding, labor, and social organization that transformed the landscape. Bartlett mentions neither women's late marriage nor their labor role in this expansionist enterprise, but he underscores the importance of the replication on the frontiers of guarantees first made to peasants in the core regions. Stressing the competition for serf farmers, he cites the use of incentives such as Herlihy mentioned in "the attempt to lure labour by creating favourable and attractive economic and legal conditions."[58] Again and again, documents reveal that migrants to villages on the expanding frontier received, in addition to land, privileges including lower rents and tithes in

---

[56] I owe thanks to medievalist Joanne McNamara, who underscored this vitally important fact in a conversation with me.

[57] Robert Bartlett, *The Making of Europe: Conquest, Colonization, and Cultural Change, 950–1350* (Princeton, N.J., 1996).

[58] Ibid., 120.

the first years of settlement plus exemption from labor services on the lord's land, thereby repeatedly replicating the conditions being hypothesized here that could have first led to women's late marriage.

Attention to the Western family pattern in early modern Europe as a mature system of interrelated features has no doubt hindered recognition that its elements likely emerged over a long period. Laslett himself argued that not all of the features would need to have appeared everywhere in the region, and that some may later have been arrested or even reversed.[59] What matters here is that there is early evidence for women's postponed marriage and that it may be explained by their productive activity. John Hajnal speculated about this possibility back in 1965, although dating it then a millennium later.

In taking what I am proposing here as the initial step of keeping daughters longer at home to contribute to a family's holdings before marriage, there is no need to imagine that the new family households had a grand plan of some sort beyond the hoped-for immediate gain of property. In fact, it seems likely that the pattern Laslett dubbed Western was the cumulative result by the sixteenth century of a range of reactions by peasants and elites alike to the special conditions that presented themselves from late antiquity in what became the manorialized region of Europe.

The risks to a family outlined earlier of postponing their daughters' marriages were not negligible in those conditions. Still, a new system of family farms with some built-in safeguards for householders in guarantees by landlords, and in communal institutions in which peasants participated, would have reduced the risks.[60] In any case, risks were bound to have been less than in the many regions where soil was poorer and tradition had long since anchored the cultural habit of girls' youthful marriage. In northwestern Europe, the system of land exploitation was new; former slaves enjoyed novel incentives; and rich, undeveloped land offered abundant work for both sexes.

A new capacity for sustained productivity, in turn, would have reduced pressures for women's early marriage as a means to ensure heirs and workers, just as protection from overlords eager to increase agricultural yields

---

[59] See Laslett, "Family and Household as Work and Kin Groups," 557–58.

[60] Richard M. Smith makes this comment about the importance of the legal instruments developing out of the manorial court and giving growing security of tenure to a person holding land: "Among the customary tenantry of later medieval England it would be ill-judged to underestimate the risk-minimizing role fulfilled by this extra-familial agency.... Just as David Thomson argues below in his paper regarding the Old Poor Law, so we may see the manorial court, albeit with its liability to influence from manorial lords, its socially and sexually biased juries, and its susceptibility to legal fashion emanating from higher curial echelons, as an integral part of the household formation system with fundamental consequences for the well-being of the elderly," in "The Manorial Court and the Elderly Tenant in Late Medieval England," 57.

would have increased confidence on the part of householders. Exposure of their daughters to sexual assaults would not, initially anyway, have been the problem it would become with the emergence of life-cycle service. If the theory here holds, adolescent daughters would long have worked exclusively for their own households, not someone else's. Life-cycle service would only have been introduced later, as land in an area became more densely populated.

While there was still an increased risk of sexual exposure for those daughters whose marriages were postponed, the evolution of new institutional ties among nonkin within manorial contexts offered substitutes for the admittedly surer protection supplied by kin within the more self-sufficient early-marriage households.[61] Manorial courts, for example, came to include sexual assault among punishable offenses. These institutions, says Judith Bennett, combined "seigneurial desire for control with local need for community regulation and mixing the lord's law with local custom."[62]

It is true that most of our data come from the later medieval period, when court records become more abundant. Yet it is clear that these institutions, requiring regular attendance by tenants and involving a large measure of their input and even control, came to address not only sexual offenses but also many other interactions among unrelated persons, including land transactions and disputes. While the courts have been seen as the lords' creations, their evolution was bound to have been influenced by an emerging household system of comparatively fragile nuclear units. Such households by themselves were unable to provide the comprehensive services for their members – including protection from sexual assault – that were literally built into ongoing multifamily households through sequestering of daughters, youthful marriage, and extended kin networks.

In the scenario here, then, growing numbers of peasant households displayed new demands for adolescent women – not as sexual booty, as in early barbarian tribes; or as reproducers of heirs, as in most other agricultural societies; but instead as field workers enriching their natal households. Later marriage for peasant women and continuing youthful marriage for women of the feudal elites can thus be seen as parallel strategies in the two groups toward the same ends: maintenance and expansion of the land that translated into family livelihood and identity. Already in the ninth-century evidence

---

[61] See Bennett, *Women in the English Medieval Countryside*, especially Ch. 2: "Studying Women in the Medieval Countryside," 18–47, for a good discussion of the role of these courts.

[62] Ibid., 20. As Bennett notes, "These local forums differed from modern courts in their familiarity, use, and form. In the twentieth century, we attend our local courts only when forced to do so by crisis or summons; in the fourteenth century, many peasants probably knew their manorial courts as well as they knew their churches. . . . And the professional expertise that so dominates modern courts was minimized in manorial courts; the lord or his representative presided over the proceedings and provided a clerk to keep the record, but business was conducted by laypeople who usually acted without the aid of lawyers or other counselors," 20–21.

from Saint-Germain-des-Prés, it is possible to interpret wide differentials in peasant holdings as a measure of the success of some household strategists over others. Most observers, though, have only dignified the elite trend as a strategy, one that by the tenth century was prompting aristocratic families to adopt patrilineal reckoning of kindred and primogeniture as opportunities for plunder were reduced by land shortage. Adoption of later marriage deserves comparable consideration as intentional behavior on the part of peasant household strategists. An agriculture based upon new incentives, after all, was bound to make territorial strategies accessible to humble families, just as to great ones.

Manipulation of peasant populations by elites from above nonetheless remains the favored scenario for the appearance of the Western family pattern.[63] Citing an influential essay published in his Cambridge Group's *Family Forms in Historic Europe*, Laslett himself suggests that Carl I. Hammer may be right in arguing that the pattern was masterminded by feudal elites.[64] Hammer bases his case on a survey from a monastery of several hundred souls in ninth-century Carolingian Bavaria, which does appear to offer the oldest evidence for several features of the Western family pattern – especially later marriage, but also nuclear households and even a kind of regimented life-cycle service.

The best explanation for the recorded distribution of residents on monastery lands, Hammer alleges, is total manipulation from above. The abbots rotated able-bodied couples onto holdings (and unmarried servants as needed).[65] Hammer postulates that a new couple's aging predecessors were moved off holdings when they could no longer farm well and either placed in service elsewhere or assigned to nonagricultural work on the lord's estate in a circulating system that denied strict hereditary land rights for servile tenants. Many young people in the meantime, he suggests, were rotated off parental holdings at about age fifteen to do agricultural or craft work. (Adolescent girls gathered in the lord's manor house in a kind of medieval sweat shop producing clothing for all residents.) Marriage, following the years of service, was thus late for both sexes.

---

[63] Peter Laslett, "Family and Household as Work Group and Kin Group: Areas of Traditional Europe Compared," 556–59, in Wall, Robin, and Laslett, eds., *Family Forms in Historic Europe*.

[64] Carl I. Hammer, Jr., "Family and *Familia* in Early-Medieval Bavaria," in Wall, Robin and Laslett, eds., *Family Forms in Historic Europe*, 217–48.

[65] In arguing for manipulation by ecclesiastical overlords as the only way to explain the data, particularly those involving the physical location of adolescent servants, Hammer in effect acknowledges his inability to entertain the idea that peasant households might have been capable of some manipulation of their own. He states that the data cannot be seen as consistent with "the natural rhythms of birth, puberty, marriage and death," but he does not recognize that feudal overlords were not the only ones capable of interfering with such "natural rhythms," "Family and *Familia* in Early-Medieval Bavaria," 245.

In proposing this model of full administrative control from above – in effect, mandating the Western family features as an alleged means of max-imizing efficiency and ensuring "a uniform socialization of dependants" – Hammer never once considers whether any of the decision making might have been conducted by peasant householders themselves.[66] Treating them as the passive objects of the lords' strategies, he says only that if handled "with some intelligence and delicacy," this system might have looked

> quite attractive to those at the bottom, in comparison with a fragmented peasant household environment and cycle. . . . It would ensure that each holding was exploited to its limit, but that no individual holding would be burdened with too many mouths to feed; that all children would be provided for, especially daughters who had access to the servile version of the aristocratic nunnery in the *gynaeceum*; and that old persons would be cared for regardless of the presence or the willingness of heirs.[67]

The key to it all, he maintains, was the inherited institution of slavery, the feature allegedly responsible for allowing lords to impose the late-marriage household model.

> The social arrangements and cultural patterns imposed by the aristocracy (including the church) on its plantation slaves for administrative efficiency may have been so deeply implanted and pervasive that they survived the decline after the eleventh century of the institutional environment which had nurtured them. The lords planned and tended, but it was amongst the enslaved masses of early-medieval Europe that the modern family emerged.[68]

Feudal elites surely played a critical supporting role, and we know they engaged in some manipulation of peasant populations. Yet it is odd that scholars persist in casting elites in lead roles as creators of the Western fam-ily system, with peasant households relegated to utter passivity for centuries. What we have already seen at both ends of the story – the ongoing incentives for settlement in the early medieval era and the extraordinary activity and calculation among the peasantry everywhere so visible at the end – argues that attention belongs instead on the limited but real options available to the early settlers and their descendants. Within the constraints of new agri-cultural structures, these householders appear to have been able from the beginning to exercise effective collective leverage. Evidence in hand may be best explained, then, by positing a decision to call on the labor of daughters, resulting in what was to become the most enduring of all the features of the Western family pattern: late marriage for women.

If a collective decision to put their daughters to work represents a plau-sible reason for postponing their marriages, we can still hardly speak with authority about the mechanisms by which late marriage was preserved or

[66] Ibid., 247.
[67] Ibid., 246.
[68] Ibid., 248.

about the intentions behind the adoption, over time, of the other features of
the Western family pattern. We cannot know, in other words, to what extent
the early actors in this drama anticipated the consequences of late marriage,
either in the short or long term. I shall argue momentarily, however, that
if late marriage was the first feature of the northwestern European family
system to appear, the adoption of the other features becomes less mysterious,
since they become alternate routes to meet the shared needs of the resulting
nuclear households in what remained an agriculturally based society. Still,
while such features did appear and become cemented in place, it is not possible to know what the actors were contemplating. The persistence of any
given feature, moreover, as with so many other historical institutions, was
likely owing to different reasons from those that prompted its adoption in
the first place. After all, while late marriage itself persisted, women's contribution to their natal families' wealth, which appears to have prompted their
postponed marriages, declined within a relatively short time; and the fruits
of their labor were increasingly devoted to separate households of their own
that they helped to create.

While it is clearly impossible to prove the hypothesis here that late marriage was the first feature among the cluster of elements that became the
Western family pattern, it is evident that despite accounts that continue to
emphasize the lead role of elites, historians are coming to recognize that members of more typical family households often devised and implemented comparable collective strategies.[69] More recent instances from societies where
documentation is stronger also reveal households adopting tactics that have
literally altered family-formation structures. In one striking example, a shift
in decision making at the household level is argued to have been critical in
the hitherto unnoticed appearance of life-cycle service in a large region of
Japan, as well as in a shift there from more complex or multifamily households to more stem-family ones, with one child, usually the first son, staying
home and importing a spouse while the rest leave.[70]

Historical sociologist Laurel L. Cornell reports that during the Tokugawa
era, when large-scale cooperative agriculture was being displaced by single-
family farming, a study on labor migration in Nishijo from the 1770s through
the 1860s showed that of the 48 percent of men and 62 percent of women
who migrated, most were unmarried and had left home as teenagers, returning ten to fifteen years later. Cornell concludes that rural householders,
confronted with population pressures threatening their holdings, had begun
sending their children out to work on a life-cycle model. Especially after

---

[69] See, for example, the discussion and citations in "Family Strategy: A Dialogue," with Leslie
Page Moch, Nancy Folbre, Daniel Scott Smith, Laurel L. Cornell, and Louise A. Tilly in
Historical Methods 20, No. 3 (Summer 1987): 113–23.

[70] Laurel L. Cornell, "Hajnal and the Household in Asia: A Comparativist History of the Family
in Preindustrial Japan, 1600–1870." *Journal of Family History* 12, Nos. 1/3 (1987): 143–62.

1850, the girls were employed temporarily in towns in the new textile industry. Women with such labor experience were over twenty-six when they returned to marry, while their sisters who remained at home married much younger, at twenty or twenty-one. Hajnal's work, says Cornell, "invites us to examine the constraints on behavior and kind of choices individuals can make."[71]

The basic argument is that as employment opportunities for adolescent women increase, their value to their natal households will rise, and marriage will be delayed. This assumes that the primary value of women to their households of origin and of marriage in preindustrial societies is as producers of children, and that their secondary value is as laborers. When we examine the distribution of mean age at first marriage for women in preindustrial Japan, we find that it is low in the underdeveloped northeast and high in the commercially developed southwest.... This transformation should also mean a decrease [which is confirmed to have occurred from the eighteenth century] in female-specific infanticide and the disappearance of differential female mortality in childhood.[72]

This argument for links between a daughter's labor and her enhanced value to her natal household is directly relevant to the case being made here for medieval Europe. Daughters' productive labor, resulting in postponed marriage, is being hypothesized as initially performed for their natal families rather than for outsiders, although there were benefits in both cases for the natal families. In Japan, motives for adopting life-cycle service also appear to have included fertility control as well as giving children unlikely to inherit land alternate means to support their marriages. Such motives were evidently not part of early medieval household rationales, although they came to be so in time.

It is not necessary to deny differences of interest or authority among individual household members, Cornell says, to show that in some circumstances, such as improved employment prospects, households can evolve effective strategies that display "the ability to identify opportunities, mobilize resources, and take advantage of them."[73] Moreover, such family activity "implies a theory of change, for as individual choices fall more and more at the boundaries of possibilities, they push the constraints into a new alignment."[74]

In the context of early medieval Europe, keeping daughters longer at home to work for their families may well have been one of those options "at the boundaries of possibilities" that embodied both risks and opportunities for the new settlers. If so, the strategy then appears to have been adopted by ever larger numbers of households, with lords absorbing some dangers from this

[71] Ibid., 147.
[72] Ibid., 156.
[73] Moch et al., "Family Strategy: A Dialogue," 121.
[74] Ibid., 21.

option by offering protection for the new households. In the end, this choice would have pushed the constraints within which households operated into an entirely different alignment. The result, in due course, would have been what we have come to call the Western family pattern.

*   *   *

If late marriage for daughters was the first of the features of the new family regime to be adopted, and for reasons postulated here, it is easier to imagine how the rest of the otherwise puzzling features of that system might have evolved. The evidence Hajnal found for more equal sex ratios at marriageable ages, for example, can now be more readily explained. It is already known that where women contribute to their natal family's wealth through work, their survival chances are enhanced. Where their value is chiefly in producing heirs, as in most early-marriage societies, the natal family does not benefit, which explains why, even now, daughters in such societies are more at risk.

It would be nice to have abundant and conclusive early medieval evidence showing that at that time, just as more recently in places including China and India, baby girls' life chances improved where productive work was available for girls and women. The data we have, however, are sketchy and seemingly contradictory. Hammer's study of ninth-century Carolingian Bavaria, for example, reports equal sex ratios. An analysis of the famous ninth-century tax census of the abbey of Saint-Germain-des-Prés by Emily Coleman, however, finds very high male sex ratios.[75] Still, Coleman argues that even at that early date, female neglect and infanticide were likely on the wane in the area.

The ninth-century Saint-Germain document, it will be recalled, lists about 2,600 couples and their children living on some 1,700 family farms. Nearly half were nuclear units, while the rest were mostly two or more same-generation couples, and Herlihy showed that marriage age was probably late. Husbands and wives are carefully recorded by name and status (*coloni*, or descendants of Roman peasants; *lidi*, or descendants of barbarians who became servile laborers; and *servi*, descendants of slaves). Children are included, often with notations as to whether they were living with birth mothers.[76]

Overall male to female sex ratios favored males by over a quarter among adults and by over a third among children. Coleman's mentor David Herlihy was loath to admit that human intervention might explain these figures, but even he later acknowledged that with all possible benign explanations taken into account, the overall sex ratio was still likely to have been around

---

[75] Emily Coleman, "Infanticide in the Early Middle Ages," in Susan Mosher Stuard, ed., *Women in Medieval Society* (Philadelphia, 1976), 47–70. Until Coleman's work appeared, the document had been used chiefly to study estate management, for as she then pointed out, "there is very little written on the most basic unit of that society – the peasant family," ibid., 47.

[76] Herlihy, *Medieval Households*, 70–71.

119 men for every 100 women.[77] Coleman's discovery of significant statistical correlations in the data fuels a compelling case for at least some female neglect and/or infanticide. She nonetheless makes a good argument that such practices were already becoming a last resort among the peasant householders.

The larger the household, she found, the higher its sex ratio – that is, the more males there were to females. On the other hand, the larger a farm, and the more families living on it, the more balanced the overall ratio of men to women became. Since sons remained more valued than daughters for hard agricultural labor, Coleman suggests that the most obvious explanation is that families allowed fewer daughters to survive on the smaller, less productive farms, where less work was available for women. There, too, she says, sisters with claims to inheritance were a greater threat to their brothers' futures.[78]

It is impossible to know whether human intervention entailed infanticide, neglect, or both. In another early medieval tax census cited by Coleman, there is information about preferential treatment for boys that may have led to differential mortality: the typical nursing period until weaning for boys is recorded as twice as long – two years – as that for girls.[79] This census nonetheless records a surplus of female over male children, 106 girls to 99 boys. The discovery led Coleman to speculate that female infanticide may already have been uncommon by this time, perhaps even "a practice governed to a great extent by cycles of famine."[80]

This suggestion that as early as the ninth century female infanticide was practiced only in extreme circumstances meshes well with the hypothesis being put forward here that households had been postponing marriage age for their daughters from late antiquity in order to benefit from their productive labor. Coleman proposes that the huge population surge from the tenth to the thirteenth centuries, when numbers shot up from about 35 to 80 million – doubling in Italy and probably tripling in France, the German lands, and the British Isles – may have been given a special boost by a new capacity to relegate female neglect and infanticide to expedients of last resort.

If one ventures to deal with pure hypothesis for a moment, is it not possible that as the technological innovations of the early Middle Ages – the three-field system, the use of the horse instead of the ox in front of the plow, the increased use of virgin land coming into cultivation – took firmer hold, the yield of the land was increased from a purely subsistence level to where it could help support more individuals, more precisely, females. This would help to account for the fact that the sex ratios become more evenly balanced in the documents in this period in a more positive way than the

[77] Ibid., 66.
[78] Coleman, "Infanticide in the Early Middle Ages," 62.
[79] Ibid., 62.
[80] Ibid., 62.

assumption of the under-reporting of women in earlier centuries. And if more females were allowed to achieve maturity, then they, in turn, could bear more children and the population of Europe would increase. This, naturally, is conjecture; yet it might suggest an avenue of approach for future investigations.[81]

Coleman does not mention women's postponed marriage or the possibility that daughters' enhanced value to their families was reflected in those more equal sex ratios, but her data strengthen the hypothesis being proposed here. If she is correct in surmising that women's lives in the ninth century were more at risk on the smaller farms, where women's work was less valuable than on larger farms where cooperating family units could deploy their labor more efficiently, then women's work in the later medieval era needs a closer look. During these centuries, improvements in productivity may not only have permitted families to let women survive in larger numbers to childbearing age, but women themselves may have been critical contributors to those very productive gains.

Coleman's analysis also bolsters the argument that farm families or their heads, and not feudal lords, were the key players in decisions leading to a new household-formation pattern, one in which women's work enabled families to permit more daughters to survive without threat of ruin. The statistical differentials in sex ratios that she finds between larger and smaller families and farms, after all, can only be explained if decision making is seen as being conducted "on the ground" by families themselves, as she assumes, rather than by clerical and lay elites, which remains the prevailing view.

Some scholars, indeed, credit the Church not only with eliminating systematic female infanticide, but also for introducing the Western family feature of young persons choosing their spouses. David Herlihy contended that by its doctrine that mutual consent is sufficient to make a valid marriage, the Church undercut lords' control over the marriages of serfs, vassals, and even their own children, and that this doctrine "by itself assured that the medieval family could never develop into a true patriarchy."[82] The doctrine was not without effect, but the claim is grossly exaggerated. In other parts of Christian Europe, as will shortly be seen, families maintained sturdy patriarchal marriage strategies, often in open defiance of ecclesiastical dictates. In northwestern Europe, the chief factor in the loss of familial control over children's marriages was most likely not the intended consequence of ecclesiastical policy but the unintended consequence of parental policy.

What has not been recognized, since we do not yet credit peasants with the strategy of postponing their daughters' marriages, is that such a strategy, in time, would have led far more inexorably than any ecclesiastical

---

[81] Ibid., 64.

[82] Herlihy's full statement was: "The Church's doctrine was a damaging blow to paternal authority within the medieval household, and by itself assured that the medieval family could never develop into a true patriarchy," *Medieval Households*, 81.

injunction to parents' surrender of control over their children's marriages. Their own reckoning of the advantages of employing their daughters' labor as intensively as their sons' works better, in short, than assumptions of lordly manipulation to explain evidence that the children of serfs came to escape patriarchal control in choosing their mates. Such an escape would hardly be welcome since peasants, no more than feudal elites, would readily opt to relinquish control over their children's marriages. Yet with their collective decision to keep their daughters at work well beyond puberty, the die would already have been cast.

Available evidence is therefore best explained by hypothesizing that peasant families, having initially delayed their daughters' age at marriage to benefit from their labor, were obliged in time to adjust to unforeseen consequences of that decision. Most obviously, putting adolescent daughters as well as sons to work resulted in more space between each generation, with households failing to replace their own kin labor at the same rate as early-marriage societies do. This in turn prompted a need for workers at times when family labor was scarce. Scattered evidence suggests that households first met this need by bringing in day laborers, a practice that slowly evolved into the life-cycle service of the early modern era. Such a system, in which families were formed, as Lawrence Stone once put it, "consecutively rather than concurrently," was in fact more efficient for meeting household labor needs than relying upon resident kin.[83] Life-cycle service, in short, could have grown directly out of the collective decision to postpone daughters' marriages.

Even before life-cycle service became widespread, young persons would have encountered more unplanned consequences in enhanced opportunities to meet and interact with one another, which would have made it increasingly difficult for parents to exert the control over their children's marriages – not to mention their sexuality – that is so effectively built into early-marriage structures. It is one thing, after all, to take in a prepubescent girl as the partner for a son who has never left home and probably never will. It is quite another to import a mature, experienced young woman in her twenties who has met one's son on her own. The practice of postponing daughters' marriages also makes it easier to understand the sparse but consistent evidence for the early dominance of the nuclear residential form. It is unnecessary to postulate some sort of natural adult predilection for nuclear arrangements, as some do, to see how extended employment for both sexes would promote pooling resources in new households, even if couples lived near parents.[84]

As for feudal elites, while they tried in many ways to control serfs, they may have refrained from much interference in both their work and courtship

---

[83] Lawrence Stone, *The Family, Sex and Marriage in England* (London, 1977), 54.
[84] See, for example, Verdon, *Rethinking Households*, for expression of the view that nuclear arrangements are a kind of "natural" preferred form.

arrangements, less because the Church forbade them than because they stood to gain from increases in surpluses through more productive use of labor. In any case, large landed families with more resources and no need to put their daughters to work managed longer to control their own children's marriages. When at the dawn of the modern era they finally yielded to their offspring a larger role in selecting spouses, it was with the aid of legal instruments enforced by states that they themselves created, in part to serve their familial interests. Elites also used new states to control their children's marriages against the claims of the Church. As for the masses of ordinary young persons, their release from patriarchal networks that continued to hold them fast in so many other societies can be recognized to have come not from the outside but from their own families' collective deliberation and action.

Finally, as for questions about why northwestern Europeans alone might have adopted a household system that made it easier for prized landed property to be dispersed, we return once again to the unanticipated effects of putting adolescent daughters to work. The resulting later marriage for women meant that in northwestern Europe, the inheritance regime that emerged was bound to take account of the reality that husbands and wives were each producers of property, and that they became partners at marriage in new households that were separate productive entities. What is called the "customary" or unwritten marital property regime that turned up in countless local variations throughout the region implicitly recognized this state of affairs, usually by creating a "unitary conjugal fund" managed by husbands but making widows heirs with both ownership and managerial rights, even including the capacity to withhold property from their own children.[85]

In southern Europe, as in other early-marriage regions, a surviving widow's capacity to manage property was rarely even at issue since when a male head of household died, another resident man normally assumed management of family property. This latter regime is generally characterized as a "lineage" type in which emphasis is placed not on the lone conjugal pair but on the natal families of the spouses and their descendants in a household. In such a system, property brought to a marriage is seen as linked to the natal lines from which it came; and it normally passes to children through the decisions of male heads of household on both sides.

In a fine recent study, Martha Howell has used the abundant marriage contracts, wills, and related documents from the French town of Douai to present a sweeping account of a major legal transition, not only in Douai but throughout northern Europe in the period from 1300 to 1550. The transition, as she characterizes it, was a shift from the conjugal or customary system of unwritten marital property law to a more lineal, even "patrilineal," written

---

[85] Martha Howell, *The Marriage Exchange: Property, Social Place, and Gender in the Cities of the Low Countries, 1300–1550* (Chicago, 1998), 6.

and contractual system. While both systems were based on the dominant nuclear household structure in the region, and while both took gender difference and male dominance for granted, they differed in how they saw women as legal actors. Customary law, says Howell, presented widows as owners and managers of property, whereas newer written, contractual law, while acknowledging women's property rights, gave them limited responsibility over their assets.[86] By the end of the period, marriage is seen less as a productive economic partnership than as an affectionate union, and women are envisioned as passive helpmates rather than as social actors.

Howell remarks that it is doubtless perplexing to see these northern Europeans moving from what she describes as a more "conjugally inflected" form of property law to one that was less so – just at the time when the nuclear household itself is widely thought, in her words, "to have taken firm demographic shape in Europe."[87] Yet she shows that such a transition did indeed take place from 1300 to 1550 in Douai and many other places, and that its authors, in Douai anyway, were not higher courts and learned lawyers but instead ordinary citizens whose motives, she argues, "lay in the way the new law allowed them to manage property and to regulate gender hierarchy."[88]

According to Howell, both of these items were seen then as precarious. The customary law had emerged, after all, in a rural context and was thus being adapted from a prior focus on landed property to an emphasis on the more transient property of early modern urban life, including equipment for household industries and even more ephemeral, portable items. Implications of the legal shift for the gender order were still more profound, says Howell, than those on property were for the legal order. Describing them for Douai, but noting their broader resonance for northern Europe, she concludes:

What changed dramatically in the shift from custom to contract in Douai was the gender code itself. The city's old custom inscribed a notion of womanhood that positioned women as creators of property, as essential elements in a conjugal social and economic unit. The new, in contrast, positioned women as carriers of property, as individuals with economic and social interests distinct from their husbands'. The first woman was thus imagined as competent and valued for her skills if feared for

---

[86] Howell writes that "In contrast to custom, which had put women in charge of property, recognizing them as property's creators (even as it subordinated wives to their husbands) and granting widows of fertile marriages full ownership of the estate, the new law tended to reduce women to carriers of property. Although the will, the marriage contract, and the emerging norms they inscribed did not deny women property rights, they limited women's responsibility for the assets they carried," ibid., 138.

[87] Ibid., 13, note 20.

[88] Ibid., 174–75. Most associated with this viewpoint on the history of the household is Wally Seccombe, *A Millennium of Family Change: Feudalism to Capitalism in Northwestern Europe* (New York, 1992).

her potential power. The second woman was imagined as not fully competent, as in need of help, protection, and supervision. Valued when obedient, she was feared for her weaknesses – perhaps for her propensity to choose beneficiaries unwisely. . . . [89]

Howell is careful, in presenting her data on Douai, to stress how slowly and unsystematically this shift occurred, citing a protracted battle between older and newer visions of family and of the gender order in the period from 1300 to 1550. She contends that a similar shift occurred throughout northwestern Europe, including in areas such as Paris and Ghent, where a contest between contrasting notions of womanhood was staged within a single legal regime. Like the women of Douai, women in these places were "caught between two different gender imaginaries, positioned both as competent and incompetent, as responsible and irresponsible, as trustworthy and untrustworthy."[90]

Returning to the alleged puzzle Howell mentions of a shift to more patriarchal visions of the legal and gender orders just when the nuclearity of households is thought to have assumed "firm demographic shape," it is possible that the shift was not really so paradoxical. Here once again, the habit of portraying the Western family pattern as a cluster of early modern features, with the nuclear household as the centerpiece, has eclipsed mounting evidence that basic elements of the pattern long antedated the era from 1500 to 1750. In other words, if the more ancient roots of women's late marriage, in particular, and of nuclear households as well, were more generally acknowledged, it would be easier to recognize the legal shift Howell outlines after 1300, along with the new emphasis on gender difference and female incapacity, as part of a broader reaction against women's long-established influence and authority in northwestern Europe.

Scholars have lately explored legal, medical, political, and religious sources that display intense convictions about women's inferiority in the

---

[89] Howell, *The Marriage Exchange.*, 233–34.

[90] Ibid., 235. Howell finds, too, that a rhetoric of affectionate, companionate marriage, nearly absent in documents from the early period, is pervasive by the mid-sixteenth century. To explain it, she points to a new fragility in the marriage pact, owing not to the urban context itself but to ever more households in Douai having ceased to be productive economic units: " . . . for talk of love and companionship exploded in Douaisien sources precisely when the old notion of marriage as economic unity was breaking down and when the marriage pact had come to seem insecure, fragile, and uneasy because it was no longer based on equivalence, but on difference. 'Love' then became the seal of marriage, not because marriage was being newly constructed as a union between a man and a woman who, as 'partners' in a household economy voluntarily chose to make a life together, but precisely because marriage was no longer such a union," ibid., 237. I will argue in subsequent chapters that the declared basis of marriage on "difference" was itself more fragile than what underlay the continuing late-marriage arrangement itself, namely, the partnership based upon a growing convergence in women's and men's life cycles and involving more than joint economic productivity, that enabled an adult couple to found and maintain a household together. See the discussions in Chapters 7 and 8.

early modern period. Yet they have not explained why such convictions were so strongly articulated – and often enough acted upon – at just this time.[91] Many accounts focus on this era as one of intense patriarchalism, calling attention to the witchcraft outbreaks. But such interpretations are undercut by compelling counterevidence, including convictions about women's positive qualities. Early modern men extolled women's wifely domestic skills, their spiritual gifts, and their companionability. The seesaw Howell so deftly describes between women's alleged competence and incompetence, power and powerlessness, trustworthiness and guile permeates portrayals of women throughout this period in these largely male discourses.

By means of case studies in the next two chapters, I contend that the wider social context for these strikingly divergent "gender imaginaries" was a protracted adjustment to late-marriage households that, by the early modern era, were increasingly obliging women and especially men to reinvent themselves. Their more parallel life cycles, and the greater dependence of spouses upon one another than in most agricultural societies, are keys to the deeper plot line of the Western gender story; and they illumine much else as well. They are part of a still untold chronicle of the Western past, embedded in an unheralded observation by John Hajnal in 1965 of which it is well now to be reminded:

The emotional content of marriage, the relation between the couple and other relatives, the methods of choosing or allocating marriage partners – all this and many other things cannot be the same in a society where a bride is usually a girl of 16 and one in which she is typically a woman of 24. These things are perhaps obvious, but they have not been much explored, at least not in histories which trace the emergence of modern Europe.[92]

* * *

Some historians enjoy it when their subjects take them by surprise. In an elegant essay published in the 1970s, Natalie Davis was intrigued to find sixteenth- and seventeenth-century Frenchwomen and men, all along the social spectrum, behaving in unexpected ways.[93] While she did not attribute

---

[91] See Sara Mendelson and Patricia Crawford, *Women in Early Modern England* (Oxford, 1998), Ch. 1: "Contexts," 11–74. The authors focus on popular as well as elite discourse about the category "woman," and their full discussion amply justifies their point that difference between the sexes was a deeply held article of faith that cut across all social groups, with men as the primary authors of that discourse. While Mendelson and Crawford expressly avoid any claim to uncover the origins of the accompanying gender hierarchy favoring men, their account provides vivid documentation of strong and pervasive beliefs in women's inferiority.

[92] Hajnal, "European Marriage Patterns in Perspective," in D. V. Glass and D. E. C. Eversley, eds., *Population in History: Essays in Historical Demography* (London, 1965), 132.

[93] Natalie Zemon Davis, "Ghosts, Kin and Progeny: Some Features of Family Life in Early Modern France," *Daedalus* 106 (April, 1977): 87–114.

their behavior to the influence of a distinctive marriage system, she was ready to pronounce it both strange and remarkable. What she discovered was that as family members, acting in family interest, these men and women were the conscious agents of far-reaching change. She then went on to suggest, contrary to all the brands of orthodoxy in her profession, that the ordinary French household in the early modern era was an important site of historical transformation.

Such heresy notwithstanding, admirers in the guild of American historians, in recognition of her gifts to their craft, elected Natalie Davis their president. Yet it was long before they paid her the added tribute of pursuing more vigorously her early insights about families and change. We still need a closer look at women's and men's behavior in medieval and early modern settings, domestic and otherwise; and we still need to ask ourselves why we persist in describing the moving forces of history in ways that either ignore the household arena altogether or relegate it to a sideshow of mirrors and marionettes.

Without trying to make her findings fit any prior interpretive mold, Davis shows how family members in this period – from the masses of peasants and artisans to the middling groups of merchants and professionals to the privileged elites – were busily devising ways to shore up family identity as well to promote individual members. They were forging these strategies, as she acknowledges, "in the face of fortune's whims."[94] But often enough, their schemes succeeded. Effective planning might be beyond the reach of the poorest in society, she says, including landless peasants or unskilled urban workers. Yet even serf families had some strategies available to them. They might, for instance, work to see that their children crowded with them under the same roof so that they could be "permitted by custom to succeed to their land when the time came."[95]

Poor sharecroppers, too, might request village status and legal title to the land they worked; and surviving petitions reveal their future-oriented habits of mind. For example, eleven such families from Burgundy, descended from a household that opened a farm for an abbey some sixty years earlier, pointed out to their sixteenth-century ecclesiastical overlords how much they had improved the land. Fearing that if the abbey contracted with other parties they would lose any hope that their children would remain to care for them when they became old, they asked for and got "perpetual and permanent habitation ... for themselves and their posterity ... born and to be born."[96]

[94] Ibid., 87.
[95] Ibid., 87.
[96] Ibid., 87. The reference is from Pierre de Saint Jacob, "Deux textes relatifs à des fondations de villages bourguignons (16e et 17e siècles)." *Annales de Bourgogne* 14 (1942): 314–23.

More options were open to those families that had accumulated a little money, some productive property, and useful connections. Davis cites a man who emigrated in the sixteenth century from a village in Normandy to Lyon, where he married a widow with connections in the printing trade. By the time of his death at fifty-three, he had become master of a printing establishment, dowried three unmarried daughters, and got a wealthy merchant-publisher to be godfather to his son. His wife then carried on in the business, even marrying one daughter to a printer more successful than her husband. She also guaranteed partnerships for herself and her young son, and the son ultimately founded a publishing dynasty in Limoges that would last for 200 years.[97]

The contention that the French family household at this time deserves to be recognized as an important site of historical transformation, that men and women there forged novel strategies for the enhancement of familial identity and goals, fits well with the more extreme claim that I am making here. That claim is that by this early modern period, the families of northwestern Europe collectively wielded a critical influence on Western society as a whole, an influence reaching well beyond households that mattered more for subsequent developments than that of any other institution or agency. The unstable family system that had come to dominate the area by the sixteenth century explains the intensified planning that Davis singles out and much else besides. By then, too, that system was placing rising pressures on family households and their individual members to become ever more vigilant in mapping out their futures.

While early-marriage societies vary widely, it remains true that planning for the future is a less urgent matter, since new marriages rarely entail the simultaneous creation of new households, and also since most young persons do not face the burden as adolescents of making a place for themselves in the world. Members of the older generation instead give them such places, along with extended apprenticeships in household management. The entire process emphasizes tradition over innovation, and also has the advantage of instilling experience and confidence by the time a son finally accedes to a family headship or a daughter-in-law takes charge of running a household.

The late-marriage system has the drawback of immediately placing the full burden of household management on newlyweds, although that system enables and encourages greater flexibility of response to new situations, inviting a certain creativity. As the sole married adults in a residence, couples are more physically mobile. They do not live daily with the accumulated weight of generations of practice passed down within the husband's family. Neither spouse is obliged to engage in what may become decades of deference to

---

[97] Ibid., 88–89.

the wishes of the resident elder generation. Yet such relative freedom comes with a large price. Without the cushion of more than one married couple in residence, members of nuclear households are chained to the constant round of activity that Davis describes.

While she does not directly acknowledge the prevalence of a distinctive family system, and thus does not credit it for the self-conscious family-oriented planning she discovers among her subjects, Davis does note a new focus on the immediate family grouping of a couple and their children. She also underscores the oddity of her findings by reminding readers that a propensity to plan for the future is hardly

a 'natural' or inevitable way for families to act. It implies a situation unlike that in the early Middle Ages, when wives in some landholding families might have closer ties to their family of birth than to their husbands; when family identity might well extend horizontally out to the third and fourth cousins with whom one consulted about immediate issues of vengeance and alliance rather than about distant prospects. It implies a situation in which the family unit, whatever its spread, conceived of its future as requiring invention and effort, rather than simple reliance on traditional custom and providence. Then the family unit must have some power to put its plans into effect, for there were other groups and persons – villagers, lords, guildsmen, city governments, clerics and monarchs – who had an interest in what parents did with their children and property.[98]

Davis is fully aware that such future-oriented strategies were not a total novelty in the sixteenth century. While she does not make the case argued here for the critical decision-making role of the peasantry, she points to how elite families from medieval times had manipulated what evolved as customary inheritance rights of wives, daughters, and younger sons so as to consolidate family holdings and enhance political positions through favoring eldest sons in inheritance. She further contends that by the sixteenth and seventeenth centuries, ever more families were applying multiple strategies, not only in the pursuit of more traditional sorts of patrimonies that could be passed on to heirs such as "lands, cattle, houses and barns," but also in the creation, consolidation, or extension of patrimonies that now came to include such portable items as "pensions, rents, offices, workshops, looms, masterships, partnerships and shares" as well as "the occupations or careers and the marriages of children."[99] Martha Howell has since shown, to be sure, that such practices were underway from at least the fourteenth century.

The growing attention to family identity and to planning that Davis reports, and the narrowed sense of familial boundaries focusing in on close kin, are just what would be expected under the constraints of the novel northwestern European family regime. Since most young people were now required to postpone marriage and childrearing until they had the resources

[98] Ibid., 88.
[99] Ibid., 92.

to set up separate households of their own, they were obliged long before marriage to engage in planning in ways that persons raised in early-marriage societies simply do not confront. Sustaining family identity from one generation to the next is hardly a straightforward task, even in societies where most people reside in more enduring multifamily households. But it presents special challenges in a society in which the successive generations reside in different households, in which large numbers of single adolescents leave home and work in other households until they marry, and in which couples are increasingly unable to take for granted either occupancy or ownership of fixed pieces of property as a glue to bind their families together over time.

The behavior Davis is describing, then, appears to be nothing less than the emergence – not just in France but in all of northwestern Europe – of an altered theory and practice of the family itself. Older views that families consisted of a mixture of particular kin and particular property, chiefly in the form of land, were being displaced. The very meaning of the term "family" was being transformed as kin groups were coming to lose even the appearance of timeless entities rooted for generations in the same ancestral soil. Davis summarizes her findings in what she modestly labels an interesting perspective on historical change, one that "has to do with its location."

Ordinarily when historians think of change emerging from the decisions of a small group, that group is made up of a king and his counselors, a party leader and his inner circle, or some other small elite at the center. When changes are perceived as emerging from the actions of large numbers of people in the middle and lower levels of society, they are explained in terms of the forces acting upon them, such as urbanization, to which they react somewhat automatically. What we see here, however, is historical change flowing from the decisions of myriad small groups, some rich and powerful, but many of only middling affluence in provincial towns and smaller rural centers. Their push toward planning, toward manipulation of property and persons for private goals, and their blending of beliefs in virtue with beliefs in stock were assisted by the growth of the state and of commercial capitalism and the professions, but were also in defiance of some of the forces of their time, both demographic and social. Some of the tools for their task, such as the family history, they forged themselves rather than receiving them ready-made from learned specialists. The extension of family planning into contraception in eighteenth-century France (in the face of strong condemnation by canon law) is another example of men and women in small groups deciding how they are going to conduct themselves.[100]

It is a mere step from these striking conclusions to the position that the emergence in northwestern Europe of the late-marriage nuclear household made a preoccupation with long-range planning a requirement if family households were to remain what they had long been there and what they continued to be in many other places around the world: namely, the preeminent

---

[100] Ibid., 108.

social institutions and the main sites of day-to-day authority for all their members. Increased effort was now demanded, under changed conditions of family formation, to ensure that such a status was maintained. What Davis is chronicling, then, are some of the means by which the families of northwestern Europe managed to guard, at least for a time, their ancient position as the chief arbiters of human destinies. What parents did with their children and property is, as she says, where attention belongs. But as those parents now came to realize, offspring and property control – or even ownership – no longer constituted the surety of a familial future. Survival from one generation to the next, to say nothing of expanding family names, power, and fortunes, now demanded that families become ever more consciously fashioned works of art, not merely at their formation but throughout their days.

Once the flurry of familial strategizing that Davis found in early modern France is seen in this light, it is less awkward to entertain the heresy of "historical change flowing from myriad small groups." The residential kin group, after all, had long been the single most important institution in societies anywhere in its influence on people's everyday lives. The early modern families that created ever more intricate strategies to guarantee their members' individual and familial futures were still functioning, albeit through altered marital arrangements and household structures, as the chief social and economic institutions. Still, the contrast with more stable multifamily structures that need less day-to-day attention will be clear from more extended illustrations in the next chapters.

The novelty for families in early modern Europe was not planning itself, nor was it the extension of planning from elites to the peasant and urban masses. In fact, the arrow of change, as I have suggested, often enough pointed the other way. Aristocratic families who turned to primogeniture to keep their landed holdings intact, for example, may well have been responding to challenges from prior property strategies of peasant families. But if neither planning itself nor evidence of planning beyond the elites was unique to families in this era, what was striking, as Davis points out, was the application of future-oriented family strategies to a broader range of activities and a wider cast of extrafamilial players. This required the cultivation of imagination, calculation, and individual responsibility on the part of ordinary people to a degree that is so far unrecognized.

An important feature of this activity – illustrated in Davis's examples, although not singled out as such – is evidence for the increased participation of women in creating and carrying out strategies on behalf of families and of their individual members. In early-marriage households, what long-range planning takes place tends to be conducted by the different generations of men, whose extended residence in natal households, surrounded by a network of male kin, enables them to act more exclusively in the interests of their paternal lineages. Men in such households enjoy the advantages of keeping their long ties with other household members and with the local community, while youthful wives imported into such settings are comparatively disadvantaged, as already noted.[101] Such built-in constraints on women's actions in these settings also make it hard for them to act on any distinctive priorities or to implement long-range strategies of their own.

Partly because households as the physical "containers" of families in northwestern Europe normally dissolved with the deaths of the husband and wife who formed them, far greater effort was required to guarantee a family's identity over time. Natalie Davis describes the rise among the middling classes in the early modern era of family chronicles, often kept by the women, as a way of creating lasting accounts of family fortunes, "of the family arrow in time, of the careers and qualities of parents, the training and marriages of children, and the near-escapes and losses."[102] Among humbler illiterate groups, an oral tradition of family exploits developed as a way of preserving memories of the whereabouts and activities of at least the last two generations on each side in a period of increased mobility and change. The planning demanded of most families came necessarily to involve more persons outside the residential kin group as well as a wider range of prizes than the familiar land, houses, barns, and beasts of the field. In time, of course, many of these prizes, old and new, would pass altogether beyond families' capacity to control, to be absorbed by extrafamilial entities that came to govern social, economic, and political activity that had once been solidly anchored within households.

Just as more general implications of a unique family-formation pattern on behavior have been little explored, Davis's calling attention to what is being argued here as one major effect – namely, intensified planning within these inherently more fragile kin units – has yet to be factored into interpretations of developments in Western history. It is true that John Hajnal's urging of inquiries into the possible role of the late-marriage system in preparing the way for economic transformation has drawn some attention, but his suggestion that women's work was the critical factor there has been little pursued.

Developments such as the transformation from an agricultural to an industrial economy and much more, then, need to be reexamined for the possible influence of an idiosyncratic family-formation system and of distinctive contributions by women as well as men. Yet since all major developments in northwestern European–based societies have long since been assigned by historians to the agency of extrafamilial entities – chiefly to institutions such as churches and states, but also, as Davis says, to more intangible economic or political "forces" – there will be resistance to such a review. It was precisely on these domestic sites, nonetheless, that a remarkable chain of historical developments was launched. Individual couples, in circumstances

---

[101] Cornell makes this point in "Hajnal and the Household in Asia," 151.
[102] Davis, "Ghosts, Kin, and Progeny," 97.

of new family formation that weakened their kinship bases within house-holds, acted to shore up their familial futures by forging more links to a wider community of nonkin. Despite their original intentions, however, these decisions would lead in time to the erosion of most of the functions that family households still perform, even now, in scores of societies around the world.

4

The Women and Men of Montaillou and Salem Village

Patterns of Gender and Power

In the tiny early-fourteenth-century village of Montaillou, perched on a hill-side in the Pyrenees, men wore their misogyny on their sleeves. In testimony before the Inquisitor, who questioned them about an outbreak of heresy in the village and its surrounding communities, they were offhand in their re-flexive denigration of women. Husbands called their wives "old women," "old heretics," and "old sows."[1] Male servants even dared to join in when masters hurled these epithets at their wives. One remarked that, like his mas-ter, he had called his mistress "Bad mother, devil!"[2] Another, learning that his master's wife had disobeyed her husband, stated matter-of-factly to the master in the wife's presence, "Women are demons."[3]

One man, insulting a local woman, declared, "The soul of a woman and the soul of a sow are one and the same thing – in other words, not much."[4] A heretic priest or "goodman," having married his pregnant lover to an unsuspecting shepherd to preserve his own reputation, announced to the new couple: "A man is worth nothing if he is not his wife's master."[5] The same goodman volunteered that the soul of a woman cannot be ad-mitted to Paradise unless the woman is reincarnated, however briefly, as a man.[6]

These examples can give only the flavor of an omnipresent misogyny in the mountain community, where men's grudging admission that a woman might be "good" or "kind" was reserved, if the testimony is accurate witness, not so much for wives as for mothers – or, failing that, for the memory of

[1] Emmanuel Le Roy Ladurie, *Montaillou: The Promised Land of Error*, tr. Barbara Bray (New York, 1979), 197.
[2] Ibid., 82.
[3] Ibid., 212.
[4] Ibid., 194.
[5] Ibid., 194.
[6] Ibid., 194.

mothers. Only the aging matriarchs were somewhat revered, and by their children rather than their husbands.

Things were different in seventeenth-century Salem Village in the Massachusetts Bay Colony. The men of the New England Puritan settlement did not express such open and casual contempt for women. Some women were even held up for praise, although less as mothers – as they had been in Montaillou – than as wives. The stereotypically virtuous woman lauded in so many Puritan sermons had attributes that many a Salem husband was prepared to acknowledge in his own wife, at least on her tombstone.[7]

Forms of abuse that the women of Montaillou appear to have encountered daily were more likely to be reserved in Salem for suspected witches; and even then, they were more sparingly employed. Cotton Mather, the renowned minister of Boston, might descend on occasion to using coarse terms for such women; he once referred to an outspoken accused witch as "this Rampant hag."[8] But his homilies generally avoided such labels and urged the godly to recognize that all women have choices: "Handmaidens of the Lord should go so as to distinguish themselves from Handmaidens of the Devil."[9]

True, even the more flattering descriptions of the ideal Puritan woman underscored all women's preordained subservience; and the conventional measure of any woman's "goodness" was her zeal to serve men. In a sermon on the role of the wife in the 1690s entitled "A Meet Help," John Cotton, Cotton Mather's grandfather, attacked blasphemers who would "despise and decry them [women], and call them a necessary Evil, for they are a necessary Good; such as it was not good that man should be without."[10] Also, one might well ask how far from the Montaillou heretic was the Puritan divine who insisted that a man must recognize that "his wife hath as noble a soul as himself," but added: "Souls have no Sexes... in the better part, they are both men."[11]

In actions as well as words, the men of Montaillou displayed their belief in a deep and pervasive subjection of women to their fathers, husbands, brothers, and even sons. Yet although Montaillou men might brand all women "devils," it was the Puritan men who were clearly more anxious about the proclivity of women to carry out Satan's work. What is more, women in Salem actually displayed these much-touted female virtues in greater abundance than did the relaxed and somewhat raffish women of Montaillou. For

---

[7] For examples of epitaphs, see Laurel Thatcher Ulrich, *Good Wives: Image and Reality in the Lives of Women in Northern New England, 1650–1750* (New York, 1982), 3.

[8] Lyle Koehler, *A Search for Power. The "Weaker Sex" in Seventeenth-Century New England* (Urbana, Ill., 1980), 405.

[9] Carol F. Karlsen, *The Devil in the Shape of a Woman: Witchcraft in Colonial New England* (New York, 1989), xvix, from Cotton Mather, *Ornaments for the Daughters of Zion* (1692).

[10] Cited in Karlsen, *The Devil in the Shape of a Woman*, 161.

[11] Ulrich, *Good Wives*, 106.

all their easy misogyny, the men of the mountain village were unprepared to dictate a female code of behavior to help keep their women in line.

What explains these differences in gender and power arrangements between these two premodern Western communities? Why were the women of Montaillou so consistently denigrated, while Salem women were praised, at least in their role as "meet helps"? On the other hand, why did the women of Salem evidently pay for this male respect by submitting to rigid rules for their behavior, rules that did not bind the women of Montaillou? Moreover, what did the women of Montaillou and of Salem, whose voices are less audible in the records, think about such treatment and pronouncements by their men? What do we know of their own views on domestic authority and their own notions on the slippery subjects of womanhood and manhood?

Crisis would force out some answers. At the moments under consideration, both these communities were caught up in troubles that took the form of major religious upheavals: an outbreak of heresy in Montaillou and a massive witch hunt in Salem. The late medieval village of Montaillou was the last one in French territory to support Catharism, or Albigensianism, which was one of the chief heresies of the Middle Ages. Of the sixty-six men and forty-eight women from the region accused or brought before the Inquisition as witnesses, five persons – including one man from Montaillou itself – were burned at the stake. Many more were imprisoned, sent on enforced pilgrimages, or obliged to wear the yellow cross marking a heretic sewn to their outer garments.[12]

In Salem, and throughout New England in the later seventeenth century, the issue was not heresy but witchcraft, an alleged female specialty. Behavior deemed "unwomanly" might put a wife, and especially a widow, in mortal danger. In 1692, in godly Salem, several hundred mostly female persons from the Village and nearby communities were accused as witches; and in the end, fourteen women and five men were hanged for practicing witchcraft.[13] Just as the Montaillou episode was the final Cathar outbreak, the Salem one was among the last of a series of witch hunts that had begun in Europe more than two centuries before. From 1450 to 1750, there were an estimated 100,000 trials for witchcraft, and over three-quarters of the accused were female. Overall, between 40,000 and 50,000 persons were executed as witches.[14]

Visits to these two communities in crisis will show how attention to neglected differences between early- and late-marriage households and the ways they influence women's and men's thought and behavior not only offers new perspectives on the Western past but also suggests new versions of how that past might have unfolded. Since early-fourteenth-century Montaillou and

[12] Le Roy Ladurie, *Montaillou*, xiv–xvii.
[13] Karlsen, *The Devil in the Shape of a Woman*, 33–45.
[14] Robin Briggs, *Witches and Neighbors: The Social and Cultural Context of European Witchcraft* (New York, 1996), 8.

especially late-seventeenth-century Salem have been extensively studied, their tales of heresy and witchcraft will not be retold in any detail here. Rather, evidence will be reviewed with a lens on how differences in household structure can be shown to have influenced the ways people thought and acted in each place. Awareness of these differences invites challenges to prevailing views and points to more appropriate choices among conflicting interpretations, both for these episodes and for more general accounts of heresy and witchcraft in these periods.

Salem Village and Montaillou were communities of comparable size – about 250 souls in each – but with contrasting marriage and household systems. Salem displayed the late-marriage system imported to the New World by English settlers. Montaillou had the "mixed" system that John Hajnal cited as characteristic of parts of southern Europe, making it, in his view, the sort of place that might yield clues to the origins of the aberrant northwestern European or late-marriage system. That both communities had shared cultural features, including the Christian faith, had the advantage of reducing variables that might explain observed differences. But it should hardly be presumed that there was any historical progression from a late medieval "Montaillou" type to an early modern "Salem" one. In fact, long-established late-marriage structures in England ensured that fourteenth-century peasant households there functioned less like those in fourteenth-century Montaillou than like those in seventeenth-century Salem. Another factor in the choice of Montaillou was the rare opportunity, for such an early period, to draw on abundant testimony of ordinary medieval villagers of both sexes.

Sources cited here have already been used to illustrate the lives and worldviews of residents in each place, but attention to contrasting household structures and their influence on behavior exposes much more. Not only does it tell us why women might have been singled out as responsible for crises in one village while being exempt from suspicion in the other, it also shows how evidence of wider patterns of gender and power can be better understood as the effects of different marriage and household patterns. Crises in both places featured conflicts about spiritual as well as earthly power; and by laying bare the tensions in each community, they expose what was true in noncrisis times, namely, that women and men perceived themselves and their most vital interests quite differently. Such differences have been partially explained for Salem; but in Montaillou, where women's and men's worldviews stood even further apart, no adequate explanation has been offered. What is more, while the women and men of Salem had more similar views of self and had more in common regarding both their earthly and heavenly priorities, it was in Salem, not in Montaillou, that adult women were literally more at risk for their lives at the hands of men.

* * *

It is thanks to two men that the tiny village of Montaillou has been rescued from historical obscurity. The first is Jacques Fournier, Bishop of Pamiers in southern France from 1318 to 1325 and later Pope Benedict XII. Fournier supervised the Inquisition in his diocese and saw to it that the account of his victory over local heretics was preserved. The 114 women and men whose testimony is contained in the Inquisition Register in the Vatican were mostly peasants, artisans, shepherds, servants, and small shopkeepers. Theirs is a precious record of how ordinary people acted toward one another, what they thought, and what they felt in a medieval community nearly 700 years ago.

The second man responsible for saving Montaillou from oblivion is Emmanuel Le Roy Ladurie, who brought its long forgotten residents to life in a remarkable book, *Montaillou: The Promised Land of Error*, which became a best-seller in France in the mid-1970s.[15] Using Fournier's register, Le Roy Ladurie presents villagers' views on children, marriage, sex, work, death, love, and more. He shows that illiterate peasants in this isolated community engaged in lively debates about the meaning of life and salvation and that they held an astonishing array of opinions. Yet his account of why women and men in Montaillou thought and acted so differently is less than persuasive. He is aware that there were gender divisions, but he regularly ignores his own evidence that women and men held opposing views on everything from sexual relations and family loyalty to religious heresy – and that each had good reasons for doing so.

Unsurprisingly, documentation for Salem Village is far richer than for Montaillou, whose residents in this account will be presented almost solely through Le Roy Ladurie's study of Fournier's register. For Salem, by contrast, many original sources survive, and there are growing numbers of studies on New England family life and on colonial women.[16] The Salem witch hunt of 1692 is itself one of the most exhaustively studied episodes in American history, even though a remarkable recent analysis by Mary Beth Norton shows that despite all the prior research, extraordinary riches remained in the records that both alter and enliven interpretation.[17] Yet for all this, it has only been with the burgeoning of women's history studies in the past generation that scholars realized that it might be necessary to explain why, throughout the early modern era, women were held responsible for so many of society's ills.[18]

---

[15] The original French edition was titled *Montaillou: Village Occitan de 1294 à 1324* (Paris, 1975).

[16] A full bibliography is available in the excellent recent study by Mary Beth Norton, *Founding Mothers and Fathers: Gendered Power and the Forming of American Society* (New York, 1996).

[17] Mary Beth Norton, *In the Devil's Snare* (New York, 2002).

[18] For a full recent discussion, see Elspeth Whitney, "International Trends: The Witch "She"/ The Historian "He": Gender and the Historiography of the European Witch-Hunts." *Journal of Women's History* 7, No. 3 (Fall 1995): 77–101. Whitney presents a rich bibliographical discussion without, to be sure, addressing the argument to be presented here about the links between the rise of witch hunts in the late medieval era and the appearance in northwestern Europe of the late-marriage system.

The early-fourteenth-century village of Montaillou was located in a principality close to the present-day border between France and Spain. It was ruled by the Counts of Foix, whose representatives kept order and collected rents and other manorial dues. Other outside authorities to whom the villagers were subject included the spies of the Church's Inquisition, the tithe-collectors for the diocese, and finally, the French monarchy itself, which would ultimately absorb the principality into the kingdom. Although the late Count of Foix had gained favor with the villagers by encouraging their resistance to the Church's tithes and to the royal officials, his death in 1302, and the ascendance of royal agents in his court, helped the diocesan authorities renew their onslaughts. The inhabitants of Montaillou were suspected of being ripe for an outbreak of heresy.

When the revival of Catharism swept the mountain community and led to a long session of the Inquisitorial court between 1318 and 1325, those summoned to testify were mostly accused heretics, identified with the help of local priests and villagers. Information was extracted from them by threats of excommunication or imprisonment. Although a few of the witnesses were nobles, priests, or notaries, most, as indicated, were humble persons earning their living by working the land. Catharism itself will be discussed more fully in the next chapter, but its features are worth outlining here.

In Montaillou, the heretical faith that was Catharism permitted a wide range of convictions blending Catholic with earlier folk beliefs. Cathars saw themselves as true Christians but questioned the authority of the Catholic priests in everything from tithe collecting and the regulation of sex and marriage to the proper route to salvation. They singled out a priestlike elite of male teachers, the *parfaits* or goodmen, who theoretically abstained from meat and sex and who traveled about the countryside as missionaries, preaching to secret gatherings of the faithful. Unlike the goodmen, their followers had no dietary or sexual restrictions. As one heretic blithely put it, "Since everything is forbidden, everything is allowed."[19] (He was the village priest who played both sides of the street, and his views were loose even by Cathar standards.) Still, at the end of their lives, these heretics were obliged to pay a high price. When they were judged to be dying, Cathars had to undergo total and suicidal fasting, a process they believed would guarantee their salvation.

As for its more mundane organization, the village of Montaillou was laid out along a hillside in traditional Mediterranean style, with tiered houses surrounded by the plots of each family. Above the village was the Count's chateau, and just below lay the parish church and the cemetery. To the south, beyond the surrounding forests, lay the pastures of the shepherds, who formed a kind of subcommunity of bachelors, many of whom were younger sons of the village employed by neighboring owners of large flocks. No longer serfs, or even strictly dependents of the lord, the families of

[19] Le Roy Ladurie, *Montaillou*, 171.

Montaillou could bequeath and even sell their land freely, although the land market was not very active.

All the villagers including the priest were from old local families, and only a handful enjoyed even moderate wealth. The few artisans there were still engaged in some agricultural work; and since money was in short supply, they were often obliged either to accept goods for their services or to be patient about cash payment. Bartering was common, as was sharing of scarce items, such as cooking pots or draught animals. Peddlers carried in a few things, including wine (which could not be produced locally due to the cold climate), needles, olive oil, and sugar. Although the village did export some items, such as sheep and squirrel skins, it was close to being a subsistence economy.

The primary unit of the village was the "ostal," a local term meaning both family and house. Ostals were at the center of social and cultural life; and, as Le Roy Ladurie reports, for Montaillou villagers, "the family of flesh and blood and the house of wood, stone or daub were one and the same thing."[20] As was usual in such communities, the public and private aspects of daily life overlapped. Despite the influence of the outside authorities of Church, lord, and monarch, village leadership on a day-to-day basis came from the heads of the forty or so ostals. The Clergue family, owners of the largest ostal, had special influence in the village. One brother, a priest, represented the ecclesiastical arm; and another, as the Count's bailiff, represented the secular one. But these deputies of the outside world derived most of their power locally by manipulating rivalries and alliances among the households. The handful of female heads, mainly widows, might enjoy more prestige than other women, but they did not belong to the male club of village elders. Such women, in fact, often turned over the actual management of ostals to their sons or sons-in-law.

Although most ostals were nuclear in form, which was the late-marriage feature in an otherwise early-marriage system, household membership varied with the life cycle of the family. An elderly parent or some other relative might be included, although more than one married couple was rare. Life-cycle service was not a pattern for Montaillou youth. If families needed to replace the functions of an out-marrying sister and had no in-marrying sister-in-law, they might hire a servant girl; or, when their own children were young, they might engage a plowman or a shepherd. Although they often resided in their employers' households, most such servants were not members of Montaillou families and usually came from poorer households in nearby

---

[20] Ibid., 24. In his study of late medieval Essex, which also addresses the fourteenth century, Lawrence R. Poos remarks that in the English case, there was no such strong identification over time between members of a particular family and particular residences. "One looks in vain in this district for any sign of the exclusive identification by the extended representatives of one lineage with one *domus* epitomised by the residents of early-fourteenth-century Montaillou in southern France," *A Rural Society After the Black Death: Essex 1350–1525* (Cambridge, 1991), 86.

towns. Some servants, though, were the illegitimate offspring of villagers, such as Mengarde, natural daughter of the bailiff, who lived in her father's ostal and made bread and washed shirts for the itinerant heretic priests.[21]

Unlike other places, where equal division of property among sons, or even among sons and daughters, was the rule, Montaillou's customs allowed fathers to "advantage" one child, usually the eldest son. Other sons took their portions – movable property and perhaps cash – and left. The men of the clans protected their property against the claims of outsiders by practicing village endogamy or "in-marriage." Among forty-three of fifty village couples named in the register, both partners came from Montaillou families, while for each of the remaining seven, one partner had been born there. Only if there were no sons might a married daughter remain in her natal ostal. Her husband was then adopted into her family, taking its name to perpetuate the ostal's identity. Daughters were married young, usually at the onset of puberty; and at marriage they received dowries of household goods, animals, and money, but rarely land. Parents or relatives chose their mates from among eligible sons of the village; and these grooms were older, usually in their mid- to late twenties.

A few younger sons might be lucky enough to set up their own ostals; some married into ostals with no sons; and others took religious orders. Yet most younger sons joined the itinerant community of celibate (if not chaste) shepherds. Despite downward mobility, they appear to have found the male camaraderie and vagabond outdoor life attractive. Even for those who left, however, and few went far away, ties to the ostal of their birth remained strong. For all men the birth ostal provided their primary source of emotional strength and identity. Sons waged blood feuds in its name; and heresy, when it came, made its conversions not by individual but by ostal.

The "mixed" households of Montaillou – nuclear in form but with early marriage for women – do not appear to offer the clues John Hajnal anticipated in 1982 when he cited the potential of southern European households, with features of both early- and late-marriage systems, to lead us to the origins of the Western family pattern. What they do demonstrate, however, is that it was entirely possible for a society, most of whose households were nuclear, to behave in practically all ways like a traditional early-marriage, multifamily society. Nuclearity, once again, does not appear to be the feature of the Western family pattern that mattered most, despite the early and sustained attention by historical demographers to that single feature. The example of Montaillou helps to confirm the argument here that women's late marriage was the single feature of northwestern European family arrangements that mattered most for generating distinctive behavior, attitudes, and power relationships among the denizens of its households.

---

[21] Le Roy Ladurie, *Montaillou*, 42.

Despite the dominant nuclear residential pattern in Montaillou, the continuing practice of parents' control of their daughters' marriages made it far easier for households there to remain on the same property generation upon generation, thus helping to ensure the maintenance of other early-marriage features as well. Making certain that new brides were a decade younger than their husbands, after all, made it easier to insist that they move into the existing households of their grooms' families. In Montaillou's case, despite ceasing to reside in their natal ostals, most of the younger brothers continued to live nearby, to remain single, and to maintain regular involvement with their birth ostals.

Late marriage for women, by contrast, was far more disruptive of household stability than nuclearity. By automatically limiting the number of potential male heirs, and by separating the generations more in time – thereby making it more likely that widows would inherit property – late marriage for women made it much harder for male lineages to keep property in the male line. These features of the household-formation system had real effects on the range of male kin upon whom any man might call for various purposes, limiting their number in the late-marriage societies and restricting their capacity to guard particular pieces of landed property over time.

Aside from women's late marriage, what was distinctive in northwestern Europe, as noted earlier, was a combination in the manorial regions of two factors: first, the availability of rich land that long offered productive work for as many as could be employed, female as well as male; and second, a system of farming that was at once collective and decentralized. These factors helped protect family households from the risks evident in most other agricultural settings of the decision to postpone daughters' marriages in order to benefit from their labor.

In Montaillou, as in most early-marriage societies beginning to shift from a prior self-sufficient agricultural system to a more regionally based, commercialized one, men rather than women were the ones first integrated into the new system – in the persons of those younger sons who became shepherds employed by neighboring large landowners. The process varied over time and from one early-marriage region to another; but since women typically continued to marry much younger than men, the result was that in most such societies, men were introduced far sooner than women to changes in new market structures and extrafamilial institutions. While a gap between women's and men's exposure to wider worlds was also present in northwestern European societies, it was far less pronounced than in most agricultural settings around the world.

* * *

So much, then, for the bare outlines of life in Montaillou. Salem, Massachusetts, was a vastly different collection of true Christians. Founded in 1626 as a commercial and fishing settlement, Salem had a fine harbor that soon made it the busiest port in the colony next to Boston in trade with Europe and the West Indies. A growing population of Puritan immigrants prompted Town selectmen in the 1630s to make grants of interior farmland to settlers; and these farmers of what became known as "Salem Village" increased the Town's tax revenues and supplied food for its traders and merchants. Established on separate homesteads scattered throughout the Town's hinterland, married couples and their children, resident servants, and hired laborers tamed the wilderness, raised crops, fought the Indians, and strove to live up to the stern commands of their Puritanical faith.[22]

At first, larger numbers of male settlers pushed women's marriage age down relative to that of English women. At twenty or twenty-one, a typical Salem bride was four or five years younger than her English counterpart; but she was still far older than the typical Montaillou bride had been. Women's average marriage age, moreover, rose to the mid-twenties as the second and third generations brought more balanced sex ratios. By the end of the seventeenth century, Salem, like some of the other older settlements, had more women than men.[23] It also came to resemble English patterns in another way as increasing numbers of Salem women became destined never to marry. By contrast, testimony covering over a quarter century in Montaillou revealed the more typical early-marriage situation: every eligible daughter mentioned in the record was married.

Soon after their community was founded, separatist impulses arose among the Villagers. The farmers petitioned for their own meetinghouse and minister, which Town authorities finally granted in 1672, but without formal church status. Villagers fell to fighting among themselves; and although a determined group succeeded in gaining church status by 1689, petitions for separate town status were denied. By the 1690s, the Village was only about a fifth the size of the faster-growing Town. It had failed to resolve conflicts over its ministers and its secular government, and it seethed with hostilities created by dividing original properties for the many second- and third-generation sons.

In addition to Village–Town conflict and generational tensions, the Village itself was divided between traditional farmers to the west, who resented being landlocked by neighboring communities, and a more dynamic population of eastern Villagers blessed with the best lands and proximity to the roads and waterways with access to Salem Town. It was these persons who could take most advantage of new economic opportunities. Compared to Montaillou, with its simplified and informal leadership by heads of ostals,

---

[22] In addition to the material from Karlsen, this summary of life in Salem Village draws upon the background discussion in Paul Boyer and Stephen Nissenbaum, *Salem Possessed: The Social Origins of Witchcraft* (Cambridge, 1974).

[23] See the discussion in Karlsen, *The Devil in the Shape of a Woman*, 202–6.

Salem Town and Village had more complex governing structures, a more diverse economy, and a far more unequal distribution of landed property and other wealth.

While Montaillou remained a stable and isolated village of intermarrying peasants organized in family clans, Salem – both Town and Village – had a rapid turnover of settlers, an active land market, and an ever-growing involvement with the outside world. Although all local governing posts, ecclesiastical and secular, were restricted to male household heads in both communities, Salem men could not count on the easy translation of their positions as heads of households into recognition and status in the community, as men could do in Montaillou. Influence for Salem men depended upon many more factors, including family background, education, training, godly behavior, naming to local office, substantial property ownership, and, increasingly, wealth from trade.

For most women in both places, the arenas where power might be exercised were the informal ones of household and community, although in each village there were female networks that enhanced women's influence. The church also offered a more formal arena to exert some limited authority, but Montaillou women do not appear to have had even the modest women's religious organizations of other late medieval communities. In Salem, on the other hand, the meetinghouse was a site of women's religious activity and a stage for female one-upmanship, even though there, and in other institutions as well, men were busily creating formal posts to which men alone were eligible to be named, underscoring women's exclusion from an expanding public sphere.

Failure to take into account that societies in which women marry early promote separate life cycles for the sexes and foster attitudes far more divided by sex than those in which women marry late, interpreters of these and other premodern settings have drawn some questionable conclusions. For example, on the basis of the more open and casual misogyny in Montaillou, including the easy acceptance of men's physical violence against women, Le Roy Ladurie declares that women there surely went "in danger of rape, perhaps in even greater danger than elsewhere and in other ages."[24] Such a view might appear strengthened by the fact that in seventeenth-century New England, and in "old" England from as early as the late thirteenth century, rape was a capital crime and any woman in the kingdom, regardless of status, could bring formal charges.[25] Yet as will shortly be seen, it was in Salem, not Montaillou – and more generally in late-marriage societies rather than early-marriage ones – that women, married as well as single, went in greater danger of rape.

[24] Le Roy Ladurie, *Montaillou*, 149.
[25] See John Marshall Carter, *Rape in Medieval England: A Historical and Sociological Study* (Lanham, Md., 1985).

Similarly, other evidence from daily life, interpreted without reference to household structures, has led to even more basic misconceptions about women's lives in the premodern Western past. For example, the discovery that many women in the early modern era from 1500 to 1750 had independent economic roles, often running their own breweries or dairy establishments, has led some commentators to proclaim the period a kind of "golden age" in which women exercised significant economic and social power. This halcyon era preceded an alleged decline in the modern industrial period, in which most married women not only ceased productive labor but allegedly lost status and were confined to the home for more than a century.[26] This rosy assessment of ordinary women's lives coexists uneasily with another view of the early modern period that still enjoys support from some newer social historians as well as some older political ones. That is that far from being a golden age, this period was one of severe patriarchal repression involving widespread and genuine setbacks for most women.

The ways overlooked differences in household structures worked to mold shared patterns of social activity can go far toward resolving these and other contradictory assessments of gender and power in premodern settings. In addition, as a closer look at life in these two communities reveals, the women of Montaillou, who spent their days in more sexually segregated surroundings, were bound to envision the world and themselves very differently from their men. Even in Salem, where women's and men's lives ran along more parallel tracks, women, in particular, still had enough common experiences to define an identifiable set of female priorities spilling across social ranks.

Visits to these two communities will also illustrate ways in which the late-marriage system came to have a profoundly unsettling effect on relations between the sexes, and on men in particular, during the early modern era. Differences are clear from the ways conflict played itself out. In both places, there were not only clashes among men, but between women and men as well as among different groups of women. In Montaillou these clashes were more open, straightforward, and even brutal than in Salem. But it was in Salem that they generated more ambivalence, anxiety, and sexual hatred.

* * *

Predictably enough by now, life in Montaillou divided more neatly than in Salem into two sexual "universes." Women and girls, men and boys, occupied themselves with different tasks in different places. Women usually stayed inside or close to the ostal. There they tended hearth fires, prepared meals, cared for poultry and livestock, gathered kindling, washed clothes, spun

---

[26] See Judith M. Bennett, "History That Stands Still: Women's Work in the European Past." *Feminist Studies* 14 (1988): 269–83. Also see the comments by Bennett in the introduction to her *Women in the Medieval English Countryside: Gender and Household in Brigstock Before the Plague* (New York, 1985), 3–9. Other works on this topic are cited in Chapter 7.

wool, combed hemp or flax, grew vegetable gardens, and minded small children. Women worked in the fields only during planting and harvest seasons.

Not that women never left their ostals. Much of their work, as their testimony reveals, was conducted in one another's company. Wives, daughters, servant maids, and widows who headed ostals regularly shared household goods, used a well-to-do neighbor's oven for baking bread or cooking pork, or even traveled together to nearby villages to sell poultry or eggs. Women also met at the spring, where they fetched water and carried it in jars on their heads. They were usually the ones who put the wheat to be ground on the backs of mules and took it to the nearby mill. A few poor widows from the village made their living as peddlers, selling wine or cheese and serving as professional messengers among the local villages. For the most part, though, women's responsibilities kept them closer to the domestic hearth than men's did.

Since the village proper was largely female territory during most of the daylight hours, women had occasion to develop solidarity among themselves and to evolve some cliques, such as a network of more influential matriarchs from the three most prominent Cathar ostals. The Inquisition added heresy to the special influence of their ostals as common bonds; and these women sent parcels to whichever one of their number was imprisoned. Another group, wives of the "middling" Montaillou farmers who formed the backbone of the village, were united by friendship, family intermarriage, and "fellow sponsorship," that is, having served as one of the six female relatives, friends, or servants who were witnesses for a bride at her wedding. Regular interchanges among women usually transcended the limited social divisions. The chatelaine herself mixed easily with even the poorest peasant women. She once declared that she had at least five close female friends, including maidservants, in whom she could confide all her secrets.

The Inquisition infused an element of danger into the curiosity typical of the village women, who might dare to ask a heretic friend how the Cathar goodmen could save souls, or even to check out rumors of itinerant Cathar missionaries hidden in someone's cellar or barn. But exchanges more commonly provided information about the daily goings-on in one another's ostals. Since they might share or withhold what they knew, women derived a kind of power from these exchanges. Also, since they were no worse educated than the men, their views could not readily be dismissed as ignorant chatter.

By contrast with women's work, the daily work of men, more seasonal and more physically strenuous, took them away from their ostals to smallish plots of two to ten hectares, where they plowed and harvested oats and wheat and dug up turnips. It was men and boys alone who went pheasant or squirrel hunting in the nearby forests or trout fishing in the rivers. A few men combined agricultural or pastoral labor (the second most important male occupation) with artisanal work. For example, the village had a cobbler and a weaver. But when one of the few tools needed to be fixed or when a roof shingle needed to be replaced, it was the men's task to seek out a nearby blacksmith or carpenter. As soon as they were old enough, village boys accompanied their fathers to the fields or watched over their family's sheep. Occasional extended visits to corn markets and sheep fairs, as well as trips to the larger towns, were made mostly by the men.

Work relationships were not an exclusive outlet for social exchange for men, as they were for women. Small groups of men from different ostals might meet in the evening to play dice or chess, or to sing and listen to the shepherds play their flutes. All-male dinners appear to have been fairly common, although no all-female dinners are reported. Since Montaillou was close to the *cabanes* of the bachelor shepherds, many of whom were sons of the village, men would often hold gatherings there. They also met in the street or in the village square, especially on Sundays, where talk might turn to religion or perhaps to collective action against the Church's tithes.

Testimony rarely mentions mixed groups of young people. That daughters married early and so many young men migrated to the pastures helps explain their limited social interaction, although occasionally young people are reported dancing on feast days, singing and playing games, or enjoying pranks during a harvest. The one institution that brought the community together, regardless of age, rank or sex, was Sunday Mass. Save for the most convinced male heretics, most villagers continued to attend Mass. Reasons included simple sociability, preserving their reputations against the Inquisition, and – for the majority of the more or less faithful – helping to ensure salvation. It is not reported whether the sexes were segregated during services, as in Salem; but accounts of mixed evening gatherings for the Cathar missionaries show a marked segregation by sex and age. Before a meal, the adult men might share a drink of wine together, while the women, who were not offered wine, prepared the food. The men were then seated at the table; and after serving them, the women joined the younger children by the fire. Boys there accepted and shared the blessed bread passed to them from the table by the master of the house. After dinner, with children put to bed, the women sat apart from the men, perhaps carding wool, while the Cathar visitors preached.

It is hard to know what the villagers thought about these separate sexual universes. When such dining arrangements are described, or when it becomes clear that women alone were responsible for apparently denigrating tasks (such as the chore of delousing people, a procedure often conducted outdoors amid lively theological discussion), or when witnesses report that the bells in the parish church tolled fewer times for a woman's death than for a man's, it might be imagined that the women felt resentful or oppressed. But there is no hint in their testimony that they did. For the time being, the most that can be said is that daily life in Montaillou reflected the rooted gender hierarchy that is characteristic of early-marriage societies.

In Salem, the sexual division of labor, on its face, was similar. Women's work had the same domestic focus, and men usually worked away from the family hearth. Farm wives presided over dairying, raising and slaughtering of small animals, cider- and beer-making, and baking. Townswomen might purchase their products from local merchants or directly from farm wives who traveled from Salem Village, but even townswomen had agricultural duties. They often kept small gardens and a cow, some chickens, or a few pigs. Townswomen joined farmwomen in spinning, at least when children were small, since spinning combined well with child care. Townswomen were also more involved in trade, often working with their husbands in a hardware shop, a bakery, or a mill. On occasion, normally as widows, they ran shops or businesses on their own.

The common domestic focus of women's work among Montaillou and Salem villagers hardly comes as a surprise, but caution is needed in interpreting this enduring tie between women and domestic duties. In a desire to find women's assigned inferiority embedded in the locales they frequent as well as in the tasks they perform, some have been eager to name the domestic realm itself as the culprit in explaining the subordination of women. Even Le Roy Ladurie appears to subscribe to this view: "Women's inferiority was linked to their physical weakness and their specialization in what were considered inferior jobs (cooking, gardening, carrying water, childbearing, bringing up children)."[27]

A problem with this argument is exposed by the high value commonly attached to the household realm itself in early-marriage societies. In Montaillou, after all, the ostal was no inferior region; it was instead the quasi-sacred center of the pride of each family clan. For the theory to be plausible, women there would be expected at the least to enjoy more prestige than in a place like Salem, where many more institutions already competed for the loyalty of villagers, and where the hopes of a lineage were not so tied to the survival of a single family property. Yet we know that it was the other way around – that it was in Salem that women were accorded greater honor, deference, and respect. While specific work and the places people perform it can surely affect the attitudes of each sex toward the other, they hardly do so in the same automatic way across all societies.

There will be time to explore further the puzzle of women's apparently universal secondary status, but there is more to be learned here first by comparing the work worlds of the sexes in these two communities. Contrary to widespread views, what matters most about those worlds is not the actual work that women and men did or even where they did it. It is instead the ways that they felt about work and, more to the point, the reasons they felt as they did. Here, the contrast between Montaillou and Salem could hardly be greater. In Montaillou, men and women alike did not view work with

[27] Le Roy Ladurie, *Montaillou*, 255.

any special reverence. We are told that whenever they could, they took it easy. They were fond of naps, and they are often portrayed as interrupting their labor for a chat or a spur-of-the-moment visit. Reality obliged most of them, as manual laborers, to work hard at certain times. Still, says Le Roy Ladurie, "work in itself was not a source of earthly consideration. For a peasant to farm his own land well was merely to show that he was not mad."[28]

By contrast, in Salem and in New England as a whole, a conscious and articulated ethic of work was almost synonymous with the Puritan faith. Nurtured on English soil, this well-known ethic has been linked to a break-down of rural stability, a demographic explosion that doubled England's population in less than a century after 1550, and enormous urban growth – all of which prompted newly uprooted people to seek new forms of social or-der, new routes to livelihood, and new means of self-affirmation. An intense focus on planning for the future, already recounted in the French context, was exaggerated in the English one, where proportionally more landless peo-ple were obliged to scramble to reinvent themselves and find new ways to support their households. The process has been singled out for generating identity crises, especially among men.[29]

If these developments are perceived through a wider lens that includes the prior emergence of a unique household system throughout the entire northwestern European region, then the rise of anxiety over identity – taking acute forms among certain groups, and among men more than women – makes more sense. After all, what limited stability there was in the medieval era, when more families controlled individual properties and when kin were often near at hand, was fast disappearing. For any given man, the extent of male kin of his own and previous generations who could be counted upon for support was already limited; and the established practice of circulating among households for work further restricted the occasions for interacting with his few male relatives. Men who were increasingly reliant on their own resources confronted additional challenges as population rose dramatically from the mid-sixteenth century.

---

[28] Ibid., 339–40.

[29] The most original of these studies of which I am aware is contained in the work of Philip J. Greven, especially in *The Protestant Temperament: Patterns of Child-Rearing, Religious Experi-ence, and the Self in Early America* (New York, 1977); and in *Spare the Child: The Religious Roots of Punishment and the Psychological Impact of Physical Abuse* (New York, 1990). In addition, Greven's remarkable portrait of a tortured New England poet and divine in " 'Some Root of Bitterness:' Corporal Punishment, Child Abuse, and the Apocalyptic Impulse in Michael Wigglesworth" in James A. Henretta, Michael Kammen, and Stanley N. Katz, eds., *The Transformation of Early American History: Society, Authority and Ideology* (New York, 1991), 93–122, presents a kind of template for understanding the afflicted, anxious, tormented, and probably physically abused Puritan man in mortal conflict with earthly and heavenly fathers.

Far from being the poorest of the new landless populations, many of those attracted to Puritanism might have expected to control property of their own. But as manorial structures decayed and market economies grew, they found themselves forced to make their way in a world in which adult livelihood was less predictable.[30] Men, who were the ones most immediately affected by reduced expectations for inheritance, were especially responsive to the idea that worthiness could be validated through the pursuit of any honorable vocation. They were the ones most in need of the alternate anchors for identity offered by a trade or profession, even though these might turn out to be as insecure as land had become. An ideal of industry was held up to women as well; but a woman's single vocation was to be a meet help, the subordinate partner of her husband. It was for men alone that the notion of work as a divine calling assumed special force and meaning. As Michael Walzer, an authority on Puritan ideology, noted, "Men accepted the discipline and received in return, as it were, a godly sense of self-importance."[31]

Long before Puritans sailed for the New World, there were signs in northern Europe, and especially in England, that ever fewer men might expect to inherit land. In places such as northern France, where feudal institutions had been established centuries earlier than in England, and where peasant families had had longer to devise collective strategies to secure a hold on their property, late marriage and nuclear residential arrangements had been less disruptive of household continuity. In England, however, less tangible items sooner replaced control of land as a badge of full manhood. Even community itself came to be envisioned abstractly, as a willed bond among like-minded souls rather than as a physical settlement of dwellings and fields. Here is John Winthrop, the first colonial governor of Massachusetts, describing to settlers on board ship to the New World the goal of a godly community built on faith and work: "[We] must delight in each other . . . rejoice together, mourn together, labor and suffer together, always having before our eyes our commission and community in the work, our community as members of the same body."[32]

Despite being the focus of such fervently expressed loyalties, the family households of New England were, in truth, far more fragile entities than the enduring ostals of Montaillou. The products of what was, in effect, a successful heretical movement, the Puritan settlements rested not on the identity of householders' blood and property over time but on the free "covenant" of believers, dedicated to a new contractual social order built on faith,

---

[30] There is a large literature bearing out this description of the Puritan male type, including two classic studies by David Underdown: *Revel, Riot, and Rebellion: Popular Politics and Culture in England, 1603–1660* (Oxford, 1985); and *Fire from Heaven: Life in an English Town in the Seventeenth Century* (New Haven, Conn., 1992).

[31] Michael Walzer, *The Revolution of the Saints: A Study in the Origins of Radical Politics* (New York, 1970), 214.

[32] Boyer and Nissenbaum, *Salem Possessed*, 104.

self-discipline, and industriousness. Within a few generations, this striking vision had been dimmed by the reality of what Puritans were fond of calling the "old Adam" of prideful self-interest. (Later generations, in due course, would ease conflict by sanctifying this self-interest as entrepreneurial spirit.)

By the seventeenth century there were many places where men had long had to accept less tangible criteria than control of property as an anchor for their identity, but the adjustment was especially trying in Salem Village. At first, the availability of apparently unlimited land, an undeveloped trade sector, and relatively few women – whose fertility in recent memory had threatened men's chances for landed inheritance in the Old World – had meant that men might hope to regain the stability of an earlier order, in which heading a household meant controlling the destinies of offspring and perhaps playing a leadership role in a community. There were even places in New England where, for a time at least, fathers were better able to unite family and property than their own fathers had been able to do in old England.[33] But Salem Village was not one of those places.

Like other communities in the region, Salem supported many forms of nonagricultural work that had long offered a livelihood for men in northwestern Europe. The piece of property handed down with luck and pain in the male line, so critically important in Montaillou, was no longer paramount. Not only had most families' literal control of land already been reduced, that asset had been diminished even further in Salem relative to other New England communities due to the high importance there of trade.

Dramatic mercantile expansion by the 1680s actually reduced farm assets to less than a tenth of all wealth in Salem's County of Essex. In Salem Village, population pressures in the second and third generations meant that the average landholding decreased to half of what it had been at mid-century. Only those Villagers in the east, who took advantage of alliance with the Town merchants, could maintain or strengthen their positions. For the rest, even the land they had could not prevent downward mobility.[34] By comparison with the men of Montaillou, whose daily work was controlled by male clan decisions, the work of Salem Village men increasingly involved interaction with men outside their families. Farmers came to specialize in producing grain or beef for the export trade as well as commodities for Town consumption, so success depended upon ties with townsmen who were shippers and local distributors. Even decisions about what crops to plant or animals to raise were not made by male blood relatives within a household, as in Montaillou, but instead by a whole network of unrelated men, including outsiders who might be unknown to the Villagers and perhaps even live across the sea.

---

[33] See the classic study by Philip J. Greven, Jr., *Four Generations: Population, Land, and Family in Colonial Andover, Massachusetts* (Ithaca, N.Y., 1970).
[34] Boyer and Nissenbaum, *Salem Possessed*, 86–91.

Entering a trade or a profession meant establishing ties with its practitioners, often leaving home for training, and then gaining enough capital, or perhaps a salaried appointment, to carry on. By contrast with the handful of men's occupations in Montaillou, dominated by agriculture and shepherding, over fifty occupations were available to men in colonial New England.[35] All this had effects on power relationships among men, limiting the ways fathers could control sons and shifting dependency ties among men from male family members to male outsiders. If young men in Salem were now able – with or without parental blessing and support – to prepare for a trade or profession, they also had to recognize that their position in life might depend less on their families, more on outsiders, and finally, more on themselves.

Contrasts in women's work lives were less stark between the two communities but still highly significant. The mountain woman's tasks varied less from one generation to the next; and her female chores were first learned from women in her father's clan and then from women in her husband's. Many a Salem woman learned her first serious housewifery as a servant working for a neighbor, or even for a stranger from a nearby community. More important, while their most typical labor involved tasks commonly held to be women's work, Salem women are often cited as engaged in what was ordinarily understood as men's work, whereas Montaillou women never are.

Too little attention has been paid to colonial women's daily boundary crossing from female to male tasks – and probably too much to the dozen or so trades a minority of these women took up, including midwifery, innkeeping, school teaching, millinery or dressmaking, and small-scale domestic production of dairy or other food products. Commentators intrigued by these entrepreneurial "women of affairs" have even framed discussions of women's position in colonial society around allegations that their independent economic activity was responsible for women's enhanced status.[36] While they are correct in pointing to evidence for men's new appreciation of women's contributions – here and in northwestern European societies more generally – they have missed its source. That source lay not in the still exceptional activities of those few women of affairs running their own businesses, and certainly not in the daily tasks associated with women's work that were similar to those of women in Montaillou, but instead in the boundary crossing itself – that is, in the overlapping of women's and men's day-to-day activities.

Claims that work offered a kind of universal elevator of women's status miss the point for the subjects in this setting. Salem women can hardly be said to have benefited as yet from the upholding of work as a measure of worth. That notion was only beginning to take root in the early modern era and was then, in any case, a project in which men, not women, were the

---

[35] Koehler, *A Search for Power*, 128.
[36] Again, see Bennett, "History That Stands Still."

intended beneficiaries. It should be recalled, after all, that Montaillou women themselves did their full share of work. Some were even women of affairs, albeit on a smaller scale than Salem women. Still, the work they performed made no positive contribution to their stature in men's eyes. In both cases, how women were perceived was far more influenced by their specific roles within two very different family and household systems. What counted more than anything else in generating the relatively greater respect women were accorded by men in Salem was the unique position of the housewife within the late-marriage household.

Most useful in clarifying this point is a look at the boundary-crossing men's work that women did – what they thought about it and why they did it in the first place. In examining women's daily lives in colonial New England, Laurel Ulrich has shown, for example, that a wife might carry on transactions at a husband's grist mill so that he could be freed to work in the fields. In a husband's absence, a wife might negotiate with his creditors and business associates, manage his farm, or run his shop. In coining the term "deputy husband" for this role, Ulrich is quick to note that interpreters have exaggerated its importance, with claims that colonial women had power that their descendants somehow lost. To the contrary, she says, such women were only doing what was expected of them as their husbands' helpmeets; deputy husbands at most reinforced "a certain elasticity in pre-modern notions of gender."[37]

These two roles [homemaker and surrogate husband] were compatible in the pre-modern world because the home was the communication center of family enterprise if not always the actual place of work. As long as business transactions remained personal and a woman had the support of a familiar environment, she could move rather easily from the role of housewife to the role of deputy husband, though few women were prepared either by education or by experience to become "independent women of affairs."[38]

It is doubtless true, as Ulrich argues, that women's activity as deputy husbands neither undid their dependence nor was regarded by them as more desirable than their female tasks. Far from taking particular pride in performing men's roles, she says that what pride they took from their work came chiefly from their more traditional activities, including child care and domestic chores. Still, Ulrich's interpretation, which takes late-marriage household arrangements for granted, ignores the fact that from a comparative standpoint, the performance of men's work by women was something both novel and anomalous. Women doing men's work, in fact, set late-marriage societies apart. It is a major example of the overlapping of women's and men's lives that is being argued here.

[37] See Ulrich, *Good Wives*, Ch. 2: "Deputy Husbands," 35–50.
[38] Ibid., 50.

That women were initially uncomfortable doing work normally assigned to men is hardly surprising. The praise for women that colonial men were touting in new prescriptive literature was not for doing men's work. It was instead for cultivating so-called womanly roles and virtues. The actual men's work women did was subsumed under the rubric of "helpmeet," a term that disguised the uncomfortable reality, for men, that women were often performing tasks that, officially at least, belonged to them.

Women did men's work in Salem not because they preferred it to women's work, or even because men wanted them to do it, but because their situation as one of two adults in economically independent households gave them no choice to do otherwise. The context of marital interdependency on which household survival rested in Salem by that time, and in northwestern European-based societies generally, regularly required women to do men's work. As men's reliance upon a network of male kin and on landed inheritance as determinants of their fates diminished, they came to recognize, if not to acknowledge, that their most immediate allies were their wives. They may have preferred to turn to a father or a brother for help in handling their affairs, and they often did so when they could. Yet circumstances beyond their control had loosened the bonds that in places such as Montaillou united the worlds of livelihood and male kinship. As more men were obliged to make livings on their own, they had to turn to their wives, the only partners who now fully shared their destinies.

The elasticity of gender roles in such households is nonetheless strange in one obvious sense. Women more readily did men's work than men did women's work. Mary Beth Norton has remarked of colonial New England, for example, that the divide between women's and men's work was a sort of semipermeable membrane that women more readily passed through than men. Even when men ran households by themselves, certain tasks considered essential that women usually did, such as butter-making and poultry-raising, just did not get done.[39] I will return to the issue of this semipermeable membrane in Chapter 6 in discussing the long-standing puzzle of the general subordination of women in most societies. But in the meantime, it is worthwhile to sum up preliminary answers to questions raised at the outset of this discussion.

First, the respect extended to Puritan wives can now be better explained. Ironically, it derived not from those "female" qualities of meekness and submission that men had begun to praise in women, but instead from men's unarticulated but uncomfortable awareness of their new dependency upon wives as deputy husbands. This role often demanded just the opposite in female behavior from that called for in the formal rhetoric – that is, assertiveness and even aggressiveness. Yet the reasons men now employed such rhetoric

[39] Mary Beth Norton, *Liberty's Daughters: The Revolutionary Experience of American Women, 1750–1800* (Boston, 1980), 13.

are clear. They wished to differentiate women's behavior from their own and to underscore a wife's secondary position in the domestic partnership.

It is also easier to understand why blatant misogyny of the sort on display in Montaillou was not so fashionable among Puritans. If a livelihood depended upon her competence to act responsibly in his stead, it was risky for any husband to call his wife a sow, at least in ordinary circumstances. At the same time, however, men were in a quandary. Now that more of their identity and self-worth were invested in the day-to-day activities of work, rather than in a vanishing bond between kin and property, any woman who performed the work men usually performed was automatically more subject to men's suspicions and anxieties. It thus became important constantly to remind wives that whatever their specific tasks, their first duty was to be meek and subordinate helpmeets.

That the men of Montaillou are never recorded in the testimony prescribing women's behavior is now easier to understand too. It was not that they never voiced any concerns in other areas about how people should act. Montaillou men regularly took time to spell out their views on proper neighborly behavior, appropriate behavior toward the poor, acceptable sexual liaisons, and more. They are never heard promoting desirable female behavior because they did not have to. Appropriate behavior from men's viewpoint was already largely ensured by clan structures that they themselves controlled.

In Salem, if men praised women and accorded them formal recognition, it was because the unique late-marriage structure gave wives enhanced domestic influence and authority. While that structure was also responsible for an overall weakening of family households relative to other social institutions, a theme that will be pursued in later chapters, the point here is that a more shared division of power between husbands and wives is implicated in the increased attention to gender roles and boundaries so evident in the early modern era, as well as in the solicitousness of men toward women's vitally important household roles. It would be going too far to label the emerging relations between husbands and wives "democratic," but in matters large and small, the shared decision making among spouses was something historically novel.

*   *   *

An obvious way to see how gender and power interact in a society is to look more closely at evidence for spousal abuse and gender violence. Such practices, more often directed by men against women, have in recent years been shown by scholars to provide insights into the nature of male power in the family and its uses to enforce the subordination of women and children. Yet here once again, household structures have been little explored or compared in efforts to explain differences in patterns of domestic violence. There have been enlightening historical accounts that reveal, for example, how in premodern Western societies, neighbors and wider communities were actually expected to intervene in a family's business, whereas in the modern era, once the family became a more private institution, victims of domestic violence had to rely more for protection upon frail ideologies of love and respect for others. Only in recent years, as one historian points out, have activists worked to make domestic violence the public issue it once was.[40] Longer-term differences in such matters, especially those between early- and late-marriage societies, nonetheless remain little examined or understood. Montaillou and Salem offer an occasion to identify and compare them.

Since we have already noted that men in Montaillou were more verbally abusive of women than men in Salem were, it will come as no surprise that they openly claimed a right to treat women violently and displayed a casual acceptance of wife-beating. "Every married woman could expect a fair amount of beating some time or other," says the historian of Montaillou.[41] An encounter between a villager and a local woman with an infected eye is cited by Le Roy Ladurie as typical: "Hey, Guillemette," shouted the weaver, "what happened? Did your husband beat you?" "No," she answered, "there's just something wrong with my eye."[42]

Christian teachings might be invoked against wife-beating, though usually to little effect. One man, for example, upbraids his son-in-law for cruelty to his daughter, reminding him that the holy scripture bids men to be peaceful and gentle. The son-in-law, however, dismisses him: "It's your daughter's fault. She is bad-tempered and a gossip." Repeatedly in testimony, even women who declare affection for their husbands report that they are terrified of being beaten or even killed by them.

Only one serious attempt to end the abuse of a wife is recorded in the register, which suggests women's lack of recourse against violence in the male-controlled clan system. In that case, a shepherd upset by a brother-in-law's systematic beatings of his sister traveled to his natal ostal in Montaillou to arrange with his male kin a plan to kidnap her. From his testimony, it is clear that the dishonor being brought upon his natal ostal was at least as disturbing to him as the physical harm suffered by his sister. Soon afterward, the brother carried out his plan, entrusting the sister to close friends in a town not far away. The rarity of such rescues is underlined, though, by the man's expressed fear of his sister's husband's kin, as well as by a friend's warning that if he failed to provide a secure hiding place for her, his sister might well "become a whore at everyone's beck and call."[43] There was no

---

[40] For an excellent discussion with a good set of bibliographical references on the topic, especially for England and the United States, see Susan Dwyer Amussen, " 'Being Stirred to Much Unquietness': Violence and Domestic Violence in Early Modern England." *Journal of Women's History* 6, No. 2 (Summer 1994): 70–89. The preceding summary was based upon Amussen's article.

[41] Le Roy Ladurie, *Montaillou*, 192.

[42] Ibid., 192.

[43] Ibid., 193.

possibility of returning her to her natal ostal either, since it was understood that in that event, the sister's husband and his male kin would seek violent revenge on her entire family.

A man's right to beat his wife was formally recognized in many contemporary compilations of customary laws. For example, one from thirteenth-century Beauvaisis declares: "It is licit for the man to beat his wife, without bringing about death or disablement, when she refuses her husband anything." Another from mid-fourteenth-century Bordeaux states that a husband who kills his wife in a fit of rage will not incur any penalty if he confesses and takes a solemn oath of repentance.[44]

Legally, as already noted, matters were different in Puritan Massachusetts. A wife there had protection against "bodilie correction or stripes by her husband, unlesse it be in his owne defence upon her assalt."[45] Cotton Mather declared that for "a man to Beat his Wife is as bad as any Sacriledge. And such a Rascal were better buried alive, than show his Head among his Neighbors any more."[46] A number of such rascals did dare to show their heads in colonial New England; but the sanctions, legal and religious, seem to have had some effect. Then too, while wives could hardly be said to give as good as they got, nearly a third of the 185 persons tried for abusing their mates in New England between 1630 and 1699 were women.[47] In addition, a number of women there reported abuse and sought aid from church elders and neighbors, while others ran away from violent husbands or filed petitions that cited beating as grounds for separation or divorce.

In practice, New England's magistrates were more lenient with wife-beaters than husband-beaters, continuing the English practice that had permitted the "lawfull and reasonable" correction of a wife.[48] Wife-beaters got off with admonitions and fines, while women presumptuous enough to beat their husbands were liable to be whipped. Unlike the residents of Montaillou, however, Puritans were less prone to mention spouse-beating in casual conversation. When they discussed gender violence with any openness, it was apt to be the supernatural sort carried out by witches doing the Devil's work.

Despite a reputation for quarrelsomeness, no Montaillou wife appears in the testimony as a husband-beater, and none is reported to have run away. In

---

[44] For a discussion see Jean-Louis Flandrin, *Families in Former Times: Kinship, Household and Sexuality* (Cambridge, 1980), 123.

[45] Cited in Norton, *Founding Mothers and Fathers*, 73, from the Massachusetts Bay Colony's first comprehensive legal code of 1641.

[46] Koehler, *A Search for Power*, 49.

[47] Ibid. See also the discussion in Norton, *Founding Mothers and Fathers*, 77–80. Norton notes that proportionately more women were likely to have been brought before the authorities since their actions were directly counter to beliefs in divine sanction for women's subservience to their husbands.

[48] Norton, *Founding Mothers and Fathers*, 74.

the larger nearby towns, women on occasion are reported to have taken the initiative in leaving an especially brutal husband; but the rigid clan system in Montaillou offered women no such option. Of the fifty marriages traceable in the testimony for a twenty-five-year period, actual separation is mentioned only twice. In one case, a husband ordered his wife out because she refused to join him in heresy; and since she was illegitimate, there were no male clansmen prepared to rush to her aid. In the other, a woman returned to her natal ostal with her dowry after it was confirmed that her husband was impotent.[49]

Women in Montaillou also turn out to have been in less danger of rape than women in Salem, despite Le Roy Ladurie's statement, noted earlier, that women were at special risk there.[50] It is true that his allegation at first seems to fit this volatile society; but the New England data show it was there, and in late-marriage societies generally, that women are bound to be more at risk than in early-marriage societies. Le Roy Ladurie's own account shows, in fact, that the victims of rape in Montaillou belonged to a restricted group: servants from outside the village, illegitimate women, and poor women who were alone. Attacks on such women, after all, were not likely to dishonor any men from one of the ostals. These same women were prey to the subtler seductions of men such as the priest, the chief womanizer of the village, who used his family connections and spiritual authority in a long string of female conquests. That one partner even recalled him as a sensitive lover is a comment on the usual sexual violence that unprotected females might encounter: "Another of his mistresses recalls with pleasure how, when he deflowered her among the straw of the family barn, he did not offer her any violence. This was in contrast to certain rustics who would have made no bones about raping her."[51]

In Montaillou, rapists did have to choose their victims with care. One man from the second wealthiest family in the village was imprisoned and obliged to pay the Count's officials twenty livres, a sum equal to half the price of a house, for foolishly attempting to rape the wife of a notary. Most village women, however, were guaranteed protection from rape – although less as subjects under law than as daughters of family ostals. As girls, they were watched closely by relatives, since their virginity was part of their family's honor. Some daughters of six or seven were already betrothed; and for the rest, the arrival of a first menstrual period marked the arrangement of marriage. Once married, most (though not all) village men settled down to monogamous fidelity, offering wives the protection of their new ostal against

---

[49] Le Roy Ladurie, *Montaillou*, 201–2.

[50] Le Roy Ladurie explains that "When they were young, the women of Montaillou or Ariège in general went in danger of rape, perhaps in even greater danger than elsewhere and in other ages," ibid., 149.

[51] Ibid., 157.

rape. Yet in Montaillou, blanket prohibitions of rape, whether by secular or religious authorities, had little meaning outside of specific contexts. What mattered was whether a potential victim had access to male clan protection. As members of ostals, most Montaillou women did.

By contrast, seventeenth-century New England court proceedings show that rape was more widespread throughout all social strata, and that not only young unmarried servants but wives as well were vulnerable to sexual violence. Unlike in Montaillou, rape was not interpreted as a violation of male "property" in women – one that in practice was no crime if a victim had no male protectors. Instead it was seen, in law at least, as an act of violence against women. Not only could any woman bring formal charges, her word was likely to be believed. Of seventy-seven men tried in seventeenth-century New England for taking sexual liberties with nonconsenting women, just eight were acquitted and only two were released with simple fines. Of the rest for whom final disposition is known, forty-two received whippings and fines and six were hanged (five of them in Massachusetts).[52]

Law and procedure, however, revealed ambivalence toward the act and its victims. The Massachusetts law, dating from 1642, reserved the most severe punishment of hanging for men who raped a married or espoused woman, suggesting yet again that for Puritan men, it was as wives that women achieved their highest value. Still, magistrates' frequent use of milder terms than "rape," such as "indecent actions" or "shameful abuse," shows a desire to avoid the maximum penalty for the crime. Reporting a rape clearly required courage. Women knew that even if an assailant were convicted, recovery of their own reputations was next to impossible. John Cotton went so far as to recommend that victims be required to marry their rapists, remarking, "it is worse to make a whore, than to say one is a whore."[53] In addition, the popular belief that rape could not lead to pregnancy meant that no pregnant women brought rape charges and that most victims waited at least two months before reporting a rape.

Reluctance to bring charges, not just as women before men but also as servants before masters, also contributed to underreporting, even though unmarried servants made up more than a third of the victims, while they were no more than a tenth of all adult women. One servant whose master's visiting brother had pulled her onto his bed one night testified that she asked him to release her but did not cry out when he raped her. "I was posesed with fear of my master least my master shold think I did it only to bring scandall on his brother and thinking thay wold all beare witness agaynst me."[54]

---

[52] Lyle Koehler presents these data and a lengthy and useful discussion of the subject, although his interpretation is very different from the one offered here, *A Search for Power*, 71–107.

[53] Ibid., 74.

[54] Ibid., 99.

Still, the unmarried servant victims are less surprising than the wives, who were thirty-five of the seventy-seven reported victims. It seems strange that rapists, who tended to be single men who knew their victims, dared to attack married women as often as they did, risking the maximum penalty. Would-be rapists in colonial New England clearly counted more categories of women fair game than they did in Montaillou, while the clans of the mountain village offered women surer if more selective protection against rape than Puritan laws and conscience.

The information here may at first appear difficult to sort out. The mountain women had a reputation for sharper tongues, but there is little sign of follow-up action on their part. New England women, who were more mindful of admonitions to be meek and obedient, were nonetheless more willing to go on the offensive in a fight and also more prepared to leave violent husbands. Montaillou women appear to have been more abused, both verbally and physically, but most had greater freedom from rape than the women in New England. While any Salem woman could report an attack and expect to be taken seriously, those women in Montaillou most subject to sexual violence had little practical recourse against would-be rapists.

Differences in the ways families were organized – and in their relative stability – can explain these apparent paradoxes. Males from the households of Montaillou retained the ability to control their women's sexuality through a combination of early marriage and enduring clan solidarity. Despite most households there having but a single married couple, other sons and male relatives lived nearby and stood ready to come to their aid and defend the family honor. (Such protection, to be sure, worked more effectively in the case of rape than in the case of more straightforward abuse and domestic violence against women.) In New England, by contrast, even if male kinfolk were close at hand, their strongest allegiances were likely to have shifted away from their natal households. Later marriage, domestic service, and geographic dispersal of the younger generations automatically increased single women's exposure to sexual assault. Similarly for wives, daily life in nuclear households necessarily entailed more exposure to the sexual advances of servants and other men.

It was not that husbands in Salem cared less than those in Montaillou if their wives were the victims of sexual assault. After all, laws that accorded the maximum punishment of death for the rape of wives were just one indicator that New England men cared a great deal about their wives, perhaps even more than the Montaillou men, whose loyalty to ostals often appears to have run well beyond their loyalty to wives. Still, their marriage and household arrangements by themselves gave the New England men less sure means to prevent assaults on either their wives or their daughters than Montaillou men had. Household heads were thus obliged to seek protection outside the surer bonds of kin, and they did so through the more fragile vehicles of law and individual conscience. It is no wonder that women in such circumstances were regularly admonished to "go so as to distinguish themselves from Handmaidens of the devil."[55] It is also no wonder that for a multitude of good reasons, many failed to do so.

Beyond showing how differences in household structures can explain otherwise confusing and contradictory evidence regarding violence and sexual assaults, such differences can also help to account for the massive and still unexplained shift by the early modern era in the ways men in northwestern European–based societies were coming to portray women's sexual and intellectual natures. As increasing numbers of single women left home to work in others' households, and as wives became obliged to serve as deputy husbands, strains developed around ancient presumptions that men in all agricultural societies had long shared about women. It is clear, however, that widespread beliefs that women are both mentally inferior and innately lascivious are far better suited to the early-marriage settings where they first appeared and where they long served as rationales for men's sequestering of women. In such settings, women's presumed mental deficiencies hardly matter, and their supposed licentious natures can readily be controlled through the mechanism of early marriage. In the late-marriage regions, by contrast, it was contrary to men's self-interest to continue to insist upon women's mental incompetence or to proclaim their inherent lust. Men were therefore increasingly obliged to devise ways to imagine women's intellectual and sexual natures that were more compatible with their own new requirements for competent wives who were governed more by reason than by passion.

Women in the early modern era, meanwhile, were not only more exposed to sexual attacks but – given their expanded mobility and independence as workers and as wives – more vulnerable to accusations of sexual immorality, from men as well as from other women.[56] A substantial literature has emerged of late describing women's new and active public defense of their honor and reputations in the period from the sixteenth through the eighteenth centuries. These studies show that while men's status and honor were also more at stake during this period than they had been earlier, men's reputations were linked to a broader range of behaviors, including their honesty and integrity, whereas women's reputations were held to be almost exclusively tied to their sexuality.

In England and the American colonies in particular, many single as well as married women actively sought redress for insults to their reputations in the courts. Although in England married women's legal agency was vested in their husbands under common law, ecclesiastical law allowed women to litigate in their own names. In the period from 1570 to 1640, to cite

---

[55] Karlsen, *The Devil in the Shape of a Woman*, xvix.

[56] For a good recent discussion with an excellent bibliography that includes continental as well as American studies, see Laura Gowing, *Domestic Dangers: Women, Words, and Sex in Early Modern London* (Oxford, 1998).

just one example, London church courts alone handled over 1,800 suits involving allegations of defamation and sexual misconduct. While men as well as women engaged in such suits, 85 percent of cases had at least one female litigant, and nearly half of the 6,000 witnesses were women.[57]

The readiness of women to go to court to defend their reputations needs to be understood in light of the peculiar marriage and household system that both promoted the women's activity in seeking redress for defamation of character and opened them to such charges in the first place. Interpreters of this rash of defamation suits, however, have overlooked the late-marriage system and ignored its critical role in setting the stage for these multiple legal dramas. They have instead explained the litigious behavior in more general terms, alleging that sexual tensions were characteristic of "patriarchal relations" during the early modern era.[58] That was true enough, but the explanation misses the reason for high sexual tensions in a marriage system that was altering time-worn habits in the relations between the sexes. The action that women, in particular, undertook in going to law to defend their names deserves to be seen as part of a broader set of initiatives women were now pursuing in household settings that were increasingly obliging them to become more dynamic and personally responsible social actors.

That women throughout this period from the sixteenth through the eighteenth centuries were coming to claim the right to refuse undesired sexual advances, and even to be credited for doing so, is a concurrent development that has also begun to be traced. Once again, however, the accounts fail to reference the ways late-marriage households literally established the critical conditions for this new behavior. In most other agricultural societies, after all, convictions as to women's more base sexual natures continued to ensure that a woman's sexuality was not hers either to withhold or deploy. While it is true that the odds against any woman's being able to fend off a determined seducer were great in this period, especially if he was a social superior, court records reveal a gradual acknowledgment of women's growing resistance to unwanted sexual advances. A late-seventeenth-century case from colonial Massachusetts recounted by Laurel Ulrich illustrates one stage in this important transition.[59]

The somewhat dubious heroine was a young Newbury woman named Mary Rolfe, whose husband, John, in spring 1663, left her and their baby behind for a fishing expedition to Nantucket. Before departing, John Rolfe arranged for a woman named Betty Webster to live with Mary, with the additional assurance that Betty's stepfather, their neighbor John Emery, would keep an eye on both woman. As Rolfe sailed out, however, two attractive English strangers, Henry Greenland and John Cordin, both physicians, sailed

[57] Ibid., 12.
[58] Ibid., 275.
[59] Ulrich, *Good Wives*, 89–92.

in and proceeded to take lodging in Emery's house. The easy manners of this pair at first captivated the two young women over a merry dinner at Goodman Emery's, but later frightened them when one night, after Mary and Betty had gone to bed, Greenland knocked on the window. Pleading that he only wanted to get out of the cold to smoke a pipe, Greenland persuaded the reluctant Betty to get up and let him in. While she was occupied in raking up the fire to get a light for his pipe, Greenland pulled off his clothes and climbed into the bed with Mary, who reportedly fainted. (Said bed, as was typical in New England dwellings, was located in "public space" next to the front door.)

What happened next has been pieced together from subsequent testimony in the county court. It appears that Greenland, who jumped out of the bed when Mary fainted, jumped back in and urged the women to lie still when a passing neighbor's servant, hearing the ruckus, knocked loudly on their door. When no one answered, the servant climbed in through a window and felt his way to the bedside, where he discovered Greenland and the distraught Mary. As this servant later testified, "The woman [Mary] and I went adore [outdoors] to Consider what was best to be done so we thought becas he was a stranger and a great man it was not best to make an up Rore but to let him go way in a private maner."[60] This they did; but the following Sunday at meeting, Mary's sister observed that she had been crying and alerted their mother, Goody Bishop, who came to visit her daughter the next day. Mary acknowledged that Greenland "with many Arguments inticed her to the act of uncleanness," but added that she, with God's help, had resisted.

Goody Bishop, insisting that "these things are not to bee kept private," asked Goodman Emery, who was a grand juryman, to bring Greenland to court; but Emery was unwilling to do so, promising only to keep a closer watch on his lodger and to lock up the hard liquor. On her way home, however, the unhappy Bishop met Emery's wife, who was more sympathetic. This pair then had a conversation with Mary and Betty that confirmed that Greenland's actions were even "more gross" than they first believed. Goody Bishop swung into action. As she later testified, after asking God's guidance, she visited a "wise man" in town who advised her to go to the magistrates. Greenland was tried by jury, convicted of attempted adultery, and fined a whopping thirty pounds. The citizens of Newbury thus supported a pious and pushy mother who was avenging her son-in-law's honor far less than her daughter's humiliation at the hands of a dazzling stranger.

In her perceptive analysis of the case, Laurel Ulrich compares this seventeenth-century real-life drama to Samuel Richardson's wildly popular novel *Pamela* (1740) of close to a century later, portraying each as markers in a transition from external to internal controls of sexual behavior in Western culture. Pamela, the maidservant heroine, resists the attempts of her rich and

[60] Ibid., 90.

titled master to seduce her and later persuades him to reform and marry her. Reading forward from what she calls the seventeenth-century "folk world" to the eighteenth-century middle-class enthusiasm for the novel's plucky heroine, Ulrich describes what was taking place at this time as the advent of a new sexual morality featuring greater female accountability.

Pamela's triumph was not in retaining her virtue but in seizing responsibility for her own behavior. Facing the tempter, she was not beguiled. If chastity was property in Richardson's novel, it belonged to the heroine, not to her father or to any other man. Using her own assets, Pamela won the title of wife. But victory over the sensual advances of Mr. B. was achieved only by overcoming the governance of Mrs. Jewkes [the old housekeeper paid to guard Pamela and eventually to deliver her over to her lecherous master], who had failed in her role as protector. It is as though Richardson were saying that the lore of the old wife was insufficient to protect a young woman in the changing world of the eighteenth century. Bereft of parents and of guardians, she must acquire a new world of values, breaking out of the ancient community of women into the sequestered paradise of an idealized marriage.[61]

The continuum from external to internal controls of sexual behavior can be traced more accurately, however, when, in addition to looking forward, one looks backward to the still submerged evolution of a distinctive family system. In most other agricultural regions, and to a lesser degree in earlier English and European manorial contexts as well, more stable family arrangements worked to keep women's sexuality under men's control – whether to protect it when it was part of their larger property strategies or to violate it at will when it was not. A sexual morality that ultimately obliged women to become more responsible for their own protection against unwanted sexual encounters brought difficulties of its own that are all too familiar. Yet it must be noted that this new morality was rooted finally in the evolution of a unique household system, one that literally obliged women to become ever more responsible actors, in sexual matters as in all else.

After all, the little drama of Mary Rolphe, Henry Greenland, and company could not have taken place in a traditional early-marriage setting, or even in a mixed setting such as Montaillou's, for obvious reasons. If a husband were leaving a young wife and baby for an extended time, special arrangements with friends and neighbors were hardly required, since resident or nearby kin – including the husband's mother and perhaps sisters-in-law – were right there, as were the husband's male relatives. Any passing stranger enjoying the hospitality of the household at this time would know full well that advances toward a wife and new mother there were out of the question, a risk not just of a fine but of horrible death. Nor would a young wife engage in the flirtation that Mary Rolfe permitted herself, an act that in such circumstances invited dishonor, at the least.

[61] Ibid., 105.

In the New England setting, the figure closest to a traditional avenger was the neighbor John Emery – not a blood relative but at least a man, and one who had given his word to Mary Rolphe's husband. In the event, however, when Emery refused to turn over to the authorities a man he had good reason to believe had tried to rape Rolphe's wife, it is no surprise that the new script for these distinctive household settings assigned the role of avenger to a female blood relative of the wife, not the husband. Women were not yet "official" public actors, but their enhanced role as partners in heading households made it perfectly reasonable for them to behave as Goody Bishop did – that is, to seek out a male magistrate empowered to take action and then to badger him into doing so.

It was already commonplace in such settings for married daughters to guard ties with their natal families and with mothers in particular, whereas most early-marriage settings make these relationships far more difficult to sustain. Modern historians picking up on later phases of these relationships in the nineteenth century have remarked that as urbanization advanced and ever more families lost their links with the soil, it was women, not men, who emerged as the day-to-day guardians of family networks and sociability.[62] What they have not recognized, however, is that mother–daughter ties, which are normally weakened if not broken by early-marriage structures, assumed unprecedented strength and importance as yet another overlooked effect of the late-marriage regime.

It is thus misleading to refer to these ties as "ancient" when speaking of the role of figures such as Goody Bishop. In intervening with authorities on behalf of a naive and wronged daughter, Bishop was playing a modern role, not an ancient one. A truly "ancient community of women" was and remains real enough in many places, but it is one in which enduring household structures still prompt daughters, wives, and mothers to follow a different and far older script – one that keeps central the welfare of the enduring male-controlled household.

*   *   *

This comparison of daily life in these two settings has shown how attention to different family structures can help explain women's and men's behavior and illuminate the power relations within households and communities. Still, differences in the ways early- and late-marriage households worked cannot alone account for a number of observed behaviors in the two communities, including, for example, the strength of the misogyny of Montaillou peasant men. Not fully explained, either, is why it was in Salem, where laws protected women from beating, where rape was treated as a crime of violence against women, and where men praised women's piety, that so many men and women

---

[62] Peter N. Stearns, *Be A Man! Males in Modern Society* (London, 1979), 48.

alike were prepared in 1692 to act on the belief that Devil-possessed women were turning their community upside down.

The excursion so far has provided some hints that will shortly be pursued while raising a still broader question prompted by the examples of Montaillou and Salem. That question is, when and why did people first come to envision womanhood and manhood as a set of changeable qualities and attributes that individuals can or should attempt to acquire, rather than as items that are presumed to be fixed or even innate? The discussion here suggests that the key to answering this question may lie in a fuller understanding of how people anywhere arrive at their working notions of who women and men are.

In Montaillou and in early-marriage societies more generally, two distinct worlds for the sexes served both to nurture and reinforce a perception that manhood and womanhood are somehow innate. Their specific features were experienced by women and men alike as fully embedded in their sex-segregated worlds. In Salem, women's and men's day-to-day worlds regularly overlapped, and the attributes of manhood and womanhood were a good deal more fuzzy. For example, while it is true that men did less women's work than women did men's, there was so much variety in men's occupations that it was far less obvious than in a place like Montaillou what men's work really was. Greater social divisions in Salem meant also that notions about womanhood and manhood varied far more by class or rank than they did in Montaillou. It is therefore much harder to detect a consensus in Salem on what women and men considered most basic to womanhood and manhood, which helps to explain why these issues were discussed there far more often.

It remains unclear why this increased fluidity in women's and men's daily activities might have prompted not only intense scrutiny of gender arrangements but also rising anxiety about the entire gender order. Nor is it obvious why men were the ones who were first to become concerned enough to parcel out a revised set of roles and qualities for the sexes, with particular attention to women. A closer look at the crises of heresy in Montaillou and witchcraft in Salem will begin to answer all these questions by forcing out what it was that both sexes, in those times and places anyway, held basic to their visions of womanhood and of manhood.

5

Communities in Crisis

Heresy, Witchcraft, and the Sexes in Montaillou and Salem

When the men of Montaillou complained among themselves about their lot, it did not occur to them to blame women for their troubles. They might label most women, including their own wives, "sows," "whores," or "devils," but in the troubled years after the turn of the fourteenth century, these peasants reserved their more heartfelt invective for the priests. One man whose anti-clerical hostility was inflamed by the tithe on sheep announced: "I wish all clerics were dead, including my own son, who is a priest."[1] Another, enraged by the bishop's agents who were sent to collect tithes on cattle, declared to his peasant cronies: "If only all the clerks and priests could go and dig and plough the earth.... As for the Bishop, let him meet me in a mountain pass; we will fight out this question of tithes, and I shall soon see what the bishop is made of!"[2]

Tithes were a recurring topic at the all-male gatherings in the village squares. "We're going to have to pay the *carnelages* [the tithe on livestock]," said one villager to some friends in 1320. "Don't let's pay anything," answered another of the men. "Let us rather find a hundred *livres* to pay two men to kill the Bishop." "I'll willingly pay my share," said a third. "Money could not be better spent."[3]

Village men with shared interests and occupations saw priests as intruders in their churches, which they considered their own property. They were angered when more orthodox clerics of the region used their power to excommunicate them for failure to pay tithes. One man told fellow excommunicants: "The church and its bells belong to us. We built it, we bought and put in it everything that was necessary. We keep it up. Woe to the Bishop and priests who drive us out of our parish church, who prevent

---

[1] Emmanuel Le Roy Ladurie, *Montaillou: The Promised Land of Error* (New York, 1979), 243.
[2] Ibid., 262.
[3] Ibid., 261.

us from hearing Mass there, and make us stand outside in the rain."[4] This man went so far as to propose that an unofficial mass be held outdoors for all people who were excommunicated.

Tithes were clearly not the only concern of these hard-pressed village men. While they cared a great deal about getting along in this life, they were also profoundly concerned about the next one. It is true that they viewed women as presenting some obstacles, to both their earthly stratagems and their heavenly ones. But the men of the Montaillou region did not take women's actual behavior seriously enough to be much concerned about it; and as already seen, the household structures they controlled go far to explain why. As their troubles mounted, those they vilified were instead outsiders – not the neighboring heads of ostals who were their usual adversaries in more normal times, but the men who enforced the policies of encroaching authorities from beyond the village, and especially the men who represented the universal Catholic Church.

In Salem, the day-to-day behavior of their own women figured large when men began to contemplate their woes. While their ministers might proclaim women a "necessary good," most men also believed that women were – at the very least – potentially dangerous creatures. It surprised no one at the time, and few since, that in the massive witch hunt that broke out in 1692, nearly three-quarters of the persons against whom formal legal action was taken were women.[5] One measure of the anxiety women might generate is the seemingly trivial set of events that ignited the outbreak in mid-January of that year. As the pastor in Salem Village later reflected, the "horrid calamity" was set off by the strange behavior of two young girls living in his own household. His nine-year-old daughter and a niece of eleven or twelve had fallen into apparent fits, complaining that they were being attacked by invisible tormenters. The pastor consulted a local physician who came up with a diagnosis that neighbors rapidly accepted: the two children, he said, had been bewitched. For their part, the girls were soon blaming Tituba, the family's female slave – a "Spanish Indian" probably from Florida or the Georgia Sea Islands – for magically hurting them.[6] Before long, older Village girls with symptoms mimicking those of this first pair began to accuse more alleged witches in the community.

The only independent eyewitness to record these developments in the pastor's household also recounted another episode from 1692 that has often been repeated in modern accounts of the origins of the outbreak. One of the ultimately forty-odd young female accusers, he said, became the victim of a "diabolical molestation" after engaging in a fortune-telling game whose

---

[4] Ibid., 261–62.
[5] Mary Beth Norton, *In the Devil's Snare: The Salem Witchcraft Crisis of 1692* (New York, 2002), 3–4.
[6] Ibid. 21.

object was to predict the trade of her future husband. Whatever the relationship of this episode to the more fully documented events involving the
two "afflicted" girls, we know that by the end of February, alarmed Salem
residents had filed complaints with their local magistrates.[7] By late spring,
scores of alleged witches named by the young accusers as responsible for
their torments – most of them women over forty (including a disproportionate number living alone) – had been interrogated by the local authorities and
were in jail awaiting trial.

In Montaillou, even though women were known to be the sex that dabbled
more regularly in witchcraft and magic, their recourse to spells, amulets, and
incantations appears to have aroused few suspicions among their menfolk.
Women supplemented their Catholicism with folk rituals and magic, which
they took less seriously than their formal faith but which they used in aid of
some special female enterprises. The chatelaine, for example, reported that
she had saved some of her daughter's first menstrual blood and concocted a
potion to bewitch a future son-in-law so that he would be faithful to his bride.
In Salem, by contrast, women using magic could hardly be held harmless. In
that community, there was force behind the pervasive belief that Satan most
often did his work "in the shape of a woman."[8]

Recent commentators on witchcraft have rightly remarked that now that
we no longer simply take it for granted that women were the chief targets
in the witch hunts of the early modern era, we must not assume that we
automatically understand the role of beliefs about women and gender in
these complex events. To argue that witchcraft persecutions were just another
instrument of male power – that witch hunts were, in effect, women hunts –
begs critical questions of time, place, and context that alone can make sense
of these episodes while ignoring that from the beginning, a number of accused
witches were men.[9] Once we have acknowledged that charges were based
on an accused witch's accepted (if, by modern standards, undemonstrated)
capacity to do harm within a community, we must confront an entire range of
data and interpretations that go well beyond any presumed blanket hostility
toward women.

Misogyny, in any case, was hardly confined to the European era of witch
hunts that ran from the mid-fifteenth to the mid-eighteenth centuries. Beliefs
in witchcraft and magic, moreover, continue to operate in many societies
even to this day. The popular link between women and witchcraft is itself

---

[7] This account is taken mostly from the Introduction and first chapter of Norton, *In the Devil's
Snare*, 3–43.

[8] Carol F. Karlsen's study, the source for much of the Salem material in this and the previous
chapter, is *The Devil in the Shape of a Woman: Witchcraft in Colonial New England* (New York,
1989).

[9] See the excellent discussion in Robin Briggs, *Witches and Neighbors: The Social and Cultural
Context of European Witchcraft* (New York, 1996), especially Ch. 7: "Men Against Women:
The Gendering of Witchcraft," 257–86.

ancient and widespread, and the popular concern regarding disobedient or disorderly women has been shown to be related less to issues such as the nature of evil or of the Devil than to the specific harm that might come to one's person or property through a neighbor's magic and malefic powers. As one commentator remarks, "The most fundamental question is not why early modern male elites thought women were particularly susceptible to the Devil's blandishments, but why early modern common people – female as well as male – thought women were particularly likely to use magical powers against them."[10] This question about the origins of a new and pervasive fear of ordinary women's aggressive power within their communities still awaits a plausible answer.

Historians have noted that there were clear differences between southern Europe, where practitioners of witchcraft were rarely pursued in formal prosecutions, and northern Europe, which was home to thousands of witch trials throughout the entire early modern era. One scholar considering the social and cultural setting of witchcraft has even speculated that the unusual family pattern in northwestern Europe – home to most of the incidents of the witch-hunt era – may help to explain why so many of the accused witches were older women, often poor widows. These women, he says, lacked the family protection more available to widows in the multifamily households of southern Europe.[11] Such protection has also been cited as available to older women in northwestern Europe before the decline in customary manorial support at the end of the medieval era, when the witch hunts there first got underway.[12]

These points and more will be supported here in an argument that the late-marriage, single-family household pattern not only helps to explain why older women were more vulnerable to accusations of witchcraft, but goes far to account for larger and still unresolved questions about the origins, character, and timing of the early modern witch hunts – as well as about the special features of the Salem outbreak. We turn first, however, to the religious crisis that was Catharism in fourteenth-century Montaillou.

* * *

In the case of Montaillou, the heresy that came to "infect" all but a handful of the forty-odd ostals turns out to have appealed most strongly to the male members of the clans. This was no accident. The chameleon heresy that was Catharism took on different colors in different places to reflect the most

---

[10] Edward Bever, "Witchcraft, Female Aggression, and Power in the Early Modern Community." *The Journal of Social History* 35, No. 4 (2002): 956.

[11] Briggs, *Witches and Neighbors*, 283–84.

[12] Elspeth Whitney, "International Trends; The Witch 'She'/The Historian 'He': Gender and the Historiography of the European Witch-Hunts." *The Journal of Women's History* 7, No. 3 (Fall 1995): 79, cited from Keith Thomas, *Religion and the Decline of Magic* (New York, 1971), 568.

pressing concerns of the declared faithful. In Montaillou, the most visible interests of men, even in ordinary times, were two: maintaining the integrity of family ostals and ensuring a route to salvation. As the men who headed the clans knew all too well, priests who represented the temporal and spiritual authority of the Church could threaten both of these cherished interests.

It might be imagined that village women would have equally strong interests in maintaining ostals and securing salvation, and that when heresy presented itself as an attractive means, in hard times, to secure these goals, they would have been as enthusiastic about the new Cathar faith as the men. But as will shortly be seen, this did not happen. Only a handful of the women displayed the fervent belief in heretical doctrines that was displayed by nearly all the men. Historian Le Roy Ladurie labels most women "passive" about Catharism, yet he misses the good reasons his own cited evidence provides for that alleged passivity. Stating that women were "more often than not governed by their emotions," he alleges that they "felt strange and uncomfortable in their new, unorthodox identity, and resistance soon stirred in hearts steeped in traditional thought and full of inexpressible feeling."[13]

Another interpretation works better than this condescending one. If women were passive about heresy because they were "steeped in traditional thought," the same ought to have held for the men: only 4 of the 250 or so villagers, after all, were literate.[14] It is more probable instead that the women of Montaillou, like the men, were perfectly capable of deciding where their interests lay, and there were good reasons for their divided loyalties. Household structures played a significant role, as they automatically ensured that a wife's attachment to her ostal would be weaker than her husband's. Also, while women appear to have been at least as committed as men to achieving salvation, Catholic doctrines turned out to match their own female priorities far better than did the heretical Cathar teachings. Women's reported attitudes and behavior reveal less a passivity about Catharism than a continued allegiance, in hard times and against the odds, to a Catholic faith that they actively chose to uphold.

Taking the men's "terrestrial" interests first, the interrogations repeatedly show that the ostal was the chief concern of the male members of each clan. Unlike women, who moved from their natal ostal to that of their husband, men had a firmer lifelong interest in their birth ostal; and usual strategies for its maintenance, as noted, included keeping heirship in the male line and marrying within the village. Even in normal times, however, men's plans might go awry. Sons might not be born or they might die young. Daughters might be too numerous, and their dowries could threaten an ostal's wealth and position. Bad harvests might destroy chances to meet obligations to

---

[13] Le Roy Ladurie, *Montaillou*, 258.
[14] Ibid., 239.

temporal or spiritual overlords; and endemic, often violent clan rivalries might compromise an ostal's status.

By the turn of the fourteenth century, there were new threats. The removal of the local lord's protection paved the way for a more systematic effort by the Church to extract wealth. What is more, between 1280 and 1305, Montaillou, and Europe generally, experienced a baby boom that put fresh strains on resources. Finally, after 1310, there were widespread food short-ages, which had been rare before then. In his study *The Great Famine*, William Jordan has recounted the catastrophic events of this pervasive famine, which occurred intermittently throughout Europe until 1322. The famine itself was the first genuine setback to rising living standards in Europe since a smaller harvest failure in the mid-thirteenth century, and it not only coin-cided with but also helps to explain the behavior of Montaillou peasants in turning to heresy.[15]

In such circumstances, men in particular were sharply reminded of ecclesi-astical constraints on their fragile strategies for their ostals. It was not simply that the Church was seen as rich and corrupt, although that view did attract many a local peasant to the ascetic Cathar faith. It was that the Church had long presented obstacles to hallowed local customs, in Montaillou and elsewhere, whose object was to keep family property intact. Given new pressures, it is easier to see why men, especially, would be drawn to heretical beliefs that could lend respectability to their anticlerical views.

Consider marriage strategy from the male head of household's point of view. The object was to contain the potential harm to his ostal from all his children, with their claims to fraternal portions and dowries. The commonest strategy was to limit all landed property to a single male heir and then to benefit as long as possible from the labor of each son. This was achieved in Montaillou by delaying the marriage of the heir (and the departure of any other sons) by means that included winking at visits to prostitutes in nearby towns and openly condoning concubinage. At least 10 percent of Montaillou couples, Le Roy Ladurie tells us, were "living in sin," many of them sons residing in parental ostals with imported female servants.[16] The Church formally forbade such unions; but Catharism would turn out, hardly by chance it appears, to be indulgent toward concubinage and to dismiss the orthodox Catholic doctrines on marriage.[17] Especially troubling to men, moreover, was the drain on ostals that daughters presented, with

---

[15] William Chester Jordan, *The Great Famine: Northern Europe in the Early Fourteenth Century* (Princeton, N.J., 1996).

[16] Le Roy Ladurie, *Montaillou*, Ch. 10: "Temporary Unions," 169–78.

[17] James A. Brundage, "Concubinage and Marriage in Medieval Canon Law," in James A. Brundage, ed., *Sex, Law, and Marriage in the Middle Ages* (Aldershot, U.K., 1993), Ch. 7, 1–17. This is a collection of Brundage's papers from several different journals with orig-inal pagination retained. This article was published in *The Journal of Medieval History* 1 (Amsterdam, 1975): 1–17.

their youthful marriages and their dowries. The issue led the heretic priest
Pierre Clergue to go so far as to justify incest:

Look, we are four brothers (I am a priest, and do not want a wife). If my brothers
Guillaume and Bernard had married our sisters Esclarmonde and Guillemette, our
house would not have been ruined because of the capital [*averium*] carried away by
those sisters as dowry; our ostal would have remained intact, and with just one wife
brought into our house for our brother Bernard [Raymonde], we would have had
enough wives, and our ostal would have been richer than it is today.[18]

Such views were extreme, yet villagers had clearly absorbed Church instruction that prohibited marriage within specified degrees of kinship. They
knew, too, that their own habit of intermarriage with local families presented problems in this regard. From the early Middle Ages, the Church had
evolved elaborate rules against marriages of blood kin and even of persons
related only by marriage. It enforced these rules either by refusing to sanction such marriages or by requiring dispensations, which cost money and
time to obtain. Encouraging out-marriage or exogamy – the practical effect
of forbidding marriages among kin – obviously made it harder for the laity
to maintain property intact by keeping it in the family.

Most commentators have nonetheless questioned anthropologist Jack
Goody's thesis that the Church's doctrine was driven from the start by a
conscious strategy to acquire more property.[19] A recent interpreter has made
a case that is more in line with the argument being made here for the strong
and continuing role of households as the major decision-making sites in this
and many other matters. Katherine Verdery maintains that rather than reflecting the Church's institutional drive to augment its property, these land
transfers were the instruments of powerful early medieval families located
chiefly in the feudalized regions of northern Europe, who used the Church
to protect their property from fellow kinsmen.[20]

Whatever the motives behind the Church's doctrines, there is no question
that by the fourteenth century, those doctrines regularly collided with the
practices of the male clan heads of Montaillou. By recognizing the validity
of marriages without parental consent, making marriage a sacrament, and
promoting respect for women and marital affection, the Church's policies
also tended to strengthen the conjugal unit, working to detach individuals
from the wider network of their kinfolk.[21] Women, whose right to inheritance was supported by the Church, often did give or will property for

---

18 Le Roy Ladurie, *Montaillou*, 36.
19 See, for example, Natalie Davis's review of *The Development of the Family and Marriage in
    Europe* by Jack Goody, *American Ethnologist* 12 (1985): 149–51.
20 Katherine Verdery, "A Comment on Goody's *Development of the Family and Marriage in
    Europe.*" *Journal of Family History* 13, No. 2 (1988): 265–70.
21 These points are underscored by Jack Goody, *The Development of the Family and Marriage in
    Europe* (Cambridge, 1983).

religious use, especially in northwestern Europe. But the families of southern Europe, including the clans of Montaillou, were able to rely upon their early-marriage household structures to help keep landed property out of women's hands. They also compromised the prohibited degrees of marriage at the limit of first cousins. A local heretic from the Sabarthes region affirmed with gusto this flagrant defiance of religious injunction: "To sleep with my second cousin? For me, that is neither a sin nor a shameful act. There is a common proverb in Sabarthes which says: 'With a second cousin, give her the works.'"[22]

Even before the arrival of heresy, it was clear that Catholic teachings appealed to women as mitigating some of the harsher features of sexual and social life. After Cathar goodmen came to town, the mountain women persisted in orthodox loyalties, reflecting their evident view that their own interests were better served by the Catholic faith than by a heretical doctrine that – in Montaillou anyway – was the tool of male clan strategy. The itinerant and self-appointed Cathar goodmen did not stop with promises that living out of wedlock or marrying their first cousins would never bar the villagers from Paradise. They volunteered to take confessions and even boasted that they were better at saving souls than the Catholic priests. "The *parfaits* [goodmen] of our sect have as much power to absolve sins as had the Apostles Peter and Paul," declared one of the heretic leaders. "Those who follow us go in the end to Heaven, and the others to Hell."[23]

Another goodman charged that the priests "do not do their duty, they do not instruct their flock as they should, and all they do is eat the grass that belongs to their sheep."[24] To the contrary, most priests in the area – with the exception of Montaillou's infamous heretic and fornicator Pierre Clergue – preached orthodox doctrine, which was what the male villagers held against them in the first place. In testimony ranging from beliefs in resurrection of the body to fasting, confession, prayer, icons, and more, it is men who are almost always portrayed cleaving to the Cathar faith as the true Christianity and women who are seen holding back. Far from being a barrier between fathers and sons, heresy became another bond between the generations of men. A shepherd testified to the intermingling of his loyalty to the paternal ostal and to the heretical faith: "Three times the house of my father and mother was destroyed for heresy; and I myself cannot cure myself of heresy, for I must hold the faith my father held."[25]

Women, on the other hand, are often portrayed asking doubting questions about the goodmen. One of the few active female heretics, the priest's mother, Mengarde Clergue, is seen in conversation with her daughter Guillemette,

[22] Le Roy Ladurie, *Montaillou*, 328.
[23] Ibid., 310.
[24] Ibid., 317.
[25] Ibid., 125.

who is confused about why, if the itinerant preachers are heretics, they can still be called goodmen. "You are a silly, ignorant girl," says her mother. "They are goodmen because they send people's souls to Heaven." "And how," the daughter replies, "can heretics send souls to Heaven, when priests hear confession and handle the body of the Lord, so that, it is said, souls may be saved?" "It is plain that you are young and ignorant," answers her mother.[26]

More commonly, it is men who attempt to persuade skeptical women that Cathar teachings are superior to those of the priests. Gauzia Clergue, wife of the namesake of the heretic bailiff Bernard Clergue, encounters a neighbor during Lent who declares that he ate some fine meat for lunch the day before. He tells her he has been advised by the heretics that "it's just as great a sin to eat meat out of Lent as in Lent. It soils the mouth just as much. So don't you worry about it." Gauzia Clergue claims she told him she did not accept such ideas. "Meat in Lent or out of Lent, from the point of view of sin it is not at all the same thing."[27] Women's allegiances, admittedly, are more evident from their reported behavior than from their pronouncements. Yet they are often seen citing Catholic doctrines in defense of their own female concerns.

It was risky for a woman to appeal to orthodoxy in a village where male control of ostals was so great and where the priest himself had Cathar sympathies. Fabrisse Rives, an illegitimate cousin of the Clergues, was thrown out by her Cathar husband for her Catholic sympathies. She then took up wine-selling and raised her daughter, Grazide, as well as she could, with some help from her cousin, Bernard Clergue, the priest's brother. Once she dared to upbraid the priest over one of his many love affairs: "You are committing an enormous sin by sleeping with a married woman," she said.[28] But Pierre Clergue dismissed her, just as he had done when she had earlier tried to report to him a clandestine "heretication," the Cathar ceremony conducted over a dying person prior to the death fast. The priest seduced her daughter, Grazide, when she was fourteen, and later found the girl a husband, even though he continued to be her lover for several years. This time Fabrisse kept quiet, telling the Inquisitors that she did not want to admit that she knew the faults of the priest and his brothers, since she was afraid that if she did, she would be ill-used by them.

Grazide herself later told the Inquisitor that until their affair ended, she had felt no sin in her lovemaking because she had experienced pleasure in the act. Women in Grazide's position, from illegitimate lines, had no access to the larger inheritance system that guarded the chastity of daughters through clan controls. Indeed, Grazide's husband consented to the relationship with the powerful priest – so long as his wife slept with no other men! Grazide

---

[26] Ibid., 257.
[27] Ibid., 314.
[28] Ibid., 157.

testified after the imprisonment of her relatives Pierre and Bernard Clergue that if she had informed on them earlier, she would surely have been beaten or killed by them. From prison, Bernard tried to persuade Fabrisse and Grazide to testify falsely to the Catholic orthodoxy of his ostal, but illegitimate blood was not thick enough for this assignment. Grazide told Bernard, "Do you think anyone wants to go to the stake just to please you?" Her mother agreed. "I'd sooner Bernard were grilled than me."[29]

Among Montaillou women, vocal proponents of the heretical faith were found in only the three wealthiest households, all of which were strongly Cathar. The high status that came from their men's property and influence explains the greater willingness of these women to embrace their men's religious loyalties. Of the households in the village, eleven were strongly identified with heresy, twenty-nine showed leanings to Catharism, and just five were considered Catholic. Given this breakdown, it is significant that two of the three female-headed households were among the handful that took strong Catholic stands. (The most influential Catholic ostal had blood ties to the Bishop Inquisitor.)

Other factors contributed to the allegiance to orthodoxy that can be detected beneath the women's outward compliance with the heretical faith. For one thing, the most committed Cathar men emerge in testimony as the most rigorous misogynists. Cathar practices entailed more exclusion of women than did Catholic and earlier folk traditions. Cathars attempted to remove women as official mourners at deathbeds on the grounds that women's impurity defiled the heretical rituals. (On one occasion, Montaillou women were quick to notice that the absence of the sounds of traditional women's laments from the ostal of a dying village matriarch indicated that the woman was undergoing a secret heretication.) More revealing than the Cathar label on most of the ostals, then, is evidence that most women quietly persisted in the observances of their orthodox faith.

Testimony is full of examples of women appealing to Catholic teachings for some leverage in their daily lives, slight though it might turn out to be. They are often cited as visiting the churches to pray on days other than Sundays, even though Cathar men tried to persuade them that they could pray just as well from their ostals. Against beatings and other physical abuse, women turned to admonitions about Christian tenderness and mercy.

Catholic doctrines also offered women some defense against sexual advances. Once when a shoemaker lodging in an ostal set upon a servant woman, he insisted with the fervor of his new Cathar faith that there would be no sin in the act. The servant – who was also mistress to the landlord – reported her shock that this lodger, who was the landlord's first cousin, would dare to dismiss that kinship in making overtures to her. She knew that sex with the shoemaker counted as incest in canon law, even though her

[29] Ibid., 270.

relationship to the landlord was based on concubinage and not marriage. She angrily reminded the shoemaker, "Are you not ashamed? You forget that I am mistress to your first cousin (and landlord) Bernard Belot, and that I have children by him."[30] The attacker retreated, and the woman claimed that the experience made her renounce her own flirtation with Catharism. "I believed in the errors of the heretics until Arnaud Vital tried to rape me. But then, because of this incest, I stopped believing in these errors."[31]

Indirect evidence for women's persistent orthodoxy is men's strong interest in usurping mothers' traditional role as religious educators of daughters. Men often discussed the need for women to have an "understanding of good," namely, heresy; and their talk shows that they no longer trusted women in this teaching role. One heretic tried to persuade a shepherd that the best way to get a right-thinking wife was to become betrothed to the six-year-old daughter of one of his heretic friends: "Raymond Pierre," he said, "will nurture his daughter Bernadette so well that, with the help of God, she will have the understanding of good."[32] Women nonetheless quietly resisted men's efforts and continued to pass on orthodox convictions to their daughters.

Most important of the interests that kept women loyal to the Church were their concerns for marriage and especially motherhood. What recognition was available for women in this misogynist community was reserved for the mothers of legitimate children, especially sons and heirs, even though women might wait for such recognition until they were past childbearing age and became family matriarchs. From most women's point of view, a faith that supported and even celebrated the institutions of marriage and motherhood, while condemning concubinage, was bound to be preferable to one that gave only grudging support to the former and actively encouraged the latter.

Admittedly, few women openly opposed their men's turn to heresy, although there were some cases of stubborn wives. One disappointed Cathar, tricked by his father-in-law into marrying a devout Catholic woman, endured twenty-five years of domestic silence to avoid being turned over to the Inquisition. Women also dared to use their household roles and orthodox beliefs for more short-term ends. One wife refused her husband's request to entertain the goodmen in their ostal. Another warned that her son's marriage into an ostal infected by heresy could bring only trouble. (It did.) Yet another saw right through her husband's ruse in pretending to have a skin ailment so that he could leave their ostal – ostensibly to find a cure but in fact to visit the goodmen.

I would have liked to go to Sabarthes, to meet the goodmen in secret. So I scratched my arms as hard as I could, as if I had scabies; and I lied to people and said, "I ought

[30] Ibid., 45.
[31] Ibid., 150.
[32] Ibid., 80.

to go to the baths at Ax [-les-Thermes]. But my wife (she was very anti-Cathar) said, "No, you're not going to the baths." And she would say to people who came, "Don't go praising the baths at Ax. It will make my husband want to go there."[33]

These glimpses of domestic interchanges show that women could and did assert some authority within ostals, and that Cathar husbands took them seriously enough to reckon the threat to themselves or their heretic friends. That men often warned women not to inform on people suggests they had reason to believe women were the ones most likely to do so. In fact, a disproportionate number of informers were women from outside the village, who might use the vehicle of confession (to their own more orthodox priests) to finger heretics. In the end, the male blood relationship held out better than the marriage relationship. Husband and wife might be turned against one another, but the Bishop Inquisitor could not turn father against son or brother against brother.

In their search for salvation, women's distinctive priorities are further mirrored in their behavior. Cathar outbreaks earlier and elsewhere did attract women, often noble widows who even became "goodwomen" ministering to female believers and establishing convents. But Catharism in early-fourteenth-century Montaillou had little appeal to women as a route to eternal life. Cathar men might paint Paradise as a plentiful ostal so vast that, as one heretic declared, it "stretched from the Merens Pass to the town of Toulouse."[34] Yet their women do not seem to have been moved.

Women remained on the sidelines as male heretics argued against the devotion to Mary that had been actively promoted by the Church in the late Middle Ages. The heretics minimized the role of Mary and rejected the *Ave Maria* as an invention of the priests. In the words of one Montaillou Cathar: "God did not receive human flesh from the Blessed Mary, nor did she give birth to Him, nor was she the mother of God. . . . It is improper to suggest and to believe that the Son of God was born of a woman and was contained in such a lowly thing as a woman."[35]

Women, by contrast, appear in testimony praying to the Virgin, lighting candles for her aid in returning stolen property, and invoking the Virgin to keep heretical views away from their hearts. Far oftener than men, they are reported to exclaim: "Sancta Maria!," a popular expression suggesting the direction of their faith. Some women also made it clear that they saw the Virgin as a redeemer in her own right. A maidservant asked by a Cathar what she believed said she had faith in God and in the Virgin Mary. She added that her mother, who instructed her in her faith, warned her against the claims of the Cathar goodmen: "Do not believe, daughter, that a man

---

[33] Ibid., 222.
[34] Ibid., 283.
[35] Shulamith Shahar, *The Fourth Estate: A History of Women in the Middle Ages* (New York, 1983), 259.

of flesh, who produces excrement, can save souls. Only God and the Virgin Mary have that power."[36]

In only one arena did women take a formal stand against the men and their Cathar doctrines. That was in their resistance to the harshness of the Cathar heretication ritual and death fast, especially in the case of children. Testimony does confirm that parents of both sexes showed great affection for their children, and that mother and father alike might grieve deeply when a child died. A case from a neighboring village in which a couple's seriously ill baby daughter was hereticated, however, shows the difference there could be between a father's and a mother's response in the context of Cathar beliefs.

The ritual of heretication violated all the rules for one so young, but the father persuaded a goodman to perform the ceremony anyway. Afterward, the mother was warned that the child was not to be given any milk or meat, and the father said: "If Jacotte dies, she will be an angel of God. Neither you nor I, wife, could give our daughter as much as this heretic has given her." The mother testified that soon after her husband and the goodman left, "I could not bear it any longer. I couldn't let my daughter die before my very eyes. So I put her to the breast. When my husband came back, I told him I had fed my daughter." The man calling his wife a devil, wept and threatened her. "After this scene," she said, "he stopped loving the child; and he also stopped loving me for a long while, until later, when he admitted that he had been wrong."[37] Their reconciliation took place when their entire village decided to renounce heresy. The child survived for another year.

This mother was not alone among women in resisting the rigors of the death fast for a child. When a seriously ill young woman who, though married, had returned by custom to die in her family ostal, her mother was ordered by a clansmen after a heretication not to give the dying woman anything more to eat or drink, even if she asked for it. The mother replied, "If my daughter asks me for food or drink, I shall give it to her."[38] Another woman with a sick baby resisted when her brother-in-law suggested the child ought to be hereticated "so that he should become an angel." The mother replied, "I will not refuse my child the breast, as long as he is still alive."[39] In yet another case, a mother pleaded with her fifteen-year-old son, a shepherd who was spitting blood, not to be hereticated, as his shepherd friends were urging. "My son," she said, "do not do that; it's enough that I should lose you, for I have no other son. I don't want to lose all my possessions as well because of you." But when her son begged her to "let a good Christian come

[36] Le Roy Ladurie, *Montaillou*, 299.
[37] Ibid., 211–12.
[38] Ibid., 227.
[39] Ibid., 229.

and save my soul," she relented.[40] Hereticated in the presence of his sisters, his mother, and his brother-in-law, the boy died soon afterward.

Given their outward compliance in so many other matters, these women's reactions amounted to strong and public resistance to a Cathar ritual that they could not celebrate as men did. While they might not have the final say, given pressure from heretics or from children themselves, they were prepared to risk contradicting their men. That their single open resistance to heresy occurred in the realm of their role as mothers is understandable. It was as mothers that the mountain women felt the strongest affirmation of their contributions to the clans. And it was as mothers of sick and dying children that they were least likely to embrace the cold comforts of the Cathar faith.

Women also resisted Cathar rules against women's presence at a death bed, though the goodmen complained that even the sheets of a marriage bed defiled the ritual. Angry over the Cathars' denunciation of women, a Catholic man once upbraided a heretic with the reminder that women, too, have a right to resurrection after death. Neither in earthly nor in heavenly matters, however, did Catharism as interpreted by the men of the clans have much to offer women. Under the circumstances, their opposition to Cathar death rituals constituted no little bravery.

Heresy therefore appears to have flourished in early-fourteenth-century Montaillou because the usual methods men employed for shoring up ostals – as well as for guaranteeing salvation – were falling short in the face of more rigorous tithe collection and a population boom followed by a European-wide famine. Much of the picture of daily life seen here, however, was probably not far removed from the Montaillou scene before and after Catharism. For men, the single most vexing issue about women was their dowries. Men concluded that the Catholic authorities, by upholding women's right to dowries, as well as a set of troubling marriage regulations, were responsible for their troubles in making ostal strategy work. Difficulties over women's dowries loomed larger as men began to realize that women's religious allegiances did not transfer so readily to the brand of Catharism they were preaching. Never doubting that it was the Church that finally stood in their way, men were increasingly prepared to regard women as obstacles to their plans, especially as the Church appeared to be taking the women's side.

The puzzling intensity of their misogyny, then, appears to be owing to men's growing awareness that women did not fully share either their earthly or heavenly priorities. Worse, women were guarding loyalty to a Church whose priests were threatening to ruin their ostals. Still, Montaillou men did not show fear of the dangerous power of their women, as Salem men did. Given what testimony reveals about the extent to which household structures continued to provide built-in male control over women's lives, it would have been odd if they had.

[40] Ibid.

Before leaving Montaillou, it is necessary to pause before some disquieting evidence. Although the Inquisition register reveals much about death and death rituals, the witnesses are silent about birth and birth rituals. Especially strange is that of the eighteen Montaillou couples who married and completed their families between 1280 and 1324, over twice as many male offspring are mentioned (forty-two) as female (twenty). LeRoy Ladurie sees nothing sinister, suggesting that in male-dominated Montaillou, girls were just "under-estimated and under-recorded."[41] But if all these "missing" girls were truly part of the community, it remains puzzling that twice as many male as female children are mentioned in the accounts of witnesses during 370 long days of testimony.

If the possibility is entertained that there were actually far fewer girls than boys at this time in Montaillou, and that Montaillou parents were allowing some of their baby girls quietly to die and/or committing female infanticide to control their numbers at a time of population boom and famine, then much other information falls into place. That would explain the evident surplus of men at marriageable ages (all those bachelor shepherds), especially as we are told that no woman was left a spinster forever and that only a handful of marriageable girls left the village. Given the far younger marriage age of brides compared to grooms, if sex ratios in Montaillou were roughly equal, there should have been a female surplus at marriageable ages, not a male one.

Much other evidence portrays girls as a greater liability to households than boys, following the typical early-marriage pattern. Testimony has already been shown to be full of male resentment over daughters who took dowries away from the ostals. Also, far greater value was placed on male than female labor, and with good reason. Montaillou's agricultural system, in a poor climate, did not provide the abundant fieldwork that absorbed so much of women's labor in the richer areas of northwestern Europe. Even there, population pressures in the late thirteenth and early fourteenth centuries led to unbalanced sex ratios in favor of boys. It is hard not to conclude that in the mountain community of Montaillou at that same time, female babies were at special risk.

Catholicism had long taught the faithful that infanticide was forbidden, so the silence about infancy and birth rituals in confronting the Inquisitors may be explained by fear of exposure. We know that Cathar men in Montaillou did flout Catholic doctrine by preaching against procreation, a dogma that meshed well with the concern to protect living standards in a period of bad harvests. The Cathar death fasts assume an even more somber aspect in this light, as they may have been prompted by the desire to give religious sanction

---

41 Ibid., 204. Lawrence Stone comments on these unbalanced sex ratios and suggests that "many female infants may have been quietly allowed to die," *The Family, Sex and Marriage in England, 1500–1800* (New York, 1977), 117.

to a desperate strategy of withdrawing support from weaker members of the community who were draining precious resources in a time of famine.

Women, who are seen more often than men grieving over lost children, were comforted by male heretics who cited the very unorthodox doctrine of reincarnation to persuade them that the soul of a dead child might live again in another baby. It cannot be proved that the appeal of Catharism owed something to its consolation to troubled consciences using starvation and infanticide to defend ostals in hard times, but the evidence is strong. If responses to the threat to resources included the selective elimination of female infants, women's lukewarm attachment to heresy can be even more keenly appreciated.

* * *

The dynamic of a very different set of gender and power arrangements is on display in late-seventeenth-century Salem. Heresy in Montaillou served to uncover wide consensus on a manhood that was most deeply invested in the defense of ostals. It also exposed a womanhood that was bound most tightly to the experience of motherhood. While many other factors affected how people in Montaillou thought and acted, including their social position, age, family status, and occupation, gender appears to have been the most salient component of identity for most villagers; and clearly delineated gender priorities informed everyone's behavior. This finding is worth keeping in mind in turning to the bewitched community that was Salem, Massachusetts, in 1692.

Just as heresy was no historical accident in Montaillou, the outbreak of witchcraft in Salem was hardly the aberration some have claimed. Emerging social, economic, and political divisions between Salem Town and Village, and among Villagers themselves, have already been outlined. What is more, Mary Beth Norton has lately discovered that many of the puzzling features of the Salem outbreak that make it an anomaly – even among other witchcraft episodes in New England – can be explained only in light of contemporary Indian wars on the Maine frontier, wars that directly or indirectly involved numerous participants of both sexes and all social ranks in the Salem crisis. In the Puritan community, as in Montaillou, these internal and external conflicts were viewed through a theological lens and interpreted by acknowledged spokesmen of the faith. In Salem, however, most Villagers held to a single creed, and it was one that had ceased to be regarded as heretical. In Salem, too, most of those who came to be suspected as rebels against that creed were women, not men.

From 1689, Samuel Parris, the first minister to serve after the Village received church status, was the spiritual leader of the Salem Villagers. The embattled Mr. Parris embodied the strains built into men's lives at a time when the rules for achieving the status of adult manhood were shifting dramatically. Himself the nearly disinherited younger son of a London cloth merchant, Parris had decided to take his chances in the New World, where he first set out to enter into commerce, like his father. But when he failed to make a success of the wharf and warehouse he purchased in Boston in 1682, he took up the ministerial calling, touting it as more honorable in its ties to the stable values of rural society as opposed to the sordid ones of the marketplace. Despite quarrels with his new flock (he haggled over salary for more than a year before his appointment), Parris's ambivalence toward the commercial world resonated well with the rural Villagers' sense of being at once attracted to and repelled by the secular values of Salem Town.

Like Parris, several farmers in the church had failed at commercial ventures; and like him, they resented the prosperity of outsiders who were leading less godly lives. From 1689 to 1692 the little congregation was harangued in weekly sermons describing an encircling menace to their church, itself held up as a last refuge against the massing of devils on the outside. By the spring of the outbreak, Parris was describing an even more terrifying vision: "There are devils as well as saints...here in Christ's little church."[42]

As Paul Boyer and Stephen Nissenbaum discovered some time ago, these simmering class and status resentments played themselves out in the witchcraft episodes.[43] A number of the accused witches from the Village turned out to live on the east side, closest to the supposedly corrupting influence of Salem Town. Several of these women were married to men who, while agriculturalists themselves, had many dealings with the merchants of the Town. Others were inn- or tavern-keepers, heavily involved with the Town's commercial life. The accusers and their supporting witnesses were more likely to be women and men from the more isolated western part of the Village, many of them experiencing a resentment-filled downward mobility.

That struggles among older agricultural and newer commercial interests were reflected in divisions between witches and their accusers was simply an updated version of long-standing patterns of neighborly hostilities and resentments that had characterized witchcraft incidents in communities for many generations. Other elements that paralleled earlier episodes, both in New England and in old England and continental Europe, were the "fits" of young women alleging torment by invisible attackers as well as the disproportionately large number of quarrelsome older women among the accused witches, including women with questionable reputations. Typical, too, was the cited use by witches of *maleficium* – that is, magical powers to harm the

---

[42] Paul Boyer and Stephen Nissenbaum, *Salem Possessed: The Social Origins of Witchcraft* (Cambridge, 1974), 164.

[43] Boyer and Nissenbaum's *Salem Possessed* is the fullest spelling out of the long-standing economic and religious discord between Salem Village and Town.

property, health, livestock, and general well-being of neighbors and their children. Common elsewhere as well was that other persons who came to be accused as witches were related to these more stereotypical women, often as husbands or close kin.[44]

Other items in the Salem story, only lately spelled out in Mary Beth Norton's remarkable *In the Devil's Snare*, set these 1692 outbreaks apart and, until her study appeared have been either ignored or unexplained.[45] These irregularities include the large numbers of accusers and accused – far more than in the biggest prior outbreak in New England in the 1660s, in which just eleven persons were accused – and rivaling the major seventeenth-century outbreaks in England and Scotland.[46] Salem's outbreak also featured a geographical extension well beyond most prior incidents, with accused witches not only from neighboring towns but from the entire region of Massachusetts's Essex County.

In addition, although the accusers in earlier cases had typically been adult men, the chief accusers in the Salem outbreak were women and girls under twenty-five. In Salem, too, there was demonstrably greater readiness both to convict and execute accused witches, notwithstanding the greater reliance of magistrates on the testimony of the youthful female accusers, along with "confessions" of witches who spoke both in spectral form through the girls and "in bodily form" in their own examinations. Finally, the Salem episode was distinctive for the abruptness with which it ended, with the community repudiating by late 1692 a witch hunt it had eagerly embraced only months before.

In her study, Norton acknowledges the many features that the outbreak shared with other New England outbreaks, noting that these similarities owed much to the participants' common worldview with other colonial settlers. They saw themselves, she says, as a chosen people among the heathen who functioned in an invisible world of spirits as well as in a day-to-day world of ordinary objects and tasks – with both of these worlds being controlled by an omnipotent deity. At the same time, however, Norton contends that the anomalies that made the Salem outbreak so distinctive derived from their heretofore undiscovered connections with the disastrous frontier wars in which the Indians acted in alliance with the French Catholics.

Norton uncovers the many links of accused and accusers as well as of magistrates and governors with these devastating events, in which thriving settler communities were wiped out. She shows, in particular, that the political and military leaders who were implicated in ongoing setbacks and defeats on the frontier were the very Massachusetts men who served as key

---

[44] This summary of the similarities of Salem with earlier outbreaks, as well as of the unique features there, is based upon the discussion in Norton, *In the Devil's Snare*, 7–10.

[45] See footnote 5.

[46] Norton, *In the Devil's Snare*, 8, and note 19, 330.

officials, including judges, in the Salem witchcraft trials. The discussion here will not dwell upon either the wars or the trials themselves, but it will argue that Norton's findings and the broader interpretive framework she presents not only make it easier to understand the Salem outbreak itself but also confirm the comparative arguments being set forth here about the influence of household arrangements on gender and power relations.

It will be recalled that early in 1692 young women appeared as the first accusers of witches. The daughter and niece of the minister were soon joined by others in displays that included fits and other signs of demonic possession, behavior recently made familiar to colonists by the Boston minister Increase Mather, who publicized an earlier case of alleged possession. The girls initially accused as their tormenters three Salem "witches": Sarah Good, the homeless and destitute wife of a propertyless farm worker; Sarah Osbourne, a remarried widow of dubious reputation; and, Tituba Indian, a slave in the Parris household. Brought in by local magistrates, the accused were examined before the "possessed" young women. Good and Osbourne denied they were hurting the girls; but Tituba Indian, who practiced folk magic and was less sensitive to the dangers of admitting so in that Puritan culture, offered a detailed if contradictory account of her services to the Devil. All three were sent off to Boston to await trial.

Trial proceedings were delayed pending the arrival of a new colonial governor, but public accusations and formal examinations by local Salem magistrates continued apace, their volume owing much to refugee accusers from the Maine frontier who joined the ranks of the "afflicted" young girls and began to implicate many figures in militant conspiracies. A former minister of the Salem Village church who had moved north to Falmouth was held up as a ringleader of intrigue with the Indians. To local residents whose friends and relatives had been harmed, and whose menfolk had been sent off to fight an elusive enemy, a heightened atmosphere of fear and suspicion made the new accusations more credible, including those of colony leaders and their spouses held to have betrayed their own people in demonic alliances with the Wabanaki chieftains.

As this witch-led conspiracy grew, ever more residents of Essex County began to recall and recount bygone happenings about those among them long suspected to be witches. From April to September 1692, residents from throughout the county made their way to Salem Village to testify that this accused witch had brought death to his child, that one had bewitched a pig she sold him, and the other (in spectral form) had come into his bed at night and nearly suffocated him. One witch specialized in filling rag dolls with pins and hiding them in a wall, another corrupted the youth with homemade cider in a noisy makeshift tavern at "unseasonable" hours, and yet another had a habit of begging and leaving her neighbors' houses muttering curses. A possessed girl claimed that a woman adorned with a snake "familiar" had tried to get her to sign the Devil's book. Matrons appointed to search this woman's body for witches' teats found an "apreternathurall Excresence of flesh between the pudendum and Anus."[47]

Overall, forty-one persons – most of them young single women between sixteen and twenty-five – were "possessed" in the Salem outbreak. An estimated 200 were accused of witchcraft, and at least 144 persons (38 of them male) had formal legal charges brought against them.[48] Fifty-four persons confessed to engaging in witchcraft.[49] The Boston and Salem jails were already full of suspects awaiting trial in May when the new Governor, Sir William Phips, accompanied by Cotton Mather's father, Increase Mather, who had helped secure a new charter for the colony, arrived from England. The Governor named a special court to try the accused, and the judges swiftly got to work, even as accusations continued to mount.

The links to the frontier wars explain much of what made the Salem events anomalous – especially why so many people were charged with witchcraft, so many defendants convicted and hanged, and the testimony of the "afflicted girls" so long accepted. As Norton points out, colonists who had engaged in hostilities with the Indians and French intermittently since the mid-1670s came to attribute what became repeated and serious losses of families, livestock, and shipping not to the mistakes of their military and political leaders but instead to divine providence. God, they decided, was punishing them for their many sins.

When in early 1692 the young girls had begun to have fits similar to those recorded elsewhere – fits whose onset Norton suggests may even have been influenced by the wartime context, since the afflicted had first accused an "Indian" of torturing them – the attacks from both the visible and invisible worlds became closely associated in New Englanders' minds. Magistrates who under normal circumstances displayed some skepticism in the face of witchcraft charges were now prepared to find a witchcraft conspiracy plausible. In Norton's words, by midsummer these men were

heavily invested in the belief that Satan lay behind the troubles then besetting their colony. And with good reason: if the devil was active in the land, how could they – mere mortals outwitted by the evil angel's many stratagems and wiles – be responsible for their failure to defend Maine and its residents adequately? Unable to defeat Satan in the forests and garrisons of the northeastern frontier, they could nevertheless attempt to do so in the Salem courtroom.[50]

By mid-October, however, in the face of growing concerns about so-called spectral evidence in the girls' testimony that had been accepted by the Puritan judges as proof against accused witches, the Governor decided to suspend the court's proceedings. By that time, twenty-two women and five men had

---

[47] Boyer and Nissenbaum, *Salem Possessed*, 13.
[48] Karlsen, *The Devil in the Shape of a Woman*, 40.
[49] Norton, *In the Devil's Snare*, 3–4.
[50] Ibid., 226.

already been tried and convicted; and fourteen of the women and all five of the men had been hanged. (Another man who had pleaded innocent but refused to answer the ritual question of whether he agreed to be tried had been pressed to death with stones in a failed effort to extract his consent to a trial.) By the time a newly created Massachusetts Superior Court tried the remaining cases in 1693, many who had confessed to being witches had retracted their statements. Most of the new trials ended in acquittals, and even those convicted were reprieved.

Toward the end, despite growing numbers who had begun to express concern that innocent persons had been accused, the influential Cotton Mather continued to defend the court. It is true that several of the judges were among his wealthiest parishioners in Boston's Old North Church, including a merchant who was the largest contributor to his salary; but it does appear that Mather's confidence in the court, including spectral evidence, was sincere.[51] For the less stout of heart, however, there had been incidents that raised doubt. It had not eased matters in July, for example, when Sarah Good, convicted on spectral testimony that her apparition had harmed many witnesses, delivered this parting shot to the minister of the Salem Town church just before she was executed: "I am no more a Witch than you are a Wizard, and if you take away my Life, God will give you Blood to drink."[52]

Cotton Mather interpreted the whole affair to his congregation as a diabolical plot to destroy New England, a corner of the world the Evil One was desperate to reclaim in the last days before Christ's Second Coming. By then, however, his father, Increase, had circulated his own view that regardless of the activity of devils, spectral evidence by itself was insufficient to convict. All Boston ministers save Cotton Mather signed their names to Increase's views, criticizing a court to which father finally felt less beholden than son. The mood of magistrates, ministers, and the community shifted dramatically soon afterward. One sign among many of the changed climate was that, in 1703, convicted witch Abigail Faulkner from Andover, who had been spared the gallows during the Salem outbreak only because she was pregnant, petitioned the Massachusetts authorities formally to remove the terrible stigma of witchcraft and to restore her good name.[53]

The trials had provided many examples of tensions between fathers and sons, as well as between young and old, maidservants and mistresses, and

[51] Kenneth Silverman, *The Life and Times of Cotton Mather* (New York, 1984), 101.
[52] Boyer and Nissenbaum, *Salem Possessed*, 7–8.
[53] Karlsen, *The Devil in the Shape of a Woman*, 253. Karlsen notes that Abigail Faulkner, the daughter of Andover's minister, had begun to resemble a witch in the eyes of her neighbors after 1687, when, in the absence of a son, she was obliged to assume the management of her husband's substantial estate when he fell ill. Karlsen notes that Faulkner could not have known that the witchcraft prosecutions at that time were virtually over and that "the image of woman-as-evil was even then passing into its more purely secular form, to be played out in the class and racial dynamics of a modern industrial economy," 221.

rich and poor. Surely the most deadly of these, however, were the generalized tensions between men and women that had been brought to the surface, although not acknowledged as such. Most historians would now likely accept the much quoted statement by Christina Larner, eminent historian of the Scottish witch hunts, that "witchcraft was not sex-specific, but it was sex-related."[54] Still there is no consensus about the exact nature of the links between women, men, and witchcraft in the early modern past.

In one of many studies asking why women in the early modern era emerged as a "newly potent source of social anxiety," Joseph Klaits refers to the open intensity and pervasiveness of antifemale sentiment, especially at the beginning of the witch hunts, as part of what he dubs the "new misogyny."[55] Similarly, Robin Briggs's recent study of the European witch craze states that witchcraft was "an unfortunate mixture of fear and aggression towards women, whose passions were seen as a grave threat to husbands and society alike."[56] Yet like many commentators who have wrestled with the nature of the relationship between women and witchcraft, Briggs expresses some bewilderment about what was, in the end, a far less thoroughgoing witch hunt than might have been expected. As he says, given the evidence for a new, widespread, and long-lasting fear and resentment of women's passions in this period, it is difficult to explain not only the timing of the outbreaks but their relative mildness, with just 40,000 to 50,000 executions in a period of over 300 years.[57]

If it is recalled that these were precisely the years during which most men, in particular, were obliged to adjust to dramatic change, featuring a declining bond between landed property and male kin as well as a new and growing dependency upon the women they married, then both the timing and the relative mildness of the witch craze are easier to understand. It becomes possible to interpret witch hunts as just one element, albeit the most lethal and extreme, in a continuum of reactions to a shift in power relationships that had the effect of enhancing women's domestic authority. If there were relatively few convictions and executions for witchcraft, there was nonetheless a wider and ongoing contest for power between and among male and female protagonists. Such an interpretation has not been adequately explored as a way to explain not just the New England episodes but the entire witchcraft era, yet it works well with the evidence presented in recent accounts.

Carol Karlsen's survey of the background and development of late-seventeenth-century New England witchcraft, for example, reveals that from the time the settlers arrived in the New World, they displayed profound

54 Christina Larner, *Enemies of God: The Witch-Hunt in Scotland* (London, 1981), 92.
55 Whitney, "International Trends," 87, cited from Joseph Klaits, *Servants of Satan: The Age of the Witch-Hunts* (Bloomington, Ind., 1985), 65–74.
56 Briggs, *Witches and Neighbors*, 284–85.
57 Ibid., 399–400.

confusion over issues of gender and power, signified in the enactment of two remarkable orders by leaders in the new town of Salem in the 1630s. The first granted land, or "maid lotts," to single women as a means of attracting more women from England to the colony; and the second required all women to wear veils over their faces in public on pain of forfeiting communion. Neither practice existed in England; and neither, in the event, would long be enforced in Salem. The former was rather swiftly abandoned as threatening to create a large group of independent female landowners, and the latter was discarded as unenlightened.[58] Yet this graphic demonstration of what Karlsen calls the "ambiguities facing women" is more comprehensible in a context in which male settlers from the outset were seeking simultaneously to appease and to restrain newly empowered women.

Karlsen acknowledges, too, that the first serious confrontation in New England around women's authority was owing to women's own initiative in taking seriously the new spiritual dignity accorded to them as joint heirs of salvation. Under the leadership of Mistress Anne Hutchinson, women in the 1630s in Boston launched their own women-focused religious movement. And as Mary Beth Norton showed in her earlier, more general study of "gendered power" in the colonial period, both the civil and religious hierarchies were caught off guard by this high-ranking daughter of an orthodox English clergyman, who had persuaded her merchant husband to migrate to Massachusetts in 1634 (with their eleven children) to follow her Puritan-leaning spiritual mentor – the Reverend John Cotton, who was Cotton Mather's grandfather.[59]

Hutchinson first launched her ministry at informal all-female "gossipings" during childbirths, later adding mixed-sex meetings in her home that regularly attracted sixty to eighty followers. Tried by both civil and religious authorities, Hutchinson was excommunicated and banished for heretical teachings. One minister summed up the case against her: "You have stept out of your place, you have rather bine a Husband than a Wife and a preacher than a Hearer; and a Magistrate than a Subject."[60] In the end, even her revered John Cotton joined the other accusers, charging that Hutchinson's defiant behavior was bound to lead to sexual transgression. Soon afterward, Governor John Winthrop himself voiced the suspicion that her ability to convert apparently righteous ministers to her heresies suggested that she was in league with the Devil.[61]

The "heretical" doctrine preached by Hutchinson was simply a strong version of the Protestant idea that salvation is achieved not through good

---

[58] Karlsen, *The Devil in the Shape of a Woman*, 186.

[59] See the full recent account of the case in Mary Beth Norton, *Founding Mothers and Fathers: Gendered Power and the Forming of American Society* (New York, 1996), 359–99.

[60] Cited in ibid., 359.

[61] Ibid., 395.

works, but by God's grace alone. Yet, as commentators have noted, this so-called antinomian position had obvious appeal to women. By emphasizing the powerlessness of the individual to achieve salvation save through God's beneficence, it not only diminished the role of the male clergy as spiritual leaders but also relegated men and women alike to the subordinate status that men now insisted was women's preordained role in Puritan society. Antinomian doctrines had been created not by women but by men concerned to justify a faith that magnified God's power over all earthly intermediaries. Still, like the Catharism that became a male faith in Montaillou, antinomianism was a chameleon dogma that could readily reflect female concerns in Puritan New England.

Men's own repeated affirmations of woman's goodness and spiritual equality also help to explain why Hutchinson and her followers seemed quite unprepared for the intensity of men's hostile reactions, especially their accusations of heresy and sexual impropriety. It is true that Hutchinson implicitly acknowledged the authority men were staking out for themselves in an emerging public arena by protesting that meetings in which she had given formal instruction were "private" and restricted to women, whereas the "public" meetings with men involved no such instruction. The men did not accept that argument, however; and she and her followers thus confronted a very different situation from the male heretics of Montaillou. Their accusers were not members of an outside church hierarchy. Instead, they were their own ministers – and their own husbands.

After Hutchinson's excommunication, specifically female religious movements lost their force for some time; but that did not mean that men found no more cause for worry from the female camp. Propounding the notion that women are not more evil than men, and that they share equally in salvation, had clearly increased the challenges men faced in continuing to uphold women's subordination to them. But as already seen, these newer beliefs still coexisted uneasily with the older idea that women – the daughters of Eve – were the innately dangerous sex. That notion, after all, had once been more open and explicit. It reigned among the male villagers of Montaillou at the turn of the fourteenth century; and it was still the dominant view in northern Europe in the fifteenth century, when more formal persecutions for witchcraft got underway.

Beliefs in women's dangerous power to do Satan's bidding were elaborated near the beginning of the great European outbreaks by priests in compendia such as the *Malleus Maleficarum* (1486) that were long argued to have served authorities as "handbooks" for witch hunts. Recent research, however, persuasively discounts the influence of such handbooks. Contrary to earlier views that contrast allegedly more state-directed witch hunts on the Continent with more popular ones in England, scholars now maintain that witchcraft persecutions in both places originated not with states or other outside authorities but in popular beliefs born among troubled and resentful neighbors. Such conclusions mesh well with the argument here that although they took different forms in different places, the early modern witch hunts were one manifestation among many of the anxieties experienced by ordinary people adjusting to a marriage regime that changed the ground rules of the gender order by allotting more power to women.

Probably the closest we will come to identifying just how that process played out, for New England at least, is the analysis by Carol Karlsen of the backgrounds of all the New England women singled out as witches from the 1640s on. Karlsen argues that the origins of the trials lay in a widespread fear of economically and psychologically independent and aggressive women. She locates this fear in men's wider concern to establish social order, and although she does not invoke the underlying feature being argued here of a unique marriage and household regime, her findings are arguably better explained by that feature.[62]

First and least surprising among Karlsen's findings is that most New England "witches" were women – about three-quarters in the major outbreaks, including Salem, and nearly 90 percent in the so-called non-outbreak cases, defined as those that involved just one or a few witches. Karlsen suggests that in larger outbreaks, the "possessed" young women who dominated as accusers had less sex-stereotyped views of who might be a witch than the male accusers who dominated in the non-outbreak cases. (Now that we know about the circumstances of the Indian wars in Salem, it is also easier to explain the size of that outbreak at such a late date.) Male judges, we are told, had trouble believing that men could be witches, convicting and hanging them less often. While they might extort confessions from women, they often dismissed accused men as liars.

Although younger women might be somewhat more vulnerable in an outbreak, it was women over forty who were at all times at greatest risk. Once accused, moreover, the older a woman was, the greater the likelihood that she would be convicted and hanged. Eight of the fourteen women executed during the Salem outbreak were aged sixty or over. Women who lived alone – chiefly widows, with some spinsters and a few divorced or deserted women – accounted for nearly a third of all accused women in Salem, which made them 100 percent overrepresented given their numbers in the population. Women alone among those accused were also far more likely to be tried, convicted, and executed. It was not simply the absence of a husband-protector that put these women at special risk. Single women not serving as helpmeets to men were seen as unnatural creatures.

Karlsen is able to show how witchcraft after midcentury became another way to punish and control a whole set of female behaviors that were held up

---

[62] The following summary is drawn from Karlsen, Ch. 2: "The Demographic Basis of Witchcraft," and Ch. 3: "The Economic Basis of Witchcraft," in *The Devil in the Shape of a Woman*, 46–116.

as active threats to the social and sexual order. Allegedly unwomanly behavior, in short, was increasingly explained by summoning the submerged belief that evildoing is the special domain of women. Karlsen describes how beliefs in women's insatiable lust were summoned to explain a rise in premarital sex, illegitimate births, and adultery – all effects of postponed marriage and an increasingly mobile society. As she explains, the courts, which had earlier punished men as well as women for such sexual offenses, initially shifted more responsibility to the women; but after the 1640s, witchcraft became an alternate way to punish women for these offenses while not pursuing the men involved. A disproportionately large number of accused witches had records of fornication, adultery, or other sexually related offenses.

Midwives and healers were also vulnerable. Such women continued to be feared for their perceived power over elementary forces of life and death at times when all men are weak and helpless; but the female practitioners were also threatened by new male professionals who were beginning to claim a monopoly over medical services. The many doctors who came forward as accusers in the witchcraft cases were part of a larger effort to discredit women's traditional expertise as healers.

There is also a link between women's work in a changing economy such as Salem's and the way witches were singled out. While dairying, brewing, and clothing production still took place in the household, the growing numbers of women who had turned these activities into small business enterprises were overrepresented among accused witches. Two ran taverns in Salem. Others managed boardinghouses, kept beehives, ran breweries, or operated dairy businesses. (One was accused when two casks of her butter went bad aboard ship several days out from port.) Placing themselves in competition with men's enterprises, on however small a scale, was risky for women.

The deputy husbands who acted on their own or on behalf of their men in running farms and business ventures, hiring people, handling legal matters, and generally serving as stand-in household heads were in special jeopardy. Edith Crawford of Salem was accused after acting for years as her merchant husband's attorney and finally having the misfortune to lose the family's house and land. When the house burned soon after it had been seized, the new occupant accused Crawford of having caused the fire, saying that "hee would have Her Hanged If ther were no more wimen In the world, for shee was A witch and If shee were nott A witch allready shee would bee won, and therefore It was as good to Hang her att first as Last."[63]

Evidence of discontent with the social order ran through many of the accusations, and women were singled out for any signs of pride, aggression, or failure to subordinate themselves to their natural – that is, male – superiors. Women even confessed to making covenants with the Devil to gain power. For example, a servant stated that her discontent made her call on Satan

[63] Karlsen, *The Devil in the Shape of a Woman*, 146–47.

to perform her many chores, such as keeping the hogs out of the field and carrying out the ashes. Another young woman confessed during the Salem outbreak that she became dissatisfied with her lot after people told her that "she should Never hath [sic] such a Young Man who loved her."[64] Her solution, she said, was to take Satan as her lover. It is remarkable how often women's discontent and anger, no matter how mild, were featured in the accusations. If they muttered when neighbors refused them favors, if they complained over a husband's mistreatment, and certainly if they dared to seek redress at court for some injustice, they exposed themselves to suspicion. The language of the time is full of terms for an angry woman, including "scold," "shrew," "termagant," and "harridan." There are no comparable terms for an angry man.

Carol Karlsen discovered something else from the witchcraft data that is extraordinary. She found that of 124 accused female witches in New England for whom data are available, approximately half lived, or had lived, in families without male heirs. Since no more than a quarter of New England women were in this situation, such women were also at least 100 percent overrepresented among accused witches. Some were identified after they came into their inheritances, others accused prior to the death of the crucial male relatives. Several had been dispossessed and had taken their cases to court.

The actual amount of property women received or claimed was less important in their accusations than the fact that as women, they were seen as illegitimate heirs. As Karlsen says, as persons who "stood to inherit, did inherit, or were denied their apparent right to inherit substantially larger portions of their fathers' or husbands' accumulated estates than women in families with male heirs," such women were anomalies.[65] True, there is often no direct line from an accuser to someone who might profit, and testimony rarely even indicates that economic resources in the hands of women might be an issue. But in an inheritance system designed, in normal circumstances, to keep property in the hands of men, such women were automatically suspect.

Sarah Good, the woman who flung a warning at the Salem minister before being hanged, is a case in point. "Goody" Good had not always been a destitute beggar. Her father, a prosperous innkeeper, had left a large estate of 500 pounds in 1672 when Sarah was eighteen; and following the custom, he allotted his widow one-third and divided the rest among the unmarried children, leaving the eldest son a double portion. Nearly eleven years later, however, after the death of the two sons and the widow, who had remarried, the surviving daughters, including Sarah, petitioned the court for the inheritance not yet received. Four years after that, widowed and remarried, Sarah Good was again in court for a suit filed by a creditor of her first husband.

[64] Ibid., 127.
[65] Ibid., 101.

The proceedings revealed that her stepfather had finally given her a portion of her inheritance, but the amount was far less than what she was due. After she had used it to pay her first husband's debts, she and her second husband were reduced to begging work, food, and shelter from their Salem neighbors. When accusers said that she never attended religious services, Sarah said she had stayed away "for want of clothes." She had her pride, and although neighbors called her a "turbulent spirit," she had cause to resent both her greedy stepfather and all-male courts indifferent to her rightful claims. In the end, even her husband sided with the accusers. Complaining of her "bad carriage" toward him at her examination, he said he was "afraid that she either was a witch or would be one very quickly."[66]

Karlsen also documents men's more standard efforts to cope with the increasing pressure of population on property by limiting widows' and daughters' access to it. After 1650, Salem fathers willed less of their estates to their daughters; and by the end of the century, only about 10 percent did not discriminate in favor of sons. Besides reducing their circumstances and creating resentment, such practices lessened women's chances to marry. In addition, although before 1650 half of men writing wills left property to their widows beyond the legal dower, after then the proportion doing so dropped to under a fifth. Most of the litigation over estates after 1650 came from disputes over the right of women to inherit, even though less than 20 percent of women were primary heirs.[67]

*   *   *

Many interpreters of the witchcraft episodes have chosen to portray them as evidence for a crushing 300-year-long display of patriarchal control. Yet it seems clear enough from Karlsen's evidence, as well as from what Edward Bever has recently argued from the European sources, that the central dynamic of the early modern witch hunts was not so much relentless victimization as it was a struggle for power.[68]

Bever convincingly argues that the example of the trials themselves served forcefully to control the behavior of large numbers of women who "lived in danger that the small ways in which they acted or felt" might lead to "ostracism, jail, the torture chamber, or even the stake."[69] He also contends that while accusers could be either male or female, since the suspects were overwhelmingly female, the trials served in the end to diminish women's power and to strengthen men's. The problem with such an interpretation, however, is that it ignores the relative situations of its presumed protagonists at the outset of the witch hunts.

---

[66] Ibid., 149.
[67] Ibid., 208–13.
[68] Bever, "Witchcraft, Female Aggression, and Power," 955–88.
[69] Ibid.

It is obvious enough that as a group, men had more social power than women, whether at the beginning of the witch hunts or at the end. Yet if men's power relative to women's was already being challenged, as I have argued it was, then it is hardly clear that the witchcraft episode finally either strengthened men's overall power or diminished women's. What I have argued is that the underlying source of the witch hunts was the painful adjustment by women and men alike to a singular set of marriage and household arrangements that placed new pressures on both sexes, but especially on men. In fact, if witchcraft is seen in the same way heresy in Montaillou was presented earlier – namely, as a strategy embraced largely by men to defend their most cherished interests in hard times – some useful comparisons can be drawn.

In both Montaillou and Salem, men were aware that achieving their own goals required them to take women into account. In Montaillou, where men's main earthly goal was maintenance of their ostals, this meant ensuring that women were virgins at marriage, that they married within the village, that they produced male heirs as soon as possible, that they remained faithful to their husbands to preserve ostals from illegitimate heirs, and that they performed women's traditional work. Since custom, and especially a male-controlled marriage system, acted as the chief enforcing mechanisms, individual women had little or no personal responsibility for ensuring that these requirements were met, and thus no rules were needed for their behavior.

It was not women's actions, after all, that could threaten an ostal in the mountain community. It was instead their very existence, as infants who might threaten future livelihood with their reproductive potential and as daughters with rights to dowries. In hard times when there were too many babies, too little food, and too heavy tithes, men might be especially likely to call women devils and mistreat them, but they could hardly regard them as serious adversaries. Instead, they were persuaded that their real conflict was with a Church whose doctrines, including perhaps the doctrine upholding the sanctity of all human life, stood in the way of preserving their ostals from ruin. Yet they did not want to give up Paradise, so heretical faith became a solution.

For the Puritan men of New England nearly 400 years later, the solution in a similar male dilemma was a witch hunt. Men's own cherished priorities in Salem Village, however, were neither so visible nor so straightforward as they had been in Montaillou. Ostensibly, men's chief aim at all times was to defend the godly community of Salem. But deep economic, social, and family divisions – especially between fathers and sons – plus the absence of permanent links between the same families and the same property, meant that men had no single shared interest in something as tangible as Montaillou men did. In Montaillou, despite a single-heir system and a nuclear household structure, men maintained allegiance to their birth ostals. In Salem, however, there were enormous pressures as growing numbers of households were forced into increasingly subdivided properties. The stated Puritan goal of maintaining a godly community was a far harder one in any case than the goal of ostal maintenance that the men of the clans set for themselves, and it competed with many other less acknowledged goals.

The role of women in men's ability to achieve their aims was also less straightforward in the changing environment of Salem Village and Town. Not only were men's goals less clear to themselves, they could not take women's part for granted in the same ways Montaillou men could. In a system in which livelihood depended not on enduring clans but on partnerships between married couples, it was impossible for women and men to coexist in different universes, as in Montaillou. What mattered most to men about women in Salem was not their biological role as the mothers of male heirs, but rather their role as wives who could create with them, in whatever ways were required, the livelihood that was ceasing to be embedded in enduring family property.

For their own part, most women in Salem continued to define their highest priorities through their domestic and traditionally female roles. Childbearing and nurturing were critically important to them, even though women were increasingly made aware that from men's standpoint, it was as wives, far more than as mothers, that they achieved their highest value. Marriage itself did not correspond with the moment of biological readiness for motherhood, but instead with the moment of a couple's readiness to establish and maintain a household. The significance of this fact for what we have come to label the "social construction of womanhood" is hard to exaggerate.

Little wonder that for women, the drama of womanhood throughout the regions of the Western family pattern came to focus on some changed requirements for becoming, and being, a wife. Later marriage, and with it the knowledge that marriage might be denied them in a society with growing numbers of spinsters – as well as uncertainty regarding their future husbands and their occupations – meant that anxieties were built into young women's lives in Salem that were simply not there in Montaillou. (No Montaillou girl needed magic to help her predict the occupation of her future husband.) Generational divisions compounded social ones in tensions that younger women might feel in waiting roles as daughters, and especially as servants. These young women both resented and coveted the now more exalted position of a godly helpmeet who might, in practice, also be a harsh mistress. That some of these young women were prompted to cry down such mistresses (or their surrogates) as witches becomes easier to understand.

The male-led campaign for womanly women also promoted a novel competition over this now more "achieved" sense of womanhood. A gulf emerged between the female paragons who might approximate the ideal helpmeet and those women who, for whatever reasons, persisted in behavior that was now branded unwomanly. That some women were prepared to join men in denouncing other women as witches is hardly surprising. Still, any concerns women felt over a postponed and increasingly problematic womanhood were overshadowed by men's anxieties about a womanhood that was resisting their best efforts to name it and to distinguish its features from those of witches.

Ironically, that ordinary women by the early modern era could be held to embody the power to turn the community upside down was a measure of the appreciation men had come to have of women's influence, as well as of their capacity for independent action. No Montaillou clansman would ever have expressed such fear of women's power. Yet in reality, women's greater domestic authority in Salem, owing to their enhanced status as household partners, does not begin to explain the new intensity of male fears. Male control was alive and well in Salem, and the witchcraft outbreak itself is witness to that if any is needed. So why did men who never were in danger of losing control, in Salem or elsewhere, begin to act as though they were?

When the process of identifying witches is decoded, it emerges that the most frightening thing about witches, for men, was their ability to cross an ancient boundary between the sexes that neither they nor women realized was crumbling. Women who now regularly performed men's work, for example, did not perceive why men might be troubled by activities that they themselves found less satisfying than their female tasks. Men, in turn, did not perceive that the deputy husbands they were crying down as witches were the very ones who had now become essential to their own livelihoods.

Men continued to act as though women controlling property were literally trespassing on male turf, even though land itself was no longer as central to their own positions and influence in places like Salem as it continued to be in places like Montaillou. Finally, female sexual activity, assertiveness, and even anger were no longer features whose potential to harm men's most basic interests was contained by automatic clan controls. Women were regularly obliged to act as independent agents within marriages, and their decisions as deputy husbands might literally make or break a household. Women and men alike were responding with bewilderment to changes in the ground rules of relations between the sexes, changes that altered reflexive notions about womanhood and manhood and about boundaries dividing the sexes.

The witchcraft crisis in Salem also revealed what was true elsewhere in the late-marriage regions, namely, that men were the ones who came first to display intense anxiety over these shifts in gender ground rules, even though their anxiety is itself still only partially explained. It is not yet clear why men rather than women should have been the ones who first became persuaded that the boundaries between the sexes were shifting and required special attention.

The next chapter will address some of these remaining questions, backing away from these two communities and examining womanhood and especially manhood with a much wider historical lens. Only then will it be possible to understand more fully why the gender scene in Salem held particular terrors for men that went well beyond the desire to curb deviant female behavior and restore order that is so often held up as the explanation for the witch hunts. The devil who visited Salem in the shape of a woman did not come merely to shore up men's authority in the social order. He came because men there, and in early modern European societies more generally, wanted something more than power and control. Witch hunts, for a very long time, became an expression of their frustration at failing to get what they wanted.

6

What Men and Women Want

During another time of troubles in the relations between the sexes, Sigmund Freud once remarked to his friend and colleague Marie Bonaparte: "The great question that has never been answered and which I have not yet been able to answer, despite my thirty years of research into the feminine soul, is, what does a woman want?"[1] Freud was convinced that men's desires and concerns are always more clear and straightforward than women's. What would he have said, one wonders, about the confused and distraught men of Salem Village? Here were men who were still in charge of household and market, of church and of state. Yet often enough, they did not behave that way.

From the late fifteenth to the late eighteenth century, an era in Western history in which intermittent witch hunts were only the most dramatic feature of what has been labeled a concerted male drive to control and repress women, historians have also singled out an apparently contradictory trend toward increased autonomy and responsibility for women. So far I have argued that an underlying cause of both of these developments, although still unrecognized as such, was the distinctive Western family pattern, and especially women's late age at marriage. This eccentric set of arrangements, by the early modern era, had put women's and men's lives on increasingly converging tracks. At the same time, however, men's continued control over wives, households, and society at large was never in doubt, which is what makes their anxious behavior so very puzzling. In that period, anyway, the more apt question was not "What does a woman want?" but "What does a man want?"

While most of this inquiry focuses on the novelty of the late-marriage system – its features, likely origins, and unnoticed effects – this chapter will do something else. It will make the case that this system, and the comparisons

---

[1] Cited in Betty Friedan, *The Feminine Mystique* (New York, 1983), 113, from Ernest Jones, *The Life and Work of Sigmund Freud* (New York, 1953), Vol. II, 121.

pursued so far with the more prevalent early-marriage one, provide vital clues to a better explanation than we now possess for a long-standing mystery. I refer to the problem of why it is that most, if not all, societies have stressed the importance of difference between the sexes and have endorsed, to greater or lesser degrees, a hierarchy favoring men.

First and most obvious, the inquiry to this point, concentrating as it does on early- and late-marriage arrangements and their powerful but overlooked influence on attitudes and behavior at every stage of women's and men's lives, has shown how these arrangements play a vital role in perpetuating shared, socially constructed elements of female and male experience. Also, by illustrating just how effective early-marriage arrangements, in particular, have been in upholding male authority within households over immense stretches of time, the analysis raises serious questions about familiar theoretical approaches that insist that since a sexual hierarchy favoring men is so pervasive and long-lived, it can never be adequately explained through the study of specific social contexts alone.

Such approaches usually appeal to biological or psychological mechanisms that are allegedly universal to the species and reproduced automatically, regardless of a society's institutions or history. While not denying that such mechanisms may exist and play a role of some sort in perpetuating systems of sexual difference and hierarchy, this account so far has emphasized that it is possible to go a very long way toward explaining these features – and much else besides – through the observable, self-perpetuating elements of the enduring, early-marriage, multifamily household.

That system of household formation, after all, is the one that was experienced by most of the world's peoples throughout all of recorded history. The contrast with the more fragile late-marriage system has made it possible to appreciate just how critical early-marriage features have been for upholding unchallenged male control in households from one generation to the next. Especially significant is that youthful marriage for women and maintenance of property in the male line give men's collective power over women's lives firm and continuing institutional buttresses. When the staying power of these households is fully appreciated, it becomes less urgent to assign the familiar sexual hierarchy favoring men to inescapable biological or psychological imperatives.

Theories appealing to such presumed imperatives have nonetheless enjoyed wide recognition. The resulting debates have too often set up a false opposition between the presumed constant feature of male dominance – supposedly deriving from genetic "hard-wiring" in prehistoric times or from universal psychological processes – and all the variables of time, place, class, race, work, religion, and more. These latter are then cited as responsible for either mitigating or intensifying the effects of the alleged biological or psychological determinants, thereby accounting for differences in the nature and intensity of men's control over women in different social settings.

Such a dualistic approach effectively removes from inquiry the supposed primary source of female subordination, obliging would-be interpreters to focus their attention on variable factors presumed only to lessen or increase that subordination. Not only does the approach ignore the peculiar success of at least one ancient social institution, the early-marriage household, in upholding a gender hierarchy over immense stretches of time, it also discourages approaches that would examine the more constant and variable features of gender systems together, as interrelated elements of a single puzzle. In the 1970s, anthropologist Gayle Rubin called for a theory that could explain women's oppression in its "endless variety" as well as in its "monotonous similarity."[2] Yet so far, interpreters have tended to focus on either the variety or the similarity, but not on both.

Anthropologists, to be sure, have been more attuned than other specialists to the idea that family households that long combined most social, political, and economic functions are effective units for perpetuating notions about who women and men are and what they do. The young learned the spoken and unspoken rules of womanhood and manhood first, and most compellingly, from their elders, long before their descendants began to supplement such instruction with extra-domestic cues from schools, television, theme parks, and electronic games. Since anthropologists long devoted themselves to the remaining examples of pre-state societies, in which institutions not constructed on households and kinship are scarce, they have had less to say about the probable effects on attitudes and behavior of more recent kinship and household arrangements, including the effects of the idiosyncratic late-marriage regime.

The habit of dividing the study of gender arrangements by constant or variable features is now enshrined within academic disciplines. Psychologists and sociobiologists, for example, focus on the presumed constant feature of sexual hierarchy. Historians, sociologists, and literary scholars, by contrast, usually evince discomfort with all-encompassing explanations for male dominance, as well as distrust for those with the effrontery to propose them. They ponder the variable features of gender arrangements and tout their disciplinary missions as interpreting specific behaviors in specific settings.

Just as those in the former camp have stressed the overriding influence of nature over nurture in explaining an enduring male dominance, those in the latter steer clear of the awkward fact of a pervasive cross-cultural hierarchy that advantages males. Since the early 1980s, in fact, most feminist scholars have stopped evoking overarching theories of any sort that would account for such stubborn behaviors.[3] On occasion, they have even declared the

---

[2] Gayle Rubin, "The Traffic in Women," in Rayna R. Reiter, ed., *Toward an Anthropology of Women* (New York, 1975), 160.

[3] For an extremely useful discussion of this and related issues, see Nancy Fraser and Linda J. Nicholson, "Social Criticism without Philosophy: An Encounter Between Feminism and

search for an explanation for female subordination to be an inappropriate subject of inquiry for disciplines such as theirs, whose proper business is exploring difference and change in human affairs.[4]

What the comparison of the two family-formation systems in agricultural societies does here is to begin to break through this stale debate. Besides underscoring the awesome capacity of the early-marriage system to perpetuate perceptions that gender difference and male dominance are innate, it provides, in the features of the late-marriage variant, important clues to constructing a more fruitful approach to how gender systems operate anywhere. If the early-marriage system suggests that it may be unnecessary to appeal to unknowable entities, genetic or psychological, to explain the longevity of habits of gender difference and hierarchy, the late-marriage system invites new ways to examine together questions about difference and hierarchy that have usually been considered separately.

What now appears to set apart the years from 1500 to 1750 in northwestern Europe, the era of the full-blown late-marriage system, is a major shift, unperceived as such at the time or since, in the ground rules for the exercise of power within households. Historians have written extensively, of course, about changes in these ground rules beyond households – featuring the successful Protestant challenge to the "universal" church, a scientific revolution overturning older modes of inquiry, and new formulations of the nature of politics and the state. Such accounts of authority shifts outside households, however, have yet to be linked to findings described here about the distinctive ways authority worked inside households, as well as the ways women and men were coming to relate to one another.

Within households, as seen, men came to depend less on their own male blood relatives and more on their wives for livelihood and support, whereas outside households they came increasingly to rely on unrelated men rather than on kin networks. Women, for their part, emerged as more active if not equal partners with their husbands in decision making within households and also within their local communities.[5] Far from this development prompting greater society-wide recognition of women's shared authority with men, however, it appears at least initially to have produced a strong and sustained reaction featuring a huge rise in popular and institutionalized misogyny. Accompanying this shift was a reassessment and redefinition of the ingredients

---

Postmodernism," in Linda J. Nicholson, ed., *Feminism/Postmodernism* (London, 1990), 19–38.

[4] In her classic essay on gender, for example, Joan Scott comes very close to this position. See Joan W. Scott, "Gender: A Useful Category of Historical Analysis." *American Historical Review* 91 (1986): 1053–75.

[5] For an excellent and full recent discussion, see Mary Beth Norton, *Founding Mothers and Fathers: Gendered Power and the Forming of American Society* (New York, 1996), Sections I and II, "Gendered Power in the Family" and "Gendered Power in the Community," 27–239.

of womanhood and of manhood, led by both secular and religious male spokespersons.

The visits to Montaillou and Salem provided a chance to observe this process in microcosm, and to compare differences in men's and women's interactions in Montaillou's mixed family system, where strong material and ideological buttresses for women's subordination remained intact, and Salem's unstable late-marriage system, in which those buttresses were under heavy siege. The comparison throws into high relief behaviors and attitudes that suggest a brand new hypothesis for systems of sexual difference and hierarchy that will be pursued here. It reveals not only how dramatically the Western or late-marriage system faltered in upholding a set of separate gender roles for women and men, but also how that system sharply reduced men's ability to control women's domestic and even extra-domestic lives – even as their claims to such control increased sharply.

Exploring why and how crises on these two sites played out so differently encourages an interpretation that moves away from the tradition of considering male dominance as separate from other aspects of gender arrangements, and that tries to assess what has been at stake over time, in women's priorities as well as men's. The comparison helps to answer critical questions about the enduring as well as variable elements of human gender systems. Not incidentally, it can also help to explain why Freud's thirty years of research into the feminine soul were so frustrating for him. In asking "What does a woman want?" he was posing an unanswerable question, since he assumed that there was only and always a single correct answer.

Instead of portraying as both inevitable and unknowable the familiar sexual hierarchy that works in men's favor, this chapter will maintain that what has come to be called "male dominance" is not a constant feature of all human societies at all, but rather a peculiarly obstinate variable. It will be presented as a likely but not inevitable by-product of a common and observable social process, one shared by both sexes anywhere. Male dominance, in other words, will be argued to be a feature that is reenacted, even re-created, in different social contexts, through a process in which a sexual hierarchy favoring men is not a necessary or preordained result, although it may be a highly likely one.

In neither the early- nor the late-marriage system, in any case, does dominance over women appear to be a primary goal of men's behavior. In early-marriage societies, it is better understood as a consistent side effect of a set of family structures whose more salient aim is to maintain households and guard their property over time. In late-marriage societies, where these structures are less capable of perpetuating distinctive sexual universes as well as of shoring up family households over time, the side effect in buttresses for male authority is also sharply reduced. At the same time, however, the contrast in women's and men's behavior and attitudes in the two systems, and especially the evidence for men's rising distress as features of the late-marriage pattern were assembled, presents inviting possibilities for reinterpreting known developments.

The fortuitous appearance of the Western family pattern, indeed, opens a new avenue to understanding the perpetual re-creation of gendered selves over time, and especially the process that, for so long, has reproduced a sexual hierarchy favoring men. That process does not entail the "inevitability of patriarchy," as some would call it; but neither does it suggest that the days of male dominance will spin out any time soon. To appreciate why this is so, it is necessary first to move from the microcosm of the two Western agricultural communities to the macrocosm of the species as a whole. It is useful to pose some initial questions about those universal biological and psychological theories in order to determine what, if anything, may be worth salvaging from them.

Visits to these two villages have uncovered persuasive evidence that while it was the men, in both places, who displayed more concern about gender arrangements than the women, their concern was far more intense in Salem than in Montaillou. What is more, the level of anxiety men displayed in Salem about women's behavior cannot continue to be attributed, as it has long been, to a straightforward zeal to establish social order in a time of turmoil or to a readiness to single out women, the presumed daughters of Eve, as scapegoats. That explanation gives insufficient attention to the long prior history of witch hunts in western Europe, to which the New England outbreaks were clearly linked. More important, it gives inadequate consideration to evidence that men's primary worries, as revealed by the analysis of who was most likely to be singled out as a witch, actually concerned women's perceived infringement of gender boundaries.

Men's troubled state of mind can only be fully appreciated in the context of novel household structures whose effects were increasingly blurring the divisions between women's and men's worlds. Men appear to have been disturbed by those women who were performing activities or enjoying prerogatives that they as men identified as exclusive to themselves – everything from speaking out in public to pursuing a profession, owning or standing to inherit property, or (as most wives did) serving as deputy husbands. Comparisons between the two household systems allowed us to see that the women who turned out to be witches were often the ones most visibly engaged in activities that all women were now obliged to perform, at least some of the time. In other words, the overlapping of women's and men's worlds, whose source was a novel household form, also appears to have been a trigger for witch hunts in New England and earlier in northwestern Europe.

That men all across the social spectrum were the ones who responded most vocally and negatively to this blurring of roles and crossing of gender boundaries provides a significant clue to the larger puzzle this chapter seeks to solve. That is whether it is possible, with the help of these findings, to identify an interpretive approach to gender arrangements in any human community that can explain the more enduring features of those arrangements, especially men's favored place of power in a sexual hierarchy, without resorting to unprovable, ahistorical, universalist claims. So far, it does appear that dominance by itself is hardly an adequate answer to the question of what the hard-pressed male heretics of Montaillou wanted, nor for that matter to what the distraught male householders of Salem wanted. While in both places there were many indicators of men's superior status and greater social power relative to women, men's actual behavior and pronouncements, even in Salem, appear to be best understood not in relation to women but instead in relation to other men and their interests.

It is well here to be reminded that despite a popular focus on what is tagged a near-universal "male dominance," even the sociobiological accounts of primate and early human activity have not singled out dominance as a primary goal of male behavior. It is time, then, to take a brief look at where the universalist claims of the sociobiologists and psychologists stand, and to review what has been learned about men, women, and their desires within a far larger framework – first in the animal primate species and then, across thousands of years of evolution, in our own.

*   *   *

It may appear silly or presumptuous in a discussion focused on a millennium or so in northwestern European societies to review the disputed legacy of 70 million years of primate development. Yet given the continued appeal of arguments that would explain the prevalence of sexual hierarchy as universal, inevitable, and linked to humans' evolutionary heritage, it makes sense to undertake one of those "huge comparisons" and look at the status of such claims about our primate ancestors. Male dominance, after all, has been cited as a feature of several hundred species that belong to the primate order. As anthropologist Sarah B. Hrdy observes, "Logic alone should warn us against explaining such a widespread phenomenon with reference only to a specialized subset of human examples."[6]

Aware that chauvinists for both sexes have lately sought and found grounds for their views in the vast primate literature, Hrdy cautions that present field research provides little to console either the camp that sees male dominance as a natural state for all primate species, ourselves included, or the camp that argues that there was an original but lost matriarchal order. There is no reason to believe that women or their evolutionary predecessors have ever been dominant over men, she contends; and most primatologists and anthropologists would agree. On the other hand, while dominant behavior of males is characteristic of most primates, what is remarkable is the

---

[6] Sarah Blaffer Hrdy, *The Woman That Never Evolved* (Cambridge, 1981), 7.

variety of dominance patterns produced, as she says, by the interactions of different species with their environments.

Among the tiny minority of monogamous primates, for example, dominance behavior is minimal. The two sexes are almost indistinguishable in size and appearance; and while males normally defend territory against male intruders, females do the same for female intruders. Dominance, defined as "the ability of one animal to displace another from a resource both of them want," is rarely an issue between mates, though when it occurs, the female holds her own and may even dominate the male.[7] Lifestyles are similar, and males invest in offspring by providing food, defending them, and yielding food to mother–offspring pairs. These more "egalitarian" species are intriguing since they show that not all primates are locked into a pattern of male dominance.

The primates that anthropologists agree were our ancestors, however, are among those for whom female deference to males was a more usual way of life. Using living primates as stand-ins for some of our primate ancestors, as well as analyses of prehistoric hominid bones, specialists are concluding that humans evolved from species whose breeding systems were polygynous rather than monogamous. In the polygynous majority, males are larger than females, owing to the effects of natural selection caused by males fighting among themselves for access to harems of females. The fossil record shows that this size differential, or sexual dimorphism, among our ancestors was at least as great as the 5 to 12 percent male size superiority in existing human populations.

Still, until recently, scholars' near-exclusive focus on the evolution of males, and on the competitive tactics that ensured their control over females, meant that female behavior was both ignored and misunderstood. Their involvement in reproduction was presumed to mean that females were passive players in a drama whose chief actors were male. As recently as 1978, the first volume on female hierarchies concluded that over evolutionary time, little functional utility can be assigned to female hierarchies, and that among primates as well as humans there is scant evidence for any formalized competition among females.[8] Little attention was paid to evidence that females showed highly competitive if less visible behavior in defense of some distinctive priorities of their own.

Notions that preoccupation with nurturing has kept all females out of "politics" have been challenged by studies showing that the female's commitment to reproduction hardly precludes her active and competitive involvement in the social organization of the group. For example, females employ many competitive tactics to increase their reproductive chances. Not

---

[7] Ibid., 38–39.
[8] The point is made by Hrdy, *The Woman That Never Evolved*, 127. The book cited is Lionel Tiger and Heather Fowler, eds., *Female Hierarchies* (Chicago, 1978).

only do socially dominant females suppress ovulation in subordinates, they also exclude them from feeding sites, favor some offspring over others to maintain dominance hierarchies, and harass low-ranking females, thereby reducing their reproductive chances. Females, then, are hardly automatic breeding machines producing one offspring after another. Many interrelated biological and environmental features appear to determine an individual's chances for reproductive success. Scholars are now increasingly persuaded that competition among females is demonstrable and provides the necessary underpinning for the evolution of any primate social system.

The importance of this detour for the inquiry here is twofold. First, it underscores growing evidence of a distinctive evolutionary history for the female among primate species. While there is no consensus on just how they evolved, scholars now admit that females can no longer be seen as passive bystanders in an evolutionary process in which males were the sole actors. Second, the detour clarifies the context in which male dominance was expressed among our primate ancestors. For all males in sexually dimorphous species, it has long been obvious that greater size and strength are assets in the ability to exert control over females. But the dominance that size and strength help to confer does not now appear to have been the primary object of male behavior. Instead, dominance over females was more likely the side effect of competition with other males to determine which ones would sire the most progeny. For our primate ancestors, at least, the answer to the question "What do men want?" was not dominance over females or even over other males. It was sexual access to females and progeny of their own.

The leap from the priorities of our primate ancestors to the human historical record presents many challenges. For both sexes, by the time the historical record begins, the chief objects of behavior had broadened dramatically from, respectively, inseminating the most females to produce the most offspring and bearing, nurturing, and preserving the largest number of same. Sociobiologists (of whom Sarah Hrdy is one) have gone on to engage in more frankly speculative analyses, positing a set of programmed responses carried on from early primate behaviors and suggesting that men's common belief in women's sexual promiscuity, for example, may have its roots in a kind of universal male reaction against an early sexual receptivity of females, a behavior that Hrdy argues female primates evolved as a means to ensure the survival of offspring.[9] Yet such suggestions are not very helpful in explaining the immense variety in the historical record; and the chronology, to say the least, is awkward.

It is already known that the more draconian measures for controlling female sexuality, including removal of the clitoris and genital infibulation, whereby the lips of the vagina are surgically closed – practices that affect millions of women today – emerged embarrassingly late to plead a programmed

---

[9] See Hrdy, *The Woman That Never Evolved*, 92–93.

male response to a stored memory of primate female promiscuity. Even much older practices such as cloistering of women and male-controlled courting, marriage, and inheritance arrangements came about after hundreds of thousands of years of human evolution and are far better explained by the needs of societies in which fixed agriculture had become the primary form of livelihood.

Another problem for such sociobiological speculation comes even closer to home here: the comparatively rapid change in arrangements regarding the sexes within a single region. There is considerable difficulty in accepting a theory asserting that what we call male dominance is, in effect, a legacy from our primate ancestors, passed on through eons of evolutionary development, only to claim, as I am in the midst of doing, that in less than 1,000 years in northwestern Europe, such practices and the beliefs accompanying them were altered almost beyond recognition. Instead, what is worth keeping from these analyses is the evidence from primate anthropology for competitive female as well as male behaviors, as well as the finding that dominance among male primates was not an end in itself but rather a by-product of the striving for progeny.

That related objectives for each sex might have been expressed in these early settings and then reenacted as the species developed an ever greater capacity to manipulate its environment is hardly a startling idea, since two things remained constant: females continued to bear the next generation and males continued to father it. By the time our hominid ancestors emerged, probably well over a million years ago, and of course by the time settled agricultural communities appeared about 10,000 years ago, men and women alike had developed less straightforward priorities than their primate relatives had had. Yet while male dominance remained a feature of human societies, it arguably was still what it appears to have been earlier: a by-product of other more pressing male concerns.

*   *   *

Both the views from the microcosm of two small Western communities and the macrocosm of the primate background suggest that dominance over females does not work well as a presumed constant male priority. Growing recognition that women as well as men display characteristic and continuing priorities of their own argues that it is long past time to discard the idea that a recurring male dominance puts that feature in a kind of primary interpretive category by itself. Such a strategy gives undue attention to men's behavior as the main item to be explained among persistent male and female behaviors. By surrounding male dominance with an aura of mystery, it has also obscured recognition that a familiar and recurring process involving both sexes might have been responsible all along for the sexual hierarchy favoring men. I refer to the process of acquiring a sense of self or social identity, a shared experience of persons of both sexes anywhere.

Explanations for this process are usually set out in terms of universal psychological events that do not depend on time or place and always function in the same way. Yet in the search for salvageable materials for a more historically viable theory to account for sexual hierarchy over time, these approaches have something important to offer. Following Freud, most interpreters long focused on the process of achieving gender identity as central to the larger process of achieving a sense of self. They held that the critical phases of that process occur in infancy and early childhood and that they unfold differently for girls than for boys. For boys, there is a universal Oedipal moment in which a "normal" boy allegedly abandons an infantile sexual attachment to his mother, thereby anchoring a firm sense of his maleness, which includes the sense of belonging to the dominant sex. Girls, by contrast, lack a comparable youthful experience that confirms their femaleness, and are thus alleged to have more difficulty in achieving the gender identity integral to a healthy adult sense of self.

Revisionist feminist scholarship has since called this approach into question, arguing that Freud's model overemphasizes preparation for adult sexuality, rather than achievement of the more generalized sense of maleness or femaleness that is the real business of the early years. Revisionists stressed instead the importance of interactions of infants with the women who are everywhere their primary caregivers. They acknowledged an asymmetry in the ways girls and boys arrive at a sense of their identity as males or females but contended, Freud to the contrary, that boys are the ones who always have greater difficulty in this task. They maintained that male dominance is a byproduct of the greater complications boys face in achieving gender identity, complications created by female parenting as a universal and cross-cultural phenomenon.

The argument, briefly, is that since all infants first bond and identify with a female nurturer, boys are the ones who must renounce this identification earlier to achieve a sense of their maleness. In so doing, boys are sooner obliged to give up the primary attachment to mothers that makes achieving gender identity so much smoother for girls. Hence a boy's sense of his maleness is always more contingent and socially constructed than is a girl's of her femaleness. Subordination of women, moreover, is the persistent effect of boys rejecting mothers and femininity to achieve gender identity, a process that also prepares boys for dominant roles in a male-dominated world. While environmental features can reinforce or mitigate this built-in asymmetry, the process is bound to continue, say these experts, so long as women remain the chief child raisers.

While the argument as it stands is yet another that would isolate the monotony side of the monotony–variety dualism noted earlier, it is a marked improvement on other "universal" explanations for sexual hierarchy. By focusing on a process that involves both sexes, it redirects attention from men's behavior, and male dominance per se, to women's and men's behavior together. Also, by envisioning the quarry on the monotony side of the puzzle as a persistent effect of the process by which women and men achieve gender identity, it appeals not to a mysterious, unobservable force but to a recognizable social experience of each person in real time. Finally, by pointing to inferences that both sexes draw about their own and the other sex in establishing a sense of self, it opens the way for an account of a recurring sexual hierarchy that need not be taken on faith alone.

Unfortunately though, in appealing so heavily to unknowable infant perceptions, these psychologists appear to have sold short their fine idea that male dominance results from an asymmetrical process by which women and men achieve gender identity. If one entertains a less rigid view of the process of attaining that identity – as many psychologists by now are inclined to do anyway – it is possible to argue persuasively that later shared social experiences beyond infancy and early childhood strongly influence a person's gender identity and might have the same effect of making its achievement more problematic for boys than for girls. It could also be argued for other reasons than a universal female nurturance that achieving gender identity is bound to be easier for girls.

Admittedly, abandoning female nurturing as an all-purpose explanation for male dominance has the drawback of requiring interpreters to identify other common social experiences across societies that made it harder for boys than for girls to achieve gender identity. Yet it also has the advantage, for historians among others, of making the process more open to scrutiny over time. What that means is that the theory of a link between male dominance and the process of achieving gender identity becomes subject to validation through historical analysis in a way that claims for universal female nurturance in reproducing that dominance do not. While a common denominator in shared social experience across cultures is clearly more compelling as an explanation for this stubborn feature than, say, an inherited dominance gene, the idea that this common denominator might be women's monopoly on childrearing raises awkward issues. For one thing, we ought to see more congruity than we do between the societies in which female nurturance is exclusive and those in which male dominance is most intense.

More important, while the case that men have greater difficulty than women in achieving gender identity remains persuasive, there is anthropological evidence suggesting that this has not always been the case, not to mention historical evidence that hints that it will not continue to be so in the future. Yet it is not necessary to embrace the universal claims of the theory to appreciate that the achievement of gender identity has immense potential for an historical inquiry into the more enduring features of human sexual arrangements. It is unnecessary, for example, to think that acquiring gender identity is always harder for men in order to find reason to think that men were long subject to greater challenges in that task than women. The culturally widespread and long-lived notion that manhood, but not womanhood, is a status to be achieved is just one of many suggestive indicators here. But to enable these ideas to function effectively in interpretations of different societies through time, it is necessary to show why an asymmetry between the sexes in arriving at gender identity is not somehow built into a necessary and identical process of human development anywhere, as the scholars who presented it have argued.

The most promising course is to explore a different but related hypothesis, one that preserves the idea that a sexual hierarchy advantaging males is a by-product of asymmetry between the sexes in achieving gender identity but discards the notion that asymmetry is always a necessary feature of that process. In other words, it makes most sense to retain the possibility that some societies may foster either comparable ease or comparable difficulty for both sexes in arriving at a sense of their femaleness or maleness. Asymmetry, and male dominance in turn, are treated as features that are not automatically built into gender arrangements everywhere. Rather, both are regarded as variables, albeit particularly tenacious ones for reasons to be outlined. The results of this approach are gratifying, not only in illuminating existing bodies of cross-cultural data about women's and men's behavior over great spans of time but also in interpreting information from individual communities, including the ones visited here.

*   *   *

Those results will shortly be presented on a broader canvas, but first it is worth underscoring why this approach recommended itself. The most important clue was in the comparison of early- and late-marriage systems in agricultural societies. That exercise, in effect, entailed assessing women's and men's relative ease or difficulty in achieving a working sense of their maleness or femaleness.

The more prevalent and enduring early-marriage system, as was seen, literally creates and sustains for both sexes a far stronger sense of gender identity – not just during infancy and early youth, but at every phase of the life cycle. The tying of the onset of a girl's menstrual period to her marriage reinforces the perception of a "natural" link between bodily and social events. While men lack such an obvious event as a marker of readiness for marriage and procreation, emphasis in their case is on an "eternal" male-run household, persisting generation upon generation, and upon an all-important, abiding bond between household and land as the primary source of identity.

By contrast, the overlapping of the experiences of the sexes in late-marriage households, plus the greater fragility of households and of the link between household and property, appears to have made achieving a sense of maleness and femaleness also more problematic. What is more, every stage of the life cycle for each sex involves considerable calculation and a greater degree of individual decision making, which automatically makes it harder for those moving through the experience to perceive those stages in terms of a preordained or natural progression peculiar to their sex group. The turmoil we associate with the early modern era arguably owed much to this still unidentified process of adjustment in which men, in particular, found it necessary to articulate an altered set of gender ground rules, including a redefinition of the features of both womanhood and manhood.

As for what might explain women's apparently greater ease than men in achieving gender identity, the comparison between early- and late-marriage societies exposes the inadequacy of feminist revisionist accounts that appeal to exclusive mother nurture. Mother–daughter ties, after all, are far more tenuous and short-lived in early- than in late-marriage societies, and yet it is demonstrably in early-marriage settings that women more readily gain a firm sense of their femaleness. The Freudian model, moreover – in original as well as revisionist versions – ahistorically assumes a nuclear household as the site for an intense and universal parent–infant drama. This ignores evident complications introduced by the fact that for most of the world's peoples, the multifamily form, not the nuclear one, has long been and still remains the most common residential arrangement.

Evidence that men in both settings, but especially in late-marriage ones, expressed stronger concern about gender boundaries has already been hypothesized to be owing to their more compelling need, at least in agricultural settings, to define their own roles and positions. Yet it is unclear what might account for that need. The explanation that works best, I think, begins with the simple observation that in every human community, regardless of type, women and men are bound to use information from their environments to establish a working sense of who they are relative to others in the society.

The information individuals use in this process obviously varies from society to society, and within societies from one group to another. It nonetheless always includes observations and information about one's own and others' female or male bodies and what they do. This information is not identical for different sorts of societies, but it has changed less over time than much of the other information people draw upon to fashion a sense of who they are in different times and places. What is noteworthy in the case of agricultural societies, though, is that the information about women's bodies appears to reveal more about their social roles than that about men's bodies reveals about theirs.

The process of achieving gender identity has been more problematic for boys than for girls in agricultural societies not because women are the universal infant caregivers but because in these societies, where there is a high premium on women's reproductive functions, girls' bodies are perceived by both sexes to supply more information than boys' bodies do about their wider social roles, or what one scholar calls the "approved way of being an adult."[10] In such settings, the fact that women have a shared set of

[10] David Gilmore, *Manhood in the Making: Cultural Concepts of Masculinity* (New Haven, Conn., 1990), 1.

time-consuming social roles attached to their reproductive functions is also readily perceived as a marker of women's preordained function as mother. What is more, women's reproductive and nurturing responsibilities, in most contexts at least, worked to reinforce their more domestic social functions long before any man thought it necessary to declare that "women's place is in the home." The result has been that women's reproductive roles long worked for them in agricultural settings to validate a firm sense of their own identities as females. In many places, this is still the case.

For the majority of men in agricultural settings, however, there are no comparable counterparts in their social roles that can be so readily inferred from information about the distinctive features of their bodies. By contrast with women, whose womanhood could readily be inferred as built in and somehow natural, men were obliged to construct their manhood more exclusively from outside materials. They could and did draw inferences for their own gender identities by observing common features of women's lives, and then by making claims that their own activities and qualities were just as natural as their female counterparts' seemed to be. But manhood for men, in most historical settings, has been more contingent, more subject to outside change, than womanhood. Men have required the establishment of local consensus on what counts as manhood in ways that women, for long anyhow, have not.

It is not surprising that in identifying the ingredients of manhood in any context, men have called upon two features distinctive to themselves: comparatively greater size and strength and the absence of any bodily functions that both consume time and limit mobility. These features have enabled men to play the roles of protector and provider for mates and offspring that a recent anthropological survey identifies as consistent cross-cultural ingredients of manhood.[11] They also have enabled men to assert control over women and children and make it stick. To an obvious extent, they still do.

If what we call male dominance was a by-product of the fact that men in most of the historical era have been obliged to work more actively to construct their gender identities than women, and have called, when needed, upon their distinctive physical qualities, then we might expect to see some differences when we step back from the portrayal of the agricultural phase of the human record and attempt to take in the whole canvas. It ought to be the case that any societies in which the central and most valued male activities can readily be perceived as directly related to men's distinctive physical capacities are also societies in which men more easily achieve a sense of manhood. That, in turn, may mean that women in those societies are less likely to pay a price – in violence, sequestering, or other forms of control – that they are liable to pay in places where men have greater challenges in gaining a working sense of manhood.

[11] Ibid., 222–23.

A remarkable study by ethnographer Martin King Whyte that set out to assess women's status relative to men's in preindustrial societies appears to vindicate this hypothesis.[12] Of the ninety-three current societies included, a third were nomadic hunting societies, a third were mixed societies such as tribal groups featuring herding and/or shifting agriculture, and a third were peasant villages within complex agrarian societies. In the absence of continuous historical records that might allow a survey of stages in the evolution of human cultures, data from such contemporary societies whose features are known to have emerged at different times – for example, pottery-making and nomadic bands appeared very early, whereas plow agriculture and settled towns emerged much later – make it possible to establish a proxy evolutionary sequence within which to examine different behaviors. White selected fifty-two variables thought to be relevant to women's status on which data were available from most of the cultures.

While the analysis failed to identify a single item or cluster of items that permits a meaningful cross-cultural ranking of societies by women's status, it did show that similar attitudes and behaviors of the sexes turn up in societies of certain types. Significantly, it was those communities exemplifying the latest societal type to emerge – namely, peasant societies – that featured the most restrictions on women. Earlier chapters have already described how tying livelihood to fixed landed property tended to mean constraints on women's sexual and wider social lives. In addition, peasant societies displayed comparatively greater ritualized fear of women. In hunting and gathering societies and even in mixed societies of herding and shifting horticulture, men subjected women to less violence than did those in agrarian communities. Despite highly institutionalized male solidarity in such settings, Whyte found little support for claims that these simpler societies, with their "male bonding" forged by the hunt, generate harsh forms of male control over women. Instead, it is the agricultural societies that do that.

Important for the analysis here, hunting and warfare, as critical male activities in the earliest human cultures, can readily be identified by men as linked to their own special physical attributes as a sex. Roles that place a premium on greater size and strength suggest a kind of preordained male arena of activity, comparable to a female arena in which women's social roles are inferred directly from their bodily features. It is possible then that the limited subjection of women to male violence in the simpler societies owes something to men's greater security in such societies in the performance of activities they can effortlessly perceive as unique to themselves.

With the adoption of agriculture after the depletion of animal herds in the last ice age, the emergence of more settled and socially differentiated societies meant that hunting and fighting ceased to be activities in which most men engaged. Warfare became the specialty of a favored minority in many

[12] Martin King Whyte, *The Status of Women in Pre-industrial Societies* (Princeton, N.J., 1978).

places; and agriculture, which had been women's specialty in the simpler societies, became the primary occupation of most men, often in conditions of servitude.

While greater size and strength could still be related to many male activities, and still are, the loss of hunting as a near-universal element of the male world meant that men were henceforth obliged to find manhood in a set of shifting, socially differentiated activities including land-owning, office-holding, and priestly functions, all of whose ties to the distinctive features of their bodies were more tenuous. While a conscious anxiety about manhood itself was a long way off, it is still worth remarking that very early on, humankind lost the strongest pattern of symmetry there has ever been between the sexes in the links between bodily characteristics and social roles. And it was men, not women, who were first to be confronted with the reinvention of their gender identity.

That it was men in northwestern Europe who would also be first to express a more conscious concern about the ground rules of gender arrangements that had long been taken for granted finally begins to make more sense. They did so because at a certain point within their particular agricultural societies, what had long been the chief anchor of male identity began to give way. More precisely, as an effect of the adoption in northwestern Europe of late marriage for women, the unity of kin and property that for thousands of years had been the central focus of most men's worlds began to dissolve. On some level, men started to realize that what had been the mainstay of manhood had become unreliable. It is little wonder that they displayed confusion and anxiety for so long. Control of property had been the mainstay of male identity in agricultural societies since well before recorded history began.

Men, to be sure, had hardly chosen to invest their identity in landed property in the first place. But as the land came to represent the most secure form of livelihood for most of the world's peoples, they had had little option to do otherwise. They had made the transition from hunting through herding and pastoral systems, which had placed them in control of the larger domesticated animals. When the animal-drawn plow was developed, in about the third millennium B.C., men's long experience with animals is presumed to have made following the plow into the fields seem a natural male role, although its links to men's greater physical size and strength were hardly so obvious.

Medieval chronicles make it clear that the heavy wheeled plow drawn by a shod and harnessed horse was an established emblem for manhood whose meaning went beyond its obvious sexual symbolism. Even though far more agricultural labor was performed by women on the manors of medieval Europe than in most agricultural societies, the idea that women might use the plow itself became unthinkable. Ivan Illich has described how the portrayal of women behind a plow in late-fourteenth-century miniatures, when the plague had reduced the European population by more than a third, was a way to convey cataclysmic disaster: a society so depleted of labor that it was driven to trespass what had been elevated as a sacred barrier between women's and men's worlds.[13]

When manhood came to be invested in things that were not, like hunting, so clearly linked to physical capacities to which they might lay exclusive claim, men were obliged to guard whatever roles held most important to their identities from female "pollution." Even in hunting societies, they developed initiation rites for boys that served to mark the entry into manhood, rites that have persisted in countless forms. More dependence upon the external environment to define manhood also meant that for men, almost any activity had implications for gender identity that were not there for women. While it is true that women often performed tasks more time-consuming than the actual nurturance of infants, it is equally true that so long as they were liable to unpredictable pregnancies and nurturing responsibilities, whatever else they did could not be perceived to eclipse a female identity that clung so much more tightly to their bodies than men's male identity did to theirs.

That men continued to be more reluctant to engage in women's work than women in men's work is now easier to explain. This is not just another assertion of male dominance or superiority, as it is often held to be. For men, a larger component of identity was – and still is – derived from any activities they perform. Doing women's work, for men, in a sense is to "become" a woman, while the reverse is not the case. This explains, too, why manhood, and not womanhood, has commonly been regarded as a status to be achieved. In the ironic tale that is the history of gender identity, men's curse has remained the sense that they somehow have to prove their manhood. Women's curse continues to be the sense that they have nothing to prove.

Male dominance, then, in the bewildering variety of forms it continues to display in the human family, appears to be the stubborn accompaniment of men's effort everywhere to establish a manhood as secure as the womanhood that, until quite recently, seemed to be securely anchored in women's bodies. That womanhood itself, like manhood, is gradually becoming more detached from bodies, or more accurately from perceptions about those bodies, suggests that something momentous in the history of the relations between the sexes has gotten underway.

* * *

What is noteworthy in this approach to explaining an enduring sexual hierarchy favoring men is that it places primary emphasis on a social process that is both familiar and universal – that is, the establishment of gender identity that is repeated anew as each person constructs a sense of what it is to be male or female in a particular time and place. This process in and

[13] Ivan Illich, *Gender* (New York, 1982), 143.

of itself need not result in male dominance behaviors. Throughout recorded history when agricultural societies were the single most prevalent type, however, the process of achieving gender identity was sharply asymmetrical for the sexes, since women's bodies long appeared to women and men alike to give more information about their presumed social destinies than men's did. This meant, in turn, that men were prompted to devise notions of manhood based on inferences from their own bodily features that were likely to include various controls over women's lives.

Once again, though, it is necessary to underscore the point that it is not the physical differences between the sexes that explain the persistence of what we call male dominance. It is rather the inferences drawn by each individual from those physical features in combination with all the other information available in a given society about women and men and what they do. A gender hierarchy favoring men is not a prior "given" of some sort, but rather a constantly reenacted social process.

This approach makes it possible, for instance, to imagine societies in which physical differences between the sexes might not be construed in ways that reproduce male dominance. That few societies have approached that situation, however, is owing to the peculiar conditions required for it to occur. If the theory holds, there should be only two "pure" cases in which a society might be expected to display an absence of gender hierarchy. The first is one in which physical differences loom equally large for both sexes as a component of perceived gender identity, since women and men alike comprehend their primary activities and roles as a more or less straightforward expression of their distinctive bodily features. This state of relative gender equality or comparability was approximated in the prehistoric era. Ironically, it may have prevailed longer than any other in the history of the species. The second pure case is exemplified by the society in which physical differences, although acknowledged as such, do not bear crucially upon the achievement of personal identity for either sex, since they do not offer clear-cut or obvious links to the observable day-to-day activities of either men or women.

Since societies in which physical differences play either a substantial or a minimal role in identity formation for both sexes have been exceptional in the period of recorded history, it remains difficult to imagine that women and men might experience symmetry in achieving a sense of their maleness or femaleness. More typically, women's physical characteristics have been perceived as more definitive of womanhood than men's are of manhood, thereby placing the greater pressure on men to achieve identity, which is likely to result in various sorts of dominance claims and behaviors.

Human evolution can therefore be seen to display a shift from early hunting and gathering societies in which their physical differences played a considerable role for both sexes in identity formation to agricultural and industrial societies in which such differences played a decreasing role in that process but long remained more salient for women than for men. Anthropological findings that common indices of male dominance increased dramatically in the shift from hunting and mixed hunting and horticultural societies to complex agrarian ones could then be held as evidence that, for long, there was a widening gap between the sexes in the ease with which they were able to attain gender identity. This could, in turn, be interpreted to mean that as human societies evolved, men were the ones presented with ever more challenges in this task.

By the same token, the approach being proposed here suggests new ways to consider the more recent gender developments in Western societies that are our immediate concern. This account focuses on the later phases of the evolution of an agricultural region in northwestern Europe, a place where the adoption of a unique family-formation system caused the gap between womanhood as a perceived "natural" state and manhood as a more "achieved" one to narrow enough to be noticed as such. To put it another way, gender hierarchy finally came to be consciously questioned in this region, since for growing numbers of people, presumptions of fixedness in women's primary activities became impossible to sustain. Like men, women came to derive their declared gender identities more and more from the contingent features of time and place and less and less from a sense that those activities were merely a reflection of their distinctive physical characteristics as a sex. In the contemporary era, the result has been that womanhood has become a notion as problematic as manhood has been for centuries.

For our purposes here, attention focuses on the gradual emergence in northwestern Europe of the second of the two pure models in which a society might be expected to display an absence of gender hierarchy: namely, the one in which distinctive physical characteristics play a minimal role for either sex in the achievement of identity. We have already seen how ever more men, from the medieval era, were obliged to invest male identity in items other than property – their vocations, in particular – that were likely to bear an even more tenuous connection with the special attributes of their bodies than the tasks of managing a plow and a team of horses in a field. A significant but more subtle parallel development occurred from this period for women. With activities that increasingly brought their life cycles in synchrony with men's – beginning with the late marriage that postponed their exclusively female reproduction in favor of productive roles shared with men – people slowly and unwittingly began to qualify, though not to relinquish, the sense that women's social identities derive from their physical attributes.

Results of the entire process have only begun to become clear in the contemporary era, with its mass consciousness and yet mass confusion over sex, gender, and the meaning of womanhood and manhood. But the point here is that these things had their roots in a development hundreds of years ago, well before the modern era, when northwestern Europeans altered the usual pattern of agricultural societies everywhere by postponing their daughters' age at marriage. That occurrence, by separating procreation from the moment of biological readiness for it, initiated a process that was to blur prior perceptions of indissoluble bonds between women's bodies and their social identities. This meant that women, like men long before them, gradually ceased to be readily and credibly imagined as creatures whose destinies are inscribed in their distinctive physical characteristics. (Ironically, by the time Freud made his famous pronouncement that anatomy is destiny, the actual undoing of the links between anatomy and destiny was moving into its final stages, where it still remains.)

If the process that produces what we call male dominance is understood as a common social experience with a history of its own, then something quite significant takes place. It becomes possible for interpreters to put knowledge about gender arrangements anywhere to work more convincingly in historical explanation, accounting for known behavior that is otherwise incomprehensible. That Western societies alone from the early modern era, for example, especially stigmatized male homosexuality, even making it a capital offense in many places, becomes easier to understand. Since those societies were the ones in which other anchors for manhood had sooner become less solid, the very act of sex with a same-sex partner carried more perceived dangers for male identity. The era of the rise and decline of witch hunts in Western societies also makes more sense when it is shown to have coincided with a time in which men and women in all groups were forced to adjust to a dramatic shift in the ingredients from which they could fashion a plausible manhood and womanhood.

The theory also lends itself to fine-tuned analyses of developments in specific times and places, not just in Western societies but in any society. Identifying the likely operative mechanism for reproducing gender hierarchy as a common and observable social process undergone by everyone makes it possible to overcome what has been seen as an insuperable interpretive barrier: that is, taking into account allegedly universal genetic or psychological features of behavior while at the same time sorting through all the more accessible, variable behaviors and attitudes that constitute the more familiar business of the historian. Recognition that a sexual hierarchy favoring men is itself a variable whose very presence depends upon particular, if frequently fulfilled, conditions allows for the theory to be put to work, with both predictive and analytical power, in exploring gender arrangements as well as many other developments in any society.

What is being put forward here, however, is a tool, not a formula. It still remains the interpreter's job to decide, in any given case, what information counts most in assessing how and why people behave as they do. Yet the largest stumbling block to using gender more successfully in historical interpretation is overcome: incorporating what have been imagined as universal, unchanging features of male and female behavior into historical explanations. This one does so in a way that allows interpreters to show that the familiar monotony and variety of gender systems, the variable and apparently constant features, are in fact all variable – and that they are inter-related pieces of the same puzzle. The approach helps to vindicate the radical early insight of feminist scholars that an understanding of how gender works has something to contribute to our knowledge of what makes history run.

* * *

The preceding analysis helps to address remaining issues in interpreting life in the two recently visited villages. It helps, in particular, to clarify questions about the priorities of the sexes in each place – that is, it helps to identify what it was that women and men wanted. Not in Montaillou, not even in Salem, did men directly articulate concerns about their manhood. Such concerns were coded in their attention to property, their attachment to work, and their competition with other men for these prizes. They were also reflected in men's behavior toward women. Women, for their part, displayed less obvious but real differences in behavior that are illuminated by considering evidence for their own central interests and their ease or difficulty in arriving at gender identity by comparison with men in each village. An interpretive approach that takes into account the likely asymmetry women and men experience in arriving at a sense of their identity and considers environmental features, including household structures, that enhance or diminish that asymmetry, can take analysis of any society further and point to better choices between conflicting interpretations.

In Montaillou, for example, there had been no fundamental change in a system in which manhood continued to derive from men's collective control of their households or ostals. True, immediate outside pressures there pushed clan heads to abandon for a time their reliance upon what Natalie Davis calls the "traditional custom and providence" that governed so many societies and to embrace heresy as a means to counter the renewed pressures of the Church. The purpose of this innovation, however, was backward- rather than forward-looking: namely, to ensure an earthly future for their clans that resembled the past. Options and occupations were few. Wealth and family identity continued to center almost exclusively on the semisacred ostal. While women mattered a great deal, they were passive players in the fashioning of a family's plans. In the eyes of controlling clansmen, women counted as infants who might threaten livelihood with their reproductive potential, as daughters who needed expensive dowries, and as wives who, annoyingly but with small effect, might resist the prescribed heretical route to Paradise.

In this world of separate sexual universes where the answer to what the men wanted was ostals in this life and Paradise (resembling a very large ostal) in the next, the answer to what women wanted was different. For the most part, husbands were unable to persuade wives to give more than lip service in support of heresy, not because the women were passive and ignorant, as their historian argues, but because they knew that the Catholic Church upheld their own female priorities better than Catharism did. If men intermingled their manhood with their attachment to ostals, women defined their womanhood in such items as recognition of legitimate marriage, acknowledgment of their role as mothers, and, most of all, preservation of the lives of their children – all items the Church defended more forthrightly in this troubled period than their beleaguered husbands did.

Still, while they might rail against priests who did not "plough and dig the soil" and yet enjoyed illicit gains from those who did, Montaillou men did not have to abandon the ostal-centered lives that their fathers had led. Nor did they have to devise whole new ways to envision and then act out manhood and womanhood. The virulent misogyny in the mountain community was a signal of new strains on men's ability to achieve manhood as it had long been understood, but the clansmen knew that real women finally could do very little to obstruct their plans. Rooted beliefs about manhood and womanhood remained solidly in place.

The troubled witch hunters of Salem were less fortunate than the rough clansmen of Montaillou in being able to achieve consensus about the core of manhood. They were hardly prepared to acknowledge, since they themselves did not understand, that their openly expressed concern about women and womanhood was more deeply a concern about men and manhood. In fact, if concern over gender identity is recognized as a factor in their behavior, then their apparent overreaction to changes that did not, in reality, threaten their dominant position – not on the domestic front and certainly not on the extra-domestic one – becomes much easier to understand.

In a real sense, what was at issue in the early modern era was the loss of consensus about a manhood whose core elements had served men in agricultural societies for hundreds of thousands of years and continued to serve a decreasing but significant number of men in Western societies as well. The nerve of sexual hatred that property issues touched in Salem owed something to the fact that men there were less able even than men in other New England regions to ensure that property remained in their control.

Still, the control of family property was ceasing to be the centerpiece in what was emerging as a far more complex construct of manhood. While landed property continued to resonate deeply in men's self-definition, changing material circumstances were causing men to acknowledge other elements – most prominently their vocations – as badges of manhood. Work, in fact, was beginning to claim the status it has achieved in the modern era as the chief repository of male identity, as landless craftsmen and artisans busily joined all-male guilds and resolutely affirmed the singular importance of male brawn for performing their labors. Complicating matters for all these men, however, was the fact that a more genuine working partnership with their wives had now made women more essential to their own achievement of manhood by these emerging standards.

In the Puritan prescriptions for female behavior, and more dimly in the efforts to link male worth and male work, it is possible to discern a perception, absent in Montaillou, that male and female qualities and behavior may not, after all, be innate, that they may even be defined and cultivated. This perception of a socially constructed womanhood and manhood was part of a male-led reconfiguring of both women's and men's identities, and its arrival was no accident. In the period from 1500 to 1750, the changes that had begun with the reorganization of households dramatically altered the guiding principles of the gender order in northwestern European societies. In the process, the consensus on woman's natural subordination, and on her lustful and evil nature, began to come undone.

New family arrangements limited the materials available to men to reconstruct their own and women's gender identities even as they increased the pressures on men to do so. That in nuclear household settings women were increasingly the ones to provide men's chief support outside themselves was unsettling to men, especially given what many thought they already knew about women's corrupt, deceitful natures. Traditional views that stressed women's mental inferiority and innate lasciviousness were obviously more suited to settings in which men did not depend heavily upon women as partners in running households. But as women's value in productive work came to be recognized, and as their roles as deputy husbands became critical to the fate of families, strains developed on presumptions men had long shared about women's debased sexual and intellectual natures. Their sexual reputations were now also more vulnerable – all of which prompted a review of women's "nature" in order to bring their supposed attributes more in line with growing male requirements for reliable partners.

The process featured the slow rehabilitation of women seen earlier in the visit to Salem. Yet the intensity of men's belief in women's wickedness ensured that the route would be filled with tension and high drama. The vehicle for exorcising convictions in a degraded female nature was the witch, who now became the repository for traits that had long been presumed to be the exclusive property of all women. Maintaining genuine conviction concerning such a creature, though, requires conditions that were ceasing to obtain in the households of early modern Europe. Policing women until they reach adolescence is at least possible, but doing so until they are in their mid-twenties is a different matter altogether. In any case, the effort would have undercut the increased productive value of women that now appears to have promoted the shift to later marriage in the first place.

The cost of clinging to older views of women's nature, however consoling they might be, was simply too high once the material supports for those views began to give way. So the unruly, libidinous woman, who continues to reign in men's calculations in so many other societies, disappeared in the West – but not before she had been forced into deadly quarantine for several hundred years in the minds and bodies of tens of thousands of accused witches. By the end of the eighteenth century, men had already begun to popularize another image of woman, diametrically opposed in her sexuality, who continued to serve in altered circumstances to reinforce male identity, as well as to rationalize some new claims for male superiority.

For their part, Puritan women did not appreciate the links between their new social recognition as marriage partners and men's real need, in changed circumstances, to shore up their manhood. More shared household authority appears to have encouraged women to pursue new initiatives, especially in the religious realm, where their equality among the faithful had been strongly affirmed by male theologians. For a time, some women even dared to launch their own woman-friendly religious movements. But once their men pronounced them heretics, they suspended these activities. Soon afterward, a series of witchcraft outbreaks became part of a whole set of strategies more or less consciously devised by men to help keep their womenfolk in line.

Women did come to see that the new approval men were willing to give them was contingent upon their conforming to these new prescriptions for womanly behavior. They were also aware, on some level, that the working definition of a witch came very close to being any woman who violated these prescriptions. When the outbreak in Salem occurred, women's own competitive rivalries contributed to their willingness to perceive other women as witches and even to accuse them as such; and yet not all women were prepared to embrace the new womanly code. It even appears that some witches, in daring to display public pride, discontent, aggressiveness, and insubordination, were consciously resisting the new order. In that order, men no longer able to control women through external mechanisms built into household structures were resorting increasingly to appeals to conscience in efforts to control women's thoughts, speech, and action.

One of the accused in the Salem outbreak, Susanna Martin, was a widow who had had nine children. She was no stranger to the accusations of her neighbors by 1692 when, after young, possessed girls named her a witch whose apparition had "greviously afflected" them, eleven men and four women, all her old neighbors, came forward to bear witness against her as a witch.[14] Martin and her two sisters, the children of her father's first marriage, had tried for years after his death in 1668 to get their rightful share of his small estate, but to no avail. Not only did the magistrates repeatedly rule against the three women and their efforts to expose the obviously false will engineered by their father's second wife, but Susanna herself was twice accused and tried for witchcraft prior to the Salem outbreak. By 1692, however, with both of her sisters dead along with the husband who had faithfully defended her against the earlier accusations, the sixty-seven-year-old Martin was extremely vulnerable. She insisted nonetheless that she was not only

---

[14] The account here is drawn from Carol F. Karlsen, *The Devil in the Shape of a Woman: Witchcraft in Colonial New England* (New York, 1989), 89–95.

innocent but had led "a most virtuous and holy life," for which declared effrontery Cotton Mather pronounced her "one of the most impudent, scurrilous, wicked Creatures in the World."[15]

Protesting the allegations against her based on spectral evidence – namely, that she had tormented witnesses while she assumed a supernatural, ghostly form – Martin appealed to Scripture in pleading to the court that the apparition the girls had seen was not her own doing but the Devil's. "He that appeared in sam[uel]s shape, a glorifyed saint, can appear in any ones shape," she declared.[16] Martin even had the presumption to display amusement at the fits of her accusers, declaring, "Well I may [laugh] at such folly." Pressed by the magistrates to speculate on what the possessed girls were experiencing, she first said, "I do not desire to spend my judgment upon it."[17] Then she added, "My thoughts are my own, when they are in, but when they are out they are anothers." Susannah Martin was found guilty of witchcraft and was one of five women hanged on July 19, 1692.

[15] Ibid., 93.
[16] Ibid.
[17] Ibid., 94.

7

Interpreting the Western Past with the Women and the Households Left In, 1500–1800

In London in the 1570s, some women created a stir by adopting men's styles of clothing. Clergyman Phillip Stubbes pronounced the women's behavior nothing less than a deliberate challenge to the divinely ordained immutability of sex differences:

> The Women . . . haue dublets & Jerkins as men haue . . . , buttoned vp the brest, and made with wings, welts and pinions on the shoulder points, as mans apparel is, for all the world, & though this be a kinde of attire appropriate onely to man, yet they blush not to wear it, and if they could as wel chaunge their sex & put on the kinde of man, as they can weare apparel assigned onely to man, I think they would as verely become men indeed as now they degenerat from godly sober women, in wearing this wanton lewd kinde of attire, proper onely to man.
>
> It is writte in the 22 *Deuteronomi*, that what man so euer weareth womans apparel is accursed, and what woman weareth mans apparel is accursed also. . . . Our Apparell was giuen us as a signe distinctiue to discern betwixt sex and sex, & therfore one to weare the Apparel of another sex, is to participate with the same, and to adulterate the veritie of his own kinde. Wherefore the Women may not improperly be called *Hermaphrodita*, that is Monsters of bothe kindes, half women, half men.[1]

Stubbes was also upset about men with "womanish" dress and habits: "we have brought our selues into suche . . . effeminat condition as we may seeme rather nice dames, and yonge gyrles, than puissante agents, or manlie men, as our forefathers haue bene."[2]

To read such distressed effusions and shrug that some things never change is to miss the point. It is true enough that cross-dressing has turned up in many times and places. But it is extraordinary that a practice usually treated as a carnivalesque diversion of role reversal was held in late-sixteenth-century

---

[1] Linda Woodbridge, *Women and the English Renaissance: Literature and the Nature of Womankind, 1540–1620* (Urbana, Ill., 1984), 139–40.
[2] Ibid., 140.

London to be an outrage not only to constituted authorities at the highest levels but to the deity Himself.

The anxiety and concern to uphold "signe[s] distinctiue to discern betwixt sex and sex" was still, in the 1570s, a rather new development. It is recognizable as one of many reactions to domestic arrangements that were bringing women's and men's lives ever closer together and prompting a new unease about shifting boundaries between the sexes. The controversy about cross-dressing simmered on for over fifty years in drama, sermons, pamphlets and ballads. Male "fops" – and especially female "viragos" – were regularly held up for scorn as creatures acting against nature.

The controversy was linked to a debate between women's detractors and defenders that had long been featured in courtly circles on the Continent. What was novel by the late sixteenth century in England, though, was the expanded popular audience, the numbers of women who joined in the literary part of the battle, and a new focus on the behavior of real women and men. The largely male authors of this literature appear less distressed by the "effeminat" fops than by the viragos, although after the accession in 1603 of James I, there was a fairly large concentration of the former among royal courtiers and favorites. These were inviting targets but dangerous ones.

The English controversy came to a head in the period from 1615 to 1620. In *A Sermon of Apparell* in 1619, John Williams, one of the King's chaplains, declared that God "diuided male and female, but the deuill hath ioyn'd them."[3] He added that the creatures in male garb even dared to attend religious services, wagging feathers "to defie the World," sporting daggers, and entering God's house "as if it were a Play-house."[4] King James himself entered the fray. In January 1620, John Chamberlain reported:

Yesterday the bishop of London called together all his Clergie about this towne, and told them he had expresse commaundement from the King to will them to inveigh vehemently and bitterly in theyre sermons, against the insolencie of our women, and theyre wearing of brode brimd hats, pointed dublets, theyre haire cut short or shorne and some of them stillettaes or poinards, and such other trinckets of like moment; adding withall that yf pulpit admonitions will not reforme them he wold proceed by another course; the world is very far out of order, but whether this will mend yt God knowes.[5]

Chamberlain later stated:

Our pulpits ring continually of the insolencie and impudence of women: and to helpe the matter forward the players have likewise taken them to taske, and so to the ballades and ballad-singers, so that they can come no where but theyre eares tingle;

[3] Ibid., 142.
[4] Ibid., 143.
[5] Ibid., 143.

and yf all this will not serve the King threatens to fall upon theyre husbands, parents or frends that have or shold have powre over them and make them pay for yt.[6]

Preachers and pamphleteers needed no royal command to carry on their attacks, although the King's personal involvement in the controversy is itself remarkable. Remarkable, too, is that theatrical portrayals actually shifted to sympathetic depictions of assertive women. One heroine draws a sword to halt a quarrel between two men. Another, held up by a highwayman, pulls a pistol and demands her purse back. Men receive deserved tongue lashings from women, and women dare to court men instead of waiting to be courted. Women distinguish themselves as heads of government, commit noble suicide like men, and go to court for redress of grievances – where they argue with wit and bravado. One popular play presents a shrew-tamer being tamed by his wife.

The decline of the bitter antifemale satire that marked Elizabethan drama has been linked to pressures by a new breed of female playgoers. Prologues and epilogues reveal increased nervousness about pleasing such women. Warning that a play contained uncharacteristically negative female portraits, one prologue admitted: "Damsels, if they mark the matter through, / May stumble on a foolish toy, or two / Will make 'em shew their teeth."[7] "Damsels," in fact, were now prepared to interrupt performances, walk out on plays, and even publicly boycott authors who persisted in attacks on women.

This cross-dressing affair lends itself to reinterpretation in light of both an idiosyncratic family regime and a historically grounded account of gender hierarchy, as outlined in the previous chapter.[8] It should be recalled, first, that the female transvestite was a figure with deep roots in popular rural culture. From medieval times, festivals often featured a "woman on top" who engaged in disorderly rituals of sex-role reversal. In a classic study, Natalie Davis early revised the then-standard view that the purpose of such

---

[6] Ibid., 143–44.

[7] Ibid., 251.

[8] In an article that queries the contention that cross-dressing, at this time, points to "a sex gender system under pressure" (cited from Jean Howard, "Crossdressing, the Theatre, and Gender Struggle in Early Modern England," in *Shakespeare Quarterly* 39 [1988]: 418–40), David Cressy, in "Gender Trouble and Cross-Dressing in Early Modern England," *Journal of British Studies* 35 (1996): 438–65, dismisses the literary readings of this phenomenon that, in his view, exaggerate its significance as a sign of "gender disorder," arguing that cross-dressing in practice was "neither the subversive abomination nor the eroticized transgression that some scholars have claimed," 464. Cressy, however, spends most of his discussion on cross-dressing by men; and while he makes useful points about the dangers of "projecting present preoccupation onto the past," he dismisses rather swiftly the evidence Woodbridge first brought forward of the hostile reaction of clergy and king to specifically female transvestism, 465. The argument I am making here is that the controversy does in fact suggest what Cressy expressly denies: that strains in early modern society and questions about gender roles and identity were "more acute than at other times," 464.

ritual play was to reinforce beliefs in traditional sex and status hierarchies through comic reversal.[9] While not dismissing that notion, she suggested that in early modern societies, women dressing and acting like men in festival settings simultaneously promoted resistance to male rule.

Remarking that such festivals originally featured just male transvestism and derived from ancient fertility rites, Davis noted that they came to include women in men's clothing playing assertive male characters. In early modern Europe, there were special times set aside for such ritual play. "In rural Franche-Comté during May, wives could take revenge on their husbands for beating them by ducking the men or making them ride an ass; wives could dance, jump and banquet freely without permission from their husbands; and women's courts issued mock decrees."[10] Such "license in ritual," argued Davis, made the unruly option more conceivable to women year round within the household, and also encouraged the disorderly woman's growing participation in political disturbances, whose purpose was not to uphold the existing order but to change it.

Davis concludes, however, that the woman on top could only serve as an image that both confirmed women's subjection and promoted resistance to it at a time when women were still viewed as the disorderly sex and when sovereignty was at stake in the state, for which the small world of the family was a ready symbol, with its tension between intimacy and power.[11] The image of the unruly female faded by the eighteenth century, she says, because a deepening patriarchal order subjected real women so thoroughly that the image of the female as the disruptive sex lost any meaning.

The theoretical approaches outlined here suggest that it may be time to revisit this image of the early modern era and the disorderly woman. While the portrayal of that period as one of increased patriarchal repression remains the dominant view even now, historians nonetheless remain divided because their evidence points in opposite directions. Some, impressed by women's expanded work roles and household authority, and also by their recognition within new religious movements, have identified a rough equality between the sexes. The early modern centuries have even been painted as a kind of golden era for women, in contrast with the industrial period that followed, with its allegedly separate and unequal sexual spheres.[12] Others, though, using the witch hunts as a guiding motif, have painted the early modern period in somber patriarchal hues. The lines of argument presented here make

[9] Natalie Z. Davis, "Woman-on-Top," in *Society and Culture in Early Modern France* (Stanford, Calif., 1975), 124–51.

[10] Ibid., 141.

[11] Ibid., 150–51.

[12] See the discussion in Judith Bennett, "'History That Stands Still': Women's Work in the European Past," *Feminist Studies* 14 (1988): 269–83. Bennett takes issue with the "golden era" adherents, whose views trace back to Alice Clark's classic *Working Life of Women in the Seventeenth Century* (London and Boston, 1982), which was first published in 1919.

it easier to explain such apparently contradictory evidence while suggesting that the authority struggles that mattered most in dethroning the woman on top were more likely to have been those generated within households rather than beyond them.

This argument shifts the grounds of debate by pointing to singular domestic settings that were responsible for both the positive and negative assessments of women's status. Husbands requiring responsible partners were obliged, however reluctantly, to abandon the image of the irrational and unruly female and to refashion women's image more closely to their own. At the same time, they resisted women's new domestic authority. If the context is taken into account of a marriage pattern that made newlyweds more personally accountable domestic managers than in more typical agricultural societies, it becomes easier to explain not only the ultimate decline of the figure of the disorderly woman wearing the breeches but also her rise in the first place, in a career in late medieval and early modern Europe paralleling that of the witch.

While links between domestic and public power do seem obvious, awareness that marriage in northwestern Europe had become a peculiarly interdependent partnership between spouses makes it unnecessary to contend that women needed the public example of annual carnivals as a stimulus to challenge male authority at home. Nor does it seem likely that their subversion of the usual purposes of sex-role reversal in such festivities required the prior existence of controversy over sovereignty in the state. After all, countless contests over sovereignty were closer at hand within their own households.

Life may imitate art, but in this case it is more plausible that the bulk of the imitation was going the other way. Art, or rather popular culture, was reflecting everyday domestic life. If the woman on top in village festivals was ceasing merely to confirm the rightness of the established order of the man on top, and if she was stretching the limits ritual placed on comic sex-role reversal, it was most likely because the models for her unruly behavior had long been multiplying at home among wives who had had to become more assertive marriage partners. That the "taming of the shrews" is such a pervasive theme in the literature of the period is further evidence for this case.

Returning now to the London transvestites who were celebrated and excoriated in ballads, plays, and sermons, some preliminary observations can be made about the probable overall direction of change from late medieval times. As ever more rural girls left home, took employment in towns, and were forced to become more independent social actors, they escaped the constraints of the old village festivals. In urban settings, some women did carry on the tradition of transvestite role playing, but they selected their own seasons and their own sites for such games. They also devised their own rules.

Both the women on top in the festivals and the pistol-packing crossdressers helped to confirm the belief in the rightness of women's subjection even as they challenged that subjection, and both embodied at least the potential for serious questioning of the social order. Yet in London, where a large urban setting had long offered relative freedom to growing numbers of single female workers as well as to the wives of small merchants and tradesmen, the older ritual elements of sex and status reversal, already declining in rural contexts, disappeared. With them went their accustomed function of offering an ecstatic experience to bind the community, followed by a sober return to normal social life.[13] In the teeming capital city, the boisterous and unruly woman had burst the bonds of community-sanctioned play with sex-role reversal that had long provided a safety valve for release of tensions over issues of status, gender, and power.

Anthropologists have argued that in places where the legitimacy of the social order is being seriously questioned, the more formalized rites of sex-role reversal tend to disappear. London, by the turn of the seventeenth century, was becoming such a place. The time had passed when dominant men and all social superiors could be secure in the knowledge that the carnival would pass and the presumed natural order of things would be restored. King James made that clear in his threat, should the sermonizing fail, to fall upon the husbands, parents, or friends "that have or shold have powre" over the insubordinate women. Although these high-spirited cross-dressers never became the subjects of more than ranting against their supposedly monstrous behavior, King James and other concerned rulers and officials had already given official support to the suppression of an even more alarming female figure: the quintessential woman on top who was the witch.

When John Chamberlain raised doubts about whether the sermonizing would work, opining that "the truth is that the world is very far out of order," he had more in mind than quelling impudent women in broad-brimmed hats. Already by 1620, forces were lining up that would erupt in the 1640s in the civil war in which James' son Charles would lose his head. And already, although not for the first time, powerful subjects were arguing that the King had violated their rights. This time, however, many more ordinary men, as well as some women, would be ready to join the fray.

In standard accounts of the period, the cross-dressing affair does not get even a footnote, the King's involvement notwithstanding. This is a shame, although less for the intrinsic importance of the affair than because of the light it sheds on attitudes and behavior in places exalted and humble. We are slowly becoming aware that women wearing the breeches – real or metaphorical – had emerged as a grave concern for men at all social levels in the early modern centuries. But that is only part of the story. The concerns involving gender, status, and power that appear in high relief in episodes such

---

[13] For a useful general discussion, see Peter Burke, *Popular Culture in Early Modern Europe* (New York, 1978), esp. Ch. 7, "The World of Carnival," 178–204.

as this one were hardly confined to direct encounters between women and men. The then almost exclusively male domain of state politics bears their imprint as well, as does the history of all other areas of human endeavor. Much of it, though, remains to be written.[14]

While connections are slowly being recognized between authority structures within households and beyond them, pathways to link them have only begun to be marked out. Traffic along these pathways, moreover, is still portrayed as one-way, from public sites to domestic ones. Yet if the sovereignty of male lineages within households was being eroded as married couples came to rely more upon one another, and if that very reliance was generating new disquiet among men, not only may there be no need to name a cause outside households for the decline of the woman on top, there may be reason to look again at prevailing views that have presented the early modern era as one of confident, even strengthened, patriarchal power – in households as well as in states.

After all, if male dominion over women, and the divine order itself, could be widely perceived to be threatened by a few London women donning male attire or having their hair shorn, it is curious that both mainstream political accounts and newer social histories have argued strenuously for this period as one of self-assured and heightened patriarchal power. If shifts in domestic authority meant that children and wives alike were experiencing expanded personal autonomy and responsibility, it is more reasonable to ask whether interpreters all along have been mistaking a troubled effort to shore up paternal authority for a secure new patriarchal reality. In short, if the direction of change in power arrangements is recognized as moving more strongly from domestic to extra-domestic sites, rather than the other way around, then this and much more of the evidence already in hand starts to make more sense. Such a shift in perspective, however, makes it necessary to take another look at what was happening to notions of power and sovereignty throughout early modern societies.

So far, this inquiry has concentrated on the impact of women's late marriage on behavior and attitudes within domestic settings. Yet with discussion of how the instability of nuclear households required family members to engage in more conscious planning and establish more links with unrelated outsiders, and also with a review of the role of the woman on top, a case has begun to be made for the importance of the late-marriage pattern in shaping familiar developments in the world beyond households.

This chapter will consider the potential of these findings about the northwestern European household for reenvisioning a sample of these well-known

---

[14] A superb example of the "new" gender history that manages to bridge the fields of gender and politics in late Stuart England when, in the author's words, "'gender' (or even 'the woman question') was not a topic of discussion" is Rachel Weil's *Political Passions: Gender, the Family and Political Argument in England, 1680–1714* (Manchester, 1999), 3.

historical developments. Whether or not the argument holds that later marriage of daughters was the actual "entry point" for the cluster of family features in place by the early modern era, the fact that brides among an unfree peasantry in the manorial region were nearly as old as grooms will be argued to have had momentous consequences. Women's late ages at marriage were nothing less than a necessary precondition for the most critical developments we associate with the era – major religious upheaval, new systems of political authority, and transformed structures of livelihood.

Standard accounts tell a different story about the roots of these developments, and it is a good one. In these, leading roles in what is billed, with justice, as one of the most dramatic historical periods anywhere are played by elite men acting almost exclusively in the name of extrafamilial entities and interests. The early modern European era opened in these accounts with corruption in the "universal" Church, followed by a Protestant Reformation that divided Christendom. It ended with the world's first industrial revolution, as agricultural ways shared by human communities for millennia were edged aside by machinery, factories, and new styles of urban life. In the interim, these three centuries saw the consolidation of national monarchies, the worldwide expansion of trade and of European colonies, and a scientific revolution that upset prior visions of an Earth-centered universe. The same years also witnessed the so-called Enlightenment movement, with radical philosophies that eroded the belief in social hierarchy, as well as revolutions in which an English and a French king lost their heads.

The discussion here will outline briefly how a review of the Western past that keeps women and households in the picture might look in just three areas: the religious upheavals of the sixteenth century, the political thought and movements of the seventeenth century, and the economic transformation of the eighteenth century.[15] Recognition that, throughout the early modern era, streamlined family households displayed great vitality enables interpretation to move beyond the still fixed notion that households everywhere were overwhelmed from the outside by the rising and relentless forces of church, state, and economy. While such a characterization may work well enough to describe the impact of outside institutions on households in the modern era, it works badly for the early modern centuries. Evidence in hand is better understood if the dominant impulses for a transition that finally placed preponderant political and social authority outside the bonds of kin are seen to have come, in the first instance, from family members acting in what they understood at the time to be family interest.

---

[15] A useful introductory essay outlining the large volume of recent work on religious change in sixteenth-century England and continental Europe is Beat A. Kumin, ed., *Reformations Old and New: Essay on the Socio-Economic Impact of Religious Change, c. 1470–1630* (Aldershot, 1996), 1–17.

By keeping an idiosyncratic household system longer at center stage, where it belongs, and by holding women's activity as well as men's in focus, it is possible to see more clearly that the stronger currents of change in this period continued to flow from households to the wider society rather than from the wider society back to households. One effect is the ability to replace some of the disembodied historical forces interpreters have invented with human faces – women's as well as men's. For if there is a single theme that is bound to run through the new narratives, it is the energy of the intentions and actions of ordinary persons. Particular interpretations will vary, as they always do; but so long as they hold northwestern Europe's eccentric households in their sights, and so long as they factor in women's roles, their accounts are bound to look different from the ones we already have. An anomalous pattern of family formation ensured that most persons from an early age were required to accept a large measure of personal responsibility for their fates. They also were obliged to endure, if not to celebrate, the condition of a wide overlapping in the experience of the sexes.

*   *   *

Consider first the riddle of Protestantism. Historians have yet to satisfy themselves as to why this particular heresy, or rather collection of related heresies, succeeded in splitting Christendom for good in the period from 1500 to 1650. As usual, attention has centered on the extra-domestic sphere and on men's activities there. Older accounts have focused, with varying emphases, on ecclesiastical corruption, social and economic dislocation, weakness in the Holy Roman Empire, competition among rising nation-states, the invention of the printing press, and more.

All these factors played a part. Yet awareness that explanations built on them overlook the odd households that had come to dominate in the very region where Protestantism took hold invites another look. It is true that Catholicism remained in place in significant portions of that region; but even there, the orthodox faith was neither unchallenged nor unchanged. What is striking, too, is the discovery in recent years that throughout northwestern Europe in the late medieval period and on the eve of the Reformation, there was a huge upsurge in religious sentiment and popular Catholic piety.

Before that discovery, to the extent that the religious behavior of ordinary people was taken into account in assessing the origins of the Reformation, it was typically argued that late medieval Catholicism was decadent, out of touch, and unpopular, a view that made the success of new Reformed doctrines easier to explain. The recent confirmation that popular attachment to Catholicism was actually strong, and lay piety vigorous, raises serious questions about the older Protestant "triumphalist" account – which is that most laypersons were just waiting for a faith to come along that was compatible with their newly individualistic outlook. A number of recent studies show, to the contrary, that local populations displayed great resentment when

Protestant liturgical practices were imposed on them from above for reasons of state.[16]

While religious doctrine and practice clearly did respond to changes in the world beyond households, the features that were most critical in promoting religious divisions in sixteenth-century Europe were arguably those that had first appeared not outside households but inside them. In fact, the religious upheaval that divided Christendom may best be explained in the context of the noted upsurge in religious sentiment from the late Middle Ages well into the early modern era, a response that can most readily be understood not as the compelling appeal of any particular brand of Christianity but as a rising religious impulse that found expression in a variety of orthodox and heretical observances. The new religiosity itself is explained by the needs of householders whose distinctive circumstances help to explain not only the widespread attraction to more intense religious observance but also the ultimate success of a new heretical faith.

It has already been noted that by the late medieval period, most young persons were increasingly left to their own devices in the many tasks of selecting a spouse as well as establishing and maintaining a household. What this meant in practice was that a weakened older generation was often quite ready to welcome a faith that explicitly bolstered parental, and especially paternal, authority. By the same token, the young of both sexes, who confronted more major life decisions from an early age, were readier to welcome a divine authority that they might envision as blessing and sanctioning a multitude of choices and actions that were ceasing to flow from long-standing habit, tradition, and custom.

Variously portrayed as totalitarian and democratic, pro- and anticapitalist, and pro- and antifemale, Protestantism was none of these things, although particular Protestants were. Like earlier heresies such as Catharism, Protestantism was a protean faith that took different shapes in different

---

[16] Most closely associated with the idea of a link between Protestantism and economic transformation is Max Weber's *The Protestant Ethic and the Rise of Capitalism* (New York, 1930 [first published 1904–5]). The new literature stressing the strength of late medieval piety and Catholic observance is vast and includes key studies such as Eamon Duffy, *The Stripping of the Altars: Traditional Religion in England 1400–1580* (New Haven, Conn., 1991); Robert W. Scribner, Roy Porter, and Mikulas Teich, eds., *The Reformation in National Context* (Cambridge, 1993); Andrew Brown, *Popular Piety in Late Medieval England: The Diocese of Salisbury 1250–1550* (Oxford, 1995); Andrew Pettegree, ed., *The Early Reformation in Europe* (Cambridge, 1992); and Andrew Pettegree, ed., *The Reformation World* (London, 2000). Eamon Duffy states in his introduction that "it is the contention of the first part of the book that late medieval Catholicism exerted an enormously strong, diverse, and vigorous hold over the imagination and the loyalty of people up to the very moment of Reformation. Traditional religion had about it no particular marks of exhaustion or decay, and indeed in a whole host of ways, from the multiplication of vernacular religious books to adaptations within the national and regional cult of the saints, was showing itself well able to meet new needs and new conditions," *The Stripping of the Altars*, 4.

company. Wealthy French noblewomen, especially widows, had embraced Catharism as a means to establish religious houses independent of orthodox control, whereas in places like Montaillou, Catharism became a male dogma to shore up family ostals. Similarly, for the men in northwestern Europe who were its chief architects and most vocal practitioners, Protestantism would turn out to shore up diminished male authority within households and to magnify a supremely powerful male godhead while stripping away the saints, male and female, whose worship had largely been nurtured by faithful women.

Also novel in the gender arena were Protestants' grudging if real concessions about women's laudable rather than lustful natures, as well as their strengthened portrayal of women as equal heirs of salvation. Both of these concessions have been argued here to have reflected men's own self-interest within changed household structures that came to require more responsible marriage partners; but they nonetheless presented women with new justification for some religious initiatives of their own. Such an interpretation again shifts the grounds of the present debate on the effects of the religious upheavals on the gender order. It does not take sides on the issue of whether the Reformation itself was good or bad for women, suggesting that those who cite Protestantism for raising women's image and options as well as those who assign it responsibility for holding women back are both right, if for the wrong reasons.

Earlier commentators such as Steven Ozment, for example, took reformers' more positive pronouncements about women at face value.[17] In examining family life in Reformation Germany, rather than recognize that much of men's positive rhetoric amounted to concessions in campaigns to contain and socialize newly empowered wives, Ozment credits Protestantism itself for elevating women's social position. He is right, of course, that the reformed religion accorded women new respect and recognition as wives. He is also right that by extolling marriage over the celibate ideal, reformers challenged the medieval Church's hostility to sex as well as its deep prejudice on the subject of women's bodies. Still, his attacks on the historians of women who have focused on reformers' insistence on wifely subordination miss the mark. He dismisses them for their judgment of the past "by egalitarian standards that have yet to win a clear consensus even in the modern world."[18] In fact, their increasingly sophisticated analyses, presenting a deeply ambiguous portrait of the effect on women of Protestant theology and practice, have often exposed a highly nuanced view of women's lives in Reformation Europe, even though their portrayals, like Ozment's, often mistakenly try to pin down the "essence" of the Reformation's influence on women – in their case, usually a negative one.

[17] Steven Ozment, *When Fathers Ruled: Family Life in Reformation Europe* (Cambridge, 1983).
[18] Ibid., 99.

A remarkable and rich study by Lyndal Roper, for example, looks at women in the German town of Augsburg in the early sixteenth century and argues that, contrary to those who see the Reformation as beneficial for women, the Protestant heritage must finally be seen as one of renewed and harsh patriarchalism. Regardless of evidence of Puritan prophetesses, French Calvinist noblewomen, and women in the English war sects, she says, "the institutionalized Reformation was most successful when it most insisted on a vision of women's incorporation within the household under the leadership of their husbands."[19] Roper acknowledges that in the heady period of the 1520s, women in Augsburg could be found writing pamphlets, prophesying, and citing the apostle Paul in Galatians that "in Christ there is neither man nor woman."[20] Yet as she later shows, this was a brief shining moment. Soon thereafter urban Protestantism, with the aid of newly established male institutional networks in craft guilds led by masters in their household workshops, spearheaded a conservative shift in which women lost their public voices. Roper insists that gender relations were not simply tangentially affected by the Reformation but were at the heart of the movement – that Protestantism, "both as a religious credo and a social movement, must be understood as a theology of gender."[21]

Here once again, categorical assessments running in opposite directions – and judging the Reformation as either positive or negative for women – miss the point about the underlying household and community context that framed both the initiation and the evolution of the Protestant heresy. These and other studies offer a wealth of new information about the Reformation at the popular level, but their assessments rarely take into account the distinctive circumstances of subjects, women and men alike, who were engaged together in a larger contest over the exercise of authority, religious and secular, that involved a major gender dimension but many other intersecting features as well.

What is beginning to be understood about a late medieval era rife with popular heresies is that religion, whether heretical or orthodox, assumed a greatly expanded role in people's everyday lives.[22] Especially in northwestern Europe, as feudal institutions that had filled in for the lack of multifamily ones declined, and as people became more mobile, household governance was ceasing to function more or less automatically and was instead coming

---

[19] Lyndal Roper, *The Holy Household: Women and Morals in Reformation Augsburg* (Oxford, 1989), 4.
[20] Ibid., 4.
[21] Ibid., 1.
[22] For a discussion that explores some of these issues of popular and heretical spirituality in the fourteenth and fifteenth centuries, see Lawrence R. Poos, *A Rural Society After the Black Death: Essex 1350–1525* (Cambridge, 1991), especially 229–88, and particularly the sections entitled "Authority and Rebellion" and "Religious Nonconformity and Parochial Activism," 231–79.

to involve ever more negotiation between partners. Women and men alike sought anchors for choices that had not before been theirs to make in new appeals to a higher authority. The process took time and occurred unevenly; but by the sixteenth century, whole populations in northwestern Europe were behaving in ways that could not readily be accommodated within earlier, more un-self-conscious authority systems.

Whether they were children dealing with parents, wives with husbands, servants with masters, penitents with priests, peasants with lords, nobles with sovereigns, or princes with emperors, people were acting in ways that did not reflect the ancient, reflexive patterns of genuine patriarchy. Protestantism might be called upon to strengthen customary ties of authority or to sever them; and it could reinforce declining male authority in households or justify strengthened female influence there. But everywhere reformers stressed a more participatory, personal, lay-dominated faith that looked exclusively to interpretable Scripture as its guide, denied the intermediary role for salvation of a priestly caste, and enshrined the household as the origin and locale of earthly authority and divine worship.

Such tendencies had marked earlier heretical movements. What was new by the sixteenth century, however, was the sheer number of people seeking rationales and reassurance for the more personally accountable ways they were now obliged to lead their lives. By then, the comparatively independent position of wives as partners in household governance also helped ensure that more women than ever before would have common interests with men, as well as some peculiar interests of their own, in becoming active "heretics."[23] Kings and princes ultimately determined the fate of the new Protestant dogma in most places. But they too had to contend with subjects who could no longer take for granted habits of authority that had worked for their forebears.

Ties of kin and property that had helped forge the bonds of authority had weakened. Feudal overlords, who offered substitutes for what real domestic patriarchs did more effectively in multifamily households, were losing their power. Population expansion and urban growth were disrupting village life. Households were now more independent, mobile, and fragile units led by single couples. Reformation historians have long underestimated the spiritual yearnings they occasionally cite in catalogs of causes for Protestantism. Such yearnings were expressed in appeals to a higher authority who might be held responsible for the daunting array of choices young people of both sexes were increasingly making on their own. It is little wonder that the authority

---

[23] See Shannon McSheffrey, *Gender and Heresy: Women and Men in Lollard Communities, 1420–1530* (Philadelphia, 1995), esp. the Introduction, 1–23. McSheffrey's study of the Lollard movement, often cited as a precursor to Protestantism, elegantly demonstrates why, counter to previous views, Lollardy was a heresy that was far more attractive to men than to women. Lollardy was a very different heresy than Catharism, as she shows, but in both cases, women had good reasons for their continued allegiance to Catholic orthodoxy.

turned out to be a Supreme Being who had preordained everyone's earthly fate and eternal destination.

The hypothesis that a whole society was becoming less, not more, patriarchal, starting at the basic level of the household, best explains why religious heresy split sixteenth-century Christendom. And Protestantism, as a faith geared to individual rather than collective Christians – one that honored marriage over celibacy and sanctified the conjugal household as the center of religious and moral instruction – supplied a governing role for households that had become rather unsteady voluntary associations of couples with their offspring and servants. The focus on an all-powerful male divinity has caused some interpreters to mistake a compensatory bolstering of paternal authority for a new patriarchal reality; but in daily life, fathers had long been losing control over their children's work and marriages. While it is true that their authority in northwestern Europe had never matched that in early-marriage societies, it had been stronger in prior manorial settings. Children, meanwhile, were paying for expanded choices with new insecurity, more responsibility, and additional requirements of individual self-discipline.

Male reformers met these increasingly wobbly nuclear households head on. Martin Luther saw that ordinary sons in his time, and daughters too, could pursue desires that ran counter to parental wishes. His own father, a rich peasant, had given Martin a university education intending him to become a lawyer, but the headstrong son chose instead to become a monk. He carried his rebellion against authority to the top, with attacks on Church and state in the persons of the Pope and the Holy Roman Emperor. In the end, though, one earthly source of authority counted for Luther – not that of popes or princes, but of parents. Only if an actual weakening of parental authority is recognized is it possible to explain Luther's and most reformers' dogged efforts to shore up the power of parents while reshaping Christianity with a newly personal male godhead.

Freedom, as Luther defined it, meant that the Christian need not perform good works to achieve salvation, as orthodox doctrine required, but could rely upon faith in divine revelation through Scripture. At the same time, Luther admitted a problem. If the offices, laws, and rituals of the Church are useless for salvation, then who, he asked, guards youth from the abuse of a liberty that might lead them to rush headlong into vice? For Luther, both state and church were inadequate to this task of instilling obedience, yet young people could hardly be left ungoverned. The family, he insisted, is the solution, since it is the sole source of natural rule on earth, by contrast with what he labeled the "forced and artificial" rule of the state.[24] Declaring that the commandment to honor and obey fathers and mothers was not just the source of parental authority but of all earthy authority,

---

[24] See the discussion concerning Luther in Jean Bethke Elshtain, *Public Man, Private Woman: Women in Social and Political Thought* (Princeton, N.J., 1981), 80–92.

he predicted "the end of the whole world" if the rule of parents were ever lost.

For all authority has its root and source in parental authority. For where a father is unable to bring up his child alone, he takes a teacher to teach him; if he is too weak, he takes his friend or neighbor to help him; when he departs this life, he gives authority to others who are chosen for the purpose. So he must also have servants, men and maids, under him for the household, so that all who are called master stand in the place of parents, and must obtain from them authority and power to command.[25]

The passage is striking as much for the strident defense of parental – and especially paternal – authority as for un-self-conscious language that reveals the displacement by this time of more genuine patriarchal households. While he insists that parents alone exercise legitimate and "natural" authority, he assimilates to that authority the more contingent, nonfamilial connections that, for most people, had come to take the place of the network of kin that continued to perform these services in other agricultural settings. For example, Luther uses the term "parental authority" to describe what had actually become contractual or semicontractual agreements with a range of persons outside the household. The teachers, paid servants, friends, neighbors, and "others" he invokes in this passage were all the consciously selected successors of the kinsmen and -women who, earlier and elsewhere, surrounded the individual, and whose functions within a true patriarchal system are not "chosen," in Luther's term, but simply built in.

The domestic paternalism so marked in Protestantism has been taken as evidence that the actual powers of men as husbands and fathers increased in the sixteenth and seventeenth centuries. But a look at the mixed legacy of Puritanism in Salem Village has already raised doubts about this notion. The very urge to articulate a religiously based domestic patriarchy, not to mention the now obligatory concessions to godly wives whose independence as deputy husbands was both required and resented, suggest that interpreters have mistaken a reactive shoring up of paternal authority for a vigorous new patriarchal reality. The religious spokesmen of the early modern era expressed themselves loudly and self-righteously, but their fervor and prescriptions give them away. Secure patriarchs rarely advertise.

Luther's was, of course, only one brand of Protestantism. A minority, including some women who became prophets and religious radicals, were prepared to pursue more mystical paths.[26] For women, a declared "priesthood of all believers" might offer release from sexual as well as social subordination, although the female prophet followed a parlous route in a world in which she

[25] Ibid., 89.
[26] See Phyllis Mack, *Visionary Women: Ecstatic Prophecy in Seventeenth-Century England* (Berkeley, 1992).

might be held up as a visionary one day and a witch the next. Male Protestants mostly set out to rehabilitate paternal authority, and Calvinists made more strenuous claims than Lutherans. Insisting upon the fearful majesty of the father, they declared that Christian "liberty" meant submission to a do-mestically based political hierarchy. Lutherans endorsed state power quite apart from God's redemptive work as a bulwark against social disorder, but Calvinists affirmed the ideal of a fused state and church dedicated to earthly fulfillment of divine will. Such diversity signaled the awkwardness of the new possibilities now for variant readings of revealed Scripture, not to men-tion the multiplied occasions for clashes of conviction. The European world soon became a more dangerous place for everyone as armed Protestants and Catholics alike persuaded themselves that God Almighty marched at their side in battle.

As for the Catholic Church, it appears to have been carried along in north-western Europe by the same fervor from the laity that drove the Protestants. A recent study of the background for the bloody episode known as the St. Bartholomew Day's Massacre in Paris in 1572, in which a wave of mur-der left about 2,000 Huguenot Protestants dead in the streets, underscores the influence of popular religious fervor on both sides:

We are used to viewing the wars of the early modern period as almost uniquely the affair of princes and kings, but the religious wars were different.... As we have seen, the doctrinal differences that separated Catholics and Huguenots in the wars were not perceived by the common people as abstruse scholarly debates but rather as crucial choices between truth and error, between salvation and damnation, between God's favor and his impending wrath.[27]

While divided by specific beliefs, Catholics and Protestants alike were united in their fervor for a personal faith that had become increasingly central to their lives and is being argued here to have owed much to the pressures of expanded choices in their lives.

The so-called Counterreformation may best be seen, then, as an institu-tional effort to respond to the new popular religiosity. The Church's structure and sacerdotal commitments, however, meant that it was reluctant to hallow familial authority or embrace household religion with anything approach-ing Protestant zeal. While Counterreformation bishops have been credited, in much of France at least, with fostering deepened personal piety among the laity, that tribute is likely misplaced. The remarkable early modern develop-ment of widespread parochial observance, lasting well into the eighteenth century, owed less to hierarchical initiatives than to the same popular search for legitimate authority in daily life that fueled Protestantism. For Catholics, there could be none of the home Scripture reading that promoted literacy

---

[27] Barbara B. Diefendorf, *Beneath the Cross: Catholics and Huguenots in Sixteenth-Century Paris* (New York, 1991), 178.

as it satisfied new longings for personal direction and guidance, but there were now private confessional boxes for exchanges with priests, expanded religious instruction, and new formal catechisms.

Such expedients were less than effective. Noting the "widespread collapse of popular religion in Catholic Europe" by the end of the eighteenth century, John Bossy attributes it to the Church's tardy embrace of domestic piety. He contends that the most damaging failure of Counterreformation Catholicism was "its reluctance to admit the nuclear family or household" on the same terms that it had formerly admitted the kin group, whether in its "natural" form or in artificial ones, such as the medieval lay fraternity.[28] Only slowly did the Church hierarchy abandon its insistence upon gathering the parish faithful in a single Mass on days of obligation, yielding to the households of Catholic Europe at least some role in setting the patterns of religious observance. And although modern Catholic spokespersons came to tout the spiritual importance of the household, for long in orthodox circles even family prayers were held to be subversive.

Attention belongs nonetheless on a new religiosity among the masses, whether under Reformation or Counterreformation banners. Attention also belongs on evidence that a decline of patriarchal control within households prompted an immense spiritual searching that included a split in the "universal" Church. Religious authority, still the most respected authority available, was called upon by people with growing personal responsibility for their lives. As men and women came to terms with a world in which their places in families and communities were ceasing to be preordained by earthly fathers, they appear to have found it consoling to construe the more willful and deliberate behavior now required of them as submission to the divine will of a heavenly father.

*   *   *

In the English Civil War of the 1640s, spiritual descendants of the high-spirited cross-dressers of a generation before took to the streets yet again, this time in overt political activity that featured formal petitions to Parliament. Like many men inside that Parliament who told them to be quiet and go home, the women claimed that their actions were part of "that duty we owe to God, and the cause of the Church"; and by the late 1640s, they were prepared to combine religious arguments for women as "equal souls" with claims for secular civil rights as English subjects.[29] Some complained of religious oppression; others decried the importing of foreign goods that hurt their manufacturing. Once in 1649 when women were petitioning on

---

[28] John Bossy, "The Counter-Reformation and the People of Catholic Europe." *Past and Present* 47 (1970): 68.

[29] Patricia Crawford and Sara Mendelson, *Women in Early Modern England, 1550–1720* (Oxford, 1992), 400–1.

behalf of imprisoned Leveller leaders and forced to leave, one group returned with a document making strong claims for their own political rights. The petition suggests that the women had come to link their positions as partners in households with recently asserted claims by their husbands and fellow countrymen for membership in the wider polity.

That since we are assured of our Creation in the image of God, and of an interest in Christ, equal unto men, as also a proportionable share in the Freedoms of this Commonwealth, we cannot but wonder and grieve that we should appear so despicable in your eyes, as to be thought unworthy to Petition or represent our Grievance to this Honourable House. Have we not an equal interest with the men of this nation in those liberties and securities contained in the Petition of Right, and other ... good laws of the Land? Are any of our lives, limbs, liberties or goods to be taken from us more than from Men, but by due processe of Law ... ?

And can you imagine us to be so sottish or stupid, as not to perceive, or not to be sencible when dayly those strong defences of our peace and welfare are broken down, and trod under-foot by force and arbitrary power?

Would you have us keep at home in our houses when men of such faithfulnesse and integrity as the FOUR Prisoners our friends in the Tower, are fetcht out of their beds, forced from their Houses by soldiers, to the affrighting and undoing of themselves, their wives, children and families? ... as if we our lives and liberties and all were not concerned? ... No ... we will never leave them nor forsake them nor ever cease to importune you. ... [30]

Historians who uncovered this evidence have noted that female petitioners were less likely to promote their interests as a sex than as members of landless, disenfranchised groups. They also failed in their political aims, like the men whose activity they supported. The Puritan- and gentry-led attack on royal prerogatives confirmed Parliamentary rule, but only by the "better sort." Despite the beheading of a monarch, democratic platforms first articulated by the so-called masterless men of the religious sects went unheeded for two more centuries. Radical sectarians themselves, moreover, while welcoming women's support, shied away from the idea that their own cries for the rights of "freeborn Englishmen" had anything to do with political rights for women.

The story here that has only begun to be told is nonetheless one of the emergence of a popular egalitarian movement that was uniquely northwestern European in its origins. Traditional accounts usually present political equality as an abstract idea, borrowed by elites from the ancients, developed in intellectual circles in the early modern era, and denatured by humble folk who took it up in hopeless popular movements. This radical activity has been recounted more respectfully of late by social historians; yet even they have not fully explained the spread of democratic visions

---

[30] Ibid., 406–7.

of society in a remarkable grass-roots politicization in the early modern period.

Scholars have admitted a problem in accounting for this diffusion of egalitarian political ideals in a society that could not have been borrowing them directly from anywhere. Family historians, especially, have even argued that the domestic experience of particular groups must have prepared the way for these movements; but attention so far has focused almost exclusively on elites, bourgeois or aristocratic, as the likely prime movers in a cultural shift away from patriarchal ideals of authority.[31] Notions of "affective individualism" and "domesticity" within the households of these privileged groups are argued to have promoted a kind of domestic egalitarianism that had major repercussions beyond the household. Ignored in this promising line of argument, however, has been the domestic behavior of the masses, and the fact that their family arrangements reveal that they had long been practicing, if not preaching, a rough sort of domestic parity of their own. Many commentators remain suspicious of suggestions that there might have been familial bases of any sort for the origin and spread of egalitarian political ideas. In the words of respected legal historian Eileen Spring:

Freedom and equality . . . are not likely to have been home-grown, so to speak. There is every reason to think that they have been infused into the modern family from the outside, from the larger world of ideas, social and political. . . . It is men and women with ideas about the legitimacy of a power structure that undermine patriarchy.[32]

Such a view begs the question of why these "outside" ideas were appealed to in the first place, let alone how they became so widespread in early modern Europe. But despite the mystery over the origins of the first popular movements, there is no doubt about the later borrowing and diffusion of egalitarian political and social ideals. By now they have radiated outward from northwestern Europe to the remainder of the world; and they offer, in the words of historian Randolph Trumbach, "what there is of a common modern morality." Trumbach adds, though, that the search for the origins of this first popular egalitarian movement, far more than of the first industrial movement, "should become the most pressing item on every modern historian's agenda."[33]

There are suggestive hints in the symbolic continuum of disorderly women glimpsed here, from the raucous women on top in rural French festivals to

---

[31] See, in particular, the studies by Randolph Trumbach, *The Rise of the Egalitarian Family: Aristocratic Kinship and Domestic Relations in Eighteenth-Century England* (New York, 1978); and Lawrence Stone, *The Family, Sex and Marriage in England, 1500–1800* (New York, 1977).

[32] Eileen Spring, "Law and the Theory of the Affective Family." *Albion* 16, No. 1 (Spring 1984): 20.

[33] Randolph Trumbach, "Europe and Its Families: A Review Essay of Lawrence Stone, *The Family, Sex and Marriage in England, 1500–1800.*" *Journal of Social History* 13, No. 1 (1979): 136–43.

the streetwise cross-dressers of Jacobean London to the angry Parliamentary petitioners of the Civil War. All raise questions about the "legitimacy of a power structure" – first in the village household, then in the urban community, and finally in the state. It is true that in most accounts of egalitarian political movements, women make their entrance very late in a drama whose setting is the world beyond households and whose cast of characters is long confined to members of the male sex. In this new narrative, though, partnership households run by adult couples supply critical opening chapters that have been left out, thus long rendering the familiar public outcome harder to explain than it needs to be. Political equality for all, including women, admittedly emerges as a conscious ideal only in the later stages of this new story; but the running theme from the early medieval era is the unpremeditated undercutting of patriarchal power.

Men who continued to be the acknowledged senior partners in households were sooner ready to admit formal ideals of equality in their relations with other men than with women, but that is no news. More relevant is evidence that before equality was widely touted in what historians have isolated prematurely as the "public realm," there was grounding in daily experience to make that abstraction meaningful and to encourage its application to political rhetoric and action. That experience was more important than the growing divisions among social groups – rich and poor, privileged and unprivileged – so often cited to explain the rise of egalitarian ideas. Claims for the equality of all sinners within the Christian faith, or of all subjects before the king, also do not work very well to explain the incendiary brand of egalitarianism that emerged in northwestern Europe in this period. More important for the appearance of equality as a popular political ideal was the shared domestic governance most people had experienced from the Middle Ages.

The notion that daily experience in ordinary households set the stage for political behavior outside households is not in itself a new idea. For years, historian Philip Greven has argued eloquently that the family his colleagues keep ignoring is actually the matrix of political behavior and of most other things that matter to them.[34] What is novel here, though, is emphasis on an eccentric family type with two adult decision makers – one of them female. This type is important for understanding political developments in northwestern Europe since it represents, in effect, a voluntary association in which the adult partners agree to create and maintain a unit to support and sustain the members. That ordinary persons ultimately came to perceive the state itself as an entity whose origins and authority rested upon a voluntary

---

[34] In addition to his previously cited classic study of colonial Andover, Massachusetts, see Philip Greven, *The Protestant Temperament: Patterns of Child-Rearing, Religious Experience and the Self in Early America* (New York, 1977); and, more recently, his *Spare the Child: The Religious Roots of Punishment and the Psychological Impact of Physical Abuse* (New York, 1990).

compact – one that might be subject to renegotiation or even termination – begins to make more sense within that framework.

In an extraordinary study that is an early exemplar of the new history being called for here – namely, one with the women and the households left in – Susan Amussen examines hierarchies of gender and class among English villagers in early modern England from 1560 to 1725.[35] She declares that if we truly believe the commonplace that the family was then a central institution, the fundamental productive unit as well as the basis for the political and social order, then "we must shift our focus; both women and men must be placed in the households which shaped their experience, and the different levels of social organization – from family, to village, county, church and state – must be analyzed to understand the models they offered to each other."[36] In an investigation that assumes, as she puts it, that systems of gender and class are both "socially constructed and historically conditioned," she presents a striking account that analyzes the transformation between the sixteenth and early eighteenth centuries of the economic and political roles of both rural households and the villages in which they were embedded.

On the economic front, she outlines a shift from a situation in which most family households were the locus of production, with the open fields in many villages supporting a collective economy in which families worked together, to one in which by 1725 enclosure and agricultural development had marginalized communal agriculture and ever more family members had become propertyless wage earners. In wealthier households, women were becoming less economically active; and among the poor, women's wage labor differed more from men's than it had earlier.

Similarly, the political role of families changed. After the revolution in the mid-seventeenth century, the analogy between families and states, which had been repeated endlessly in conventional portrayals of the supposedly natural relationship of the father as king in his household and the king as father to his people, became ever more strained. Collective village policing of moral behavior in the name of social order also declined by the late seventeenth century, and the family began to lose its public functions as parish notables became responsible for controlling the poor and disorderly. Households gradually emerged as "private" realms imagined as quite distinct from the state. As Amussen points out, it was not until the late seventeenth century that a discussion of the family as separate from other social institutions even became possible.[37]

What is so valuable about her analysis is the way it fills in previously submerged features of domestic power struggles, helping to situate the more

---

[35] Susan Amussen, *An Ordered Society: Gender and Class in Early Modern England* (London, 1988).
[36] Ibid., 2.
[37] Ibid., 188.

familiar and wide-ranging contests on the nature of authority that took place in more elevated circles in the seventeenth century. Awareness that household power was more widely shared among family members in northwestern Europe, and that most wives and daughters experienced considerable independent authority, also helps to decode lively debates involving writers with political persuasions ranging from divine right monarchy to secular absolutism, representative monarchy, and republicanism. Modern commentators focused on these diverse approaches to state power have failed to explore why these writers were all so anxious to portray that power with reference to power in the family.

In a revealing account of the religious spokesmen and social commentators who both described and prescribed behavior in the state as well as on the ground level of the household, Amussen considers the rich trove of political tracts as well as the manuals for householders.[38] While most accepted some version of an analogy between family and state, the political writers tended to ignore what the authors of the manuals knew all too well – namely, the difficulty of characterizing as fixed and immovable the ways authority works in households and the ways husbands exert power over wives. In this period, as she shows, domestic power was constantly shifting and contested.

Political theorists believed they were dealing with natural and immutable relations; writers of household manuals knew they were dealing with social and mutable ones. The family failed to provide as secure a basis for the state as political theorists hoped, but it provided the appearance of one.[39]

Village wives, Amussen contends, interpreted gender very differently from the prescriptions of the manuals. Of two prime duties for women, namely, sexual fidelity and obedience to husbands, women embraced sexual fidelity and readily engaged in defamation cases such as those already described to defend their own sexual reputations. The male injunction of obedience, on the other hand, was more likely to be ignored, especially when women's economic activities conflicted with expectations of obedience.

Women re-defined their proper relation to their husbands in order to minimize its contradictions and difficulties. This process was not a conscious one on their part, nor does it represent a desire for independence from their families. Women's independence and autonomy were critical to their success as wives and mothers. But the contradictions between women's economic roles and their expected subordination were so severe that they posed a challenge to the most carefully conforming wife. As a result, they elevated the importance of sexual behaviour, more than they neglected obedience.[40]

[38] Ibid., Ch. 2: "Political Households and Domestic Politics: Family and Society in Early Modern Thought," 34–66.
[39] Ibid., 66.
[40] Ibid., 121–22.

To be sure, Amussen's account, while splendidly leaving women and households in the picture, adopts in the end what amounts to a zoom lens on an already existing portrayal of early modern societies. Like other accounts, hers argues that both the "great debate on the nature of women: were they good or bad, orderly or disorderly?" and witchcraft prosecutions themselves were finally owed not to any serious challenges to the gender order but to dramatic changes in other arenas that summoned a deep longing for social order.[41] "Women did not ask to govern, claim equality with their husbands or declare the family an irrelevant institution."[42] Instead, we are told, what mattered were multiple changes in economic, political, familial, and social arenas for which control of gender disorder became a symbol. Amussen concludes that in the end, "the hierarchies of class and gender became increasingly polarized, as the experience of women and men, and rich and poor, became ever more distinct. The experience of women and men diverged...."[43]

The historical canvas being sketched out in these pages obviously challenges Amussen's familiar conclusions. I am arguing to the contrary that the household and work structures accompanying women's late marriage had an enormous effect on gender arrangements and attitudes, one that literally shaped societal relations, structures, and developments. Analyses that avoid the premature severance of religious, social, economic, or political arenas from their familial moorings will begin to get at what is needed in the reimagining of the past that is being called for here. They will also make it easier to recognize that the shift in women's productive roles matters far less in assessing their position and relative power at this time than their continuing function as adult partners or as deputy husbands in single-family households. The experiences of the sexes, moreover, are likely to be seen as continuing to converge rather than to diverge, which brings us back to the otherwise puzzling new insistence of male political commentators, regardless of their place on the political spectrum, upon women's subordination.

Writing at midcentury to counter what he perceived as the dangerous notion in early contract theory that all men are born free and subject to no higher earthly power, Sir Robert Filmer insisted in *Patriarcha* on an identical divine source for family as well as state power, arguing vigorously the necessity of a male hierarchy in both. John Locke was almost unique among political thinkers of the time in rejecting the analogy between state and domestic governance.[44] Yet he took Filmer's arguments on the family seriously

---

[41] Ibid., 182–83.

[42] Ibid., 182.

[43] Ibid., 187.

[44] This section draws heavily on the excellent discussion of these writers in Mary Beth Norton, *Founding Mothers and Fathers: Gendered Power and the Forming of American Society* (New York, 1996), esp. Ch. 6: "Fathers and Magistrates, Authority and Consent," 293–322. That

enough to spend the whole of his now unread first treatise on government, and much of the second as well, refuting the thesis of *Patriarcha*.

That Locke took Filmer so seriously has been explained by his recognition that the restored English monarchy after the Civil War had popularized divine-right doctrines. If the moderate Parliamentary faction was to succeed in replacing the reactionary Charles II, it was necessary to discredit divine-right theory.[45] That popularity itself, however, can be better explained by its resonance far beyond a handful of privileged royalists. There was now nearly an entire population of unstable households whose male heads had reason to welcome notions that, while endorsing monarchs as God's anointed rulers of states, also proclaimed their own divinely ordained rule within households. Locke saw more clearly than Filmer where family authority had actually come to rest by the late seventeenth century in England, namely, on the "voluntary compact" between a woman and a man that he describes in his second treatise, a compact similar to that between the state and its citizens that he alleges is at the heart of any legitimate government.

This founder of modern liberalism was nonetheless hardly prepared to pursue for the family and marriage a full contractual analogy with the state, where he readily posited the right of citizens to repudiate a sovereign who violated the contract. Indeed, for Locke, the social contract constituting civil society was entered by male property owners alone, chiefly as a means to protect their property. Women had no formal standing in the polity for Locke, since he did not acknowledge them to be property owners, even though many actually were. Unlike Filmer, who envisioned a perfect parallel between rationales for rule in the household and in the state, Locke was prepared to jettison his voluntary compact on the domestic front in cases of disagreement between the partners:

But Husband and wife, though they have but one common Concern, yet having different understandings, will unavoidably sometimes have different wills too; and it therefore being necessary, that the last Determination, i.e. the Rule, should be placed somewhere, it naturally falls to the man's share, as the abler and the stronger.[46]

Filmer, for his part, was no more eager than Locke to embrace those features of his theory – in his case, appeal to the fifth commandment to "Honor thy father and mother" – that might be construed to endorse independent authority for women. Even the single widely known female theorist of the period, the well-born Mary Astell, acknowledged that "from the Throne to

---

thesis, as Norton summarizes it, was that "the historical and theoretical origins of the state lay in the husband and father's power over his wife, children and other dependents," 8.

45 See John Locke, *Two Treatises of Government*, ed. Peter Laslett (Cambridge, 1988).

46 John Locke, "Second Treatise of Government," in *Two Treatises of Government*, ed. Peter Laslett (New York, 1963), 363–64.

every Private Family," husbands are "the Representatives of God whom they ought to imitate in the Justice and Equity of their Laws."[47]

What set Astell apart was a concern about how men wielded their superior power, and in particular about how they often behaved tyrannically toward their wives. Conceding that wives must always bow to their husbands' authority, as subjects must to their sovereign's, she reconciled sympathy for a victimized womankind with belief in absolute monarchy by urging sensible women not to marry. She proposed secular all-female communities as retreats for such women, a proposal that appealed to aristocratic fathers who, with the repudiation of Catholicism, could no longer dispose of dowryless daughters in convents. Her jibes at men's contrived arguments for their natural superiority suggest again that the patriarchalism of the era was defensive rather than confident. In *Some Reflections on Marriage* (1700), she remarked acidly, "For if by the Natural Superiority of their Sex, they mean that every Man is by Nature superior to every Woman ... the greatest Queen ought not to command but to obey her Footman."[48]

If the actual shifts in power relationships within most households of northwestern Europe are kept in focus, the nearly simultaneous appearance of secular, contractual theories of government, strident defenses of divine right monarchy, and new feminist critiques of unbridled male domestic authority becomes easier to understand.[49] There was disagreement over whether authority in the family and state came from the same source, whether it was contractual or natural, of divine or human origin, absolute or limited. Yet that modern political theory began with the nature of authority in the family and ended in many different places was an expression of a new consciousness, and a new bewilderment, over prior shifts in family governance at all social levels. Neither Locke nor Astell nor Filmer (nor any other political writer of the period) was aware that shifts in the marriage and household

---

[47] Cited in Norton, *Founding Mothers and Fathers*, 59, from Mary Astell, *Some Reflections Upon Marriage* (London, 1703).

[48] Cited in Ruth Perry, *The Celebrated Mary Astell: An Early English Feminist* (Chicago, 1986), 24.

[49] In her study *Founding Mothers and Fathers*, Norton generally accepts the view that Filmer's account of the seventeenth-century world was more descriptive than prescriptive, despite the contradictions in cases from daily life in New England that she herself presents and explicates. In the conclusion she then asks, "How did the Anglo-American Filmerian world come to be replaced by one organized along Lockean lines? The answer to that key question is not clear and remains to be addressed," 405. The response, if the argument I am making here is borne out, is that by the seventeenth century, due to the evolution of late-marriage and single-family arrangements, households were already organized more along Lockean lines than Filmerian ones, and that Filmer's was an even more reactionary representation than is generally recognized. Male members of the more privileged among these "Lockean" households then proceeded to fashion states "along Lockean lines," paying special attention to their familial interests and in particular to the defense of family property that continued to resonate so strongly with male heads of households.

order had set the larger parameters of their debate over power, in families as well as in the state. And none was aware, though it was implicit in all their commentaries, that this change had had the effect of enhancing women's bargaining position, at home and in wider communities, if not yet directly in states.

The story of the first modern liberal and egalitarian political movements is not confined to English shores, of course. There were other contemporary versions, with differing casts of characters and subplots, in most northwestern European lands and in North America. Everywhere a common denominator was the experience of women and men in partnership households that promoted participatory governance and raised new questions about the legitimate bases of authority inside and outside those households. This meant that everywhere privileged family groups at the top of the social hierarchy, whose resources gave them more room to maneuver, were faced with containment and accommodation, tasks that would oblige them sooner or later to address multiple egalitarian claims of other families and groups, including claims of class, race, and sex.

The challenge to authority that came from below was not, originally at least, a challenge to monarchs or to states themselves. That challenge appeared well before new nation-states had consolidated their power and before equality had become a popular rallying cry. At first, the challenge was to elite feudal households in the medieval era, and it came from peasant households. Explanations that ignore the continuing importance of household units at all social levels and presume the priority of economic and political forces distinct from households have confused the issues. In early modern societies, neither political nor economic decision making was yet independent of the bonds of household, neighborhood, and kinship. Evidence that the behavior of households all along the social spectrum was a vital element in the evolution of new nation-states, long before it became a factor in attacks on those states, has thereby been overlooked.

Historians have painted new absolutist nation-states as the nemesis of the feudal order rather than, as one scholar suggested not long ago, the highest form of feudalism.[50] Instead of envisioning these entities as led by princes consumed by dreams of state-building, and engulfing the remnants of the feudal order, this latter and more promising approach portrays early modern nation-states as the creatures of elite feudal families, who used them to nourish and protect their most cherished familial interests. In response to challenges from peasant families whose property strategies increasingly

---

[50] See William Beik, *Absolutism and Society in Seventeenth-century France: State Power and Provincial Aristocracy in Languedoc* (Cambridge, 1985): "Absolutism must be seen accordingly, not as a modern state grafted onto a pre-modern society, but as the political aspect of the final, highest phase of a venerable, though modified, feudal society – a society in transition, if you like, from feudalism to capitalism," 339.

stymied their own activities as territorial magnates, elites in northwestern Europe contrived to erect and buttress states that could advance their interests and preserve what still mattered most of all to them: their lands. Where they could, they strove for influence in these emerging state systems and bureaucracies, in return for which they were ready to surrender local political, military, and judicial powers. Yet even where they could not effect such favorable exchanges, they were prepared to abandon much to retain control of ancestral property and the ability to pass it on, preferably in an unbroken male line.[51]

In some places, feudal elites managed to keep their lands for a very long time while gaining power in new state systems. In others, they had to be content with hanging on to their property. In still others, these families lost even that most prized item, usually to newer elites who shared their landed tastes. But everywhere privileged families that might hope to meet the challenge from below were obliged to help fashion larger political entities as defensive measures, entities whose claims typically undercut their own local power bases. To justify and maintain themselves, these state entities were obliged in turn to appeal for legitimacy to still higher authorities. Initially the authority of choice was the divine will of God, although in due course, the declared basis for rule in states would shift to more pragmatic, this-worldly sources. In the end, a number of the new states settled on the secular divinity that came to be called the "will of the people."[52]

Accounts that divorce the history of states in northwestern Europe from the history of families – all families, not just elite ones – miss the connecting thread throughout in a process that made families, and then states, consciously constructed "works of art." New state entities demanded constant thought and attention, just as the late-marriage households had done. Histories that pay more attention to these family–state ties can explain more coherently both the evolution of nation-states in early modern Europe and the appearance of popular egalitarian movements.

The emergence of the typical family as a contractual unit, with new responsibility for both adult partners, offers therefore a promising theme for future investigation in reimagining what we already know of political change in the wider world. For ordinary people, the family by the early modern era had largely ceased to be the presumed natural, enduring, semisacred mixture of property and kin that it might long remain in remote regions such as pastoral Montaillou. From the lowest to the highest social levels, the family had instead become a more consciously fashioned entity, one requiring regular

---

[51] In a study of the English case, *Law, Land, and Family: Aristocratic Inheritance in England, 1300–1800* (Chapel Hill, N.C., 1993), Eileen Spring has recently argued that the entire history of aristocratic inheritance law from 1300 to 1800 focused on limiting women's right to inherit.

[52] See the provocative account by Edmund S. Morgan, *Inventing the People: The Rise of Popular Sovereignty in England and America* (New York, 1988).

care and attention if the goals of its members, collective and individual, were to be achieved.

Even in places where many peasant families managed to hang on to productive land that they might pass on intact to heirs, tradition and custom no longer sufficed to ensure survival. Maintenance from one generation to the next demanded negotiations, contracts, and diligence. In many other places, the control of productive property ceased to be part of the self-definition of families. Already by the end of the seventeenth century in England, wage laborers comprised nearly half of the population.[53] Families were coming to rest more exclusively upon the labor, skills, money, and ingenuity that couples brought to that voluntary compact called marriage.

The lowliest of subjects, then, had experience with the stuff of daily life to nurture views on the "legitimacy of a power structure" that might differ markedly from those promoted by their betters. As more sons and daughters came to chart their own courses, their attitudes toward authority – in families and in states – were increasingly emerging from their own experience of personal responsibility for their futures. Most people negotiated contractual agreements as young single servants with employers. They did so once again as partners establishing households.

Long before the contingent nature of the marital contract was recognized in law, marriages were conducted in northwestern Europe as joint enterprises by the two adult members, each of whom had recognized and reciprocal duties and obligations. In circumstances that required both members of an alliance to work and postpone marriage until there was a sufficient economic base to establish a household, individual self-reliance was a requirement long before individualism itself became an abstract social and political ideal. A sense of equality of rights was further promoted by such arrangements long before notions of egalitarianism became the popular coin of political movements.

These later marriages, forged now through consent by the adult principals, offered themselves as implicit models to the sensibilities of political and religious reformers grappling with questions of authority. Experience in families, which were miniature contract societies unique to northwestern Europe, offers a plausible explanation for popular receptivity to the suggestion that the state itself rests upon a prior and breakable contract with all its members. And if this is so, the influence of family organization on the ways people were coming to conceive and shape the world at large can hardly be exaggerated. The lingering mystery about the origins of a movement of equal rights and individual freedom can be explained. Contrary to notions that these were imported items, it appears that they, along with charity, began at home.

---

[53] D. C. Coleman, "Labour in the English Economy of the Seventeenth Century." *Economic History Review* 8, No. 3 (1955): 280–95.

None of this is to deny that features distinctive to different regions, as well as differences among family groups at varying social levels, either hastened or retarded the spread of these ideals. But people who increasingly claimed that their governors required their consent did not snatch such notions from the air. Their behavior was nurtured in common experience, and the ground of that experience was the household.

For long, until at least 1700, religious belief remained the only context in which the vast majority could articulate their new attention to the sources of legitimate authority, whether in the domestic or the extra-domestic realm. But that situation changed, especially as new monarchs began to experience the drawbacks of grounding their own claims for legitimacy on irreconcilable versions of the Christian faith. This encompassing theme of the search for a credible authority, in households and in states, helps then to explain the paradox of the "age of faith" that was the Reformation bumping up so abruptly against the "age of reason" that was the Enlightenment.

The revolutionary movements that swept northwestern Europe and the American colonies at the end of the eighteenth century everywhere began with a more explicit notion of contract, and of a broken trust between governors and governed. By then, religious rationales for attacks on constituted authorities had been edged aside by secular ideas of natural rights. Denials of original sin and appeals to human perfectibility were used to justify all men's right to a role in the political realm. By then, too, men from all social levels were at least initially willing to decry as unnatural the prevailing divisions among men and even, in rash moments, to declare that all men are equal.

Most women and men had no sense that familial arrangements that had emerged first among the peasant masses played any part in their attitudes or actions. Men who were obliged to adjust to a world in which fathers, at best, could only launch them did not automatically embrace either individualistic or egalitarian ideals. For long, they also remained deeply ambivalent about women's enhanced positions in households and in communities. Women, for their part, were not in a position to pose a serious challenge in this period to the continued dominance of men, either inside or outside families. But as individual wives, their importance in creating and maintaining households was far greater than in multifamily settings, where households readily could and did carry on without them, especially after the birth of an heir. Despite the many differences that set them apart, however, one thing had stayed the same. None of the features that had shifted the gender balance of power in the household had altered most women's confrontation at marriage, after long years as single workers, with the familiar set of reproductive responsibilities that they shared with the rest of the world's women.

So long as women were liable to unpredictable pregnancies and related nurturing chores, whatever else they did still had to be accommodated within these parameters. Women's own priorities were thus bound to remain focused longer than men's upon domestic activities, even as men's continued concern with familial property led them now beyond the household in efforts, often frustrated, to secure it or to find acceptable substitutes. That said, however, emphasis still belongs on the dramatic but still historically invisible changes that put women's and men's life cycles on converging tracks and brought unplanned affirmative action to domestic governance. When these changes are taken seriously, it will be possible to understand more fully familiar events outside households that stand alone, and inadequately explained, in mainstream accounts.

It should be apparent by now that a novel household system, and new attention to "signe[s] distinctiue to discern betwixt sex and sex" were developments whose drama and importance rival anything in the standard narratives of this eventful era. When households and women are left in, Western history as we know it is transformed.

* * *

For the third and final example of how different history might look if the standard causal order were inverted, and if the late-marriage regime were recognized for critically shaping the world beyond households, we turn to the economic transformation of the eighteenth century, better known as the "first industrial revolution." Ethnologist Martin King Whyte declared recently that the riddle of economic development anywhere – that is, the riddle of "why some countries, groups, and individuals prosper economically while others do not" – is "perhaps the central problem in the social sciences."[54] As he says, over the years vast amounts of time and energy by scholars and policymakers have been devoted to this problem, and yet fully understanding the sources of economic development remains a pressing issue.

The riddle becomes even more confounding when scholars seek to explain the special case of the world's first region to undergo industrialization. And, as Whyte says of the already announced approach being adopted here, "the claim that family patterns may have an impact on [economic] development represents a reversal of the more usual causal argument."[55] This is an understatement. To explain industrial change in eighteenth-century Europe, and in England in particular, interpreters long looked anywhere but to the influence of family and household arrangements to make their case.

Back in the mid-1960s, for example, when John Hajnal first made his discovery of the eccentric late-marriage regime, historians were regularly framing accounts of the origins of industrial transformation in terms of a debate between the "coal school" and the "soul school." The former school maintained that access to critical natural resources – coal in particular – made the vital difference in a declared "take-off" into sustained economic

---

[54] Martin King Whyte, "The Chinese Family and Economic Development: Obstacle or Engine?" *Economic Development and Cultural Change* 45, No. 1 (October, 1996), 1.

[55] Ibid., 1.

growth.[56] The latter appealed to a cluster of attitudes and values that allegedly enabled people in a small and not very rich country to forge ahead and industrialize. Most closely associated with this view is Max Weber, a founding father of sociology, whose classic study posited a critical role for economic development of the so-called Protestant ethic.[57] Still others pointed to the role of key inventions or to the involvement of governments. By the 1970s and 1980s, many scholars claiming inspiration from Karl Marx singled out colonial exploitation and the slave trade, which became a recurring explanatory theme in accounts of merchant capitalists investing wealth from global trade and thereby promoting a new class of bourgeois entrepreneurs.

As seen earlier, until John Hajnal's discovery that late marriage and nuclear households had dominated throughout northwestern Europe long before industrialization, scholars regularly argued that such households were themselves the products of industrial change, having evolved to accommodate the needs of a mobile, urban workforce. Hajnal himself speculatively reversed that order, hypothesizing not only that late-marriage households might have been responsible for industrial transformation but also that women's distinctive economic contributions within those structures could have been the decisive factor in industrial transformation.[58]

Subsequent analyses of women's preindustrial family and work roles have failed directly to engage this suggestion that women's labor may have played a far grander role in economic transformation than has ever been imagined. Hajnal had pointed not only to the familiar argument about later marriage controlling excess population growth but also to the long period of productive work for most women prior to marriage as a time when savings would have been possible and could have contributed to a demand for consumer goods well beyond the needs of minimum subsistence. "The mere presence in the labour force of a large number of adult women not involved in child-bearing or -rearing must have been a considerable advantage to the eighteenth-century economies."[59] Now that more recent scholarship has established the likelihood that several features of the Western family pattern, including the critical one of relatively late marriage for women, were in place centuries before Hajnal first thought, there is all the more reason to investigate the cumulative effect of these young, single women's collective

---

[56] See Walter W. Rostow, *The Stages of Economic Growth: A Non-Communist Manifesto*, 3rd ed. (New York, 1990).
[57] Max Weber, *The Protestant Ethic and the Spirit of Capitalism* (London, 1930 [first published 1904–5]).
[58] See the fuller discussion of Hajnal's thesis in Chapter 1.
[59] John Hajnal, "European Marriage Patterns in Perspective," in D. V. Glass and D. E. C. Eversley, eds., *Population in History: Essays in Historical Demography* (London, 1965), 132.

contribution to the labor force, a unique phenomenon among the world's agricultural societies.

To date, the single most robust effort to implicate the northwestern European family pattern in industrial change has been made by Alan Macfarlane, who picked up and ran with the idea then current in the Cambridge Group for the History of Population and Social Structure that nuclear households might be causally linked to industrial transformation.[60] His argument was that the chief effect of postponed marriages was to release young people from the confining control of their kin, thereby liberating their allegedly acquisitive, calculating, and individualist impulses. Such a bold, even reckless, claim elicited a storm of criticism, diverting attention from more sensible parts of Macfarlane's case and from other approaches to Hajnal's idea that late marriage and women's work might have been the keys to industrial transformation. Critics of Macfarlane also wasted little time identifying communities where late marriage and nuclear households dominated, such as in rural northern France, but where, for long anyway, economic individualism was hardly rampant.

As is obvious by now, I share the view that late-marriage households were critical sites for change, including economic change that radiated into the wider society. But it will not do to contend that eliminating the constraints of multifamily households resulted in women and men alike experiencing the release of their shared instincts as economic animals. Macfarlane also excuses the male bias he openly admits in his account with the observation that since more than elsewhere the two sexes now acted as one, collapsing all differences between women's and men's behavior and taking men's more fully documented activity as the standard hardly affects the analysis.[61]

To the contrary, while there had come to be remarkable parallels in men's and women's experience that are absent in early-marriage households – a case I have argued here at what some might call tedious length – it hardly follows that priorities specific to each sex ceased to matter. A more promising approach would consider other sources for behavior than a presumed "natural" acquisitive instinct while identifying and accounting for persisting differences between women's and men's priorities. If it is recognized that an ongoing obligation to support comparatively fragile family households continued to be a prime impetus for behavior at most social levels, then it is still possible to make a credible argument that both individual and collective

---

[60] Alan Macfarlane, *The Origins of English Individualism: The Family, Property and Social Transition* (New York, 1978). He remarks that since we already know that scholars were wrong to argue that industrialization produced the nuclear household, it is time to make the case that "if the family system pre-dated, rather than followed on, industrialization, the causal link may have to be reversed, with industrialization as a consequence rather than a cause of the basic nature of the family," 198.

[61] Alan Macfarlane, *Marriage and Love in England: Modes of Reproduction, 1300–1840* (Oxford, 1986), 48.

decision making by the members of nuclear families had far-reaching consequences in promoting the first transformation from an agricultural to an
industrial economy.[62]

What marked the late-marriage region in northwestern Europe from the
medieval era, after all, was not so much the release of economic individualism but rather, as hypothesized at the end of Chapter 3, an intensified level
of calculation on the part of adult couples making decisions that created
and sustained their unstable single-family households. With that in mind, a
more plausible case for causal links between family arrangements and the
birth of capitalism can be set out while avoiding the untenable view that industrial transformation was inevitable once nuclear households turned up.
Postponing daughters' marriages to take advantage of their labor contributions, if the argument made here is sound, was an early choice made in
peasant households in anticipation of immediate property gains. There was
nothing in this development that was bound to unleash capitalist impulses.
In fact, its occurrence in the classic manorial regions of northern France was
accompanied by the early emergence there of extrafamilial peasant communal government, which actually worked to retard rather than promote
economic individualism and capitalist development.

If the original motive of peasant families was to expand their control over
prized land, then only in places where this strategy failed to bind particular
families to particular property were alternate strategies likely to be pursued.
In other words, the question that needs to be asked if we are to understand
how the late-marriage regime may have been a key factor in industrialization is not "Why did industrial transformation first occur in England?" but
instead "Why did the calculations of members of late-marriage households,
focusing on land as the chief repository of livelihood and identity, succeed
longer in France (and elsewhere in northwestern Europe) but fail sooner in
England?"

Posing the question this way makes it easier to see how industrial transformation might have been but one possible outcome in a region of unsteady
households whose ties to the land were diminishing. Acknowledging peasant
households as collections of deliberative single-family units with a fair range

---

[62] It is true that more recently, several interpreters, including Roger Schofield of the Cambridge
Group, have considered in less idiosyncratic ways the possible relationship between family
structure and economic development. I am grateful to an anonymous reviewer of this study
who referred me to Schofield's "Family Structure, Demographic Behaviour and Economic
Growth" in John Walter and Roger Schofield, eds., *Famine, Disease and the Social Order
in Early Modern Society* (Cambridge, 1989), 279–304. Schofield is primarily considering the
shifts in nuptiality within the established late-marriage pattern in England, and he argues that
"value systems regulating inter-personal relationships, more specifically the degree to which
they were dominated by 'familistic' principles, constitute a critical institutional variable that
profoundly influences not only a society's demographic behaviour, but also its potentiality
for economic growth," 280.

of options also forces recognition of a marriage system that gave considerable leverage to the masses of families in dealing with their superiors, one that put constraints on elites, old and new, and on the institutions that they, as well, were constructing in the interests of their own families. These privileged groups coexisted in northwestern Europe not with a set of established and relatively self-sufficient multifamily households but with a multiplicity of increasingly rootless and mobile nuclear units – growing numbers of which were finding ways to earn livelihoods removed from the land or to supplement their agricultural income with wage labor.

A promising inquiry, or rather set of inquiries, pursuing this line of argument was launched in the 1970s by Franklin Mendels, who, trained in both economics and demography, inspired a broad investigation of multiple European-wide instances of cottage industry, or rural manufacturing, which came to be labeled "proto-industry." This research venture, which by now has become a kind of European-wide cottage industry of its own featuring wide networks of scholars, conferences, and joint publications, is relevant for the discussion here since it places the distinctive early modern peasant household at the center of the study of the origins of industrialization.[63]

Early on, these researchers focused on the importance of the economic and demographic strategies of peasant householders being touted here. Mendels himself, citing the generally accepted Malthusian view that landed resources set limits on population growth in preindustrial contexts, described how land-deprived peasant households turned to wage work in cottage industry in the early modern centuries. This strategy became a means to marry earlier and support more children in a process that also became a major route to economic transformation. The sources of industrialization, in this view, lay not in the inventions and innovations of the eighteenth century but in a long, slow development with its roots in decision making that began in peasant households in the countryside. In a recent survey of work on this proto-industrial model, Richard Rudolph remarks that the model also puts the evolution of industry in a different light from the Marxist one, for "if the roots of industry lie in the peasant household one can see its origins and growth outside the feudal-capitalist paradigm."[64]

Subsequent studies of proto-industrialization have challenged and complicated a number of the views Mendels put forward, and have also contended

---

[63] For a summary of these studies that explores recent work on the European peasant household by a variety of scholars in different fields, see Richard L. Rudolph, "The European Family and Economy: Central Themes and Issues." *The Journal of Family History* 17, No. 2 (1992): 119–38. For a collection of recent papers on proto-industry in several European settings that includes an extensive bibliography see Sheilagh C. Ogilvie and Markus Cerman, eds., *European Proto-Industrialization* (Cambridge, 1996). The investigation is based on work originally done by Franklin Mendels that is highlighted in both the Rudolph article and the edited collection of Ogilvie and Cerman.

[64] Rudolph, "The European Family and Economy," 131.

that the proto-industrial model ignores other routes to industrialization such as urban or state development of industry. Yet the model itself hardly excludes those other routes. What is more, its emphasis upon long-term continuities in social and economic development in Europe from the late medieval era provides a valuable corrective to still prevalent views that what happened in the eighteenth-century industrial revolution was an immediate, volatile, and highly localized English event.

The object here, in any case, is not to present this proto-industrial thesis as the answer to the origins of industrial transformation. It is instead to point out that a significant strand of current research highlights the importance for economic development of deliberations within peasant households around issues of work, livelihood, and family support. These collective deliberations, as the research shows, might or might not lead to industrial transformation in particular places, although it is noteworthy that the proto-industrial areas that had actually begun to industrialize by the nineteenth century coincided with the late-marriage region in northwestern Europe. The comparative study of peasant households involved in rural manufacturing is also important, regardless of the conclusions it may ultimately provide as to the relationship between proto-industry and "real" industrialization, since it focuses attention upon households and families as crucial links between the agency of individuals and the wider institutional structures with which they interact.[65]

As for the evolution of gender-specific work roles, and of power relations around economic decision making within households in early modern Europe, research since the 1970s has been at once impressive and inconclusive. We know a great deal more now than ever before about women's as well as men's shifting work roles in the period, but our inherited interpretive frameworks for understanding gender and the distribution of power are increasingly strained by these masses of new information.[66] On the one hand, and despite mounting evidence to the contrary, scholars have continued to present early modern households as manipulated and powerless – reactors rather than actors. Such portrayals appear to have been extrapolated from later working-class households from the modern era in which economic decision making came to be controlled more often from the outside. Equally problematic, in presenting women's activity, many studies have continued to cite productive work as the prime measure of status and to mourn trends within an emerging factory system that diminished married women's productive roles, rather than to ask whether such work is always the crucial issue in assessing status.

[65] Ibid., 120.

[66] For a bibliography of a number of these recent studies, see Olwen Hufton, *The Prospect Before Her: A History of Women in Western Europe, 1500–1800* (New York, 1996), 564–614.

I have already maintained to the contrary that work emerged as a primary measure of status and social identity – and then chiefly for men – only in the early modern period itself, when control of landed property was ceasing to perform that function adequately. Also, while many women's historians have argued for a kind of gender parity in premodern households, they have made the case not on the contention here of unique single-family households but upon comparable productive work for the sexes. Yet it is inaccurate to view this rudimentary parity as the effect of the centering within households of productive and reproductive work. Both, after all, were united in the ostals of Montaillou, and in most other early-marriage settings, too; and few would describe such sites as even roughly equal for the sexes. Instead, it was the partnership structure of households in northwestern Europe that produced a more balanced power relationship between the sexes than that experienced by most other agricultural peoples.

It is true enough that married women, in particular, could more readily engage in productive work when it was based within households. Martha Howell's study of women's work in late medieval cities in northern Europe shows that capitalism itself did not necessarily curtail married women's engagement in productive work, as used to be thought, since early capitalist modes were compatible with household production.[67] What led married women to withdraw from productive work was rather the removal of such work from the household, a process she shows initially occurred more often with small commodity production than with early capitalism. Howell found, in addition, that while the later medieval era witnessed widespread extension to women of legal capacities to practice the household-based artisanal work that many entered when they moved to the cities, things changed after 1500. New laws began to restrict women's entry into trades:

I am inclined to suspect ... that the apparent rise in women's legal status from about 1200 to 1500 was a response to the need for new legal capacities required by the work women were doing. I am inclined also to suspect, however, that the changes which restricted women's legal capacities in early modern Europe were part of a prevailing effort to restrict women's economic and social autonomy so that, in this period [1500 to 1750], the direction of causality was reversed.... For example, in sixteenth-century France, community property laws were changed to insure explicitly that widows could not control their husbands' estates.[68]

If Howell is correct, and I believe she is, this reversal can be seen as yet another instance of what has been cited here as the reactive patriarchalism of the early modern era. It joins efforts ranging from new praise of wives for displaying submissive "womanly" traits, to declarations of women's divinely ordained subordination, to diverse political theories with women's secondary

---

[67] See Martha C. Howell, *Women, Production and Patriarchy in Late Medieval Cities* (Chicago, 1986).
[68] Ibid., 178.

status as a common theme, to state-sanctioned witch hunts that chiefly targeted women. The wider framework for all these initiatives was a family regime that made married women both more responsible domestic partners and unacknowledged threats to their husbands' social and sexual identities.

Recent studies of early modern and modern society are breaking away from prior explanatory models without showing much concern to present new ones. Many have been conducted by historians who have not, like the proto-industrial scholars, explicitly invoked ordinary households as likely sites for generating industrial transformation – or, for that matter, any other major extra-domestic change. At the same time, these studies are far less likely than earlier ones to present work activity as the most significant measure of status, or even as the single item presumed to merit pride of place in assessing women's behavior. Like Natalie Davis, whose study of early modern French families featured all sorts of activity, including work, under the general rubric of "planning for the future," these newer scholars have explored a broader range of their subjects' activities without feeling obliged to place them within any new interpretive frameworks. It is possible nonetheless to view much of their recent research as the chronicling of precisely the sorts of calculation – or "planning," in Davis's term – that are being presented here as mandatory for successful functioning within late-marriage settings. These historians, for example, have been especially mindful of the ways that partners within family households operated interdependently. They have also taken pains to highlight the typically less visible contributions of women to family survival and achievement.[69]

Given a family structure that made a woman one of the two adults managing a household, wives were bound to be key players in fashioning and implementing countless family strategies. These streamlined households could also hardly avoid appealing to individuals and institutions beyond themselves if they were to remain viable over time, although tactics varied with region, proximity of kin, social milieu, and much else. Experience of both sexes in dealing with unrelated persons, as servants and/or servant employers, no doubt aided family strategists in assembling their plans. While historians have long been aware of elite households and their strategies, knowledge of future-oriented activity all along the social spectrum goes far to explain the pervasive, restless activity of the early modern era. Families at every social level were teeming with plans.

---

[69] The study deservedly credited with pioneering this approach in the area being discussed here is Leonore Davidoff and Catherine Hall, *Family Fortunes: Men and Women of the English Middle Class, 1780–1850* (Chicago, 1987). This book expressly sets out, in the authors' terms, "to move beyond this public/private divide to show how middle-class men who sought to be 'someone', to count as individuals because of their wealth, their power to command or their capacity to influence people, were, in fact, embedded in networks of familial and female support which underpinned their rise to public prominence," 13.

We already know, of course, that from the medieval era, the strategies of some peasant households in acquiring land were far more successful than others – which is to say that well before early modern times, the individual households of northwestern Europe were already taking advantage of a limited but real capacity for action that differentially influenced their fates. While landed property long remained the most tangible, reliable, and popular guarantor of family (and especially male) authority and identity, as population rose from the sixteenth century, the utility of land as a carrier of status and influence was increasingly offset by newer, more volatile forms of household insurance concocted by family strategists. These included office, liquid wealth, and professional expertise, all of which multiplied avenues to social power. As ever more families extended to occupations and offices the inheritance strategies they earlier evolved for landed property, entrusting their regulation and guarantee to law and to other extrafamilial bodies in addition to states, they enhanced the power of those entities. Ultimately, too, they opened the way to claimants of these prizes who were no longer obliged, or even inclined, to place family interests first.

In her admirable recent study, *The Middling Sort: Commerce, Gender and the Family in England, 1680–1780*, Margaret R. Hunt gives an account that can be read as a crucial phase in the evolution of family households, not just as collections of workers of both sexes but as planners and decision makers. These households are portrayed reckoning their own and their children's futures and, in the process, fashioning change in broader social and economic worlds that led, among other things, to industrial transformation. The study places gender and family firmly at the heart of an analysis that explores the lives of an emerging nonelite group of shopkeepers, independent artisans, manufacturers, tradespeople, lower-level professionals, and civil servants. This concentration of roughly 20 percent of the eighteenth-century population was located beneath the smaller gentry and aristocracy but above the laboring classes and smaller shopkeepers and artisans, who were then 70 to 75 percent of English people.[70]

Hunt's study, revealing complex and conflicted domestic relationships at the beginning of the modern era, displays intense activity within this group that was electing to pursue new economic opportunities. It shows how those seeking to enter business or professional careers then were utterly dependent upon personal and family assets rather than upon investment firms, lending agencies, or other impersonal economic instruments that did not yet exist. "Early modern English business activity," Hunt notes, "relied upon the willingness of ordinary families to shoulder risks that most middle-class people today would view as unacceptable."[71] Disputing studies that identify

---

[70] Margaret R. Hunt, *The Middling Sort: Commerce, Gender, and the Family in England, 1680–1780* (Berkeley, 1996).

[71] Ibid., 23.

work almost exclusively with men, she also insists that families at this time remained "a central, even constitutive feature of eighteenth-century social life."[72]

It is intriguing to note of Hunt's study that she expressly refuses to take sides on older debates among family and women's historians about whether her period witnessed a rise or a decline in family relations or in women's position. Instead, she discovers and duly reports much evidence on both sides. In the terms already argued here in discussing religious and political change, that is just what one would expect to find in a context in which comparatively more gender-balanced structures were spreading from households to a wider world and, at the same time, summoning new forms of male-led resistance. Rejecting the reigning view among feminist scholars that the eighteenth century was a time when women's status, and family life generally, worsened owing to women's "declining involvement in household-based production and agriculture,"[73] Hunt says she is "agnostic about whether the eighteenth century witnessed improving or deteriorating family relations – or for that matter, a rise or a decline in women's status."[74]

Hunt's evidence shows, for example, that women as well as men from these middling groups enjoyed a high and growing rate of literacy. While in the population as a whole in 1500 just 1 percent of women and 10 percent of men are estimated to have been literate, and a corresponding 40 percent of all women and 60 percent of men by 1800, the literacy rate of "middling" women in the needle trades and among shopkeepers, midwives, and schoolteachers rose in the eighteenth century to a remarkable 70 to 100 percent.[75] What is more, Hunt's findings offer correctives to the widespread view that middling women in this era were economically disenfranchised. She shows that separate estates often ensured middle-class women's control over resources, and that women regularly left more legacies than men to their female relatives and friends. She also outlines evidence for women's considerable trading activity, using insurance records and other little-used sources. Hunt remarks as well that historians have overlooked evidence that many women in this period sought to escape or alter the legal and social constraints of marriage through their massive urban migrations, and she stresses the important economic role of the substantial, if declining, number of women who never married.

At the same time, her evidence reveals again and again that middling girls were groomed to contribute to their families rather than to act independently, as their brothers were encouraged to do. Standards of education were lower for them, and they were expected to work more in order to permit brothers

[72] Ibid., 7.
[73] Ibid.
[74] Ibid.
[75] Ibid., 85.

to go to school or to acquire formal training. It was not biology, Hunt argues, nor was it a purely functionalist distribution of "roles" that consigned middling women to an unequal share of their families' resources. It was instead the systematic, willful deployment of power within what she calls the "loving yet exploitative gender-system of the eighteenth-century middling family."[76]

In one sense, parents in northwestern Europe were just doing what parents in multifamily households also do, that is, attempt to ensure and perhaps enhance the future livelihood, well-being, and social identity of their offspring. But these concerns now led them, as means and imagination allowed, to invent or buttress institutions beyond their unstable households as a way to serve these familial ends. Those largely male-run and -staffed institutions then came in time to develop charms of their own, transcending the interests of the families that created them and absorbing identity and loyalties that once resided more exclusively with the kin. As is evident, this expansion of nondomestic institutions through the agency of family households was quite unlike the more typical scenario for religious, political, or economic change that has occurred since in many societies outside the northwestern European orbit – often enough through the sudden and disruptive intrusion of extrafamilial institutions imported from the West.

Concerns to maintain identity and influence obliged single-family households in northwestern Europe first to widen their circle of strategy makers to include wives as active participants, and then either to strengthen or to call into being the very outside authorities and institutions that would, in the end, compromise the family's ancient place of honor in society. Paradoxically then, activity initially undertaken to further familial goals had the ultimate effect of hastening the eclipse of family households as the prime movers of everyday life. Most historians, however, unwittingly complicit in burying the massive evidence of purposeful, family-centered activity in late medieval and early modern Europe, have persuaded us that the real action occurred elsewhere, driven by alleged "forces" – whether religious, political, or economic – that had already escaped the controlling compulsions of the kin.

Recognition that throughout the early modern era families retained immense vitality underscores yet again that as historical specialties have multiplied, the neat ways we have packaged history have often failed to reflect the ways people lived it. If we are serious about seeing societies as more coherent wholes, then what we have come to take for granted as a near-universal distinction between public and private spheres and behavior must be understood to have been a historical creation only just evolving in its modern form in this period. Systems of authority, moreover, cannot be assumed to function independently and are hardly confined to formal political arenas.

[76] Ibid., 100.

People's intentions and actions, too, cannot be explained by limiting inquiry to the influence of material and social settings. More enduring human needs to anchor identity, form attachments, and find meaning must always figure in. And yes, to understand the fate of families, and that of kingdoms as well, it will no longer do to exclude the female portion of humankind.

For the tasks outlined here, the most arduous labor is done. The evidence, or enough evidence, is in. What is needed now is a perceptual shift to help account more convincingly for what we already know. Scholars are familiar with that most satisfying of tasks here: finding plausible links between apparently unconnected bits of information. The result will be not only a fuller picture of the past but also a different one. The operative image is not the discovery of missing pieces in the jigsaw puzzle of the past, but rather a turn of the historical kaleidoscope. The colored stones collected so far will remain in view when it is held to the light, but their hues and positions will have changed.

This study has made no secret about images that are likely to appear with this turn of the kaleidoscope. A culture that gave most young couples chief responsibility for the creation and survival of new family units was bound, on that account alone, to develop beyond its households in distinctive ways. The explanation proposed for the common condition of a sexual hierarchy favoring men also lends itself to practical use here or in any historical inquiry. If this pervasive feature of social arrangements is treated as a likely but not inevitable by-product of the tasks both sexes anywhere confront in achieving a sense of personal identity, then particular hierarchical arrangements in any society can more readily be sorted out.

Finally, since the northwestern European family system promoted a remarkable commonality in women's and men's experience throughout the life cycle, and also was first among agricultural societies to surrender landed property as the chief source of livelihood and focus for ideals of manhood, novel challenges were bound to confront men in this period. There appeared for the first time a concern, even an obsession, to maintain boundaries between the sexes and ensure appropriate gender attributes and behavior. That concern, which became a hallmark of modern society, is still very much with us.

If there is something to these arguments, then the potential for reimagining the past is enormous. For if both sexes are left in when interpreters confront the imposing transformations still described in the standard single-sex accounts, and if a novel pattern of family formation is recognized as an active rather than a passive element in the goings-on outside households, the course of Western history begins to look rather different. In many ways, it also begins to make more sense.

8

The Late-Marriage Household, the Sexes, and the Modern World

This inquiry began with the continued puzzlement among scholars about Western Europe's singular role in ushering in the modern world. More precisely, it began by asking why that region was home to major changes that, from about 1500 to 1800, launched the first "models for modernity." While debate persists, interpreters have usually aligned themselves with one of two camps. The first contends that the dynamism of western Europe at this time, and the "gap" that emerged between European-based societies and others around the world, was owing to the invention there of a vigorous new system of national states. The second argues instead that the energy of early modern western European societies owed far more to their early creation of worldwide capitalist structures.

This book has maintained that what set this region apart, leading to transformation that continues even now to make its way around the globe, was neither of these so-called master processes of political or economic change. Each was obviously important; but both have been presented here as dependent upon the prior evolution within northwestern Europe of a distinctive family and household system whose most crucial feature, late marriage for women, appeared in the manorial regions of northwestern Europe at the end of the Roman Empire. Other elements of the system – that is, nuclear households, significant numbers of persons who never married, a pattern of life-cycle service, and increasingly equal sex ratios at marriageable ages – evolved in the medieval era and were in place throughout the region by the turn of the sixteenth century.

The status being claimed for the influence of these family arrangements, which were aberrant in an agricultural setting, is not trivial. What has been argued here is that these arrangements generated a set of shared experiences, attitudes, and values that profoundly affected how people in the region thought and behaved. These included the ways they interacted in households and communities, as well as the ways they set about changing or inventing their religious, social, political, and economic institutions.

If the conclusions presented here about the causes, timing, and effects of the Western family pattern are borne out, current depictions of the Western past, as well as of many global developments, are likely to require review. As that happens, it will also be useful to put to the test in a variety of historical settings the interpretive framework that has been presented here, as well as the analytical tools that have been introduced along the way. Attention here has focused more on the behavior and attitudes of ordinary householders, rural and urban, than on elites – and for good reason. It was the former groups, after all, that are being argued to have given birth to the peculiar late-marriage arrangements, and whose deliberations and actions have been presented as either overlooked or misinterpreted. Since we already have fuller information and many more studies on the elites, much of that material can now readily be reviewed through the lens of the approach being recommended here, which can also be used to inform choices between conflicting interpretations.

An example of how this process can work will suffice to illustrate this invitation to reassess current historical accounts using a new interpretive framework. A while ago in the pages of the august *American Historical Review*, medievalist Charles Wood repudiated some conclusions he had drawn in his own earlier published work.[1] The item to which he drew attention, namely, the emergence of the nation-state, was a topic already well worked over in the literature and, in the eyes of many, as settled as these things usually get. But in recognition of then new work in family history on how medieval "high politics" might be reconceived, Wood did an about-face. He declared that he and his colleagues were wrong to have propounded for so long the anachronistic idea that medieval kings saw themselves, first and foremost, as state builders.[2]

Recanting his prior characterization of thirteenth-century French monarchs' decisions to endow younger sons with newly acquired lands as part of a long-range strategy to extend royal rule, Wood affirmed that new studies show that medieval kings were not acting from state-building motives at all but from familial habits that they shared with other noble households facing similar challenges in adapting to what he calls "the more hierarchical, nuclear, and patrilineal [family] structure so newly characteristic of the era."[3] They met the challenge of these conditions – especially the difficulty of guarding the integrity of family property over time – by guaranteeing that

[1] Charles Wood, "The Return of Medieval Politics." *American Historical Review* 94, No. 2 (April 1989): 391–404.

[2] These scholars failed to pay heed, Wood says, despite being warned decades ago by their remarkable colleague, the late Joseph Strayer, who told them that no one in the medieval era, kings included, "believed that the development of national states was the chief end of man." Ibid., 393, from Joseph R. Strayer and Dana C. Munro, *The Middle Ages: 395–1500* (New York, 1959), 153.

[3] Wood, "The Return of Medieval Politics," 396.

the eldest son inherited all lands save any new acquisitions, the one sort of holding younger sons were allowed.

This property arrangement was thus an expression, in altered circumstances, of the timeworn strategy of keeping family holdings intact. Far from being innovative state-building, it was merely an adaptation of ancient priorities to a changing environment of land shortage, population rise, and nuclear residential arrangements. The monarchs' goals, says Wood, were the same as those of all noble households: "to maintain and enhance purely family resources, not to create the institutions of a lasting French state."[4] He might have added that they also mirrored the strategies of peasant families in the manorialized regions, who for similar reasons had switched at around the same time to a single-heir system for their primary holdings.

Evidence that behavior toward property in the late medieval and early modern eras is best understood as emanating from family concerns – particularly those of male heads – is part of the case being made here that throughout this period, the dominant motor of conduct remained household interest. Royal and noble households had the same obsession with maintenance and identity that animated the peasantry. What set the former apart was the wider range of strategies and resources at their disposal.

Since the sustenance of monarchs and nobles, as well as their ability to engage in the state politics and war-making peculiar to their set, depended upon peasants, whose circumstances allowed them to devise some effective strategies of their own, it makes little sense to keep interpreting elite behavior as political and active and peasant behavior as economic and passive. Analysis works best by keeping the household decision makers and their interests – political, economic, and more – in focus, whether one is inspecting the top or the bottom of society. Contests might be resolved differently in different locales, but even where peasants were early forced to abandon familial property and set up landless households, as happened in England, they were not without options.

The scholarship on medieval kingship is closer to an understanding of what was really happening, Wood says, when it portrays the new monarchs not as self-conscious state builders but as family resource managers on a grand scale. "The growth of what we think of as government... might better be termed the creation of a whole series of administrative procedures."[5] Political manipulation was never absent, but neither was it absent from the calculations of peasant households. While outmatched in power and influence, peasants were still key players, along with the mightier noble households, in collectively setting some limits on the capacities of "government" to control "society."

---

[4] Ibid., 397.
[5] Ibid.

In making this case, Wood approvingly quotes W. L. Warren's 1987 study of governance in England from the Norman conquest of 1066 to the late thirteenth century:

Nowadays we tend to think that the kind of society any state has is determined by the type of government it has. In the Middle Ages, the type of government it was possible to have was largely determined by the kind of society over which it was trying to rule. Government was more about controlling and managing society than about changing it. It is true that government developed at the will of enterprising rulers; but a successful ruler was like a gardener training an apple tree: he might prune and cut back, select and encourage, but he could work only with what was already there.[6]

Such analyses of medieval governance do not, to be sure, expressly characterize "what was already there" in northwestern Europe as a unique collection of calculating, mobile, and volatile late-marriage households. Yet by arguing that imperatives of family interest rather than state-building still directed monarchs' actions in the late medieval era, and by recognizing that nuclear households were already dominant, these studies of high politics are corroborating the altered framework outlined here for reconceiving how northwestern European societies evolved from the medieval era.

That framework hardly assumes that all interests are household ones or that all household members have identical priorities. (Despite the late-marriage pattern's tendency to bring the life cycles of the sexes together, women and men, in Salem and elsewhere, still displayed clear priorities of their own.) Yet this approach starts from the premise that interests deriving from experience in distinctive household settings remained strong enough in late medieval and early modern times that their explanatory potential should be exhausted before any behavior or development is assigned to other sources.

Such an approach makes it easier to assess the interactions between government and society and to trace the ways that already weakened kinship ties and manorial structures were giving way to ever more extra-domestic institutions that claimed people's loyalties and informed their actions. Looking first at what was happening within households also makes it easier to see how late marriage, while hardly dictating identical outcomes, helps to explain resemblances in the ways northwestern European societies evolved. Households in different groups are also the appropriate place to begin to assess claims about women's and men's relative status. As will be seen, had there been more scrutiny of early modern households, there might have been fewer dubious assertions about the reality of "separate sexual spheres" of

---

[6] Ibid., 403, from W. L. Warren's introduction to his *The Governance of Norman and Angevin England, 1086–1272* (Stanford, Calif., 1987), 1.

the sort that permeated discourse from the late eighteenth century and have misinformed interpretation ever since.[7]

The plans and schemes of the modest householders that have engaged our attention throughout most of this study were hardly, then, carried out in a vacuum. Monarchs and feudal elites devised their own strategies, and for long they too were acting on behalf of their family households. That the boundaries between groups of households were more permeable in northwestern European societies than in the caste systems in many other agricultural societies owed a great deal to weaker, less stable family structures that demanded constant attention from individual members. Group, rank, and later class divisions were real enough, but they have been exaggerated. Such divisions were hardly so sharp or so enduring as the more rigid social demarcations of early-marriage societies.

By adopting primogeniture, using their more extensive resources to prolong control of children's marriages, and manipulating land through the states they created to serve their family interests, elites might become dominant figures in new national structures, as described earlier. They might also continue to marry their daughters young. Yet in one example among many of practices set by the masses "trickling upward," the daughters of these groups came in time to wrest at least a veto power over the spouses chosen for them. By the dawn of the modern era, even elite parents were forced, as peasants had been centuries before, to surrender direct control of their children's marriages and content themselves with a lesser arsenal of connections, wiles, and bribes.

It is true enough that the habits and strategies of elite households also trickled downward. Early merchants and industrialists, for example, despite having acquired their wealth in trade, often refashioned themselves as large landowners – with titles if they could arrange it. Then too, as legal historian Eileen Spring has argued in a persuasive if controversial study of aristocratic inheritance in England from 1300 to 1800, the landowners' legal history from beginning to end "is much to be seen as the effort to overcome the common law rights of daughters.... From the entail, to the use, to the strict settlement, what landowners were above all seeking was a means of dealing with the problem that female inheritance posed."[8] Taking issue with a spate of historians, including Lawrence Stone, who have portrayed aristocratic women as increasingly favored in property settlements, Spring recounts English legal arrangements from the thirteenth through the eighteenth

---

[7] For an excellent discussion that traces the historiographical enchantment with the separate spheres doctrine in the past thirty years, see Linda Kerber, "Separate Spheres, Female Worlds, Women's Place: The Rhetoric of Women's History." *Journal of American History* 75 (June 1983): 9–39.

[8] Eileen Spring, *Law, Land, and Family: Aristocratic Inheritance in England, 1300 to 1800* (Chapel Hill, N.C., 1993), 35.

centuries as one long tale of the creation of impediments to female inheritance of landed estates. While Spring's conclusions run counter to a number of respected studies, they are fully in line with the many examples of reactive patriarchalism identified here – and are echoed lately in Martha Howell's survey of women's property rights and inheritance in continental northwestern Europe from 1300 to 1550.[9]

In the end – it hardly comes as a surprise – the male elites, old and new, who were wise enough to recognize the importance of shoring up their family households managed for some time to carry the day, both against challenges posed by female heiresses-at-law in their own circles and by poor and middling householders seeking to expand their own social and political power. These latter groups naturally made far more headway in places such as the new United States, where the elites they confronted were less powerful and entrenched than those in Europe. Yet the wider point here is the constraints that unique household structures placed upon the behavior of all elites. Privileged groups throughout the late-marriage regions were pressed not only to compromise with their challengers from below but also to engage in the perpetual activity of defensive family maintenance that has already been recounted for more ordinary householders.

As seen in the previous chapter, a minority of the families no longer making a living from the land emerged as the ones whose frenetic activity and sacrifice on behalf of their own households' survival would make possible the first transition from an agricultural to a commercial and industrial society. These increasing numbers of urban dwellers, whether from professional and mercantile families or artisanal or unskilled wage-earning ones, confronted more dramatic change than either the rural masses or the upper-class elites. The middling families, in particular, were also the ones first prompted to pay new attention to the changing ways the sexes were coming to relate to one another at the dawn of the modern era. This time around, one thing would be different. Men would no longer be so alone in what would emerge as a more conscious project for both sexes of redefining the meanings of womanhood and manhood.

Critics might entertain the argument presented so far here that the Western family pattern had immense influence upon developments both within and beyond households in the years from 1500 to 1800. At the same time, however, they might ask whether those features can be held to have significantly affected the modern period – and contemporary developments – as well. While they might admit the impact of later marriage for women into the present era, such critics could well argue that so much else has happened that was driven by institutions that have shaken loose from prior household influence that we must look elsewhere to explain most of the change in the

---

[9] Martha Howell, *The Marriage Exchange: Property, Social Place and Gender in the Cities of the Low Countries, 1300–1550* (Chicago, 1998).

past 200 years or so, or to make any predictions about where the world is headed.

The critics would have an obvious point in that there has been a steady diminution in those years of the influence of household arrangements upon other institutional structures in the societies of the Western family pattern. It would nonetheless be hasty to write off the likelihood of other persisting effects of those family arrangements into the modern era. It would also be hasty to presume, as most scholars still do, that the bulk of behavior in the modern era is owing to the straightforward working out of eighteenth-century political and industrial transformation – thereby discounting practices, values, and habits of mind with a more ancient lineage.

This concluding chapter will consider just a sample of the evidence for the vital and continuing influence on behavior of these idiosyncratic northwestern European family and household arrangements. It will stress how, even now, the ways people live their lives in the United States or England as compared to southern France or Italy, for example, and the values they espouse concerning self, family, and community owe a great deal to continuing cultural habits deriving from different marriage and household regimes. The chapter will compare persisting northwestern European features with those – especially in southern Europe – that derived from early-marriage households. It will then look briefly at recent global shifts in early-marriage household structures and the causes of those changes. The comparison will reveal the tenacity of characteristic features in both settings and will suggest why some long-standing elements of household structure, especially in the traditional early-marriage regions, are gradually giving way.

Attention will then turn from reviewing the fate of late-marriage structures in the modern era to examining the related issue of the status of the "gender order." In a period that witnessed the birth of the first organized women's movements as well as the discovery of women, family, and gender as factors in historical development, the gender order has become a territory that is at once familiar and hotly contested. Controversies abound, even though we now know more about these topics, especially in modern Western societies, than we have ever known before. The controversies lie in assessments of what was actually happening to women and men within and beyond families; in endeavors to fix the influence of biological as compared to social factors in creating identity and informing behavior; in attempts to assess the origin and success of nineteenth-century doctrines proclaiming separate spheres for the sexes; and, more recently, in efforts to sort out the changing weight of gender as one of many components in the identities of contemporary women and men.

Not only does the deviant family-formation system provide an invaluable tool for assessing contradictory claims about the modern gender order, it is also responsible for a development that has yet to be recognized for its high significance. I refer to the fixation of people in European-based societies these days on issues of sexuality and gender identity. While most tend to take this development for granted, it will be argued here to signal a momentous event-in-progress, which is nothing less than the final phase of a crumbling of consensus about the vital importance of differences between the sexes, including the importance of a hierarchy favoring men over women. The consensus itself has been renewed within human societies for countless generations; but its days now appear to be numbered, and for good historical reasons. This development has vital implications for those who would act to influence policy, local and global, about issues related to households, families, and livelihood. Just as more than a millennium ago when peasant households stirred themselves into action, there is again room at this time for some unlikely parties to seize a critical historical moment.

*   *   *

A recent analysis of family ties in modern western Europe presents a striking example of another of those "huge (but not stupendous) comparisons" recommended by Charles Tilly and employed throughout this inquiry. This one compares and contrasts contemporary family systems in the northern and southern regions and concludes that these systems "are neither good nor bad, but they are not neutral either."[10] In this piece, David S. Reher contends that many of the differences that distinguish western European societies today derive directly from distinctive family regimes that worked to create and embed a number of these repeated and predictable behaviors that are "not neutral." Presenting this information is useful, he says, since "doing so may enable us to rediscover the importance of the family, an institution apparently given up for dead by many students of contemporary society."[11] For purposes here, Reher's analysis is very telling, since he expressly states that the geographical demarcation between what he labels the "weak" and "strong" family regions of western Europe coincides with the one John Hajnal singled out between the northwestern European late-marriage region and the southern region of mixed households that, as seen in Chapters 3 and 4, long displayed primarily early-marriage features.

While it is easy to recognize in contemporary Western societies, as Reher says, the (mostly northern) areas where families and family ties appear quite weak and the (mostly southern) areas where they are rather strong, few people today, including few politicians and public planners, recognize that the relationship between the family group and its members has many

---

[10] David Sven Reher, "Family Ties in Western Europe: Persistent Contrasts." *Population and Development Review* 24, No. 2 (June 1998), 215. In this section, the comparative material in this article is essentially paraphrased, as it offers an excellent, and rare, comparative summary of the status of the behavior and "family ties" promoted in early- and late-marriage societies, or what the author terms "strong and weak family societies," by the modern era.

[11] Ibid., 215.

implications for the ways a society functions as a whole. Among the most important of the enduring features of family life that he cites, for example, is that centered on the process of young family members setting up households of their own. These days in the "weak family" regions of northwestern Europe and North America, young persons typically leave home to start lives on their own when they have acquired sufficient maturity to pursue studies or to take jobs after secondary school. By now, saving for a permanent household may well be less important than the need to establish an independent life; and as Reher says: "Often these initial forays into the adult world are made while sharing housing with friends and colleagues who are at a similar stage of their own lives."[12] It may not be until years later that young people marry and again set up another household, this time usually with the aim of launching a lasting relationship with a partner and starting a family.

In Mediterranean Europe's "strong family" societies, by contrast, this process of leaving home is very different for young people, in that departures usually coincide much more closely with marriage and finding a steady job. The years from the late teens until marriage are normally passed in the parental household, even if young people have jobs. As a result, leave-taking from the parental home, finding steady work, and marrying – events that in northwestern Europe are typically separated and occur in stages – are closely intertwined in the Mediterranean societies. "In fact, an excellent indicator of the labor market and unquestionably the best one for the rate of family formation in southern Europe would be the incidence of first marriages among young adults."[13]

We have already observed earlier phases of these diverging practices deriving from different family structures in places such as Montaillou and Salem Village, but it is noteworthy that up to the later nineteenth century in England, owing to the continuing practice of life-cycle service, most young adults aged fifteen to nineteen had already left home more or less permanently. The first round of modern European censuses in 1851 shows English servants at 7.1 percent of the total rural population and 3.2 percent of the urban population. If lodgers are included, the percentages rise to 12.1 in rural areas and 14.3 in urban ones. Servant figures are also high for Belgium – 11.9 percent of the total population in 1890 – and quite high for France, at 6.5 percent in 1872. Figures for southern Europe are in sharp contrast, with under 3 percent in Spain in 1860 and 2.2 percent in Italy in 1861. Reher concludes that until the later nineteenth century, between 50 and 80 percent of young people were servants before marriage in the weak-family regions, compared to just 15 to 30 percent in the strong-family areas of the south.[14]

---

[12] Ibid., 204.
[13] Ibid., 205.
[14] Ibid., 206.

In recent years, and despite the decline of life-cycle service in northwestern Europe, there is little evidence that these differences between the two regions have much changed. It is true that there has been an increase in southern Europe in the age at which children leave the parental household, but this has been paralleled by an increase in the age at marriage. Comparative figures for men and women aged twenty-five to twenty-nine still living with parents in 1994 in Greece, Italy, and Spain were over 60 percent for men and between 30 and 50 percent for women. By contrast, in France, Germany, and the United Kingdom, only 25 percent or less of men and just 10 to 12 percent of women in the twenty-five to twenty-nine age group were still residing in their parents' homes.[15]

The consequences have continued to be that in southern Europe, the family assumes many roles that are foreign to northwestern European households. Times of economic hardship, for example, tend to be more equally shared by the entire family group in the south, whereas economic difficulties are borne more fully in the north by young adults themselves. We have already seen, too, that from earliest times in the north, aid to the weakest members of society came from public and private institutions outside the family, epitomized in England by the sixteenth-century Poor Laws, while in the south, family and individual charity – supplemented by organized religious charity – were far more important. Such differences still exist today, despite the growth of institutional supports that have accompanied economic modernization.

In Spain's 1991 census, for example, close to half of the people older than age sixty lived with one of their children. In the weak-family settings in the Nordic countries and in North America, by contrast, only about 10 percent of older persons live with a child, and the rest live in public or private nursing homes paid for by public funds, insurance policies, or personal savings. In a recent survey within the European Union of residential preferences of elderly persons no longer able to live on their own, an average of nearly three-quarters in Spain, Portugal, Italy, and Greece stated that coresidence with children was the preferred option, whereas only a quarter said so in Denmark, Finland, Sweden, Great Britain, and the Netherlands.[16]

Each family system has generated what are by now familiar justifying values for its members. In the weak-family areas, for example, values attributed to the individual and to abstract individualism have tended to predominate; and leaving home early is touted as important for learning autonomy. In the strong-family areas, however, loyalty to the family group is held up as the critical value in the socialization of the young. In old age, such values in weak-family societies translate into an internalized desire to preserve physical

---

[15] Ibid., 223, note 21, from Fernandez Gordon, *Eurostat Labor Force* (*Survey*, 1997), Tables 1 and 2.

[16] Ibid., 210.

and economic independence as long as possible – an attitude so widely held in the United States, for example, that as Reher points out, those elderly persons who live with their children most likely come from strong-family ethnic backgrounds.[17] In southern Europe, by contrast, insisting upon independence as a matter of principle is held to be foolish, and the vast majority of elderly are in constant contact with their children.

The differences in the attitudes and values still on display in contemporary northwestern European families and among families in the Mediterranean region come as no real surprise in themselves. What is remarkable, as I have maintained throughout this study, is their longevity as well as their probable early origins in distinctive family and household structures. Those on display in northwestern Europe did not originate at the dawn of the industrial era, as many still suppose, but have likely been evolving over more than 1,000 years. Such attitudes and values were also given new life, as argued earlier, by being enshrined in novel extra-domestic religious, political, social, and economic institutions. These were created throughout the early modern centuries by persons raised within these eccentric family households who appear to have initially envisioned such institutions as instruments to strengthen and shore up their own families' futures.

These weak-family attitudes and values evolved and coexisted in northern Europe with the more typical cluster of attitudes and values that characterized the Mediterranean region, whose household system is itself a version of a still more antique family regime, whose exemplars in eastern Europe, and especially in Asia, assign even greater weight to the extended kin within family lineages and clans. The point that the two systems, while neither good nor bad, are "not neutral either" may be obvious enough by now, but a few points are worth summing up here about their current status before turning to recent events affecting these ancient family systems – as well as to some speculation about where they may be headed in the future.

First, as David Reher, the chronicler of the present standing of the two systems remarks, it is the strong-family societies that exhibit greater cohesion as well as higher levels of social, if not political, conservatism. While some have assigned this behavior to religion, it is more likely that the family system itself is responsible. A prototypical contemporary example of this greater cohesion in southern European societies is the far lower incidence there of homelessness than in places such as the United States, where, despite higher living standards and lower levels of unemployment, uprooted or destitute people are far more liable to be left to fend for themselves than to be absorbed into family households.

Another example of this cohesion is the evidence that despite rising recent levels of divorce and teenage pregnancies in southern Europe, high percentages of single mothers end up living with their own mothers – over 30 percent

---

[17] Ibid., 212.

with children under eighteen in a 1991 study in Spain and nearly half of those with children under six. (Interviews confirmed that even without coresidence, grandmothers in Spain were likelier to live nearby and aid daughters with child care and support in finding jobs.) By contrast, only 9 percent of all single mothers and 16 percent of never-married mothers in Britain between 1991 and 1993 continued to live with their parents. Similarly, the massive entry of women into the labor force in recent years has been shown in southern Europe to have been eased enormously by grandmothers' willingness to care for the children, a practice that has never been as widespread in the north.

Other documented features of weak-family societies include higher levels of reported loneliness owing to the frailer safety net of family support, which continues to translate into higher levels of suicide in northwestern Europe and North America by comparison with southern Europe. This greater isolation of individuals has been typically compensated for in weak-family societies – with their greater physical and social mobility – by people's habit of forming extrafamilial networks of civic associations for a multiplicity of purposes. This movement struck that acute French observer Alexis de Tocqueville very forcefully on his visit in the 1830s to the then-new United States, a place that lacked the conservative presence of the more family-oriented titled elites who still exercised significant social power in the albeit weak-family societies of northwestern Europe.[18] Reher sums up his findings as follows:

Weak-family societies, then, tend to be associational societies with a deep civil component, and strong-family ones tend to be more passive societies, at least in terms of the importance of individual initiatives within them. The sense of individual responsibility for collective norms and needs, so essential for the concept of democracy and civil society in the West, is often conspicuously absent from southern European societies, while in northern societies it is an integral part of the social fabric. In sum, the countries of northern Europe and of North America have well-developed civil societies that thrive on individual initiatives, but with a dark side shown by their lack of social cohesion and by the desperation and anguish so prevalent in them. They are tough societies, but they are also dynamic ones. Mediterranean societies are more pleasant, more comfortable, more conformist, more oriented toward the family group, and less dynamic.[19]

Such societal norms, while lasting, are not forever. Their resilience into the present era is nonetheless striking, although looming demographic trends – and related effects of transformation through globalization – have persuaded some observers that in the case of western Europe as a whole, a kind of convergence may be underway. That is, rates of family change in the north

[18] Alexis de Tocqueville, *Democracy in America* (New York, 1945) 2, Book 2, Ch. V, "Of the Use Which Americans Make of Public Associations in Civic Life," 114–18.
[19] Reher, "Family Ties in Western Europe," 217.

are predicted to slow down, while those in the south will likely continue to accelerate for some time to come. A variety of indicators already show that despite the occurrence of similar trends throughout western Europe, fertility and marriage are declining at higher rates in the south, and the number of children born out of wedlock is rising faster. There, as well, children and women are acquiring more autonomy with respect to the family group, and women have now entered the labor market in substantial numbers.

The demographic reality that everywhere families have fewer children and more elderly members in itself presents a special challenge for the strong-family households in southern Europe – and much of the rest of the world as well – since support of the elderly in such households is tied to having enough children to ensure that support. In weak-family societies the same demographics prevail, but there they pose a challenge for those societies as a whole more than for individual families.[20] Scholars have also pointed to an alleged diminution of the associational and civic traditions within weak-family societies in recent decades, which may point to convergence there as well.[21]

It should be recalled that in the case of northwestern Europe, we are looking at a singular example of a region that, in a sense, had the accidental luxury of setting its own pace in arriving at what are now recognized as the trappings of modernity. The process through which it did so – which is being argued here to have been largely "from the inside out" through the dynamic activity of unstable households operating at all levels – was very different from the ways modernity has since arrived in most other settings around the globe, where it has more typically been imported into a variety of sites beyond households. In many ways, nonetheless, the results from a demographic perspective have begun to look quite similar. One major effect, for example, is that the average age at first marriage for women, in particular, has already increased markedly in all global regions. In Africa, Latin America, Asia, and eastern Europe, the average age of women at first marriage was in the low twenties in 1997, whereas in western Europe and North America, it had risen yet further to the high twenties.[22] The appearance of other late-marriage or weak-family features also suggests that there may be something to the convergence being argued for western Europe's two major household regions.[23]

[20] Ibid., 219–20.

[21] See, for example, Robert Putnam's *Bowling Alone: The Collapse and Revival of American Community* (New York, 2000).

[22] *The World's Women 2000: Trends and Statistics*, United Nations Social Statistics and Indicators, Series K, No. 16 (New York, 2000), 25.

[23] Ibid. See especially the excellent demographic discussion in Ch. 2: "Women and Men in Families," 23–51.

Still, it is not our purpose here to try to determine whether a convergence of household patterns will ultimately take place in western Europe or globally, even though it is noteworthy that, like many largely demographic analyses and comparisons, Reher's very useful one still lacks an assessment of gender arrangements that might make it easier to make such a call. On an obvious level, for example, one might ask how long the "grandmother effect" will last anywhere if ever more women engage in full-time work and men's domestic responsibilities do not change. Yet rather than speculate about whether a theory of convergence makes more sense than one that envisions a continuing north–south divide in western Europe or, on the global level, a continuing divide reflecting the embedded cultures of early- versus late-marriage systems, it is more helpful to review recent studies that, for the weak-family, late-marriage societies, anyway, address both household demographics and gender arrangements together, attempting to assess the nature and direction of change in the modern and contemporary eras.

The exercise does not require new research, since the modern period in the late-marriage societies has been extremely well mined of late by new historians of women and gender. Still, because these scholars were not conducting their inquiries with attention to the probability that a peculiar family-formation pattern must have influenced the behavior of their subjects, the conclusions they have drawn, even when they have been examining the same data, have often varied widely. In the section that follows, I review the diverse findings about women's and men's lives in the modern era and make the case that the new interpretive approach outlined here helps not only to illumine these findings but points to appropriate choices among conflicting analyses of households and of women's and men's status, roles, and options in modern times.

*   *   *

Among scholars of the new women's history that expanded so rapidly since the late 1960s, the modern era – that is, the period since the late eighteenth century – swiftly assumed pride of place. European-based societies, and the United States in particular, emerged as the chief objects of study. Scholars took advantage of an unprecedented garrulousness about gender and identity that is the envy of those who study these topics in periods when their subjects are less voluble. Yet despite countless new studies, crucial issues remain in dispute. Historians now know far more for this period than any other about women and men from all social strata, what they did and what they believed. But they remain deeply divided on how to interpret what they know.

Early investigations were not only profoundly influenced by the revived women's movement in these same societies, they were also informed by one or the other of the two "master narratives" already encountered for the modern West, namely, that highlighting the new state makers, on the one hand, and the new capitalists, on the other. Proponents of the former, persuaded that the spread of democratic ideals and forms of government is the true centerpiece of the modern era, usually pointed to the expanded recognition of women's rights by governments from the mid-nineteenth century onward as the major influence on the sexes of a wider democratic movement unleashed from the late eighteenth century. Women's new struggle to gain entry into the polity was portrayed as the crucial element in a push for equal rights with men. Champions of this school often cited steady, if contested, advances toward equality for women in education, property-holding, employment, entry into the professions, and more. They contended that the overall effect was to reduce gender inequality in areas where it remained, narrowing the gap between women's and men's rights and options.[24]

New social historians, by contrast, were more likely to challenge such conclusions and argue that economic rather than political transformation deserves top billing in interpretations of the modern era. They also often maintained that far from narrowing the gap between the sexes, economic change actually widened that gap and heightened the differences between women's and men's social lives. These interpreters cited, in particular, a new division between the sexes caused by altered systems of production that isolated married women in the home, resulting in the loss of their prior ability to combine productive and reproductive roles there.[25] The family household itself was often held up in these early accounts as an institution that stifled women's advance at every turn.

Commentators from this camp usually argued that the nineteenth century saw renewed patriarchal domination and a hardening of gender segregation that only began to be undone in the last decades of the twentieth century. Even the later and more subtle analyses from the 1980s of middle-class women's lives, for example, reiterated a theme of intensified segregation of the sexes. In her pioneering study of bourgeois women in northern France, Bonnie G. Smith makes a compelling case that despite these women's location in "a scientific and industrial society with a democratic political configuration," the prototypical "bourgeoise" inhabited a world apart focusing on childrearing, domesticity, and deep religious faith.[26] Concluding their

---

[24] Early models for this point of view can be found in pioneering studies of suffrage in the United States by Eleanor Flexner, *Century of Struggle: The Women's Rights Movement in the United States* (Cambridge, Mass., 1959); and William L. O'Neill, *Everyone Was Brave: A History of Feminism in America* (Chicago, 1969).

[25] Famously, Alice Clark, *The Working Life of Women in the Seventeenth Century* (London, 1919), argued that this transition had already effectively taken place in the seventeenth century, a position that was initially widely accepted, along with the negative implications for women's status. Since then scholars including Margaret Hunt (see the discussion in Chapter 7) have respectfully contested Clark's pioneering study as well as its conclusions about women's status in industrial society.

[26] Bonnie G. Smith, *Ladies of the Leisure Class: The Bourgeoises of Northern France in the Nineteenth Century* (Princeton, N.J., 1981), 15.

account of English middle-class life in urban Birmingham and rural East Anglia from 1780 to 1850, Leonore Davidoff and Catherine Hall state that by the mid-nineteenth century, English women "found a world more rigidly divided into separate spheres for men and women. The tensions were deeper, the opportunities less."[27] Mary Ryan paints middle-class women's domestic seclusion in nineteenth-century Oneida County, New York, in even starker terms:

The importance of this sexual segregation cannot be overemphasized. On the one hand, as historians of women have often pointed out, isolation in a single, common sphere could nurture a self-conscious female identity and foster strong loyalties among women. Such a heightened consciousness of sex was a precondition to the development of the women's rights movement. On the other hand, sex segregation tended to mire women in a world that was remote from the public spheres where men continued to wield power. The women of the nineteenth century, in other words, were caught in the contradictions of that problematic notion of "separate but equal."[28]

Of these two early schools of thought about women in nineteenth-century northwestern European societies – one of which identified (and often celebrated) a progressive, upward trajectory that brought women's and men's lives closer together and the other of which described (and usually deplored) a downward trend that divided the sexes and deepened women's subordination – the latter long claimed more numerous and enthusiastic adherents. By the 1990s, however, with the accumulation of complex analyses of women's lives around the world, plus a changed intellectual climate in which the grand teleological approaches to the past, whether liberal/progressive or socialist/Marxist, were falling out of favor, debate subsided. Without actually bridging this huge interpretive divide, the new historians of women and gender began to sound a strong cautionary note about further attempts to assess women's overall status or to identify a prevailing direction of change in their lives. Scholars calling for more refined theoretical approaches also urged the abandonment of efforts to explain the evidently constant, cross-societal condition of women's subordination to men, advising researchers to focus instead upon the change that has ever been at the heart of historical investigation.[29]

Such admonitions were all well and good to the extent that they discouraged crude and ahistorical generalizations about womankind as a whole. But to the degree that they delegitimated efforts to draw even circumscribed

[27] Leonore Davidoff and Catherine Hall, *Family Fortunes: Men and Women of the English Middle Class, 1780–1850* (Chicago, 1987), 453.

[28] Mary P. Ryan, *Cradle of the Middle Class: The Family in Oneida County, New York, 1790–1885* (Cambridge, 1981), 240–41.

[29] See, in particular, Joan Scott, "Gender: A Useful Category of Historical Analysis." *American Historical Review* 91, No. 5 (December 1986): 1053–75.

conclusions about the direction of change in particular women's lives, or discouraged attempts to find plausible historical explanations for the persistent cross-cultural hierarchy favoring men over women, they stalled vital inquiry into still unanswered questions of high importance.

Women's history from the 1990s has largely steered clear of earlier controversies and instead has featured highly focused inquiries that often employ experimental theoretical and interdisciplinary approaches while avoiding appeals to any overarching interpretive frameworks. Several scholars have also continued to produce broader compendia of women's experience that tend to emphasize description over explanation.[30] That recent work engages the earlier paradigms much less, however, is not simply owing to the fading of prior ideological enthusiasms but also to an implicit recognition that neither of the earlier contending, if contradictory, assessments of the nineteenth-century gender order explains very well the complex evidence that continues to accumulate.

In this interpretive impasse, the new approach outlined here offers a chance to review these mounting data to see whether it can provide a better fit. The first observation, of course, is that scholars from the outset failed to consider the possibility that the particular political or economic changes that they chose to privilege in their accounts might have deeper common roots. Late-marriage households, after all, simultaneously generated a habit of independent behavior on women's part while creating a more equivalent power relationship between couples within households. By basing their diverging appraisals of the trajectory of women's lives on modern, extra-domestic events, however, both the "political" and "economic" approaches have, in effect, foreshortened by hundreds of years the time span during which critical developments had long set women's lives, as well as men's, on a peculiar path. This foreshortening has meant not only that the appraisals themselves were likely to be flawed but also that the eighteenth-century industrial and democratic revolutions have been made to bear far too much weight in explaining subsequent change – not just in the sexual order but everywhere.[31]

Because most married women initially withdrew from productive work when the household ceased to be a site of production, many historians have declared that women's status plummeted in the nineteenth century rather than recognize that for the time being, the loss of productive roles hardly

---

[30] See, for example, Olwen Hufton, *The Prospect Before Her: A History of Women in Western Europe, 1500–1800* (New York, 1996).

[31] The recent account of French feminism and political rights by Joan W. Scott, *Only Paradoxes to Offer: French Feminists and the Rights of Man* (Cambridge, 1996), is highly original in its analysis of the paradox of nineteenth-century feminists confronted by the simultaneous need to accept as well as deny sexual difference in politics, but like the other analyses of feminism in the period, it sees the roots of that development in the modern era, within the Enlightenment and revolutionary periods.

altered what had always mattered more for married women's relatively high status in those late-marriage or weak-family societies, namely, the partnership between husbands and wives that was literally required to keep their households afloat. What changed in the nineteenth century, then, were the terms of that partnership, under which for some time wives withdrew from productive work but nonetheless moved into more exclusive control of household management and childrearing. New doctrines of "separate sexual spheres" touting men's patriarchal dominance did make it seem that modern men benefited from enhanced household power. Yet awareness of the longer-term trend of the challenge to men's authority raises questions about what was really happening at the dawn of the modern era, just as men's new assertion of their power in the sixteenth century did earlier.

As for the related controversy over whether women's and men's lives were actually moving closer together or further apart, a review in light of the late-marriage evidence points to a far stronger case for their moving closer together, although not for the reasons the original proponents argued. While there was public political activity in the nineteenth century that ultimately, after many skirmishes and confrontations, brought the formal "citizenship" rights of women and men closer together, the more striking and immediate evidence for the convergence of women's and men's lives occurred on the same site as before: namely, the household. Despite assertions of a widening gender divide, a hardening of sex roles, and renewed patriarchy, the weight of the evidence points to the persistence and even acceleration of the centuries'-long trend already recounted here: that is, overlapping of men's and women's lives and erosion of the gender hierarchy.

On the domestic front, and despite an increased separation of home and workplace as well as an intensive effort to promote gender difference and the notion of separate gender spheres, there was a weakening of the remaining material props for distinctive roles for women and men, as well as for male dominance. Even on the extra-domestic front, the "men only" signs – many hastily tacked up from the late eighteenth century – were violated with increasing regularity, if not always with impunity. While it is true that in these newly "democratic" societies gender itself was touted as a more conscious category for pigeonholing experience and anchoring identity, the grounds for labeling particular traits or activities "female" or "male" became ever more flimsy and arbitrary. In assessing what was actually happening from the late eighteenth century to the turn of the twentieth, it is well to recall the words of a great Victorian, W. S. Gilbert: "Things are seldom what they seem. Skim milk masquerades as cream."[32]

While the discussion here recognizes the usefulness of the now widely used term "gender" to distinguish "the culturally specific characteristics associated with masculinity and femininity from biological features (male

---

[32] W. S. Gilbert, *H. M. S. Pinafore*, 1878.

and female chromosomes, hormones, as well as internal and external sexual and reproductive organs)," it has argued that the distinction is itself not only historically contingent but best understood within a long evolutionary framework.[33] As outlined earlier, a useful way to understand how the social and biological characteristics are related and work together is to trace the ways women and men over time have arrived at, and acted upon, a sense of femaleness and maleness.

The key here was recognition that the biological elements of gender identity as well as the cultural ones are "socially constructed" in that both are comprehended through people's perceptions of their environments, which always include observations about men's and women's bodies and what they do. This approach made it possible to see why, throughout the long agricultural era, women achieved gender identity comparatively easily, since their bodies appeared to give stronger cues than men's to their primary social tasks in such settings – in women's case, reproduction of heirs. Adoption of an aberrant late-marriage regime in northwestern Europe, moreover, further increased the challenges for men in achieving gender identity by blurring boundaries that were reinforced elsewhere by early-marriage structures. The overlapping of women's and men's experiences in late-marriage areas, in turn, meant that beliefs in gender difference and male dominance became harder to uphold as built-in features of the human condition.

The diverging political and economic accounts of the nature and direction of change affecting the sexes in the modern era can usefully be reviewed, then, with the two related hypotheses developed here: a specific one about the effects of a unique late-marriage pattern that put women's and men's lives on increasingly converging trajectories, and a more general one applicable to any society about the mechanisms that reproduce the sexual hierarchy in any social context. These hypotheses go far to explain otherwise paradoxical evidence that even as women's and men's life cycles demonstrably moved ever closer together in the nineteenth century, epic if finally unsuccessful campaigns were launched to uphold distinctive spheres for the sexes and to generate new rationales for a hierarchy favoring men over women.

These linked hypotheses explain best why talk about the sexes was on so many more lips by the modern era. They also explain why it was in the Victorian period that men's near monopoly on naming male and female qualities and defining boundaries between the sexes was first seriously challenged by women. They can account, too, for why women took over whole regions of this talk then and why men slowly fell silent on prior claims for their superiority in the sexual order. Finally, they can show why many women in

---

[33] Mary Hawkesworth, "Confounding Gender." *Signs: Journal of Women in Culture and Society* 22, No. 3 (1997), 650.

the modern era came to embrace a dogma of their own that upholds innate differences between the sexes, and why even now they are loath to let that dogma go.

* * *

A brief discussion here can only serve to outline how the voluminous historical data now available on the sexes in the nineteenth century can best be read as a demonstration, on the one hand, of how women's and men's lives were continuing to move closer together and, on the other, of how that very movement was again summoning new forms of resistance. Initially the resistance came from men, but as the nineteenth century wore on, men were joined for the first time by women in a new and shared concern to guard distinctive identities rooted in perceived gender difference.

It is important to recall the undermining by the later eighteenth century of what had evolved as a kind of compromise on men's status. Despite a novel family pattern that had already generated substantial power sharing between spouses, men until then gave no evidence of recognizing a shift in dominant male roles that they still held to be just as "natural" as subordinate female ones, although it is true that they were less inclined to claim automatic male superiority as they once had. With corollaries appropriate to rank or group, the basics of manhood were still held to be property ownership, control of a productive enterprise, or entry into a trade or profession that could be held up as a godly, masculine "calling" – plus family headship and protection and control of wives and children. The case was buttressed by reminders of men's advantages in size and strength, plus a declared monopoly on rational thought.

While changes in family organization had already forced men's accommodation by introducing the seeds of equality and individualism into the household, it was not until after 1750 that shifts affecting the gender order were increasingly thrust into consciousness. Population explosion, egalitarian political movements, and economic shifts that touched men, in particular, in all social groups forced awareness that there were problems with notions of manhood that had been altered tacitly and with little fanfare from the medieval era. For the first time, the idea of preordained male and female attributes, and a sexual hierarchy in men's favor, was openly suspected of having some mortal origins. The result was a novel, more conscious focus on the gender order. There were some scattered women's voices, such as Mary Wollstonecraft's. But as usual, men led.

Social historians have chronicled how reorganization of production made adult livelihood more dependent than ever upon the efforts of children rather than upon the legacy of parents. What is less noticed are strains upon patriarchal ideals informing families and other institutions such as artisan guilds and live-in domestic service. The effect was that everywhere young men were realizing that fathers and surrogate fathers who had exacted an extended period of deference and dependency in return for the promise of adult security and livelihood were increasingly unable to deliver.

For most in the poorer ranks, dreams of controlling productive property were wiped out by the late-eighteenth-century population expansion; and although heading a family was possible at an earlier age through expansion of wage labor, it counted less as a badge of manhood since public power of any sort was ceasing to derive from household headship. For urban laborers, too, the premium on masculine strength was steadily being devalued with the advent of the machine age. Even in more affluent middling and upper social ranks, securing livelihoods in crowded professions was difficult. Men who were ever more dependent upon women and less able to guarantee the future of children were also less likely to regard themselves as the natural protectors of either, let alone draw much comfort from the idea that they held a monopoly on rationality. Few men after the mid-eighteenth century could overlook the fact that forces beyond their control were diminishing their claims on some, or even most, of the familiar ingredients of manhood.

Unsurprisingly, middle-class men, whose lives were subject to the most change, were the first to conclude that the ground rules of the sexual order needed some attention. Their most vigorous response to shifts that put new pressure on male identity was what became known as the "doctrine of separate sexual spheres," which evolved from the mid-eighteenth century. What is odd is that interpreters continue to mistake what was essentially a renovation job, using perishable materials over an already shaky foundation, for a shiny and impregnable new edifice.

The very spelling out of gender spheres signaled men's new unease about change that they sensed had compromised their manhood, at least by the familiar criteria. Greater attention to women's domestic sphere should not obscure evidence that as before, the chief concern of the men who articulated these ideas was for their own positions, not women's. It stretches credulity to think that these middle-class spokesmen's first concern was the mobility and earning power of the main group of women actually leaving home then – that is, poor, single wage earners. It is equally implausible that initially, anyway, men were motivated by fears of *Wanderlust* among women of their own class, most of whom were not going anywhere. What makes more sense is that at a time when the quietly refurbished components of male identity had once again become problematic, manhood had to be redefined; and despite all the changes that had enhanced women's household authority, men could not fail to notice that women remained the sex subject to unpredictable pregnancies and accompanying nurturing tasks. In circumstances that now obliged more men to make a living outside households, men could elevate motherhood as the core of an allegedly female sphere, asserting women's preordained confinement to the household while dubbing everything else "men's sphere."

The emerging middle classes came to subscribe to a familiar set of related tenets that spread up and down the social scale: Society consists of two distinct and firmly separated spheres. The sphere of home and family is the natural realm of women and children, while that of business, politics, and public life is the natural habitat of men. The two spheres are governed by distinct values appropriate to their functions and embodied in the innate qualities of women and men who, respectively, are their denizens. Men are active, quick-witted, rational, and aggressive in roles as breadwinners and protectors. Women, who have purer religious and moral sensibilities, are passive, nurturing caregivers and natural homebodies. Motherhood is the enduring basis of women's femininity, although proper women (this chiefly in the Anglo-American renditions) have no sexual feelings at all and are animated by maternal instincts alone.

This portrayal is familiar. What is less noticed in the new rhetoric, however, is the ground it formally gives away in portraying women's "natural" qualities. The prior fading of the lustful and disorderly woman has been recounted as a consequence of men's new requirement for responsible wives and work partners. Yet by the time men outlined the new doctrine of the spheres, the limited gender equality that had been endorsed in Christian and especially Protestant teachings had been reinforced by secular arguments from the Enlightenment. These conceded that women and men have common personality traits and that some women may even have superior talents. Such admissions and praise made it harder for men to bar women from places or activities they wished to guard for themselves, as suggested by this tortured "Discourse on Female Influence" from 1837:

That there are ladies who are capable of public debate, who could make their voice heard from end to end of the church and the senate house, that there are those who might bear a favorable comparison with others as eloquent orators and who might speak to better edification than most of those on whom the office has hitherto devolved, I am not disposed to deny. The question is not in regard to ability, but to decency, to order, to Christian propriety.[34]

By the late nineteenth century, as such exhortations went unheeded, the new science was seized by men eager to prove woman's incapacity owing to her reproductive organs and small brain size.[35] Such notions had damaging effects, and a good deal of the first phase of the new women's history was devoted to exposing their harmful influence. Yet what remains poorly

---

[34] Jonathan F. Stearns, "Discourse on Female Influence" (1837), excerpted in Aileen S. Kraditor, ed., *Up from the Pedestal: Selected Writings in the History of American Feminism* (New York, 1968), 49.

[35] The documentation here is overwhelming. Early studies include those by Ann Douglass Wood, Carroll Smith-Rosenberg, Regina Morantz, and Elizabeth Fee in Mary S. Hartman and Lois Banner, eds., *Clio's Consciousness Raised: New Perspectives on the History of Women* (New York, 1974).

understood is that men, in propounding such arguments, were in full retreat from prior stronger claims. Having long abandoned more powerful positions that invoked women's base nature as a rationale for witch hunts, they were settling for what was, by comparison, benign containment.

A related example of skim milk masquerading as cream in the new gender pronouncements is the switch declared in the Victorian era in male and female sexuality. Not only were women pronounced passionless; men, who had long portrayed themselves as the sex more capable of rational control over sexual impulses, were now depicting themselves as the ones with barely governable lusts.[36] Here again, the habit of confining explanation to change that occurred only from the eighteenth century obscures the critical nature of this shift. Interpreters may be correct to argue that denying women sexual feelings served the new middle-class goal of limiting family size.[37] Yet a novel emphasis upon men's sexual appetites points to something deeper: namely, men's search for new anchors for their identities. Touting their stronger sexual impulses, however, meant fully abandoning the reassuring idea that libidinal lapses are the fault of lustful, seductive women. This move, a retreat for identity's sake, gave men less leverage while handing women an excuse to turn aside unwelcome sexual advances.[38]

Other evidence about daily life in middle- and even working-class households raises yet more questions, both about the validity of alleged setbacks for married women in the home and about the reality of a supposed new divide between women's and men's worlds. While the nineteenth century is

---

[36] Nancy F. Cott, "Passionlessness: An Interpretation of Victorian Sexual Ideology, 1790–1850." *Signs: Journal of Women in Culture and Society* 4, No. 2 (1978): 219–36.

[37] Peter N. Stearns, *Be Man!: Males in Modern Society* (New York, 1979), 88–90.

[38] In her study of early Victorian sexual purity in America, Carroll Smith-Rosenberg notes that anthropologists have long been aware that in unstable societies where some groups are losing the power to control or coerce, at least by the old roles, it is common to see the creation of fantasy systems in which specific behavior is magically punished. Pointing out that fathers whose sons were moving outside the rural and mercantile economic structure could no longer prepare their male offspring for an ordered world, she suggests that they attempted to retain control through a variety of reform campaigns, from vegetarianism and temperance to antimasturbation, making the rootless youth and his body both the symbol of danger to the social body and the target of a reformist cause. These alarmed propagandists portrayed the male orgasm as raging and wild, and masturbation as a degenerate habit that leads to insanity as well as effeminacy and even overt homosexuality.

Anxiety was not the only response to the changes men confronted in this era. Smith-Rosenberg remarks: "The vision of another – of a free – young man danced charismatically through the 'Jacksonian' imagination. Joyfully embracing change and christening it 'progress,' the autonomous young man of the frontier was the mirror image of the moral reformer's dangerous and endangered youth...the young man on his own, reinforced by liquor, his faithful dog, and his gun." See Carroll Smith-Rosenberg, "Sex as Symbol in Victorian Purity: An Ethnohistorical Analysis of Jacksonian America," in John Demos and Sarane Spence Boocock, eds., *Turning Points: Historical and Sociological Essays on the Family* (Chicago, 1978), 212–47.

still viewed by many as a nadir for women, some studies that richly deserve a second look have long pointed to women's enhanced power and autonomy, not beyond households but within them. As early as 1974, Daniel Scott Smith tried to call attention to what he labeled "domestic feminism."[39] He argued that by the end of the nineteenth century, middle- and working-class women alike had expanded authority in the household, owing chiefly to a radical decline in marital fertility.

The average number of children born to white American women, he noted, fell from 7.0 in 1800 to 4.2 in 1880 and then to 3.6 in 1900, at a time when over 95 percent of married women were not employed outside the home.[40] Fewer children, Smith persuasively argues, automatically enhanced these women's chances for social participation and personal development. He also makes the case that these impressive decreases in fertility were achieved far less by contraceptive devices than by "methods" of abstinence and withdrawal, contending that although both partners agreed on limiting fertility, women were the more active decision makers. Evidence he gives for wives' dominant role in family planning includes an intriguing comparison of sex ratios of last children in small and large families in Hingham, Massachusetts, from 1821 to 1860. Presuming that women then were likelier than men to be satisfied with female children, he shows that the smaller families were far more likely to contain only girls or to have a girl as the last child.[41]

Others have contributed to the case that married middle-class women and, more slowly, married women in the new working classes attained more power and autonomy within households in the nineteenth century.[42] In addition to the remarkable and little-known influence on family planning within marriage, women whose husbands were now typically in offices or factories during most daylight hours assumed more independent direction of all aspects of domestic management. They also took responsibility in new areas of family health, welfare, and consumer spending. The decline in marital fertility enhanced the overall quality of life and permitted more involvement in community activities.

Even the allegedly house-bound middle-class women cited previously were deeply involved in their communities, especially through voluntary associations.[43] Bonnie Smith's portrait of upper-middle-class French women, for example, shows participation in religious organizations dedicated to improving working-class women's and children's lives. The middle-class

---

[39] Daniel Scott Smith, "Family Limitation, Sexual Control and Domestic Feminism in Victorian America," in Hartman and Banner, eds., *Clio's Consciousness Raised*, 22.

[40] Ibid., 122.

[41] Ibid., 127–28.

[42] See, for example, Patricia Branca, *Women in Europe Since 1750* (London, 1978).

[43] Katherine Lynch, "The Family and the History of Public Life." *Journal of Interdisciplinary History* 24, No. 4 (Spring 1994), 677. Bonnie Smith kindly drew my attention to Katherine Lynch's work.

Englishwomen that Davidoff and Hall portray withdrew from business only as firms became more professionalized; and then they were likely to form charity associations, where their networks helped to build a sense of citizenship.[44] Paying attention to women's activity in civil society, then, belies the case for total withdrawal of women into the privacy of the family household. As Katherine Lynch argues:

Whereas the exclusion of women from formal political life was realized in both ideological and actual terms, recent research focusing (either implicitly or explicitly) on civil society has suggested that women's relegation to a private, domestic sphere in the nineteenth century may have been more of a "dream" about the family, more a statement of desire on the part of many social observers, than of women's actual social life. When we sever the equivalence sometimes drawn between public life and formal politics and expand our notion of the public to include life in civil society, links between women's public and private roles become more obvious, and the family's status as both a public and private institution becomes clearer.[45]

Scholars now may be readier to accept as reality the rhetoric of a gulf between the private familial sphere and public life in the nineteenth century, since their own perceptions are influenced by today's more stark separation of domestic and public life. In the nineteenth century the family household was still, though to a diminished extent, a public institution. But since then, as Richard J. Evans puts it, the family's "incorporation into a private sphere removed from society has been followed by its removal from history in a wider sense and its incorporation into a de-politicized history of private life."[46]

If and when the history of the family, and of women in particular, is reintegrated into the history of civil society, and even more when it is recognized that for hundreds of years, women as deputy husbands were partners in managing households in northwestern European societies, it will be easier to understand why their nineteenth-century descendants not only continued to expand their authority within households but were also prepared as the century progressed to take the next step and demand fuller participation in the formal political realm. The process is made to look too simple by the assumption that women's public activism was born only in the late eighteenth century. It is true that women then picked up men's slogans of individual rights and of "maternalism," turning both to their own purposes in the first massive rights and reform movements to benefit themselves. It is misleading,

---

[44] Ibid., 676.

[45] Ibid., 675.

[46] Richard J. Evans, "Politics and the Family: Social Democracy and the Working-Class Family in Theory and Practice Before 1914," in Richard J. Evans and W. Robert Lee, eds., *The German Family: Essays on the Social History of the Family in Nineteenth- and Twentieth-Century Germany* (London, 1981), 256, cited in Lynch, "The Family and the History of Public Life," 672.

however, to suggest that women would have experienced the success they did if they had not had their very own, very long tradition as responsible and independent actors to draw upon.

This point is especially important now that studies are multiplying on women in societies outside the northwestern European orbit. The absence of a comparable tradition of independence and public activism for women in many societies, often an impossibility given the nature of early-marriage, strong-family household structures, makes it easy for interpreters from weak-family societies to imagine that such women must somehow lack the gumption to champion their interests. At the same time, the deterioration of households and communities in northwestern European-based societies makes it harder for people there to recognize the importance of new and powerful, if frequently local, activism by women in many places around the world, since neighborhoods and villages are no longer seen by such interpreters as genuine public sites. Portrayals based upon a foreshortened historical record, and ignoring differences in behavior conditioned by differences in household arrangements, distort the experience of all women.

*   *   *

Moving from the nineteenth century into the twentieth and the contemporary era, more evidence can be marshaled from recent work on northwestern European and North American societies that supports the thesis here that women's and men's lives continued to move closer together, as they had been doing for centuries. Well before women in the later twentieth century returned in massive numbers to the workforce, domestic authority for wives was enhanced in the working classes, for example, where in the absence of family-controlled property, social networks and even living arrangements were increasingly based on proximity to a wife's kin rather than to a husband's. The reactions of men to such developments slowed but did not alter the underlying direction of change. It is true that like middle-class men, who had acted to shore up their identities through exclusive new social clubs, chambers of commerce, professional societies, and academic institutions, working-class men fled their female-ascendant homes when they could for refuge in bars, sporting clubs, union meetings, and male-only spectator events.[47] By the later twentieth century, however, many of these sexually segregated institutions and patterns of socializing were themselves fading away.

Men's evident discomfort over the de facto surrendering of day-to-day domestic authority by the turn of the twentieth century fueled their reactive efforts to shore up control of the world outside the home. That men were obliged to admit women's position now as domestic managers, and even to praise them for it, complicated matters, just as being more exclusively

---

[47] See Stearns, *Be a Man!*, Ch. 4, "The Emergence of the Working-Class Man," 59–78.

mother-raised than previous generations of men placed them in a double bind in coping with women's rising demands. As early as 1900, women had succeeded in so deforming men's original intent in the doctrine of separate spheres – that is, the defense of a "natural" male sphere – that they were confronting men in a whole series of extra-domestic clashes on territory long held to be safe male preserve.

Armed with the legitimating rationale of defending their domestic sphere, many women claimed new ground as their own as they embarked on campaigns for extending women's education, enforcing temperance, rescuing prostitutes, and achieving broad-based rights and suffrage goals. They created a plethora of voluntary associations in which they made common cause across class and racial boundaries by appealing to the needs of a female sphere that they declared united all women. The strategy, while imperfectly realized, was not even available to men, who had long since ceased to have a set of roles transcending the boundaries of rank, class, and race that could be portrayed as offering a plausible common identity.

It was nonetheless women's own push to control their fertility that did more than anything else to foster a continuing convergence of their life experience with men's and promote the further erosion of credible bases for gender hierarchy. This was the single development in the modern era that made the most difference in altering women's overall social position. It mattered more than their expanded autonomy in managing households, or their stronger participation in civic life, or even their ultimate reabsorption into the full-time workforce, although all were related. Yet if the focus remains on those things, as it has so far, the real novelty of the modern era is eclipsed.[48] Women in northwestern European societies, after all, had been set apart since the medieval era by their comparatively more independent activity beyond households as well as their extensive productive contributions. These were hardly new with the industrial era, although they have frequently been presented that way.

What stands out as the real hallmark of the contemporary era is rather the final stages of the undoing of ties between women's reproductive functions and their capacity to exercise fuller roles in society. The process began centuries before with postponed marriage, which had had the effect of expanding women's social experience, multiplying their productive tasks, and – for most women – reducing the number of children they bore. This time, however, a renewed and rapid decline in fertility owed much to women's direct agency. It was one more instance, and a dramatic one, of the activist habits that women had had to acquire as mistresses of vulnerable, unstable

---

[48] Just such an emphasis upon the supposedly key factor of women's expanded household roles in their new autonomy is argued in Julie A. Matthaei, *An Economic History of Women in America* (New York, 1983). See my review "Capitalism and the Sexes." *Raritan: A Quarterly Review* (Summer 1984): 123–33.

households that had long demanded regular interventions and midcourse corrections.

The modern era has typically been portrayed as the time when northwestern European and North American women, propelled by the changes of the democratic and industrial revolutions, finally made their debut on the historical stage. Yet if the reimagining of the past being urged here is taken seriously, these last two centuries may instead come to be seen as at once epilogue and prologue – the end of a phase in which women's agency was confined to household and community stages that were informal arenas of power, and the beginning of a phase in which women could shift attention to an ever wider world, including multiple public arenas that many more men had entered long before them. As unmarried workers for a decade or more of their lives, most women had long since learned to cope with a degree of independence at a young age. They had also made singular contributions for nearly a millennium to the accumulation of wealth in society that may have been a critical precondition for industrial transformation.

One irony here is that long-range planning, risk-taking, personal responsibility, and independence have yet to be recognized as mass behaviors generated by the demands of life in distinctive sorts of households – in other words, as normative conduct required of everyone in late-marriage, weak-family settings. To the contrary, these features have been held up as evidence of a peculiar European genius, a mistaken view that has bolstered many a chauvinist case for the superiority of Western civilization. Since maintaining unstable households, let alone enhancing their assets, quite literally depended upon these qualities, it is hardly surprising that they turned up with some regularity in the humblest households, and in the behavior of women as well as men.

Failing to exhibit these qualities during youth might well increase one's likelihood of falling into the marginalized state of involuntary bachelor or spinsterhood that befell up to a fifth of early modern persons. Yet it is also true that a society that long made survival possible for unmarried persons made the single lifestyle an easier one by the later twentieth century, when improved education and living standards made singleness a more genuine choice. The option of remaining single also permitted some women to pursue full-time careers that until lately were nearly impossible. Daniel Scott Smith has remarked that such women likely had more impact than their small numbers suggest. In 1940, for example, nearly a third of forty-five- to forty-nine-year-old female college graduates in the United States were unmarried.[49]

Awareness of the late-marriage pattern is also helpful in sorting through recurring claims that we have abandoned the "traditional" family that was

[49] Smith, "Family Limitation, Sexual Control and Domestic Feminism in Victorian America," in Hartman and Banner, eds., *Clio's Consciousness Raised*, 120.

once the norm and remains the ideal for many, with a male breadwinner and a female homemaker. This family form, however, was approximated for only a relatively short time in the early industrial era in northwestern European societies, when the relocation of productive work away from family households meant that married women with small children were obliged, at least temporarily, to withdraw from such work or to work part time. Far from being traditional or natural, this novel domestic form of male breadwinner/ female homemaker lasted as the dominant household type for barely more than a century. By now, most married women with children in these societies have resumed what are arguably more traditional roles, for them at least, as full-time members of the workforce.

Keeping a focus on the weakened but hardly defunct family household as a continuing site for change well into the modern era, this revisionist account has presented the household's continuing viability as a base from which women, in particular, were enabled to move into wider social arenas. For wives, if less so for their husbands, households well into the twentieth century remained locations of innovative activity and sites for the enactment of power. In a fascinating account of myth, ritual, and family values entitled *A World of Their Own Making*, John Gillis describes how as real families in northwestern Europe and the United States became more threatened and fragile entities, the symbolic families created chiefly by the cultural work of women within households came to exercise ever more power, if only in their grip on their members' fantasies.[50] He shows that pervasive images of "home sweet home," along with many family rituals imagined to be of earlier origin, including birthdays, anniversaries, white weddings, and more, were modern inventions introduced chiefly by Victorian women.

While lip service was paid to the domestic patriarch, husbands who had left home for daily employment more than a century before their wives did so increasingly concentrated their energies on power bases they were creating beyond households. While the women who followed men into these arenas have yet to achieve parity with them, there is little question that the contemporary era is witnessing the continued overlapping of women's and men's lives. Evidence is there in the data on women's employment, education, sexual behavior, and self-consciousness regarding their roles and rights. Men retain formal ascendance on the domestic front and real ascendence on the public front, but women have moved into the lead in articulating discourse around topics of gender and power. The first women's movement in the mid-nineteenth century was arguably a by-product of the more dramatic changes men were experiencing then, but the second women's movement of

---

[50] John Gillis, *A World of Their Own Making: Myth, Ritual, and the Quest for Family Values* (New York, 1996).

the later twentieth century was created by women finally experiencing even more dramatic changes in their own lives.

The most enduring trend in the sexual order within northwestern European-based societies has been the increased overlapping of women's and men's experiences from the medieval to the contemporary era. With variations in timing for different groups, each phase of the life cycle came to display a more synchronized pattern for the sexes. That women from early to mid-adulthood continued to be subject to unpredictable pregnancies long remained the single item that could be construed to mean that the sexes have separate, even preordained, destinies. But once reliable fertility control became possible and women were more able to pursue education, employment, and other activities freed from the interruption of unplanned pregnancies, it became increasingly difficult to guard the perception of a primary female destiny residing in motherhood

What is more, when women achieved significant capacity to control their fertility, the opportunity arose for a new sort of single sexual standard. From the early modern era, such a standard had been based, as recounted earlier, upon sexual abstinence outside marriage for both sexes, challenging the double sexual standard that reigned in early-marriage settings, where a woman's sexuality is more controlled by her own and her husband's kin. Now a new single standard has emerged, uncoupled from the institution of marriage and based on mutual sexual fulfillment rather than mutual abstinence. The potential of this standard to advance sexual equality remains imperfectly realized at best, however, because it has appeared at a time when women's social and economic bargaining power is still well outmatched by men's.

Men and women in northwestern European and North American settings also have yet to come to terms with the notion of marriage as a fully realized partnership, especially now that supports to uphold it continue to weaken. Households have ceased to be productive units, and children have long been net economic liabilities rather than assets to parents. Marriage itself has emerged as a breakable and renegotiable contract, even though most people still sign up at least once. The ultimate fate of the late-marriage households that for so long provided a stage for women to expand their experience and authority remains unclear. With every new census, as residential units with two or more persons related by blood or marriage continue to decline, it becomes ever more problematic to construe marriage as a necessary feature of households.

A process that placed women's and men's lives on converging trajectories, and has occurred over many centuries, always needs to be recalled in assigning any given change to specific individuals or groups. Whether we are looking at change in the sexual order, as here, or at other sorts of change, as in the previous chapter, a still invisible marriage and household system can now be recognized to have set crucial parameters within which most historical actors and their supporting casts prepared for their roles. While praise or blame is still in order for many performances, awareness of the agency of ordinary women and men who did the stage-setting as well as much of the behind-the-scenes script-writing makes it necessary constantly to reimagine what we think we know happened, and to reconsider what the springs of behavior for all the players truly were.

The most striking conclusion regarding women's place in the sexual order, for example, flies in the face of still-reigning opinion among most historians of women. That conclusion is that throughout the period from the Middle Ages until well into the twentieth century, the institution of the household was a vitally important base for women's creative agency, serving both to weaken a hierarchical order favoring men and to promote a more shared set of activities and traits for the sexes than in other comparable societies. The household, in other words, was the single most important institution for realizing whatever measure of equality women in northwestern European–based societies have come to possess. This was so despite the fact that for the bulk of that long period, neither women nor men consciously promoted a formal agenda of equality between the sexes.

By the second half of the twentieth century, the household had largely ceased to perform this still overlooked function. Since historical opinion has already fixed the image of the nineteenth-century household as at best a place where newly isolated women learned to take advantage of the special "bonds of womanhood" or, at worst, as a repressive domestic backwater, it is not surprising that households continue to be portrayed as places where women's energies and ambitions are always thwarted.[51] While most married women have now returned to the workforce, some critics noting continuing challenges are asking whether women will ever achieve equality with men, while others are asking whether equality is what they should be after. What is clear is that whatever women do next, households will no longer provide their launching pads.

Anxious Victorians, at the eleventh hour, fashioned and embellished a rambling, twin-domed edifice enshrining separate spheres for the sexes, dedicating it to gender difference as *the* master social division. They would surely be dismayed to behold the present decay of their gilded habitation. A nineteenth-century period piece, it once commanded the obsessive attention not just of run-of-the-mill talents, but of the finest minds of the era. Yet almost overnight, it came to be seen as something of an embarrassment, even a joke. This reversal is owing to the fact that the doctrine itself was always, to borrow the words of commentator Katherine Lynch cited earlier, "more a statement of desire on the part of many social observers" and "more of a

---

[51] See Nancy F. Cott, *The Bonds of Womanhood: "Women's Sphere" in New England, 1780–1835* (New Haven, Conn., 1977). Cott's is a subtle account of the mixed experience of middle-class women, whereas others, including more popular accounts, placed most stress on the negative effects of households on women.

'dream' about the family."[52] It was an effort to tie a system of gender differentiation to a division that, as has been argued here at length, never existed in northwestern European societies to the extent that it did in so many other places – namely, the division between households and a wider world.

While it is true that even in late-marriage settings women were more identified than men with households, a case has been made here that already by the early modern era, the denizens of those households had had to become ever more actively involved outside them merely to accomplish what early-marriage households readily achieved through their own kin networks. Parents in the comparatively permeable households of northwestern Europe not only sent out their daughters and sons at tender ages, but also harbored at home legions of unrelated servants who were resident ambassadors from the wider world. The nineteenth-century attempt to equate women with households and men with the outside world, then, far from being the huge success it has been declared by too many commentators, was doomed from the start. The boundaries between households and the world beyond them had long been blurred, and the traffic of women across them had been heavy for centuries.

It was not, as is occasionally claimed, that admittedly weakened households were themselves collapsing. Households were and remain responsible for many functions that continue to be vitally important, if increasingly ill attended. But the declared identification of women with the household, and their confinement there, had long been a dream in northwestern Europe. Although discourse on separate sexual spheres largely disappeared by the later twentieth century, people became more preoccupied than ever at that time with sorting out contested ground rules of the gender order and with determining once and for all who women and men really are. Their endless deliberations on these topics, however, have rarely been recognized for the critical cultural work they are performing. These interchanges are shaking to the roots deep-seated notions about gender that have been with us as far back as we can reckon.

*　　*　　*

This brings me to some final comments on the gender order. The first large hypothesis explored here – namely, an extended argument that the strange late-marriage pattern in northwestern Europe had huge but still unrecognized consequences – has been seen to be helpful in sorting out conflicting views about whether the sexes in the modern era were moving closer together or being driven further apart. The second and related hypothesis is about the mechanisms that appear to be responsible, in this or any society, for perpetuating beliefs in the importance of differences between the sexes and of a hierarchy favoring men. If one assumes that this hierarchy is not a

[52] Lynch, "The Family and the History of Public Life," 675.

permanent feature of human societies but instead a variable whose presence depends upon particular, if frequently fulfilled, conditions, it becomes possible to put knowledge about gender arrangements to work more convincingly anywhere in accounts of social change over time. Identifying a plausible social/psychological explanation for this obstinate feature of human behavior means, in other words, that it is no longer necessary to view the sexual hierarchy in any society as either historically inaccessible or inevitable.

If the hypothesis is pursued that the gender hierarchy is rooted in differences in the ease or difficulty with which the sexes achieve gender identity, there should, as noted, be only two circumstances in which a society might display an absence of conviction in the gender hierarchy. The first such case is one in which observable physical differences loom large for both sexes as a component of identity, since women and men alike are able readily to comprehend their primary social activities as a more or less straightforward expression of their unique bodily features. This case does appear to have been approximated, perhaps even for thousands of years, in prehistoric hunting societies. The second "pure" case, the first example of which I propose is emerging now, is exemplified by a society in which physical differences, although acknowledged as such, do not bear crucially upon a larger sense of individual identity for either sex, since they are not seen as obviously tied to the primary activities or roles of either women or men.

The long history of the species was then argued to display a shift from the earliest societies, in which physical differences played a large role for both sexes in identity formation, through agricultural and industrial societies in which such differences played a decreasing but asymmetrical role in that process, in which women's distinctive physical features were long perceived as more salient for their social identities than men's. The account here has, of course, paid most attention to the later phases of this process in one agricultural region in northwestern Europe, where it has been argued that the appearance of the aberrant late-marriage regime resulted in the gap between womanhood as a perceived natural state and manhood as a more achieved one finally narrowing enough to be noticed as such. To put it another way, presumptions of a fixedness in women's activities owing to their bodily features finally became impossible to sustain – either for male or female perceivers.

The process was gradual; but by the modern era, especially as women gained the ability to control conception, they finally experienced what had happened to men so many generations before. That is, their gender identities came to derive more from the contingent features of time and place and less from their distinctive physical characteristics. It is true that even as middle-class women in the nineteenth century succeeded in limiting fertility through heroic measures of abstinence or guilty recourse to inadequate contraceptive devices, they were still likely to insist that woman's chief end in life is motherhood. Even feminists of the era who argued that women had the right to choose when to conceive a child were reluctant to endorse artificial contraception, urging mutual self-control instead. Convinced of a special maternal instinct, they recoiled at the consequences for the family of separating sexuality from reproduction. As one historian put it, voluntary motherhood was "a tool for women to strengthen their positions within conventional marriages and families, not to reject them."[53]

By the later twentieth century, however, the picture had changed dramatically. Women's increased access to education and employment, plus the availability of reliable means to prevent conception and to secure safe, legal abortions, were prompting ever more women and men alike to abandon their conviction in a proposition that once seemed self-evident to all: women's primary fate as mothers. In historical terms, women's bodies were finally ceasing to be imagined as the eternal carriers of their destinies, whereas the comparable event for men had occurred thousands of years before.

Despite this immensely important development – a capstone of the longer trend argued here to have brought women's and men's lives closer together – the magnitude of the transformation in process in the ways we perceive the sexes remains neither acknowledged nor understood. This is no doubt because even now the effects are so partial, so puzzling, and so contested that it may seem not merely pretentious but downright absurd to insist that what is happening is a momentous development, that we are finally abandoning the conviction that differences between the sexes are vitally important. I think, nonetheless, that this is so, and that it matters a great deal, not just for the ways we try to understand the past in European-based societies, but also for the ways in which we attempt to imagine, and then create, a global future.

It is important to underscore that if the framework being argued here holds, it is the belief in the importance of differences between the sexes, even more than in male superiority and dominance, that has mattered most and endured longest. That belief has been reenacted and renewed for as long as the species has run – well before upstart agricultural societies promoted not merely difference between the sexes but also a new claim for men's natural priority in the sexual order, a claim that many have since taken as the more serious of the two. By now, though, even as growing numbers have come to be suspicious of that more recent claim, many continue to infer from the physical differences between women's and men's bodies a whole parade of notions about who women and men are and can (or must) be, although it is hard to explain why declaring these differences remains so important. Like the "voluntary motherhood" advocates of the nineteenth century who proclaimed maternalism the core of women's identity even as they embraced the means to tame its liabilities for the fuller lives beckoning to them, many

---

53 Linda Gordon, "Voluntary Motherhood: The Beginnings of Feminist Birth Control Ideas in the United States," in Hartman and Banner, eds., *Clio's Consciousness Raised*, 68.

people continue to insist that some differences between the sexes matter, or at least ought to matter, even as they labor to dismantle the remaining material and ideological props that sustain their influence.

The tale that has been told here has focused upon only a millennium or so of developments argued to have played a critical role in undoing an ancient consensus about the importance of difference between the sexes. It helps to explain women's apparently schizophrenic response to their new capacity to control conception. Despite all the other changes that the late-marriage system generated that blurred the boundaries between the sexes, most women right into the present era could still plausibly infer a core female identity attaching to perceived links between their bodies and their social roles. Unlike men, who lost the closest thing to a comparable anchor for identity as societies of fixed agriculture replaced hunting societies, women have only lately been obliged to confront the implications of giving up what long served as the most compelling basis for their identities. By the modern era, indeed, when men were finally driven to define their own beleaguered gender identities by negation, motherhood became a mainstay, in the doctrine of the sexual spheres, not just for women's identities but for men's too.

While it is true that from the beginning motherhood itself was less central in the lives of women in late-marriage societies, most women, even by the second half of the twentieth century when sure contraception became available, were barely beginning to perceive motherhood as something voluntary – a choice among other choices, even an important choice, but no longer a destiny. Their confused response in such circumstances, and men's, too, was hardly schizophrenic. What was and is happening, after all, is something still new in the history of the species. For growing numbers of both sexes now, and for the very first time, evident physical differences between women and men are ceasing to serve as plausible markers of social identity. Those differences are obviously still real; but since the chief activities of men, and now of women too, can no longer be readily perceived as an expression of what their bodies do, the function of those differences as primary signifiers of the self is slipping away.

The noted increase in talk about the sexes, then, is owing to this extraordinary decline of notions of femaleness or maleness as components of personal identity. That people are talking about differences between the sexes more than ever before is nonetheless often taken to mean the opposite, that such differences have somehow become more salient. Yet just as men in the nineteenth century, and then women, entered into desperate discourse about the need to guard separate sexual spheres even as the last credible vestiges of support for such spheres were vanishing, we are now clinging to our conviction that differences between the sexes are crucially important. In the context of developed societies where most of these conversations are taking place, however, the bulk of the declared cream turns out yet again to be skim milk. We are finally surrendering gender as a vital component of identity.

Such a development might be more welcome not only if it were more complete, but also if it had been more deliberate. Instead, it appears to have emerged in northwestern Europe as the largely accidental result of an anomalous late-marriage system that lacked the built-in structures that to this day work all too well to perpetuate gender difference and hierarchy in early-marriage settings. For long as the late-marriage system evolved, there was no conscious aim to diminish gender differences or to make the sexes more equal. To the extent that these things occurred – and they did – they were unplanned and often unwelcome, especially to men but often enough to women as well.

Men long responded to the compromising of boundaries between the sexes by periodically redefining the ingredients of manhood and womanhood, all the while quietly surrendering ground shored up in the last round of claims. By the time large numbers of women consciously entered the game of defining gender differences in the nineteenth century, many were ready to put a positive reading on these gender-equalizing trends, and some were even prepared to embrace new movements for women's rights.

If the origins suggested here for the idiosyncratic late-marriage pattern are sustained, however, it bears reminding that daughters' marriages were postponed in the first instance in the service of patriarchal land strategies. The weakness of resulting single-family households then prompted the invention by their residents of countless expedients and institutions to assume religious, political, and economic functions that could no longer be borne by weakened households. In new investigations based on these findings, items such as Enlightenment ideals, the growth of nation-states, and capitalist transformation will obviously survive as major narrative elements; but all will turn out to owe rather less than has been imagined to the isolated activity of elite men educated in the classical tradition. When all is said and done, these things and more that historians have singled out to value in societies with northwestern European roots – and many continue to deserve their respect – must also take into account the agency and creativity of untold numbers of poor, illiterate persons, women as well as men, who invented as they went along countless ways to prop up the precarious and unstable households that they had inherited. In the process, they laid the groundwork for some utterly novel religious, political, economic, and cultural configurations.

Epilogue

It was essential in the preceding pages, which revisited some major unresolved historical controversies of the past generation, especially around the role of western Europe in prompting major global change after 1500, to paint with a broad brush. The object was to make a case for the importance of the largely ignored late-marriage pattern, identify a plausible source for its origins, and describe how different some key developments in the Western past would look if that pattern were taken seriously. A postscript remains to be added, however, about the versatility of this interpretive approach for many other sorts of investigations, large and small. There are potential uses not only for reviewing some perplexing historical and contemporary issues within the European and North American context, but also for assessing such items as the debate on a convergence of weak- and strong-family systems in a global context.

A long perspective on household systems and an even longer one on how gender arrangements work can help, for example, to explain the more extreme reactions in an ongoing contemporary debate over abortion that periodically erupts into violence. Awareness of the peculiar proximity of the sexes promoted by the late-marriage system, as well as of the nerve of anxiety and hatred that has been exposed again and again at times when male identity (however constructed at the time) was under pressure, makes it possible to understand more fully a controversy whose capacity to call forth such visceral responses is otherwise extremely puzzling.

There is a plausible link between this controversy over legalized abortion in the United States (and increasingly in other northwestern European countries as well) and events such as the Salem witch hunts over 300 years ago, in which so many women, in particular, were perceived to be challenging men's divinely ordained authority. It can be said, though, that in the former case, the perpetrators of the more brutal and violent forms that such reactions have taken are now confined largely to the fringes of society, rather than to its mainstream, where they were still located in Salem. With

an appreciation of the long and often painful history in which power struggles around manhood and womanhood were a recurring theme, it is easier
to explain vigorous and even violent antiabortion action at a time when, in
the eyes of a fearful minority, the differences between the sexes, including
a supposedly preordained male superiority, are all being obliterated. The
tenacity of belief in gender difference, after all, has always been greatest in
the enduring perception that motherhood is the core of women's identity.

Another example of a baffling historical development that becomes more
comprehensible in light of findings here is the long and unique northwestern
European tradition of anathematizing male homosexuality. This intensely
negative reaction has already been described as linked to the special male
anxiety over manhood, unleashed in late-marriage societies in particular as
one more effect of men's perceived increasing and uncomfortable proximity
to women. This helps to explain the timing of the episodes of strongest repression that occurred, predictably enough, at the dawn of the early modern
era – when most northwestern European countries adopted the death penalty
for sodomy between men – with subsequent peaks of repression in the late
nineteenth century and again in the late twentieth. All three periods marked
broader efforts to redefine and anchor manhood even as reliable materials
for doing so were becoming ever more scarce. It is also noteworthy that only
in recent years have lesbians acquired an unenviable equality in parallel status as a targeted group. This helps confirm the wider case here that only as
motherhood ceased to provide a credible core identity for all women could
other identities begin to be taken more seriously for particular women.

Shifting to some global implications of this revisionist analysis, we turn
to some issues raised earlier about the fate of late-marriage societies versus
early-marriage ones and to evidence that these household systems, which
have long been distinct, may now be converging. What emerged first from
the recent review of weak-family households since the eighteenth century
was confirmation that women's and men's lives persisted in their centuries-
long trend of moving ever closer together. That is, contrary to allegations
that a new gap emerged in the nineteenth century between women's and
men's spheres that, in effect, moved women's and men's lives closer to the
more segregated worlds of the sexes in early-marriage societies, what actually happened was a continuation of the long-established trend toward ever
greater correspondence between the lives of women and men.

On the other hand, since the mid-twentieth century in southern Europe,
as well as in many of the more traditional early-marriage societies elsewhere,
the trend has been a reverse of the earlier pattern, with a shift toward the
weak-family household model. Many demographic and life cycle features
that first marked women's experience in northwestern European societies –
including later marriage, declining fertility, expanded employment, increased
literacy and education, and new domestic empowerment for women – have
now emerged as clear trends in growing numbers of societies around the

world, often enough through governmental or extragovernmental initiatives that, whether intentionally or not, have promoted them.

The findings here should nonetheless give planners new reasons to be wary of the capacity of these Western "models" to effect rapid, predictable, and desirable social change, especially if goals include expanding the options of women as well as men in societies where sharp gaps remain between the sexes, not simply in access to employment but also in indices that include literacy and education, nutrition, health care, life expectancy, and survival rates from ages zero to three. Planners who hope to compress major change into the space of two to three generations, and who often see traditional multifamily households in many parts of the world as obstacles to their goals, need at the least to be aware that the largely unplanned economic development of western Europe occurred over a far longer stretch of time than the 150 or so years that is usually presented. For some time now, the voices of many policymakers around the world have also been raised to urge more attention to local conditions as well as to the involvement of local populations, women as well as men, in any intended changes. The findings here obviously confirm these sentiments.

To take just one example, a comparatively mild one, of problems that can arise when major change is introduced with insufficient attention to existing household arrangements, the Republic of China on Taiwan was transformed in less than fifty years from a poor agricultural society into a prosperous industrialized one, accompanied by huge changes in women's lives. Owing to state-run family planning, the birth rate declined dramatically from over 6 births per woman in the 1950s to just 1.77 in 1995.[1] Women's employment outside the home expanded greatly and stood at 46 percent in 1997. The overall literacy rate was 93 percent in 1991, with no significant difference in the rates of women and men under sixty-five, although among those over sixty-five who were illiterate, 29 percent were men and 71 percent women.[2] Female undergraduates at the college and university level jumped from 11 percent in 1950 to 48 percent in 1997.[3] Women's age at marriage rose to the mid-twenties, and urbanization reduced the number and power of extended families, while major growth in nuclear family households increased many women's domestic autonomy.[4]

At the same time, however, the state countenanced some serious negative effects that were disproportionately borne by women. The family planning program that targeted residents of rural regions with large families resulted

[1] Lan-hung Nora Chiang, "Women in Taiwan: Linking Economic Prosperity and Women's Progress," in Louise Edwards and Mina Roces, eds., *Women in Asia: Tradition, Modernity and Globalisation* (Saint Leonards NSW, Australia, 2000), 231.
[2] Ibid., 232.
[3] Ibid., 233–34.
[4] Ibid., 243–44.

in fertility declines that triggered a sharp increase in female neglect and infanticide in a society in which sons remained more desired than daughters, both as heirs of family property and as supporters of elderly parents. Technologies such as ultrasound and amniocentesis were used, along with induced abortion, to guarantee sons, practices that have also been widely documented in both India and mainland China. Meanwhile, as of 1994, three-quarters of Taiwan's aged persons lived with their children, mostly with married sons.[5] Despite improvements in education and access to the professions, the double burden of working women is especially hard for wives, who remain almost totally responsible not only for domestic chores and child care, but also for elder care. A survey from 1995 on the values of married women showed that they overwhelmingly cite the family as the place where they hope to gain the greatest fulfillment, an irony given that changes to date have arguably made realization of that goal harder for them than it was before while ensuring continued disincentives to a stronger commitment to the workplace.[6]

The fact that crucial changes in social, political, and economic arrangements, as well as shifts in the sexual order, stretched back over many hundreds of years also meant that northwestern European societies had time to adjust to all these changes – far more time, in fact, than has previously been imagined. This realization makes it even easier to appreciate the unsettled reactions that have occurred when contemporary societies have had very little time to absorb major change, especially change introduced from the outside. The analysis here of shifts in the sexual order, and of men's greater dependence on features of the external world in anchoring their manhood, also helps to explain men's often stronger reactions to change, including their appeal to religious fundamentalism to restore lost values, real or imagined. In northwestern Europe, after all, it was not even outside change but rather the "inside" change of postponed marriage that simultaneously enhanced women's domestic power and summoned widespread efforts to control women's behavior, including witch hunts that were allowed for 300 years to run a gruesome and leisurely course.

That some sort of convergence between weak- and strong-family systems has lately been taking place does appear to be the case, although arguably, what matters most are the terms under which that convergence is occurring and what, if anything, can or should be done. While that is a subject for another inquiry, a final, related, and sobering implication of the findings from this one needs to be mentioned, as it bears directly on the matter of what should be done. I refer to the fact that most of the changes that have been argued in these pages to have brought women's and men's life cycles ever closer together, ultimately making it possible even to imagine a still fuzzy abstraction labeled "gender equality," have occurred through developments

---

[5] Ibid., 231–32.
[6] Ibid., 238.

that made women's day-to-day lives look far more like men's than they continue to look in most other societies. The effect, in northwestern European and North American contexts, has been that the very notion of equality between the sexes has been "gendered male" in ways that most interpreters still do not recognize, since they remain unaware of the lengthy historical experience behind the emerging concept of gender equality.

This investigation has spelled out just how long this process of women's increasing conformity to men's life cycles and values has been going on. Postponing marriage from medieval times meant that single daughters, like sons, worked longer at productive tasks. Comanaging nuclear households that called upon women to play the role of deputy husband emphasized and rewarded the male rather than the female tasks in which women in early-marriage societies engage more exclusively. Motherhood itself not only arrived later for women in northwestern Europe, it was also a less exclusive and all-encompassing experience than for women in most other agricultural societies. Women involved more extensively in productive work, both single and married, bore fewer children. The years of childrearing were fewer, too, since children of both sexes usually left home for good as teenagers. Women, we know, were also less honored by men in their roles as mothers than they were as wives and household partners, even though there is abundant early evidence that when women expressed priorities of their own, they placed stronger emphasis upon their roles as mothers than men did.

Initially, at least, it can hardly be said that women made active choices to be less involved in childrearing or in caring for the older generation in order to engage more fully in men's work. Still, the effect of later marriage in nuclear household settings was inexorably to oblige couples to identify or create a whole range of extrafamilial practices and institutions to fill in for them in helping to raise children and care for the elderly. Life-cycle service, maintenance contracts, and other expedients very soon came to substitute for the roles that women in early-marriage settings still play in many other places. In due course, as men's activity moved increasingly outside the household, and as the ideal of equality came to permeate public discourse, this ideal came to be associated almost exclusively with activity in the public realm. It was no accident that by the twentieth century, what equality of the sexes came to mean in practice was that women should be allowed to do whatever it is that men do. The frantic nineteenth-century proponents of separate sexual spheres, who surely deserve much of the ridicule that has come their way, at least recognized that despite the massive expansion of activity beyond households, vital functions were still being conducted within them that were fast losing credible champions.

The longevity of this still unrecognized development that the very notion of equality between the sexes for women is gendered male provides yet another reason for the slowed advance to a more genuine equality for women in late-marriage, weak-family societies. Since their challenges in these societies are so very different, and often appear to be less basic and compelling than the needs of women in early-marriage, strong-family societies, they are often made to appear trivial. Yet the usefulness of household analysis in both instances is to demonstrate the extent to which distinctive challenges confronting women in both weak- and strong-family contexts derive from inherited household structures that have rarely been identified as such and whose influence has not been directly addressed – whether it is in the continuing deep devaluation of women, which is more likely to occur in strong-family settings, or in the persistent discounting of children, the elderly, and all those who work with and serve them, which occurs more typically in the richer, weak-family societies. Awareness of the roots in distinctive family structures that have informed both of these behaviors may ultimately help to eradicate them, since to some extent, anyway, their perpetuation is owing to their embeddedness in unexamined behaviors that, even in the case of weak-family societies, are themselves very old and often appear to have taken on a life of their own.

There may, in short, be some appropriate practical consequences from an exercise that has focused on identifying the likely causes and results of the late-marriage pattern in northwestern Europe. The good news is that while too many households by now have become fragile, isolated, and stressed, many extra-domestic institutions, including governments and workplaces, are also showing the disturbing strains of a past that has set them apart from families and households, often quite deliberately. What this suggests is that just as peasant couples long ago managed to take their shaky new nuclear households in hand and find ways to make them work better – a task that in their case meant inventing the extra-domestic institutions they needed to do so – men and women located now within strong institutions beyond their weakened households have more than enough power, if they choose to use it, to change the course of history. They can insist that those institutions start to play a more active role in making their lives both within and beyond those institutions more whole, more secure, and, yes, more genuinely equal.

That women and men together have managed to evolve, quite unwittingly at first, the means to end a system of gendered power relations does not mean that the end will be coming any time soon. We can persist in parceling out activities and qualities based on ever more haphazard gender rationales that will work for a time to uphold that weakened system, or we can acknowledge that the game is finally coming to an end and work to hasten the day. So far, we have only ensured that so long as the game of naming women's and men's activities, traits, and natures lasts, women will be dealt in. Yet that is hardly a small thing.

Index

adolescence
  comparison in early- and
    late-marriage settings, 53–57
  in contemporary northern versus
    southern Europe, 250–56
  in medieval northwestern Europe, 71,
    83, 92
  sexual behavior during, 57–64
  see also Ben-Amos, Ilana Krausman;
    Bennett, Judith M.; Gillis, John R.;
    life-cycle domestic service; Hajnal,
    John; Hanawalt, Barbara; Laslett,
    Peter; McDonald, Michael;
    servants
adulthood and old age
  comparison in early- and
    late-marriage settings, 64–68
  widows and widowers, 66–67, 68; in
    Montaillou, 117; in Salem, 168–71
  see also early-marriage households;
    late-marriage households; *sati*;
    witch-hunts
agricultural societies
  constraints on sexual behavior in, 81
  effects on sexual stratification in, 80
  models of household formation in,
    82
  origins of, 79–80
  see also early-marriage households;
    late-marriage households; Western
    (or northwestern European) family
    pattern

Amussen, Susan, *An Ordered Society:*
  Gender and Class in Early Modern
  England, 222–24
Astell, Mary, 225–27
authority
  concern about from late medieval era,
    39
  connections between domestic and
    extra-domestic sites of, 202–41
  of fathers in Western family pattern,
    65–66
  of husbands and wives in early- versus
    late-marriage settings, 66–67
  links between domestic and public,
    218–31
  of popular religion in late medieval
    and early modern era, 213–15, 218
  search for credible bases of in late-
    marriage societies, 227–31
  of women in late-marriage
    households, 69; in seventeenth-
    century Salem Village, Chapter 4,
    111–43; in *Utopia*, 68–69; in
    nineteenth-century late-marriage
    societies, 265–68
  see also early-marriage households;
    gender and power arrangements;
    late-marriage households

Bartlett, Robert, *The Making of Europe:*
  Conquest, Colonialization and
  Cultural Change, 89–90